FRENCH-CANADIAN
SOURCES

A Guide for Genealogists

FRENCH-CANADIAN
SOURCES

A Guide for Genealogists

Patricia Keeney Geyh

Joyce Soltis Banachowski

Linda K. Boyea

Patricia Sarasin Ustine

Marilyn Holt Bourbonais

Beverly Ploenske LaBelle

Francele Sherburne, SSND

Karen Vincent Humiston

Ancestry®

Library of Congress Cataloging-in-Publication Data

French Canadian sources : a guide for genealogists / Patricia Keeney
Geyh ... [et al.].
    p. cm.
Includes bibliographical references and index.
  ISBN 1-931279-01-2 (hardcover : alk. paper)
  1. Quebec (Province)—Genealogy—Handbooks, manuals, etc. 2. French
Canadians—Genealogy—Handbooks, manuals, etc. I. Geyh, Patricia
Keeney

CS88.Q4 F74 2002
929'.1'0720714--dc21

            2002005751

Dedication

Oftentimes we genealogists, in discovering the identity of our ancestors, find ourselves speaking the names of men and women whose names have not been spoken by a human tongue for generations. We learn of the work, loves, hates—in short, the lives of people who, until now, have completely passed from the memory of the living world. And in recording their stories, we insure that they will never again be nameless and unknown.

In the same manner, as we record the events of our own lives and the lives of our children and grandchildren, we guarantee that they too will always have a name, a personality, an identity for future generations to know and appreciate.

And so we dedicate this book to those thousands of men and women, alive and dead, whose names we now know, and to those thousands for whom we still search.

Table of Contents

Preface

The path leading to the actual publication of this book on French-Canadian genealogical research was a long one. Initially the publications committee of the French-Canadian/Acadian Genealogists of Wisconsin thought it might be a good idea to pull together all the articles relating to research that had been published in the *Quarterly* over a period of some fifteen years.

When we looked at them, however, we realized that they needed radical revision. Then we decided that we needed to write many completely new articles on subjects that had never been covered in the *Quarterly*. Time passed and every month we met and worked on chapters in THE BOOK.

As we became more and more satisfied with what we were doing, we contacted Ancestry and to our delight they were interested in publishing what we had done.

This book, then, has been a collaborative effort on the part of the eight members of the publication committee that has lasted over six years. We sincerely hope that our English-speaking French-Canadian cousins will find its contents useful and will share with us the joy of genealogical research.

The address of the French-Canadian/Acadian Genealogical Society, Inc., is P.O. Box 414, Hales Corners, Wisconsin 53130-0414 . The website is <http://www.fcgw.org>.

Acknowledgments

Acknowledging those who were of help to the authors of this book is difficult, largely because of the danger of skipping someone. Nonetheless it is essential that we mention some without whom this book would not have been completed.

Daniel Olivier, research librarian at the *Salle Gagnon* in Montreal, has been of tremendous help. He has corrected errors in some articles, provided new information and been available for help at the *Salle Gagnon* as well as on the phone and on the Internet.

Marie Dorice Hebert Dougherty and Richard Walker, both now deceased, provided an invaluable service in helping to translate old French documents.

Margaret Schutz and Susan White helped us find church records to transcribe and translate. Nelda Womack and her Canadian cousins took time to help with some of the transcription and translation. Kateri Dupuis worked with us scanning some documents.

James Hansen, research librarian at the Wisconsin Historical Society in Madison, Wisconsin, has been ready with advice whenever needed and graciously let us include his bibliography to fur trade records.

Our two editors at Ancestry Publications, Jennifer Utley and Matthew Wright, put up with us neophytes to the publishing world and finally made our dream of a published book come true. David Ouimette spent a great deal of time previewing the book and made many useful suggestions. His help was essential.

All of us are especially grateful to our friends and family who have put up with our eternal conversations about THE BOOK and who listened to the same "stuff" over and over.

Introduction

The introduction to this book can be found in the following four chapters. They are important because they acquaint the genealogist with the culture and history of those living in a Gallic society. They also provide basic information needed by all genealogists.

The first chapter, "It Is Time You Come Home," provides the reader with a general overview of French-Canadian history and genealogy. This is followed by an historical timeline into which researchers can fit the lives of individual ancestors, learning what was going on in the larger world around them. This chapter should encourage genealogists to read the history of this land.

The chapter on the seigneurial system is important because it explains the system under which the French Canadians lived and because many of the records to be used are generated as a part of the seigneurial system.

Naming patterns are a significant problem to many researchers. Name changes that occurred within Quebec and after leaving Quebec can cause great confusion. "*Dit* names," a unique phenomenon in this part of the world, are explained. Those living in the twenty-first century are used to the concept that a name is either spelled correctly or incorrectly. Unless an involved court process is initiated, one keeps the same name. Everyone in the family has the same surname. This is not the way it has always been, either here or anyplace else in the world, for that matter. This chapter discusses naming patterns specific to French Canadians.

Once the introductory chapters are studied, it is time to go on to the sections covering secondary sources of information, and then primary sources.

Chapter One

"It Is Time You Come Home"

—Words of a Montreal cab driver when he discovered his passengers were French-Canadian genealogists from Wisconsin

By Patricia Keeney Geyh

Welcome to the world of the French-Canadian genealogy. As the Montreal cab driver said, "It is time you come home." Come home to Quebec.

Hundreds of thousands of people born and raised in the United States are descendants of the intrepid French men and women who came to North America in the sixteenth, seventeenth, and eighteenth centuries. The genealogists among their descendants are invited to follow them back, identify them all, and learn about them through the records of their lives.

In order to truly appreciate these people, and to value the records about them that still exist in such huge quantities, it is essential that there be an understanding of the people themselves and the history they created.

The French, along with many other nations of Europe, were fishing the Grand Banks off Newfoundland from the late 1500s. The important season of the year for the fishermen was before Lent, early enough to catch and salt the fish and then get back to port in Europe to sell their catch to the many Roman Catholics who ate fish in huge quantities throughout Lent. This process of salting and drying the fish often took place on land, especially in Newfoundland and Nova Scotia.

In 1604 Pierre du Guast, Sieur de Mont, and Samuel Champlain established a base in what is now Nova Scotia. The base was called Port Royal, the land was called Acadia and the settlers came from France. These French and their descendants remained in Acadia for many years. In 1713 their land in Nova Scotia was ceded to the English. In 1755 the English

1

uprooted the Acadians and dispersed them throughout the east coast of what is now the United States, as well as back to Europe. Some escaped into the forests of northern New Brunswick, Quebec, and Prince Edward Island. The Acadians, especially those repatriated to France, were most unhappy and, because of their difficulty in adjusting, they eventually became an expensive charge on the government of France. The French government made an agreement with Spain to allow the Acadians to be settled in Louisiana. There, with some of the other Acadians from throughout the colonies, they settled in the bayous where their descendants live today. They are known as Cajuns.

In 1608 Champlain established a separate French settlement in what is now Quebec City. Here, at the top of cliffs overlooking the St. Lawrence River, was established one of the major French-Canadian settlements. Initially the purpose of this settlement was to search for a route through the continent and on to China. If not successful in that, the settlers were to find gold and silver, just as the Spanish had done in Central and South America. Almost immediately it became obvious that neither of these goals would be achieved, and two other goals were established. One was to obtain as many furs as possible to be sold in Europe, especially for beaver hats. The second was to convert the "savages" to Roman Catholicism.

Since these goals required working with the natives, one of the first things Champlain did was send some of his men to live with nearby friendly tribes. The French learned to speak their languages and acquired many of the skills required to live and travel successfully in the vast wilderness of New France.

The French and the English

At about the same time that Champlain established Quebec City, the English were sending colonists into what became the Thirteen Colonies. Here, however, entire families emigrated right from the beginning. They formed towns and farmed the land. The colonies on the eastern seaboard of what is now the United States were in an area that restricted their travel. The ocean was to the east, the French to the north, the Spanish to the south and the Appalachian mountain chain to the west. There were only a few natural openings through these mountains. One of the most famous was the path created by the Hudson River going north and then the Mohawk River going west, eventually leading into Lake Erie. It was along this valley of the Mohawk that the United States in 1825 completed building the Erie Canal. The second famous path was in the south and was known as the Wilderness Road. It was made famous by Daniel Boone and other explorers of his time. During the first hundred years or so of settlement, most English colonies tended to stay east of the Appalachians.

In contrast, the French were located on a highway of rivers, connecting with other such highways as far as the French could explore. The immense territory claimed by the French king was sparsely inhabited. They had occasional settlements, primarily trading centers.

It is this very difference between the colonies of the two nations that some historians suggest was a major cause of the defeat of the French by the English in North America.

Initially the Indian tribes came to Montreal to exchange furs for trade items brought to North America from France. As hostilities between these tribes and the Iroquois increased, the western tribes were no longer willing to travel to Montreal. The French had to go to them in the wilderness of the interior. From this necessity, the *voyageur* was born. These hearty men were hired by fur companies to make the journey to remote outposts to trade for and transport furs.

Additional settlements were established further up the St. Lawrence River, the largest ones being Trois Rivières and Montreal. Initially most of the French arriving in Quebec were missionaries, members of the military, explorers, or traders. Some wives came with them, but relatively few. After some years, the French king, wanting to keep the soldiers in New France when their term of service was finished, recruited women to go to New France to marry the men there. From 1663 to 1673, nearly 800 of these women, nicknamed the "Daughters of the King" because their dowry was paid for by the king, made the arduous journey across the vast ocean to a land of uncertainty. Robert Giffard, a very early settler, recruited families to come to North America and a few others of the major landowners brought families to settle the land.

The few French-Canadian settlements that were established could be found scattered along the rivers and in the early years were used primarily as trading posts. Each Frenchman owning or leasing land wanted to be located directly on a waterway. Today, flying over Quebec, one still can see the farmland set out in long narrow strips, one end touching the river. A plat map of Green Bay, Wisconsin, one of the early French-Canadian settlements, shows the land laid out in that fashion—long narrow strips of land with one end touching the bay. Their highways throughout the continent of North America were rivers and streams, their vehicle of choice was the birchbark canoe.

After the explorers and missionaries came the aforementioned voyageurs, exploring and trading with various Native American tribes. There were several types of canoes, but two were used most frequently. Those traversing large bodies of water, such as Lake Superior, would travel in a Montreal Canoe, which was thirty-three to thirty-six feet long. Eight to ten voyageurs paddled the canoe. It carried three and a half to four tons of cargo, including the voyageurs and their small packets of personal property.

The North Canoe was used on smaller waterways and only four to six men paddled. It was twenty-four to twenty-eight feet in length and carried about one and a half tons of cargo including the voyageurs and their packets.

When a waterway became impassable it was sometimes necessary to portage. This meant the men carried the cargo—between 250 and 400 pounds at a time—using a trump line, or a portage collar, as a sling.

The voyageurs were usually small men, about 5'6" in height—there was no room for larger men in the canoe. They were strong men who sometimes worked as many as eighteen hours a day. During the day, they had short rest periods—long enough to smoke a pipe.

These breaks became known as "pipes." The voyageurs were cheerful and happy men, proud of the work they did and full of joy. They often sang. In fact, those men with very good voices were paid more, as the beat of the music set the rhythm of the paddles. The voyageur often came from a long line of voyageurs before him. It was a proud vocation and the sons of voyageurs dreaded nothing more than the possibility of growing to be tall men.

The more experienced men were called "winterers." Their lives took them far out into the wilderness where they would spend the winter with the Native American tribes. Many had Indian wives. When the spring came they loaded the furs in their canoes and headed for the rendezvous. Here they turned over the furs, sang, danced, and eventually returned to the deep forests.

The "porkeater" was the less experienced voyageur who traveled from Quebec to the rendezvous and then returned to Quebec with the furs provided by the winterers. Porkeaters spent winters in Quebec.

The French-Canadian voyageurs continued their work into the English regime and even when the United States took over the fur trade in that country. However they rarely settled in one place for long.

Except for the settlements scattered on the waterways, there is nothing left of them but a memory, a shadow flitting through the forests. Wearing leather and bright-colored wool sashes, they were gallant when facing a lady and cheerful when faced with back-breaking work. They followed the wild game west as civilization encroached on the animal habitat in the east. Eventually the popularity of beaver hats waned and the fur-bearing animals became scarce. The voyageur tradition died out.

The vast majority of the *Québecois*, however, were not fur traders. They stayed in Quebec, farmed the land, settled the villages, mined the ore, and hewed the trees. In times of economic depression they sometimes headed south to the United States for employment. Although many would return home when jobs became available in Quebec, many stayed in the United States and their descendants have multiplied and spread throughout the entire country.

After the explorers and voyageurs, the next wave of French Canadians to come into the United States was the lumberjacks. Wherever they worked they were the finest "jacks" available. Coming down from Canada into the United States, they then traveled west as the forests were cut down. Many settled along the way, but others kept coming from Quebec and traveled west to the Pacific.

Some of the time they came with their families, or they married women living near the lumberjack camp. They bought small farms near the forests, and in summer they worked there and raised a family. During the winter months, when the underbrush had no leaves and the ground was frozen, they cut down trees, slid them into the frozen rivers and waited until the spring thaw to begin the drive down the river. Many remained in the United States, and their descendants now live throughout the nation. They also went west in Canada and settled from the prairie provinces all the way to the Pacific.

During one economic downturn the Canadians came into the eastern states to work in the mills. Consequently many of the mills in New England were staffed by French Canadians. *Québecois* children as well as men and women were effectively incarcerated in these sweat shops, struggling for survival. These people settled in Maine, Massachusetts, Rhode Island, and other eastern states where there are still vigorous French-speaking communities. Further inland, in the Midwest, many French Canadians became so absorbed in the Anglo community that they lost their French identity. Nevertheless, their religion remained constant.

Throughout their history French Canadians have been shepherded by the missionaries and priests of the Roman Catholic Church. These priests, with their crucifixes and their missals, were the constant in the lives of all the *Québecois*. They cared for their spiritual needs and recorded highlights of their lives—baptism, marriage, and burial. Because of the relatively small number of French who came and stayed in Canada, these priests recognized the importance of keeping track of family relationships and obeying the mandates of the church as they related to consanguinity. Some of these priests began the recording of family histories and extractions of marriage records that French-Canadian genealogists now use with such enthusiasm.

Many thousands of the descendants of these people find that French-Canadian genealogy is a fruitful and engrossing avocation. This book is designed to assist researchers by providing detailed explanations about many primary and secondary sources available to those who are willing to learn how to use them. Because much of the most valuable information available is in French, many non-French-speaking genealogists hesitate to go to them for information about their families. It is the purpose of this book to help those researchers use these resources.

To begin research on any family it is necessary to start in the present and go back one generation at a time. Non-Canadians researching French-Canadian ancestors will begin in the land to which their ancestors emigrated, and this usually means the United States. The object is to learn about the family living in America and also to learn the name of, and information about, the immigrant ancestor. It is then necessary to locate the exact place of origin because, like most places throughout the world, the majority of primary records are generated in the local communities.

The first step is to contact as many living relatives as possible and ask for any information they may have: stories, newspaper clippings, old photographs, holy cards, etc. Once their records have been photocopied and returned, it is time to enter the information on the standard genealogy forms, whether on paper or included in a genealogical software program.

Now is the time to plan a research strategy that will help you locate the specific place of origin of the immigrant ancestor. What information has already been obtained? What essential information is missing? Where is the best place to go to find the missing data? These questions should be asked over and over again throughout the entire research process in order to keep focused on reasonable and appropriate goals.

At this point genealogy reference books become important. There are many basic "how-to" books available for United States research. Several of these are listed at the end of this chapter. It is important to purchase a good basic text on United States research as this will speed up the process and help to avoid common mistakes.

Once the immigrant ancestor and his/her place of origin is located, it is time to learn some of the details of French-Canadian genealogy. And genealogy in Quebec is not the same as other such research. The reasons for this difference are based on these three facts:

1. Women in French society do not lose their maiden names. They are called by their married names socially, but in all official civil and church records they are known by their maiden name. The identity of their spouse may be mentioned, but not necessarily. This usually carries over to their tombstones.

2. An extraordinarily large percentage of French-Canadian records have been preserved.

3. Since the middle 1800s the French Canadians have been carefully tracing their families back into France and also indexing a huge proportion of the primary records. In Quebec these are called *répertoires*. Repertoires of marriage records exist, which give the names of the bride and groom as well as the names of the parents. The women's maiden name is given. Using these repertoires, one can sometimes go back a number of generations in one afternoon.

French-Canadian genealogy then, begins with building a framework of marriages going back as far as one can go. Once this is done, the researcher goes to the primary records to confirm the information in the repertoires and to fill in all the additional information on each family. Many genealogists gain a great deal of data from various sources on the Internet and, of course, this is an excellent secondary source of information. Just as with any other secondary source, however, it is important to verify the data by locating the appropriate primary records.

This book will describe in detail many of the French-Canadian secondary sources and how they can be used. It will also discuss the use of many of the available primary records. When studying these records it is important to note that the names of the parents of an individual are often written in parentheses after that person's name. When this is done, only the first name of the father is given. It is assumed that his surname is the same as that of his child. This is followed by the maiden name of the mother—for example: "Pierre Douville (Joseph and Julie LaChance)." Pierre's father is Joseph Douville and his mother is Julie LaChance.

It is most important to join a genealogical society. If there is a French-Canadian society available, that is terrific; however at this beginning stage it is just as important to join a local society where experienced researchers will be glad to aid beginners. Genealogists are generally a very helpful lot.

In addition to names, dates, and places, good genealogists will collect as much information as possible about the life and times of their ancestors. In order to do this it is necessary to know what was happening in the world at the time these ancestors lived. The timeline that follows this chapter can be used to place a family in a given period in history in a given place. Setting family events (births, marriages, deaths) on such a timeline and then adding events that occurred in their immediate communities is the beginning step to understanding the world as it was seen by them.

It might also be a good idea to check local newspapers to discover the clothing that was popular in a given period, and the furniture that was used. This might mean photocopying ads from the late eighteenth- through the early twentieth-century newspapers. Another resource is the inventory found in probate records. Here one can learn about every piece of clothing, every item in the house that an ancestor owned at the time of death. One might even consider going back to visit the places the families stopped on their migration to their new homeland—step by step, generation by generation—through the United States, back, perhaps, into Ontario and then into Quebec. The family stories must be recorded. A picture of real human beings will emerge.

But none of this can be done if those names, dates, and places are not known, and this book will help the descendants of French Canadians acquire that information. This book will not discuss United States research, nor does it cover Acadian records. It is written to help the genealogists who wish to use Quebec records and give them the information they need to decipher the records written in French, to learn about their ancestors who lived so many hundreds of years ago.

A Sampling of Basic Genealogy Texts

Greenwood, Val D. *The Researcher's Guide to American Genealogy*, 3rd Edition. Genealogical Publishing Company, 2000.

Szucs, Loretto Dennis and Sandra Hargreaves Luebking, editors. *The Source: A Guidebook of American Genealogy*, Revised Edition. Ancestry Inc., Salt Lake City, 1997.

Rose, Christine with Kay German Ingalls. *The Complete Idiot's Guide to Genealogy*. Macmillan Publishing, New York, 1997.

Chapter Two

A Timeline for French-Canadian Genealogists

By Marilyn Holt Bourbonais

This timeline can serve as a brief chronological framework of French-Canadian history and therefore as an aid in understanding the outside forces influencing the lives of early French-Canadians. The dates are believed to be correct, and were included only after consulting several historical sources. This timeline is not intended, however, as a substitute for a good text in the history of Quebec. Some researchers take such a timeline and insert the dates of events in the lives of their own ancestors thus creating a "personalized" family timeline. The dates in bold type record events in United States history, allowing the American genealogist to place these familiar dates and events with those occurring simultaneously in Canada or France.

1492	**Columbus discovers America.**
1534	Cartier discovers the Gulf of St. Lawrence and claims the Quebec region for France.
1539	Roman Catholic pastors in France are required to keep baptism registers.
1539	The beginning of French Protestantism.
1547	The earliest reference to whaling in Labrador is made. By the 1550s Basques are whale hunting along the coast and into the St. Lawrence River.
1559	Many Protestant pastors begin to keep baptism and marriage records in France.

8

1565   **St. Augustine, in what is now Florida, is founded by the Spanish. This is the first European settlement in what is now the United States.**

1572   St. Bartholomew's Day Massacre results in many Protestant Huguenots leaving France.

1579   The Catholic church in France begins to require that marriage and death records are kept.

1598   Edict of Nantes grants religious freedom in France. (Many Protestant records date from this year.)

1603-1663   New France is controlled by various companies authorized by the king to bring settlers to the colony and establish a government.

1604   Pierre du Guast, Sieur de Monts, and Samuel Champlain establish a base at Port Royal, Acadia (Nova Scotia).

1607   **The colony of Jamestown, Virginia is founded.**

1608   Champlain settles near Stadacona, an Indian village, and that settlement eventually becomes Quebec City. French explorers, military personnel, and eventually settlers come to live here.

1617   Louis Hebert, wife Marie Rollet, and children arrive at Quebec City. They are the first permanent settlers in what is now Quebec.

1618-1648   Thirty Years War. The English and French are fighting in Europe, and at times this conflict spreads to North America.

1620   **The Mayflower lands at Plymouth in what is now Massachusetts.**

1621   The first Catholic parish register is started at the parish of Notre Dame de Québec.

1629   The English capture Quebec City and hold it until 1632 when it is restored to France by the Treaty of St.Germain-en-Laye.

1634   Trois Rivières is founded by Sieur de Violette.

1634   Jean Nicolet lands in what is now Wisconsin.

1639   Ste. Marie Among the Hurons, the first French settlement in what is now Ontario, is established by the Jesuits as a mission settlement. It is abandoned in 1649.

1640-1668   Quebec is at war with the Iroquois.

1642   Paul de Chomeday, Sieur de Maissonneuve, founds Ville-Marie de Montréal, the pre-cursor to modern-day Montreal.

1655	The English briefly capture Port Royale in what is now Nova Scotia. Both France and England claim Acadia.
1660	A trading post called LaBaye is established at Green Bay, Wisconsin.
1660	Placentia is established by France in Newfoundland.
1663	King Louis XIV takes over the government of New France and establishes a Sovereign Council to govern the colony. Quebec becomes a royal province.
1663-1675	*Les Filles du Roi* arrive in New France. (The dates vary a few years in either direction, depending on the authority providing the information.)
1665-1668	The Carignan-Salieres Regiment, *Les Troupes de la Marine*, is sent to Quebec to defend against the Iroquois. Many men in the regiment remain in Quebec after they are discharged.
1666	The first census of New France is undertaken by the *Intendant,* Jean Talon.
1670	The Hudson Bay Fur Trading Company is founded by the English.
1673	Louis Joliet and Pere Jacques Marquette explore the Great Lakes area and travel down the Mississippi until they near Spanish territory.
1685	Fort St. Nicolas is established at what is now Prairie du Chien, Wisconsin by Nicholas Perrot.
1685	The Edict of Nantes is revoked by the French government, causing thousands of Protestant Huguenots to leave France.
1689-1697	King William's War, the first French and Indian War, pits New France against New England and New York. The Treaty of Ryswick in 1697 restores all possessions to the way they were before the hostilities. In Europe this was called the War of the League of Augsburgh.
1699	French colony of Louisiana is formed.
1702-1713	Queen Anne's War, the second of the French and Indian Wars (known in Europe as the War of the Spanish Succession) ends with the signing of the Treaty of Utrecht in 1713. By the terms of this treaty, France surrenders to England the Hudson Bay region, Newfoundland and Acadia (the part now called Nova Scotia).
1703	The Sovereign Council is replaced by the Council Superior, the body that governs New France from that date.
1711 & 1734	Edicts of Marly regulate seigneurial land and free it from some of the feudal restriction existing in France.
1718	New Orleans is founded by France.

10

1744-1748	King George's War, the third of the French and Indian Wars, ends on 18 Oct 1748 with the Treaty of Aix-la-Chapelle. Once again the borders are returned to the previous boundaries; Louisburg is returned to France. In Europe it is called The War of Austrian Succession.
1749	The British found Halifax as a military garrison.
1749	Many French Canadians migrate to the Detroit region.
1754-1763	The last of the French and Indian wars, called The French and Indian War, ends with the Treaty of Paris. Canada and Louisiana, east of the Mississippi and excluding New Orleans, go to the British. In Europe this war is known as The Seven Years War. This conflict marks the end of the French regime in North America.
1755	The Acadians are expelled from Acadia by the English and scattered to Europe, New Brunswick, New England, and the southern colonies of what is now the United States.
1759	Wolfe defeats Montcalm on the Plains of Abraham, outside of Quebec City. This results in the capture of Quebec City by the British.
1762	France cedes its portion of Louisiana to Spain.
1774	The Quebec Act results in the establishment of the early province of Quebec. Wisconsin is considered part of that province. The Quebec Act also guarantees religious and linguistic freedom in the province.
1775-1783	**The American Revolution.**
1779	The Northwest Fur Trading Company is established by the British.
1783	**The Treaty of Paris officially ends the American Revolution. Under the treaty, Britain gives up all territory east of the Mississippi River and south of the Great Lakes, not including Spanish-owned Florida. This region becomes the United States.**
1783-1784	Over 30,000 Loyalists migrate to Canada as a result of the American Revolution.
1791	The Constitutional Act divides Quebec into Upper Canada (now Ontario) and Lower Canada (now Quebec).
1796	Detroit and Michilimackinac pass from British to American hands.
1800	Spain cedes Louisiana back to France.
1803	**The Louisiana Purchase is transacted between the United States and France.**
1812-1813	**The War of 1812.**

1815	The American Fur Trading Company takes control of Michilimackinac from the British.
1821	The Northwest Fur Trading Company and Hudson Bay Company merge.
1832	A cholera epidemic strikes Quebec.
1837-1838	In the Rebellion of 1837-1838 the French in Lower Canada rebel against British control. Also called Patriots' Rebellion.
1840	The Union Act joins Upper Canada and Lower Canada under one government. Lower Canada is then called Canada East, and Upper Canada is called Canada West.
1847	A typhus epidemic brought over by immigrants strikes Quebec. Many, largely Irish, are quarantined on Grosse Ile, where thousands died.
1857	Queen Victoria names Ottawa the capital of Canada.
1860-1864	**U.S. Civil War.**
1867	The British North America Act creates the Dominion of Canada. Canada East becomes Quebec; Canada West becomes Ontario. New Brunswick and Nova Scotia also become part of the Dominion of Canada.
1870	Manitoba becomes part of the Dominion of Canada.
1871	British Columbia becomes part of the Dominion of Canada.
1873	Prince Edward Island joins the Dominion of Canada.
1905	Alberta and Saskatchewan become provinces in the Dominion of Canada.
1949	Newfoundland and Labrador join the Dominion of Canada.

Chapter Three

French-Canadian Naming Patterns

By Karen Vincent Humiston

The topic of names is of concern to any genealogist. Today one tends to think of one's name as being set in stone. This was not the case, however, in past times. Many ancestors could neither read nor write; therefore, the spelling of a name depended largely on the scribe who happened to record it. Other name changes occurred when people crossed the border into an English-speaking environment. The tracing of family lines is further complicated by the French-Canadian practice of adopting "*dit* names," or alternate surnames, for their families. An understanding of the practices and forces at work in the use of names is essential to successfully recognize and identify the ancestors in the records researched.

Maiden Names

One French-Canadian practice that is very helpful to genealogists is the use of a woman's maiden name in official records. In the past in the United States women almost always took the surname of their husbands. Thus, a woman born Augusta Merriweather who married a man named John Smith would be referred to in various records simply as Augusta Smith, or even as Mrs. John Smith. This practice may be considered valuable in establishing family unity, but it does nothing for the genealogist who would like to know more about the wife's identity and familial origins. In Quebec the situation was quite different. While a French-Canadian woman generally used her husband's name in social settings, she was always referred to by her maiden name in official documents, whether civil or sacramental. Consider the example of Angelique Guibault who married Andre Jodoin in 1801. After her marriage her neighbors knew her as Madame Jodoin. However in such documents as the sacramental records of her children, notarial records, censuses, and her burial records—the sources most likely to be used by the genealogist—she is always referred to as Angelique Guibault. Obviously this is a boon to the researcher since the maiden name is crucial to tracing the maternal line.

Dit names

Anyone who delves into French-Canadian genealogy to any extent will confront the uniquely French-Canadian phenomenon called the "*dit* name." The practice of adopting an alternative surname was extremely common in Quebec and continued well into the nineteenth century. The word *dit* (or *dite* in the feminine case) is a form of the word *dire* (to say) and can be loosely translated as "that is to say," or "called." Thus an ancestor whose name is recorded as Antoine Emery dit Codere can be read as Antoine Emery, called Coderre. The dit names sometimes followed the family through the generations: to make life more interesting for the genealogist, however, their use was sometimes inconsistent. Some families always used the dit name in combination with the original surnames, while others used it only occasionally. In many cases the dit name eventually replaced the original surname completely. For example, the individual named Jean Francois Toupin dit Dussault may also appear in a record as Jean Francois Dussault, Jean Francois Dussault dit Toupin or as Jean Francois Dussault.

When novice researchers first confront the startling fact that their family did not always go by the same surname, they may be puzzled as to the reason for what seems to be such an abrupt "name change." There is a temptation to speculate rather wildly why the family would suddenly want to hide its identity. These theories often involve the French Revolution or other such cataclysmic events. For those who are hoping that the discovery of a dit name points to the existence of a really juicy story about their ancestors—sorry. In reality, these changes generally happened somewhat slowly, and for much more mundane reasons. An example is Andre Jarret de Beauregard, who arrived in New France as an officer with the Carignan-Salieres Regiment. In Andre's case, de Beauregard referred to his ancestral home in the French province of Dauphine, and his sons and grandsons adopted the Beauregard name in addition to Jarret. In time, Andre's descendants, most of whom lived in Vercheres or Champly Counties, became extremely numerous. Some branches of the family began using new dit names, perhaps to distinguish them from their many cousins. Some of the descendants of Andre's youngest son, Vincent Jarret dit Beauregard, gradually adopted the surname Vincent. This change did not happen overnight; the first record of its use was actually in 1776, while the Jarret name continued to be used occasionally as late as the 1870s. Today, however, there are many descendants of Andre Jarret de Beauregard who are called Vincent without any awareness that their family ever went by any other name. In most cases the reason for the adoption of a particular dit name is lost forever. The critical fact, in terms of genealogical research, is that such a name did in fact occur.

Obviously dit names have great significance for the genealogist, because one must be aware of them in order to recognize an ancestor in the various records being researched. The researcher who reaches a dead end should suspect that a dit name may be the cause. There any number of sources to which one can turn. Both René Jetté's *Dictionnaire genealogique des familles du Québec* and Msgr Cyprien Tanguay's *Dictionnaire genealogique des familles canadiennes* (Volume 7) provide lists connecting French-Canadian names with their possible dit names and other variants. Other more extensive sources include Robert J. Quentin's book, *The* dit *Name: French Canadian Surnames, Aliases, Adulterations, and Anglicizations,* and René Jetté's *Repertoire des noms de famille du québec des origines à 1825.* Once into the actual church records, the researcher will find that if a family used a dit name, both surnames (original and dit) are frequently recorded by the priest.

Spelling Variations

While the use of dit names is a problem unique to French-Canadian research, there are other name problems that eventually confront any genealogist. One of the most common is spelling variations. Today the spelling of a name is viewed in black and white terms: it is either correct or incorrect. If a surname is spelled differently, it is thought that the individual "couldn't be related." This rigidity about spelling, however, is a fairly recent development. Even if the ancestors could read and write, record keepers in past times simply did not place much importance on spelling. A particular priest may have recorded Beauregard as Bogard or Jarret as Garrais.

Even more dramatic changes in spelling often occurred when French Canadians crossed the borders into the United States. Here English speaking record keepers recorded the names as they heard them. Pariseau became Perrizo and Lefebvre became LaFave. For this reason it is very helpful to have a basic understanding of French pronunciation in order to recognize these variations.

Another type of name change that occurred when French Canadians immigrated to the United States was the anglicization of their names. In many cases, this was simply a matter of translating the name into English. Examples of such changes would include Boisvert to Greenwood, Roi to King, Boucher to Butcher, and Renard to Fox. In other cases, the name was anglicized by changing it to a similar sounding Scottish or English name. Thus Boucher became Bush, Rabouin became Roberts, and Belaire became Blair.

Given Names

The spelling of given names was actually more consistent than that of surnames. However, the use of nicknames and variations was common. Angelique in one record may be Angele or Desanges in another, and Frederic Rabouin was occasionally referred to in records as Derique. Given names were often anglicized when the families immigrated to the United States. Some of these changes were fairly straightforward, such as Pierre to Peter or Jean to John. Others were not so obvious, such as Narcisse to Nelson, Apolline to Polly, Hilaire to Eli.

Not only did the form or spelling of names vary in French-Canadian records, in some cases the given name itself was completely changed. The most frequently encountered instance of this is the use of the name Marie. Many, if not most, girls were baptized with the name Marie either by itself or before another name. A girl who was called Marie Therese on her baptismal record may be referred to in subsequent records as Marie, Marie Therese, or Therese.

The use of one or more middle names could also add to the confusion, especially in the nineteenth century. A child baptized as Philippe Hippolyte George might later be referred to as George Joseph or even as Paul. Obviously these changes can be disconcerting to the genealogist. In extreme cases one must rely on dates, places, and other family clues to confirm whether two different names might actually apply to the same person.

As in many other cultures some parents gave a child the same name as a sibling who had died at an earlier time. When there are too many Jean Baptiste's in a given family, it is well to check for this possibility.

The usage of names was not always as chaotic as the above examples may suggest. It is critical, however, to recognize that such changes occur, both with given names and surnames. If researchers are aware of the various processes and practices at work, they will have a much better chance of recognizing their ancestors in various records and of tracing the current surnames to their French-Canadian roots.

Some Aids for Discovering Name Variations

Gassette, Veronique. *French-Canadian Names: Vermont Variance.* Vermont Historical Society, Montpelier, 1994.

Jetté, René. *Répertoires des noms de famille du Québec des origins à 1825.* Institut Généalogique J.L. et Associes, Inc., Montréal 1988.

Jetté, René, *Dictionnaire généalogique des familes du Québec des Origines à 1730.* University of Montreal, Montreal 1990.

Quintin, J. Robert. *French Canadian Surnames, Aliases, Adulterations and Anglicizations.* Robert J. Quintin Publications, Pawtucket, Rhode Island, 1993.

Tanguay, Cyprian. *Dictionnaire généalogique des familles canadiennes, dupuis la Foundation de la colonie Jusqu'a Nos Jours,* vol. 7. Euse Senécal & Fils, Imprimedurs-Éditeurs, Montréal, Canada, 1888.

Chapter Four

Feudalism and the Seigneurial System in New France

By Patricia Keeney Geyh

Long before Europeans came to the continent of North America the feudal system was significant in social and political matters throughout Europe. Exact origins seem to be lost in time, but feudalism did become strong as the Roman Empire disappeared. The system is based on the relatively simple principle of land and protection in return for service. The absence of a strong central government made it necessary for powerful men in each community to preserve order and provide protection, food, and necessities for their dependents. Dependents, in return for grants of land and protection, were to provide the powerful men with service and support, especially in times of war.

The immediate dependent of a lord, having been granted a large piece of land, could, in turn, distribute some of that land to his followers. There developed then a military hierarchy where each dependent was liegeman to his immediate feudal superior.

The dependent also assumed nonmilitary obligations, and these were called manorial or seigniorial obligations.

French Feudalism

In France, as the centuries passed, one of the lords became more powerful than the rest and was named king. As each succeeding king assumed the throne, his power became greater, until it was absolute. All the other lords were liegemen to him. The king, then, set up armies and developed new systems of warfare that protected the entire country. The military responsibilities throughout the feudal hierarchy disappeared; an extensive system of personal relationships based upon the tenure of land remained. "No land without a *seigneur*" was an axiom of this system. It became a tool of the French monarchs by which they maintained absolute control over their lands and people.

As time went by in France, many of the lords—or seigneurs, as they were now called—departed from their estates and went to the larger towns or the capital, leaving their land in charge of a bailiff. Many of these seigneurs were born, lived to a respectable age, and died, never having visited their land. All they wanted was the income from it. They had no contact with their dependents. It is at this time that many of the extreme abuses of the seigniorial system in France began to develop.

Feudalism in New France

When New France was settled the seigniorial system was, naturally, employed to govern it. Initially the French monarchy granted control of all of the lands claimed by France in the Northern Hemisphere to one man or one company, with the condition that seigeuries, or feudal properties, be granted to individuals and that the land be developed.

The first three grants were made on the advice of Champlain. The first grant, made in 1623, was to Louis Hebert. Hebert's seigneury was called the *Seigneury de Sault au Metelot.* Three years later the size of this grant was extended.

The Barony of Cap Tourmente was the second seigneury, and it was granted to Guillaume de Caen in 1624. Caen stayed in New France only a short time.

In 1626 the Society of Jesus (Jesuits) was granted the *Seigneury de Notre Dame des Anges* which is located along the River Charles near Quebec City. The Jesuits eventually became the largest single landholder in the colony.

In 1627 a monopoly of the fur trade and exploration rights was turned over to The Company of New France (Company of One Hundred Associates) on condition that they transport settlers and develop seigneuries in North America. From that time until 1674 control of New France switched from one trading company, to the crown, and then to another trading company. Little settlement and development of the land was accomplished inasmuch as the companies were primarily interested in the fur trade and any exploration that might lead to a route to China. Finally in 1674 the crown took over direct management of the colony. The seigneuries already issued were confirmed and validated. The seigneurs were then liegemen directly to the king instead of to a company. This relationship continued until 1759 when England defeated France and took control of all that is now known as Canada.

During this time of the French regime, the king and his ministers issued many edicts designed to encourage settlement and adjust the seigneurial system as it existed in France to the circumstances in New France.

The king also worked to encourage fair treatment for those responsible to a local seigneur. It is interesting to see how many of his edicts were ignored. It was, after all, a little difficult in those days to enforce a regulation from the other side of the Atlantic Ocean.

Life Under Feudalism

To truly understand the life of the settlers in New France it is important to consider the relationship that existed between a seigneur and the king and the relationship between a seigneur and those living on his land.

The relationship between a seigneur and the king depended to some extent on the type of seigniorial grant he had received. There were several types of seigniorial grants given: (1) grants *en franc aleu noble*, (2) grants *en franc aleu roturier*, (3) grants *en franc aumône* or *frankalmoign*, (4) grants *en fief* or *en seigneuri*.

Grants En Franc Aleu Noble

Grants *en franc aleu noble* were actually freeholds and not really feudal at all. The only obligation placed on the person or organization receiving such a grant was that he/it should render fealty and homage to the king. If these grants were made to an individual, that individual was named to the nobility. Actually, no individuals received land *en franc aleu noble*, and only two such grants were made at all.

These two grants were made to the Jesuits. Because title to property held by the Jesuits was in the name of the general or head of the order, every time they changed administrators they would have to change the title. If the land held was held *en seigeurie*, they would have to pay a *quint* or mutation fee (discussed later), at the time the title changed. Under *grants en franc aleu noble,* this tax was avoided.

Actually, most of the grants to the Jesuits were made *en seigneurie.* In 1678, the king issued a royal edict eliminating any taxes on lands granted to them.

Grants En Franc Aleu Roturier

The second type of grant made was *en franc aleu roturier.* This grant did not bring with it any rank in the nobility, but was otherwise the same as a grant made *en franc aleu noble.* In other words, it was for all intents and purposes a freehold. Few of these seigniories were given and, when they were, there was usually a good reason. Such a grant, for example, might be awarded if a particular parcel of land was difficult to settle because of frequent Indian attacks.

Grants En Franc Aumône or Frankalmoign

A grant *en franc aumône,* or *frankalmoign,* is the third type to be considered. A good many of these were given to religious, charitable, or educational organizations. The organization receiving the grant would be expected to render fealty and homage, and assume responsibility for performing some specific acts such as saying masses at a given time, converting "savages," tending the sick, etc.

Grants *En Fief or En Seigneurie*

The fourth type of grant was *en fief* or *en seigneurie*. Most large grants fell under this category. Those terms were used synonymously in New France. Most large grants were seigneurial grants, and this was the basic unit of the colonial land tenure system. The seigneur receiving such a grant assumed several responsibilities:

1. He must perform the ceremony of fealty and homage *(foi et hommage)*. In New France the ceremony involved the visit of the seigneur to his feudal superior, or that superior's representative. This was usually the king's representative in Quebec City. On bended knee the seigneur would pledge fealty and homage. This ceremony would occur with each new succession to the throne and with each change of land tenure.

2. Within forty days of receiving his grant, the seigneur was required to send to Quebec an *aveu et denombrement*. Such information was sometimes additionally required, by terms of the grant, on a regular basis (i.e., every twenty years) as well as whenever the seigneury changed hands.
   - The *aveu* was a map of the seigneury, either graphic or verbal.
   - The *denombrement* was a detailed description or census of the seigneury including the amount of improved land, the number of subgrants, the number of settlers, the *rente* and *cens* for each settler, the amount of produce, livestock, etc.

3. An obligation distinct to New France was *jue de fief*. It required the seigneur to subgrant his land to settlers who would live on the land.

4. When a seignieury changed hands (*mutation* of ownership) a *mutation* fee or *quint* was payable to the crown. It usually was one-fifth the value of the seignieuy. The crown then usually rebated one-third of the *quint*. The *quint* was payable by sale, gift, or inheritance of the seigneury. The only time it was not required was when the land was inherited by a direct lineal descendent.

5. The last of the seigneur's duties to the crown was military duty. He and his dependents (those living on his seigneury) were to be prepared to perform military service as needed. As time passed a captain of the militia was assigned by the King's representative. The captain reported directly to that representative and not to the seigneur. It was the captain's responsibility to be sure that each person able to bear arms was trained and equipped to do so.

Other conditions in *grants en seigneurie* varied from one grant to the other. Many required the seigneur to build roads along river frontage. Some limited his rights to that river frontage (this was done to encourage a fishing industry). Seigneurs were required to permit their dependents to appeal seigneurial decisions to a higher authority. Other provisions might prohibit the seigneur from trading with the Indians (since the crown wanted to control that trade). Still other grants might prohibit an individual seigneur from setting up tolls to cross bridges, use ferries, or a road.

One important fact to note is that in the change of ownership of any land grant, the king retained the right to refuse the new owner his title to the land. In the large majority of cases this ratification of new title was a mere formality, always granted. The existence of the royal privilege, however, did emphasize that the king retained ultimate authority in the distribution of land in New France.

Having received a seigneural grant, the seigneur was encouraged and eventually mandated to subgrant his land. This was generally done in one of two ways.

First was a concession *en arrière-fief*, which in reality created a new seigneury, but one under the jurisdiction of the seigneur of the larger seigneury and not directly under the king. The person granted the sub-seigneury was required to perform the obligations that the crown imposed upon the seigneur himself, but when pledging fealty and homage, filing the *aveu et denombrement* and paying the *quint,* he was dealing with the seigneur and not with the king.

This form of subgrant was rarely made because it was unprofitable to the seigneur. When made, it was usually granted to relatives or to settlers of importance who arrived at times when the crown was not issuing more seigneuries. The *seigneurie en arrière-fief* could be subgranted. Some, however, were too small to make this practical.

The majority of seigneurial sub-grants were for farms held *en censive* or *en routure*. In New France, for all practical purposes, those two terms could be used interchangeably. Land held *en censive* or *en routure* could not be sub-granted and the man who held them was theoretically a *censitaire* or a *roturier.* These terms were considered pejorative by the French in Quebec, who had lived in the demeaning feudal system in France, and they insisted on being known as *habitants.* The land the habitant was granted was called a *routure.* The land retained by the seigneur for his own personal use was the *seigneurial domain.*

What duties and obligations were imposed on the habitants by the seigneur?

1. The *cens* was an annual token payment intended, in large part, to indicate that the land was held *en censive* and could not be subgranted.

2. Most habitants paid a *rente* that was a much higher charge than a *cens,* and was supposed to be revenue producing for the seigneur. This *rente* was paid with money or was paid

in kind (grain, capons, etc.). Some had no proof of their land grants. They had been given the right to the land from the seigneur by word of mouth, or merely with a *chit*; there was no formal contract. If problems arose between the seigneur and the habitants, it was the latter who fared the worst.

3. The *corvée* was the obligation of the habitant to work from three to six days a year for the seigneur without pay. In addition, there were royal *corvées* at unspecified times that required habitants to work on public projects, such as road building.

4. *Droit de pêche* granted the seigneur all rights to fish in the waters of the seigneury and in the St. Lawrence. The habitant had to pay for the right to fish in the river in front of his house—or in any waters of the seigneury. This took the form of a small cash payment or a percentage of the catch. This right was frequently not exercised by the seigneurs, who found it too difficult to regulate fishing.

5. Many seigneurs did, however, reserve the *droit de bois de chauffage*, which was the right to harvest timber on the lands of the habitants.

6. When there were common lands for pasturage in the seigneury, there was a charge for using it. This charge was either stipulated in the original land grant, or in a separate contract. By 1700 there were commons on one-third to one-half of the settled seigneuries.

7. The seigneurs also had the *droits de banalités*. The *banal* rights as found in France granted the seigneur the right to set up a monopoly of services on his seigniory and compel his dependents to use these services at a price he set. The French *seigneurial banalities* might include the right to build and charge for grist mills, cork factories, hemp factories, saw mills, and bake ovens.

In Canada the only *banal* right enforced was the privilege of building and charging for the use of a grist mill. This was often a *banal* right more desired by the habitant than the seigneur. In most cases it was not a money-making project, but it was necessary to produce flour and the habitant insisted on it. A great deal of conflict arose over mills. The seigneur complained that he was losing money. The habitant said that the mill in the next seigneury was closer or that the mill he was compelled to use didn't work properly, etc.

At first the seigneur attempted to enforce his *banal* right to build bake ovens in which habitants had to bake their daily bread for a fee. This was largely discontinued since distances needed to travel each day to bake bread were prohibitive.

8. The *lods et ventes* were charged whenever a *routure* was sold out of the direct line of succession. The seigneur was entitled to one-twelfth of the sale price. The seigneur retained

Terms Used in This Chapter

Arriére fief

A seigneurie granted within a larger seigneurie, and obtained from the seigneur of the larger seigneurie, rather than from the king.

Aveu et denombrement

A list of the landholdings within a seigneurie, including the buildings, cleared land, and livestock on them, and the dues with which the landholdings were charged. This list was required of the seigneur after any change in seigneurial control, or on request of the intendant. The *aveu* was a map of the seigneurie, either graphic or written.

Banality

A charge which a seigneur levied for a service provided.

Cens

A token cash payment always levied on *rotures*, and on no other type of landholding.

Censitaire

One who paid a *cens* for a *roture*. Called a *habitant* in Quebec.

Droit de retrait

The right to take over land which had been sold by paying the purchase price within a specified time to the buyer.

Foi et hommage

A statement of vassalage owed by a seigneur to a seigneur of higher order from which he held his land, or to the king.

Lods et ventes

A tax of one-twelfth of the sale price that was levied on a sale of a *roture* out of the direct line of succession.

Quint

A tax of one-fifth of the sale price of a seigneurie.

Rente

A charge which a seigneur frequently levied for a *roture* held from him.

Roture

A concession of land that could not be subconceded and that was held by a *roturier*—called a *habitant* in New France—from a seigneur.

Roturier

One who held a *roture*. Called a *habitant* in New France

the right to buy the *routure* at the sale price within forty days of the sale. In other words, he had the right to refuse to allow the sale of land and to buy it himself at the sale price.

The seigneur wanted this privilege in order to protect himself when he felt that the habitant buyer and habitant seller actually exchanged more money than they declared. This would lower the *lods et vents* due the seigneur. The seigneur, within forty days, could buy the property at the price agreed upon by the habitants (which he assumed was considerably less than the amount actually paid) and thus thwart the tax-evading habitants.

The habitants also owed the seigneur certain honors. The seigneur had the best pew in the parish church and always marched just behind the *curé* in church processions. The habitant had to stand in his presence and doff his cap as the seigneur went by. The carriage of the seigneur was given precedence on the road.

The habitant had to render fealty and homage to the seigneur when the habitant first obtained his land and upon each subsequent mutation of ownership. In addition, on the first day of May, the habitants and their families had to appear before the manor house and plant a maypole near the door. In some seigneuries the *routure* grants specified that the habitants must put up a maypole outside the door of the manor house and dance and celebrate. This custom has been read about by many in the twenty-first century with smiles as they contemplate this quaint and joyful event of the bygone days. The habitant, however, was not always delighted with the idea.

Summary

During the French regime in Canada, the seigneurial system was part of the framework of society. Much of it was contractual, much of it was traditional, and all of it reflected a paternalistic and sometimes repressive attitude toward persons lower in the feudal hierarchy. The seigniorial system certainly did not encourage independence, group problem solving, or pride of ownership. It became necessary for the individualist, the free thinker, the malcontent, to slip off into the forest and head west and south.

Bibliography

Adair, E.R. "The French-Canadian Seigneury." *Canadian Historical Review* 35 (1954): 187-207.

Harris, Richard Colebrook. *The Seigneurial System in Early Canada A Geographical Study,* Madison: University of Wisconsin Press, 1966.

MacKirdy, K.A., J.S. Moir, and Y.F. Zoltvany. *Changing Perspectives in Canadian History. Selected Problems,* revised edition. Don Mills, Ontario: J.M. Dent & Sons (Canada) Lt., 1971.

Monro, William Bennett. *The Seignorial System in Canada, A Study in French Colonial Policy.* Longmans, Green, and Co., 1907.

Parkman, Francis. *The Old Regime in Canada,* 27th edition. Boston: Little, Brown, and Co., 1892.

Finlay, J.L. and D.N. Sprague. Th*e Structure of Canadian History,* 2nd edition. Scarborough, Ontario: Prentice-Hall, Canada Inc., 1944.

Zoltvany, Yves F. ed. *The French Tradition in America.* New York: Harper & Row, Publishers, 1969.

Secondary Sources

Secondary sources are those that were generated well after the event that is described. In other words, extracts of records, newspaper articles, genealogies, family stories, much of the information on the Internet, and other such information are considered secondary sources. Some of these are carefully organized; an example of this is a published extract of all the records in a given parish. Others come in a hit or miss fashion; gossip, newspaper articles, and family stories are examples of this.

The number of organized French-Canadian secondary sources available is phenomenal. Because of this, the genealogist generally turns to secondary sources as a beginning point. It is important, therefore, to learn about these sources and then carefully plan a research strategy.

The main reason for using secondary sources is to find where the primary documents can be found. In the United States, French-Canadian genealogy begins by going back generation by generation until a couple is located who was married in French Canada. Then, turning to the secondary sources, the search begins to locate the time and place where that marriage occurred. From there, continuing back in time, a framework of marriages is built using these secondary records. Having accomplished this, it is time to go to the primary sources, to confirm all this information and to add to it.

The recommended place to begin is the *Loiselle Quebec Marriage Index*. This is a master index covering all of Quebec and in many cases takes a person back several generations immediately. From here it might be advisable to refer to the appropriate *repertoire,* or index. Most of the rest of the secondary sources described in this text cover only records through the French regime—perhaps going up to the end of the eighteenth century. They will be used when research has brought the family tree back to that period.

This book contains chapters on a large number of these secondary sources, and it is worthwhile to read them all. Please note that the number of pages devoted to discussing a given record is not related to its importance. Because one chapter is longer than another does not mean that it is therefore more significant. Some sources are easier to describe and/or less complicated. They just might be more important than the others; then again, maybe not.

So find that couple married in Quebec and delve into the impressive treasure trove of secondary sources described in the next several chapters.

Chapter Five

The Loiselle Quebec Marriage Index

By Patricia Keeney Geyh

The *Loiselle Quebec Marriage Index* is one of the most important French-Canadian secondary sources. It is the largest of all *répertoires* (indexes) of marriage, which are so common in French-Canadian genealogy.

In French tradition, which certainly includes French Canada, women did not lose their maiden names when they married. In all legal matters and on all official documents, they retained the name they were given at birth. When searching for the parents in a marriage record, for example, one will find the maiden names of the mothers. Extracting this marriage information from *répertoires* makes tracing a French-Canadian family back through the generations relatively easy.

Overview

The general method of doing French-Canadian genealogical research is to build a skeleton of marriages from information found in such an index, and then go to the original records to obtain the primary information needed to complete the search. Most of these indexes usually record only the marriages in a given parish, town, or county.

The Loiselle Quebec Marriage Index, however, includes most of the marriages in all of Quebec, from its founding into the 1900s. Given in master alphabetical order for the entire province, and in some cases beyond, it includes the names of both the brides and the grooms. It is available on microfiche at the Quebec Archives and some libraries throughout the United States. It is also available on microfilm at The Church of Jesus Christ of Latter-day Saints' Family History Library in Salt Lake City, Utah, and its network of Family History Centers.

The Family History Library originally put the index on film in the 1970s. Since that time the Quebec National Archives, Ste Foy, Quebec has recorded many more marriages in this index. Obviously, none of these additions appear on the original set of 165 rolls of film. Fortunately the Family History Library cameras have again been busy in Quebec, and these additions are now available on a supplemental set of fifty-one rolls of film. Both sets of indexes are in alphabetical order. (see Appendix H)

Researchers interested in French Canadians who settled in the Midwest will be especially pleased with this supplement inasmuch as it includes many predominately French-Canadian parishes in Ontario. Many Quebec parishes that were not in the original group have also been indexed into the 1900s. In addition, the supplement includes some parishes that had appeared in the original index but only through the 1860s or 1870s. Many of these have been further indexed into the 1900s.

The fiche edition is constantly being updated and additional fiche can be obtained from the National Archives of Quebec.

Using *Loiselle* on Film

The microfilm is a reproduction of the 3" x 5" cards used to record marriages in Quebec, parts of New Hampshire, New Brunswick, and Ontario. In using the Loiselle index on film, one searches an alphabetical listing for a particular surname. Within a given surname the cards are in alphabetical order by first name. All those that have both the same surname and the same first name are listed in chronological order by date of the wedding. But, while the Loiselle index is an invaluable resource, there are certain things to watch out for. For instance, there are the usual errors of alphabetizing where, for example, Jeanne is placed before Jean. In addition another problem frequently occurs. Upon reaching what should be the end of the file for a given surname (with the first name of Zacharias, for example) one finds the same surname again, with the first names going from A through Z—different people, different dates, same surname. It is almost as though two separate files were photographed—one right after the other.

There are two 3" x 5" cards filed for each marriage, one for the groom and one for the bride. These are interfiled in one huge alphabetical index. Each card is usually typed and includes the date and place of the wedding. It also notes the names of the bride and groom as well as the names of the mother and father of each. If any parent of the couple was dead, that fact was noted. All women are called by their maiden names. If either the bride or groom or their parents are from another parish, the card indicates the parish from which they come. If the bride and/or groom is widowed, the record of the marriage gives the name of the previous spouse rather than the names of the parents. To find the names of the parents of a widow(er) it is necessary to find the indexed entry for the first marriage.

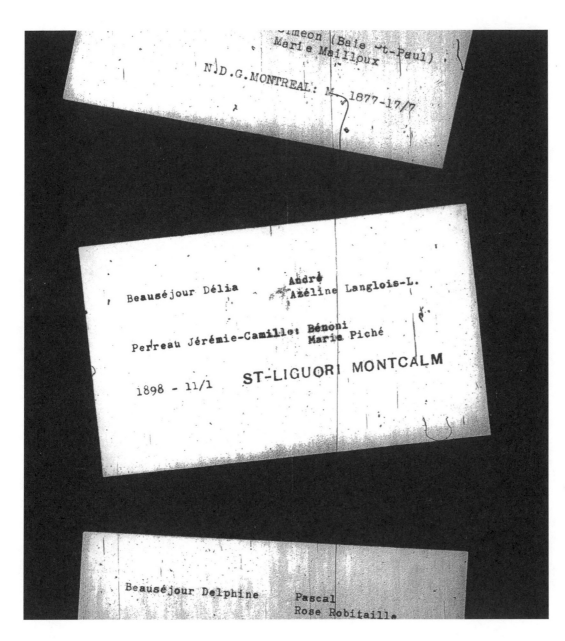

A portion of film #543731 of the Loiselle card index.

Using *Loiselle* on Fiche

There are differences between the fiche edition and film edition of the Loiselle index. First, there is a separate index for the brides and for the grooms. The number of fiche for brides is considerably less than for grooms, which would seem to indicate that many of the cards for the brides were not included in this index. It is nonetheless important to refer to the brides index if the marriage is not located in the grooms index.

Second, the cards on the fiche are in a different order than the cards on film. On the grooms index, for example, the cards are filed in alphabetical order by surname of the groom. Within that surname they are filed in order of the bride's surname. If there is more than one couple where the surname of the groom and the surname of the bride are the same, they are then filed alphabetically by the first name of the bride. If more than one couple falls in this group, they are then filed chronologically.

On the fiche a separate section is devoted to those who became priests, nuns, or sisters.

Research Strategies

Consider the obvious value of this index. The researcher, with the names of a couple married in Quebec and the approximate time of their marriage, looks in the Loiselle index, on film, alphabetically under the surname of the groom and then within that surname alphabetically to the first name of the groom. (If using the fiche, the researcher would look under the maiden name of the bride, after having found the surname of the groom.) Once an entry is found it provides, among other information, the name of the parents of the groom. The researcher, who is already searching on the reel of microfilm that includes the surname of the groom, turns again to the file and finds the listing of the groom's parents' marriage. That entry, in turn, gives the names of the parents of that couple. The researcher searches once again to find the record of the marriage of this next set of parents and so on, back generation upon generation. Obviously the same process will be used when tracing the bride's parents, grandparents, great-grandparents, etc.

There are other ways that the *Loiselle Marriage Index* can be of benefit to genealogists. Family tradition indicated to one researcher that her great-grandfather, Pierre Hubert Douville, was born in St. Casimir, Quebec, on 4 April 1838. He married Rosanna Hoy in Wisconsin, meaning his marriage will not be found in Loiselle. In checking information about St. Casimir, it was found that no parish was located there as early as 1838. Using the Loiselle index the researcher traced back all the families named Douville who were married in St. Casimir after the church was founded. In short order it became apparent that all the Douvilles listed as being married in St. Casimir were descended from couples who had migrated from Ste. Anne de la Perade. At this point a check was made of the original parish records of Ste. Anne de la Perade, and the baptismal record of Pierre was quickly found. In addition to the usual information, the record indicated that he was born in St. Casimir.

At times family records in the United States provide the birth date of a French-Canadian immigrant, but intensive research gives little extra information about his home and family in Quebec. Some researchers using the Loiselle index have noted places of marriage of people with the same surname. Frequently the overwhelming majority of people with a given surname come from relatively few parishes. By referring to the microfilms of the appropriate parishes' records for the correct time period, these researchers have been able to locate the birth record of their ancestor. This is an especially good method when in Salt Lake City at the Family History Library, or at the Quebec National Archives, where all the films are immediately accessible. (See Appendix H for Loiselle Marriage Index microfilm numbers at the Family History Library.)

Chapter Six

Using *Répertoires*

By Linda K. Boyea

Genealogists searching for their French-Canadian ancestors are fortunate to find numerous *répertoires* (indexes) available to aid in their research. These useful publications are indexes to Quebec parish records, and there have been hundreds of *répertoires* published.

The great majority of these *répertoires* are indexes of marriage (*mariage*) records only. Because French-Canadian marriage records contain the maiden names of all the women listed (bride, mothers, sisters, witnesses), marriage records are an invaluable tool for the French-Canadian researcher. A few of the *répertoires* are indexes of baptism (*baptême*), or burials (*sépultures*), and some are a collection of all three events.

Some *répertoires* contain minimal information. For example, a marriage index generally lists the names of the bride and groom, the date, and the names of their parents. A lucky researcher may find a marriage index that includes additional information, such as the parish of bride or groom when different from the one being indexed. Sometimes a baptismal index also lists the birth date.

One répertoire may cover a single parish *(paroisse)*; another may include the records of several parishes. A third may include the records of all the parishes in one county *(comte)*. A répertoire may record the events of a few years, or it may span centuries.

Répertoire Format

The events in a few *répertoires* are listed chronologically. *Répertoires* of this style usually number the events and contain an alphabetical index at the back of the book.

The information in most *répertoires* is arranged alphabetically by surname. However, under each surname the events may be listed in chronological order, or in alphabetical order by the first name of the proband listed in the original record. A proband in any record is the person about whom the record is written. They could also be listed in alphabetical order by the spouse's surname. Some marriage *répertoires* index just the man, but others will also index the woman.

Example #1

Taken from *Mariages de Notre-Dame-de-la-Prairie-de-la-Madeleine, Laprairie, 1670-1968.*

BOYER

Jean	vf Marguerite Dumay	07-01-1736	AGUENIER, M.Anne
Félicité	Jean & M.Anne Maguanier	13-10-1773	ASSELIN, Toussaint
M.Hypolite	Louis & M.Angelique Duquet	30-01-1797	ASSELIN, Frs-Clovis
-			
-			
-			
Jean	Antoine & Marie Perras	14-07-1722	DUMAY, Marguerite

In this répertoire each marriage is indexed twice, once under the groom's surname and once under the bride's surname. Only one set of parents is listed with each entry. The parents of M. Anne will be found with her listing under the surname Aguenier. Likewise, the parents of Toussaint and Frs-Clovis will be included with their listing under the surname Asselin.

Under the surname heading, in this case Boyer, marriages are listed alphabetically by the surname of the spouse. In the event of duplicate surnames, as in the name Asselin, the marriages are then listed chronologically.

Instead of listing the parents of Jean, this entry shows that Jean is a widower of Marguerite Dumay as indicated by "vf." Because that marriage also took place in this parish, it can be found further down the list under the same surname heading Boyer. That entry gives the names of Jean's parents, indicating that this was Jean's first marriage.

Example #2

Taken from *Mariages de la Paroisse de St-Antoine-de-Pade de Longueuil 1701-1980*

1046.BOYER, ANTOINE	28-01-1754	BOURDON, ELISABETH
Jean & f.Marguerite Demers: Laprairie		f.Pierre & Elisabeth Lavoix
1047.BOYER, PIERRE	14-07-1738	BOURDON, MARIE-ANNE
Antoine & f.Marie Perras		Pierre & Marie-Anne Goyan
vf Marie Gervais: Laprairie		
1049.BOYER, MAGLOIRE,mn	06-02-1855	DAVID, LUCIE, mn
Michel & f.Geneviève Ménard:Laprairie		Louis & f.Suzanne Benoit

In this répertoire the information is only listed once, under the man's surname. Each marriage is given an index number. Within a given surname the marriages are recorded alphabetically by the surname of the wife; if two women have the same surname they are further listed alphabetically by the first name of the bride. The entries for Bourdon, Elisabeth and Bourdon, Marie-Anne illustrate this point. Those who are unsure of the surname of the groom can look to the back of the book where the brides are listed alphabetically and the marriage index number is given.

This répertoire includes the information that a parent had died prior to the marriage, (f.), and lists the name of the previous spouse, (vf/ve). It also gives the parish of those who are not from St. Antoine, but from the parish of Laprairie. The third entry lists both participants as minors, (mn). The abbreviation (mj) would mean that they were of age.

Although it is very helpful to have this extra information listed, the researcher must realize that the absence of qualifying information does not mean the opposite is true: perhaps Antoine or Elisabeth are minors, even though this information isn't given for this record.

Example #3

Taken from *Répertoires de Mariages de Cap-de-la-Madeleine, (Comte de Champlain), 1673-1920*

BOURASSA

Jean-Baptiste		Ursule Desrosiers
Marie-Anne	29-09-1794	Pierre Arsenault
Judith	17-10-1791	Jn-Baptiste Ames-Jolibois
Joseph		Louise Cormier
Augustin	27-06-1825	Julie Gariepy

In this répertoire the marriage of a couple is listed under the names of their parents. There are two entries for each marriage; one under the parents of the bride and one under the parents of the groom. In turn, the marriage record of the parents is found under the names of their parents if they were married in that parish. In this way family groups are kept together. The researcher who does not know the names of the parents must go to the surname and look through the entire list of children until the right family is located.

In the example above Jean-Baptiste Bourassa and Ursule Desrosiers are the parents of Marie Anne and Judith. The marriage of Marie-Anne and Pierre is also found beneath the listing of Pierre's parents, under the surname Arsenault.

These are only three examples of the way information can be presented in the various *répertoires*. Many other styles will be found, but most are easily understandable. Some may appear confusing at first, but with a little study they can be comprehended.

Using the *Répertoires*

Although these indexes are written in French, non-French-speaking people can interpret the information easily. Most *répertoires* will include a list of abbreviations of names and places used within the index. Some *répertoires* also include a history of the parish, giving a wealth of information to the lucky researcher who can read French.

The records of a particular parish may be listed in several *répertoires*. For example, the marriage records could be indexed alone, or they might also be in an index that includes all the baptism, marriage, and burial records for the parish. A third répertoire may index the entire county, including this parish. Still another répertoire could cover the early years of parish records, which are later included in a répertoire containing all parish records up to the 1900s.

Researching all the *répertoires* that include a particular parish can lead a researcher through the years to current times. Because families often stayed in much the same area, these *répertoires* can help fill in names and facts for family members that would otherwise remain unknown. Many *répertoires* give the locations of people who were not from the parish and can therefore lead the researcher to another parish or locality.

Special Problems

Dates listed in *répertoires* are almost always written day-month-year. However, this is not an absolute standard. The careful researcher will write out the month when recording information from these indexes to avoid confusion at a later date.

Although several variations in the spelling of a surname may appear in the original parish records, surnames are often standardized in these indexes. Some *répertoires* will list all variations that are included in the records as part of the heading, but others will not. A knowledge of French pronunciation can be useful in finding a surname that has an anglicized spelling. When looking for an individual in these indexes it is necessary to research any dit(e) names as well as all the alternate spellings.

The researcher cannot make assumptions based on the absence of information. In example #2, the third entry noted that both bride and groom were minors. It is tempting to then assume that if this fact wasn't mentioned, then the participants must have been of legal age. But the compilers of the *répertoires* only listed information that was included in the original record. For whatever reason the priest did not include this information in the original record. Of greater importance to the researcher is the inclusion or absence of information regarding previous marriages. In many cases widows and widowers are only listed as such if the previous marriage took place in the same parish. A marriage may look like it is a first marriage in a particular répertoire because the previous spouse isn't listed but, in fact, it may be the second or third marriage for that individual.

Although much information can be gleaned from the *répertoires,* these publications are best used as a guide, directing the researcher to the original record. It must be remembered that these repertoires are a secondary source, and therefore there is always an additional possibility of error. Also, and most important, researchers will want to find the original record, which usually contains other valuable information such as the witnesses to the marriage and their relationship to the bride and groom, or in a baptismal record, the names of the sponsors and the birth date.

Not all *répertoires* are available locally. In the United States, libraries in areas with people of French-Canadian heritage will generally have a good selection. The library of the Wisconsin Historical Society in Madison has an excellent selection. Most large Quebec libraries will have quite a few *répertoires*, including a complete set of those *répertoires* relating to their area. Many have been microfilmed and are available through the Family History Library in Salt Lake City and its Family History Centers throughout the world.

Chapter Seven

Tanguay's *Dictionnaire Généalogique des Familles Canadiennes Depuis la Fondation de la Colonie Jusqu'a Nos Jours*

By Patricia Keeney Geyh

Msgr. Cyprien Tanguay, considered the father of French-Canadian genealogy, is the author of the seven-volume magnum opus, *Dictionnaire Genealogique des Familles Canadiennes Depuis la Fondation de la Colonie Jusqu'a Nos Jours*. Although it has recently been superseded by other more accurate dictionaries, it is still the best known and most frequently used secondary source of data for French-Canadian genealogists. Written in French, it nonetheless can be easily deciphered by those who do not read that language.

Overview

This huge work is written in two parts. The first part is entirely contained in volume one. It encompasses records of French-Canadians married before 1700 and was published in 1871. In this one volume the families are listed alphabetically from A to Z. The second part is in the next six volumes and was published between 1886 and 1890. It covers, in large part, French Canadians born, married, and died during the entire French Regime, which ended in 1764. In some cases it continues on towards the end of the 1700s.

Alphabetically, names beginning with "A" start in volume two and names beginning with "Z" end volume seven.

The *Dictionnaire* does not merely chronicle the marriage records of Quebec, but groups the families together, generation by generation, giving dates and places of baptism, marriage, and burial. Tanguay did this long before computers, photocopiers, telephones, e-mail or fax. It is natural, therefore, that these volumes contain more mistakes than usual in this day of computer technology. Errors or not, Tanguay dealt with 1,220,000 dates of baptism, marriage, and burial, organized into 122,620 articles, and the result has been astonishingly useful for many years.

In addition to the genealogical information about the French-Canadian families, there are various tables and charts of more or less interest, depending on the individual researcher. Of special interest in volume seven is an alphabetical table of surnames and their variations and *dit* names. Although this is certainly not a complete listing, it may be useful when attempting to locate a missing ancestor whose name has changed.

Codes and Symbols: Translating Tanguay

Learning to decipher the essential data in the *Dictionnaire* can be done quite easily. What little difficulty there is involves understanding the codes and symbols, and a few French words. First, the articles on each family are organized alphabetically by the original family surname. Within a given surname, the individual nuclear families are more or less organized by the date of the husband's first marriage. At the beginning of each listing of a given surname is a list of the variant names which people with this surname may have called themselves, e.g. dit names.

A practical example of how to use Tanguay's book is beneficial. Look at the article written about Pierre Brosseau in figure 1 on the following page. (see #1). On the first line appears the date of marriage of Pierre and his wife. The year is printed in large dark numerals, with the date and month of the wedding appearing in similar print and in parentheses. Next to the date is the name of the parish, *Laprairie*, in which they were married. The parish name is coded with superscript 3. During the rest of this article, Tanguay will substitute superscript 3 for the word Laprairie, as a form of shorthand. If a second parish were named several times in this record, it would have its own superscript code. It is important to note that superscript 3 stands for Laprairie only in this article. For other Brousseau families on this same page there are other superscript numbers for Laprairie. They are arbitrary numbers assigned by Tanguay and have no significance beyond the individual article.

The second line (see #2) provides the name of the husband, in this case, Pierre Brosseau. Just preceding the name of the husband is a Roman numeral. This numeral indicates the generation of the husband. Pierre is a second-generation French Canadian. To the right of the name of the husband is a single bracket, followed by the Christian name of the husband's father and the father's generation. Pierre's father was Denis Brosseau, who was a first-generation immigrant to New France.

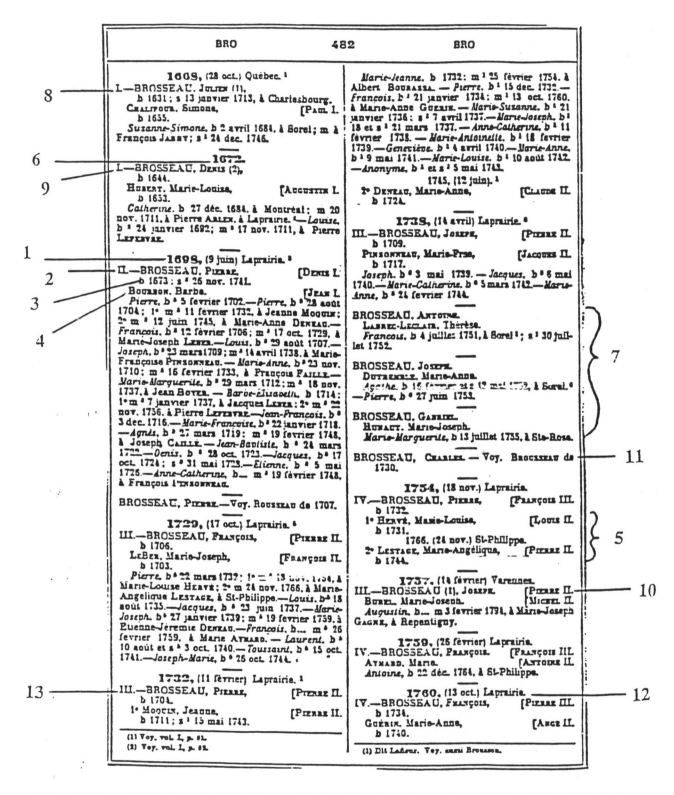

Figure 1. Tanguay's Dictionnaire Généalogique des Familles Canadiennes Depuis la Fondation de la Colonie Jusqu'a Nos Jours, *vol. 2, p. 482.*

The third line (see #3) indicates that Pierre was baptized in 1673. To check the complete date of the baptism it will be necessary to check the record of his father. That record will be either in this volume or in volume one. Pierre died at Laprairie (note superscript [3]) on 26 November 1741.

Next is listed the wife of Pierre (see #4) and the name of her father. Barbe Bourbon was the daughter of Jean Bourbon, a first-generation colonist.

Then follow the names of Pierre and Barbe's sixteen children, each name printed in italics. Baptism and burial information is given as well as marriage information including the name of the spouses.

Some men married more than once, and referring to #5, one can see how this is indicated.

There are other significant issues to be aware of when using Tanguay. Refer to #6 and note that in some cases Tanguay does not provide the day and month of a marriage, but the year only. This indicates that Tanguay did not actually find a marriage record for that family and that he is only estimating the date of the marriage. Some experts say that as many as 80 percent of these estimates are in error. Not only is the year of the marriage often wrong, but frequently the names of the parents of the husband and wife are also in error.

Abbreviations Used in Tanguay

"b"	*baptême* or baptism
"m"	*mariage* or marriage
"s"	*sépulture* or burial
"n"	*naître* or born
"voy"	*Voyez* or look (at)

At other times Tanguay did not even attempt to guess the date of the marriage or the names of the parents (see #7). Since he was unable to tie in these families with the rest of the Brosseau family, he merely cited the information that he had.

When Tanguay wished to footnote an item of information, he placed the number of the footnote in parentheses (see examples #8, #9 and #10). When Tanguay referred the reader to volume one, this indicates that much more information about that nuclear family is available in that volume. At times, in volumes two through volume seven, Tanguay did not cite the first generation at all, but simply referred to the article in volume one. A great deal of other information was provided in the footnotes. Example #10 shows a referral to a footnote that indicated that Joseph Brousseau sometimes went by the name Lafleur and also refers the reader to the article on the name Brousson.

Often names were spelled differently in different church records. Apparently Tanguay found a record for a Charles Brosseau but was able to establish that this man descended from people with the name Brousseau. Tanguay therefore refers the researcher to the records of families with the name Brousseau (see #11).

Research Strategy

How does one trace a line back in Tanguay? Assume that the researcher has identified Francois Brosseau, who married Marie Ann Guerin in 1760. Searching through the

Dictionnaire, the family is found (see #12). Note that the father of Marie Anne is Ange Guerin, a second generation Canadian. To trace the Guerin line, it would be necessary to turn to the record of the family Guerin in Volume Four. Note also that Francois' father is Pierre, a third generation member of the Brousseau family.

Now search for Pierre, who is in the third generation (see #13). This Pierre Brosseau was married twice. In searching through the names of the children, it can be seen that Francois was a child of Pierre and his first wife, Jeanne Moquin. If there were several Pierres in the third generation, it would be necessary to check through the names of the children and find the correct set of parents.

This Pierre Brousseau in the third generation was the son of Pierre Brousseau, a second-generation French Canadian (see #1).

Denis Brousseau, a first-generation immigrant, was the father of Pierre in the second generation (see #9). When looking for Pierre to be listed as a child of Denis and Marie Louise Hubert, one does not locate him in the article appearing in volume two. When referring to volume one, as suggested in the footnote, Pierre is indeed noted as part of this nuclear family.

Special Problems

It is important to be aware of several other problems when using this set of volumes. First, Tanguay did not cover, in whole or in part, the following parishes: Point Claire, Rivier des-Prairies, Point-aux-Trembles de Montréal, Boucherville, Cap-de-Madeleine, Saint Louis de Lotbiniere, and Saint-Pierre du Sud.

Also, in whole or in part, the following counties were not included: L'Assomption, Berthier, Deux-Montagnes, Joliette, and Terrebonne.

Tanguay usually did not specify the trade or occupation of the men at the time of marriage, nor did he indicate whether or not the parents of the couple were alive at the time of the marriage. This information was usually given in the church records.

The place names are sometimes unclear or inaccurate, especially when referring to places in France.

Researchers may find information about an individual in the entry for the individual's parents' that is not found in the individual's entry. The researcher, for example, may know the name of the parents of a great-great-grandmother, and the name of her husband, but not be able to find an entry for that marriage under the name of the husband. However, looking in the entry for the parents of the woman, a researcher may find the needed information amongst the children's records.

Conversely, some children are missing from their parents' records. It just depended on the records that Tanguay extracted. To quote Fr. Archange Godbout, "....there is no mention, or scarcely any, in his dictionary of abjurations, illegitimate births, or of capital punishments. Our history is a splendid one, we agree, but on consulting Tanguay, we could well ask whether it is human."[1]

Since the time of the publication of this tremendously useful work, many French-Canadian genealogists have published additions and corrections to it. The best known is *Complement au Dictionnaire Genealogique Tanguay,* edited by J. Arthur LeBoeuf. This book is discussed in the next chapter.

Summary

While there are many problems associated with using Tanguay's works, it is very important to understand the tremendous value of this collection of genealogical information. With these books, the researcher can shortcut the trial and error system sometimes used in tracing a given family as it moves from one place to another. Using Tanguay as a guide, genealogists can go immediately to the correct church records and obtain the primary information necessary to accurately document their work. It is readily available and, with a little practice, it is easy to understand. This is an excellent secondary source and if wisely used will quickly lead the genealogical researcher to the primary records that are so abundant in Quebec.

1. A comment of Father Archange Godbout as quoted by Roland J. Auger in "Tanguay's Genealogical Dictionary," *French Canadian and Acadian Genealogical Review,* vol. 3, no. 4, p. 221.

Leboeuf's *Complément au Dictionnaire Généalogique Tanguay*

By Patricia Keeney Geyh

J. Arthur Leboeuf's two-volume work entitled *Complément au Dictionnaire Généalogique Tanguay* is an essential reference tool for genealogists using any of the seven volumes of Msgr. Cyprien Tanguay's *Dictionnaire Généalogique des Families Canadiennes Depuis la Fondation de la Colonie Jusqu'a nos Jours*.

Overview

Msgr. Tanguay's set of seven volumes of French-Canadian genealogies has been a major tool for genealogists for the past 100 years. It is certainly the most readily available secondary source for Quebec family history. Most major libraries have a set. With these books, the researcher can shortcut the trial and error system sometimes used in tracing a given family as it moves from one place to another. Using Tanguay as a guide, genealogists can go immediately to the correct church records and obtain the primary information necessary to accurately document their work.

Msgr. Tanguay worked, however, in the pre-computer era. He also lived and worked before the age of automobiles, and when train travel was limited. Even today, with the use of computers, errors in published works are common. In Tanguay they are legion.

J. Arthur Leboeuf, in his *Complément au Dictionnaire Généalogique Tanguay*, has collected thousands of additions and corrections to Tanguay's monumental work. Many of these entries have been written by Leboeuf himself. Others have been provided by authorities from all over Quebec. This work is divided into two series or books. Each is complete in itself.

The first book (series) of the *Complément* is in master alphabetical order. In addition, at the top of each right hand page is given the volume of Tanguay in which the surnames below it can be found. Footnotes are indicated by the conventional superscript numbers.

At the end of each entry the specific page is given of the volume in which Tanguay entered the information that is being amended. Additional entries provide new information about people who are not listed in Tanguay. In this first book (series) Leboeuf indicates this with a footnote, stating "*Pas dans Tanguay*" (not in Tanguay). Leboeuf also lists the page in Tanguay on which this entry should have appeared.

The second book (series) is also in master alphabetical order, with the volume of Tanguay stated at the top of each page. When a name does not appear in Tanguay, however, this is indicated with an asterisk (*) or with an "X." "C" indicates that the entry is a correction of something in volume one of Tanguay's *Dictionnaire*. A number in parenthesis corresponds to the name of the genealogist who provided the correction or addition. The key to these numbers is located at the beginning of the second book (series).

These two series were compiled over a long period of time and published as Leboeuf went along; for this reason, in some libraries, it is possible to find the series in seven or eight different booklets. They can also be found collected together in one binding. It is important to note, however, that even when put together in one binding, the *Complement* is set up in two books or series, each alphabetized completely within itself. When looking up a name, be sure to look in both series

Codes and Symbols: Translating Leboeuf

Looking at to the pages reproduced in this chapter and then going back to Tanguay, a good deal of new information can be learned about this family.

Note that on page 28 of the First Series, which is reproduced in figure 2 on page 46, there are only three entries for the Brosseau surname, and Denis Brosseau is listed first. His father, Jean Brosseau, and his mother, Perrine Gobin, are noted as is his place of origin in France. Leboeuf also states that a marriage contract between Denis and Jeanne Auber (Pierre and

The following abbreviations are used in Series One of Leboeuf

Abbreviation	Meaning
Bce	Beauce
Bte	Baptiste
c.	contrat (contract)
c.m.	contrat de mariage
I.J.	Ile-Jesus
I.O.	Ile d'Orleans
m	mariage, marie (marriage, married)
M., Mie	Marie
Mtl.	Montréal
p.	page
Pte	Pointe
Que.	Québec
Riv.	Riviere
St	Saint
t	tome
T.R.	Trois-Rivières
v	Voir (see)
vf	widower
vol.	volume
vve	widow

BRODEUR, Jean-Baptiste, et Marie Viau: erreur de nom[28], p. 479.

BRODEUR, Charles, (Jean-Bte et Marie Hébert) m 3 oct 1766 St-Charles-sur-Richelieu, à Judith Bougret (Jean-Louis et Marg. Chicoine), p. 480.

BROSSARD, Pierre, et Louise Leblanc[29], p. 481.

BROSSEAU, Denis, (Jean et Perrine Gobin) de St-Sébastien de Nantes, France, m (c. Ameau, 6 nov 1669), à Jeanne Auber (Pierre et Judith Aumond) de Paris[29a], p. 482.

BROSSEAU, Gabriel, et Marie-Joseph Hunaut: mauvaise lecture[30], p. 482.

BROSSEAU, Jacques[31], (Françoise et Marie-Joseph Leber) m 4 août 1766 Laprairie, à Marie-Joseph Lefebvre (Pierre et Marg. Moquin), p. 482.

BROUILLET, Michel, (Jacques et Renée Vaisine) du Poitou, m (contrat passé au Fort St-Louis, en la maison du seigneur du lieu, 3 nov 1670) à Marie Dubois (Guillaume et Isabelle Lasoeur) de Lisieux, en Normandie, France, p. 484.

BROUILLET, Pierre, m 22 nov 1706 Riv.-des-Prairies, à Louise Boulard, p. 484.

BROUILLET, Joseph, (Gilles et Marie Bricault) m 8 août 1729 Riv.-des-Prairies, à Agathe Mersan (Jean et Anne Fronsac), p. 485.

BROUILLET, Jean, (Bernard et Marie Chartier), m 5 nov 1731 Pte-auc-Trembles de Mtl, à Thérèse Lorion (Jean et Anne Tessier), p. 485.

BROUILLET, Antoine, (Gilles et Marie Bricault), m 27 nov 1733 Pte-aux-Trembles de Mtl, à Anne Mersan (Jean et Anne Fronsac), p. 485.

BROUILLET, Michel, (Bernard et Marie Chartier), m 6 juin 1735 Chambly, à Louise Renaudet (Jean-Bte et Marguerite Ménard), p. 485.

BROUILLET, Pierre-Laurent, (Pierre et Louise Boulard), m 10 avril 1736 Chambly, à Marguerite Lefort (Jean et Marguerite DeRousson), p. 485.

BROUILLET, Robert, (Bernard et Marie Chartier), m 10 fév 1738 Pte-aux-Trembles de Mtl, à Catherine Lorion (Jean et Anne Tellier), p. 485.

BROUILLET, Louis-Julien, (Jean et Madeleine Richard), m 17 nov 1738 Verchères, à Elisabeth Huet (Jean-Joseph et Anne Gareau), p. 485.

BROUILLET, Gilles, (Gilles et Marie Bricault), m 3 fév 1739 Chambly, à Marguerite Robert (Jacques et Jeanne Dumets), p. 485.

BROUILLET, Jean, (Jean et Françoise Leclerc) m 6 fév 1741 St-François, I.J., à Jeanne Dessureaux (Jean-Bte et Jeanne Baribeau), p. 485.

BROUILLET, Jean-Baptiste, (Pierre et Louise Boulard), m 13 fév 1741 Chambly, à Françoise Lefort (Jean et Marguerite DeRousson), p. 485.

BROUILLET, Joseph, (Jean et Madeleine Richard), m 11 fév 1743 Ste-Geneviève de Batiscan, à Marie Veillet (Jean et Catherine Lariou), p. 486.

BROUILLET, Charles-Alexis, (Gilles et Marie Bricault) m 26 sept 1746 Pte-aux-Trembles de Mtl, à Angélique Sicard (Barthélémi et Catherine Belisle), p. 486.

BROUILLET, Jean - Baptiste, (Joseph et Agathe Mersan) m 19 fév 1753 Pte-aux-Trembles de Mtl, à Marie-Jeanne Mersan (Joseph et Marie Foran), p. 486.

BROUILLET, Alexis, (Pierre et Geneviève Arrivée) m 7 janv 1765 St-Pierre-les-Becquets[32], à Anne Turcot (Joseph et Elisabeth Arseneau), p. 486.

BROUILLET, Jean, (Jean et Marie Veillet) m 29 juill 1771 Ste-Geneviève de Batiscan[33], à Angélique Hayot (François et Véronique Baribeau), p. 486.

BROUILLET, Julien, (Jean-Bte et Catherine Migneron) m 15 nov 1790 Pte-aux-Trembles de Mtl, à Françoise Desroches (Nicolas et Thérèse Venne), p. 486.

BROUSSEAU, Joseph, m (c. Saillant, 21 sept 1769) à Marguerite Pelletier, p. 488.

BROUSSON, François - Xaxier, (Etienne et Madeleine Papleau) m 8 nov 1760 Ste-Geneviève de Batiscan, à Anne Lefebvre (Jean Bte et Marie-Joseph Papleau), p. 490.

28–N'existe pas: les enfants sont ceux de Jean-Bte Brodeur et de Madeleine Charron, dont la mère était Marie Viau.

29–Même couple que Pierre Brassard et Louise Leblanc, mariés à Montréal, le 22 oct 1742, voir Tanguay II, p. 451.

29a–Ce contrat aurait été annulé; un autre contrat est passé devant Ameau, le 15 oct 1670, avec Madeleine Hébert (Guillaume et Marguerite Meunier).

30–C'est Gabriel Brazeau marié à Josephte Hunaut à la Pte-aux-Trembles, de Montréal, le 21 oct 1754, voir Tanguay II, p. 458.

31–Pas dans Tanguay.

32–Pas dans Tanguay.

33–Pas dans Tanguay.

Figure 2. Leboeuf's Complement au Dictionnaire Généalogique Tanguay, *Series One, page 28.*

Note the entry in

Judith Aumond) was written by the notary Ameau. Footnote 29a indicates that this contract was probably annulled, and that a new contract was written by Ameau between Brosseau and Madeleine Hubert (Guillaume and Marguerite Meunier). When referring to the original article in Tanguay, the researcher discovers that, thanks to Leboeuf, Denis, a first-generation immigrant, has now identified his parents. In addition a previous marriage contract was probably annulled. The footnote in Leboeuf has also provided the exact date of the marriage contract between Madeleine Hebert and Denis, instead of the erroneous estimate given by Tanguay.

Referring to page 75 of Series Two, which appears in figure 3 on page 48, the information given for Denis Brosseau in series one is repeated. Note in the entry in Series Two there is a capital "C" which indicates that the information amends that in volume one of Tanguay.

The second entry on this page is a correction of the information given about Gabriel Brosseau. In Leboeuf it is stated that Tanguay made a poor reading *(mauvaise lecture)* of the original records. Footnote 30 refers the researcher to page 458 Volume Two of Tanguay to the article for Gabriel Brazeau.

The third entry in Series Two gives information about Jacques Brosseau and footnote 31 tells us that this name was not found in Tanguay at all.

The second entry is for Joseph Brosseau and indicates that this was a poor reading by Tanguay. The researcher is referred to Tanguay's Volume VI, page 171 and the surname Ossant.

Notice the entry for Brodeur, J.Bte, son of Pierre and Archange Petit. Look at the coding that shows he was married a second time (2°) to M. Joseph Brouillet.

Abbreviations and Codes Used in Series Two

Abbreviation	Meaning
veuf	widower
veuve	widow
P	page
cont.	contract (sometimes followed by name of notary)
X	name did not appear in Tanguay
*	name did not appear in Tanguay
2° m	married the second time
mauvaise lecture	poor reading

Research Strategy

Begin with Tanguay. Find out all the information about the family recorded there, and then enter this data on pedigree charts and family group sheets.

Next look in each of Leboeuf's two series to find any additions and corrections to Tanguay.

Using the names, dates and places from these two sources, refer back to the primary church records and notarial records to confirm and add to the data.

Baudoin), m le 26 sept 1796 à Verchères, à Madeleine Benoit (Paul et Madeleine Jarret), 2º m le 15 oct 1804 à Verchères, à Judith Meunier (Pierre et Marguerite Lussier), 3º m le 14 juil 1814 à St-Mathias, à Geneviève Sicard (Jacques et Marie Tessier), P. 480, X.

BRODEUR, Pierre (J.-Bte et Josette Hébert), m le 15 janv 1798 à Beloeil, à Marie-Louise Loiselle (Prudent et M.-Louise Tétrault), P. 480, X.

BRODEUR, Louis (Augustin et Marg. Bousquet), m le 22 janv 1798 à Beloeil, à Marguerite Cadieux, (Jacques et Marg. Halde), P. 480, X.

BRODEUR, Charles (Amable et Marie Brunelle), m le 15 oct 1798 à St-Denis-Rich. à Marie-Louise Choquet (François et M.-Louise Bousquet), 2º m le 12 oct 1801 à St-Denis-Rich. à Marguerite Dudevoir (Claude et Agathe Joubert), P. 480, X.

BRODEUR, J.-Bte (Pierre et Archange Petit), m le 15 oct 1798 à Chambly, à M.-Joseph Tessier dit Major (Jean et M.-Joseph Cournoyer), 2º m le 6 fév 1809 à St-Mathias, à M.-Joseph Brouillet (Gilles et M.-Louise Brouillet), P. 480, X.

BRODEUR, J.-Bte (Ignace et M.-Reine Malard), m le 12 nov 1798 à St-Hyacinthe, à Desanges Jarret (J.-Bte et M.-Louise Fortier), P. 480, X.

BRODEUR, J.-Bte (J.-Bte et Josette Hébert), m le 7 oct 1799 à Beloeil, à Véronique Adam (Prudent et M.-Louise Bousquet), 2º m le 25 juillet 1803 à Beloeil, à Elisabeth Casavant (François et Marie Tétrault), P. 480, X.

BROSSARD, Paul (Claude-Marg. Bisaillon) m 13 nov 1773 Laprairie, Marie-Anne Lefebvre (Pierre-Marg. Moquin) *, P. 481.

BROSSEAU, Denis (Jean et Périnne Gobin, de St-Sebastien de Nantes, Bretagne), m le 15 oct 1670, contrat Ameau, à Marie-Madeleine Hébert (Guillaume et Marguerite Meunier, de Nantes-sur-mer, Bretagne, P. 482, C. Le contrat 6 nov 1669 aurait été annulé.

BROSSEAU, Joseph et M.-Anne Dutremble. Mauvaise lecture voir Vol. VI, page 171 - OSSANT, Joseph-Marie, m le 7 janv 1750 à Sorel, à M.-Anne Desrosiers, P. 482.

BROSSEAU, J.-Pierre et M.-Joseph Guertin. Mauvaise lecture - Voir Vol. VII, ROLLAND, Jean-Pierre, m le 10 nov 1760 à Verchères, à M.-Joseph Guertin, P. 483.

BROSSEAU, Antoine (Pierre et Marie-Anne Deneau), m le 10 nov 1788 à Lacadie, à Marie Laure-Lord (Honoré et Hippolyte Garceau), P. 483.

BROSSEAU, Antoine (Antoine et Marie Laure-Lord), m le 26 fév 1821 à St-Luc, à Louise Moreau (Hippolyte et Elisabeth Letartre), P. 483.

BROUILLARD, Pierre-Toussaint (J.-Bte et Thérèse Badaillac), m le 26 août 1788 à Yamaska, à Claire Blanchard (Jean et Catherine Forest), P. 483, X.

BROUILLE-LAVIOLETTE, Michel (Jacq. & Renée Vaizière, de Gouex, dioc. de Poitiers, soldat de Carignan, Cie Petit) & Marie Dubois (Guill. & Isabelle Lasoeur, de Lisieux Norm.) Fort-St-Louis 3 nov 1670.

BROUILLET, Jean (Bernard et Marie Chartier), m le 5 nov 1731 à Pte-aux-Trembles, Mtl, à Thérèse Lorion (Jean et Anne Teilier), r. 485, C.

BROUILLET, Jean (Jn & M.-Mad. Richard) & M. Veillet (Jn & Cath. Lariou) Cont. Rouillard 10 fév 1743.

BROUILLET, Joseph (Joseph et Marie Veillet), m le 7 sept 1767 à Ste-Geneviève-de-Batiscan, à M.-Joseph Desaulniers (Lesieur) (Charles Lesieur et M.-Joseph Lefebvre), P. 486.

BROUILLET, Pierre (Pierre et Marguerite Lefort), m le 26 oct 1772 à Beloeil, à Charlotte Imbault (Paul et Charlotte Cavelier), 2º m le 19 juil 1784 à Beloeil, à Marie-Renée Daunet (J.-Bte et Marie-Joseph Pépin), P. 486, X.

BROUILLET, J.-Bte (Michel et Louise Renaudet), m le 21 nov 1774 à Chambly, à Marie Bourassa (Frs-Albert et M.-Jeanne Brosseau), P. 486, X.

BROUILLET, J.-Bte (Gilles et Marguerite Robert), m le 22 janv 1776 à Beloeil, à Françoise Larrivée (J.-Bte et Frse Larchevêque), P. 486, X.

BROUILLET, Clément (Chas-Alexis et Angélique Sicard), m le 26 janv 1778 à Sault-au-Recollet, à Marguerite Fortin

Figure 3. Leboeuf's Complement au Dictionnaire Généalogique Tanguay, *Series Two, page 75.*

Summary

Even with the thousands of corrections published in the *Complément,* researchers will continue to find errors in Tanguay. All written records contain mistakes, especially secondary sources. This only serves to emphasize the necessity for genealogists to check Leboeuf carefully but even then to go back to original sources, thus eliminating as many erroneous interpretations as possible.

Chapter Nine

Dictionnaire Généalogique des Familles du Québec des Origines à 1730 by René Jetté

By Joyce Soltis Banachowski

Dictionnaire *Généalogique des Familles du Québec* by René Jetté, published by the University of Montreal in 1990, has rapidly become one of the foremost secondary sources of French-Canadian research. In it, Jetté has made additions and corrected many of the errors of Tanguay. Like other genealogical sources, however, it is not the ultimate source; it should lead one to verify information for an individual family by researching primary sources. Jetté has compiled genealogical information from parish records, census reports, marriage contracts and other notarial records, registers of the sick of Hôtel Dieu, Quebec, confirmations, periodicals, books concerning clergy and other notable professions, seigneuries, religious institutions, and a number of other secondary sources. Although written in French, it can be deciphered by those who do not read that language. A copy of Jetté appears difficult to understand on first glance. Upon closer examination, one will note that these are mostly names, dates, places, and many abbreviations and symbols which can be learned quickly.

Overview

This *Dictionnaire* is an alphabetical listing of families by surname from the founding of the colony in the 1600s to 1730. Besides information regarding births, marriages, and deaths of individuals in family groups, it contains a variety of other information of interest to the researcher: places of origin in France of *habitants*, whether parents of the bride and groom are deceased at the time of marriages, censuses of 1666, 1667, 1681, 1686, 1688, 1699, 1700, and 1716, *engagements*, occupations, relationships with others, deaths by drowning or Indian attacks, confirmation, dates of arrival, military activities, illegitimacies, annulments, religious orders, Protestants, and abjuration dates. By checking parentage, one is able to use Jetté to trace several generations. Occasionally, ascendancy charts tracing habitants' families in France are included.

Using Jetté

The *Dictionnaire* is arranged alphabetically by surname, then chronologically by given name. Each family entry has several parts beginning with the name of the male spouse, followed by marriage information, the name of the female spouse, the children, second and third spouses, marriages, and children if there are any, and finally ascendancy information.

All dates are given with the day first, followed by the month, then the year.

Looking at the sample entry on page 52 (figure 4), one can see that each family entry begins with the male surname, in bold letters, followed by the first name. Other possible spellings and *dit* names are also included. Following, in parentheses, are the names of his parents. Sometimes the symbol † appears indicating a particular parent is deceased. The occupation of the parent is also included within the parentheses. Following the parentheses is additional information about the husband (see A and F of the sample). The kind of information found here varies from entry to entry. At the end of this part of the entry, in brackets, one finds abbreviations representing sources of information that Jetté used. A listing of the abbreviations for secondary sources is on page xxiv of the "Sources" section found at the beginning of the book.

The second part of the entry gives information concerning the marriage—the date, place, and, in parentheses, the marriage contract date and notary (see example B).

The next part of the entry gives information concerning the wife. It follows the same format as the male entry (see example C).

Abbreviations and Symbols Used in Jetté

ar.	(arrondissement) department divisions
archev.	(archevêché) archdiocese
b.	(baptême) baptism
C.N.D.	Congrégation Notre Dame
ct	(contrat) contract
d.	(décès) death
ev.	(évêché) diocese
m	(mariage) marriage
n.	(naissance) birth
rec.	(recensement) census
rec. 66	1666 census
rec. 67	1667 census
rec. 81	1681 census
rec. 88	1688 census
rec. 99	1699 census
rec. 16	1716 census
rem.	(remariage) remarriage
s.	(sépulture) burial
v.	(ville) city
(…)	(nom des parents inconnus) names of parents unknown
†	(feu, feue) deceased
	indicates number of marriage, 1-first marriage, 2-second marriage, etc.

PILOTE, Léonard (...) de St-Nicolas, v., ar. et év. La Rochelle, Aunis (Charente-Maritime); d Beauport et s 03-12-1665 Québec; confirmé 10-08-1659 Québec, 40 ans.
⚜ m vers **1654**, La Rochelle
GAUTHIER, Denise (...) de St-Nicolas, v., ar. et év. La Rochelle, Aunis (Charente-Maritime); 45 ans au rec. 67; 60 ans au rec. 81; rem. 1667 Robert LEFEBVRE.
1. *Marguerite* n vers 1655, 12 ans au rec. 67, 26 ans au rec. 81, m 1671 Jean DROUARD.
2. *Jean* n vers 1657, 10 ans au rec. 67, 24 ans au rec. 81, m 1678 Marie-Françoise GAUDRY.
3. *Pierre* n 03 Beauport b 04-03-1663 Québec m 1694 Marie-Jeanne BRASSARD; au rec. 81, à Québec, domestique du Séminaire.

PILOTE, Jean (Léonard & Denise GAUTHIER) au rec. 81, à Lauzon.
⚜ m 27-06-**1678** Québec (ct 31-05 Gilles Rageot)
GAUDRY, Marie-Françoise (Nicolas & Agnès MORIN) d entre 21-10-1710 et 04-11-1714, Sillery.
1. *Marie-Agnès* b 14-01-1680 L'Ancienne-Lorette m 1698 Pierre HÉDOUIN.
2. *Jean* n 05 Lauzon b id. 13-10-1681 L'Islet m 1710 Catherine BRASSARD; *ENFANT NATUREL* (mère inconnue): Ludovic b Tadoussac 25-07-1709 Saguenay. ← J
3. *Marguerite* n 24 b 26-08-1683 Lauzon m 1699 François LAMBERT.
4. *Pierre* n vers 1686, 30 ans au rec. 16, m 1716 Louise CHALIFOU.
5. *André* n 12 b 14-07-1687 Sillery.
6. *Marie-Françoise* n 06 Lauzon b id. 09-07-1688 Neuville s 25-12-1694 St-Nicolas.
7. *Ignace* n vers 1690 s 15-02-1700 St-Nicolas (9 1/2 ans).
8. *Madeleine* n vers 1692 m 1715 Michel MARIÉ.
9. *Louise-Charlotte* n vers 1694 m 1714 Michel RICHER.
10. *Jeanne-Françoise* n 15-11 b 08-12-1696 St-Nicolas m 1715 Jean-Baptiste RICHER.
11. *Joseph* n 06-04 St-Nicolas b 03-05-1699 St-Augustin m 1726 Barbe RANCOURT.
12. *Marie-Anne* n 29-03 b 03-04-1701 St-Nicolas m 1724 Antoine TREMBLAY.
13. *Charles* b 04-07-1703 St-Nicolas m 1730 Ursule TREMBLAY (jumeau).
14. *Jacques* b 04-07-1703 St-Nicolas (jumeau).

PILOTE, Pierre (Léonard & Denise GAUTHIER).
⚜ m 11-01-**1694** Québec (ct 26-12-1693 Chambalon)
BRASSARD, Marie-Jeanne (Jean-Baptiste & Jeanne QUELVÉ).
1. *Marguerite* n 06 b 07-11-1694 Québec m 1715 Joseph RACINE.

PILOTE, Jean (Jean & Marie-Françoise GAUDRY).
⚜ m 21-10-**1710** Québec (ct 20 Dubreuil)
BRASSARD, Catherine (Jean-Baptiste & Jeanne QUELVÉ).
1. *Marie-Catherine* n 03 b 04-08-1711 Québec.
2. *Jean-Baptiste* n 05 b 06-10-1712 Québec.
3. *Marie-Michelle* n et b 03-07-1714 Québec d et s 06-11-1716 id.
4. *Louis* n 14 b 15-08-1716 Québec.
5. *Marie-Angélique* n et b 14-02-1718 Beauport.
6. *François-Louis* n et b 27-07-1722 Québec d et s 08-08-1722 id.
7. *Jean-François* b Chicoutimi 11-09-1724 Tadoussac

PILOTE, Pierre (Jean & Marie-Françoise GAUDRY) au rec. 16, à la basse ville Québec; huissier au Conseil Souverain 12-05-1730.
⚜ m 30-09-**1716** Québec (ct 16-08 Duprac)
CHALIFOU, Louise (Paul-François & Jeanne PHILIPPEAU).
1. *Marie-Louise* n et b 21-07-1717 Québec.
2. *Charlotte* n 17-08 Tadoussac b 27-09-1718 Québec.
3. *Pierre* n 05 b 06-06-1720 Québec.
4. *Paul* n 03-10-1722 Québec.
5. *Joseph-Charles* n 17 b 18-06-1726 Québec.
6. *Marie-Angélique* n et b 13-05-1728 Québec d et s 09-09-1730 id.
7. *Marie-Josèphe* n et b 21-04-1730 Québec.

PILOTE, Joseph (Jean & Marie-Françoise GAUDRY).
⚜ m 27-07-**1726** Québec (ct 08 François Rageot)
RANCOURT, Marie-Barbe (Joseph & Françoise DAVEAU).
1. *Joseph* n 20 b 21-07-1727 Québec d 06 s 07-08-1727 id.

---

2. *Joseph* n et b 22-08-1728 Québec d 20 s 21-12-1729 id.
3. *Antoine* n et b 19-11-1729 Québec.

PILOTE, Charles (Jean & Marie-Françoise GAUDRY).
⚜ m 22-10-**1730** Québec (ct 12 François Rageot)
TREMBLAY, Ursule (Michel & Geneviève BOUCHARD).

PIMPARÉ dit *TOURANGEAU*, Charles († Pierre & † Anne CHAQUENEAU) de St-Symphorien, v., ar. et archev. Tours, Touraine (Indre-et-Loire); 27 ans en 1724; soldat de la compagnie de LIGNERY, puis tisserand. ← F
⚜ m 18-07-**1724** Montréal (ct 17 Jean-Baptiste Adhémar)
BOURS dit *LACHAPELLE*, Marie-Louise (Antoine & Marie-Anne VANDANDAIGUE).
1. *Marie-Louise* n 04 b 05-09-1724 Montréal s 10-01-1727 St-François Î.J.
2. *Thérèse* n et b 17-11-1725 Laprairie.
3. *Charles* n et b 18-05-1727 Rivière-des-Prairies s 16-08-1728 St-François Î.J.
4. *Charles* n 16 b 17-10-1728 St-François Î.J. s 22-04-1730 id.

PINARD, Louis (Jean & Marguerite GAIGNEUR) b 12-07-1634 Ste-Marguerite, v., ar. et év. La Rochelle, Aunis (Charente-Maritime); s 12-01-1695 Batiscan; frère de Marie m Dominique GAREAU; aux rec. 66 et 67, au Cap-de-la-Madeleine, maître chirurgien; au rec. 81, à Champlain; cité 08-09-1647 Québec. [DBC I 563, AG-LaR] ← A, B
⚜ m 29-10-**1658** Trois-Rivières (ct 11-06-1657 Ameau) → B
HERTEL, Marie-Madeleine (Jacques & Marie MARGUERIE) d entre rec. 67 et 25-11-1680, Champlain. ← C
1. *Marie-Françoise* n 15 b 16-11-1664 Trois-Rivières m 1682 Martin GIGUÈRE.
2. *Claude* n vers 1667, 14 ans au rec. 81, m 1694 Marie-Françoise GAMELIN; engagé Ouest 23-08-1691.
3. *Louis* n vers 1669, 12 ans au rec. 81, m 1698 Madeleine RENOU. → D
4. *Marguerite* n vers 1671, 10 ans au rec. 81, m 1692 François REICHE.
5. *Marie-Angélique* n vers 1677, 4 ans au rec. 81, m 1699 Jean NIQUET.
6. *Madeleine* n vers 1679, 2 ans au rec. 81.
⚜⚜ m 30-11-**1680** Champlain (ct 25 Adhémar) ← G
PÉPIN, Marie-Ursule (veuve Nicolas GEOFFROY). ← H
1. *Antoine* n et b 10-05-1683 Champlain m 1708 Marie JUTRAS; engagé Ouest 28-07-1704.
2. *Louis* n et b 16-08-1686 Champlain.
3. *Michel* n 24 b 25-10-1688 Champlain d et s 27 id.
4. *Guillaume* b 24-11-1689 Champlain m 1720 Marguerite LECLERC.
5. *Marie-Ursule* n 27 b 29-03-1692 Champlain m 1714 Michel JUTRAS. ← I
6. *Jean-Baptiste* b 20-10-1694 Batiscan m 1724 Agnès GAUTHIER; engagé Ouest 28-04-1716 et 22-04-1726.

Ascendance de Louis PINARD:
2. Jean PINARD, de v. et ar. Cognac, év. Saintes, Saintonge (Charente); marchand bourgeois; m 21-08-1618 Ste-Marguerite de La Rochelle (ct 21-04 Combault).
3. Marguerite GAIGNEUR.
4. Louis PINARD, marchand.
5. Gabrielle MESNARD.
6. Jean GAIGNEUR. ← E
7. Guillemette RAYNIER.

PINARD, Claude (Louis & Marie-Madeleine HERTEL); chirurgien. ← K
⚜ m ct sous seing privé 10-10-**1694**, déposé 14-03-1695 Pothier (La Pérade)
GAMELIN, Marie-Françoise (Michel & Marguerite CREVIER).
1. *Marie-Louise* n ... m 1717 Jean-Baptiste MONGEAU.
2. *Marie-Madeleine* n 21 d 24-02-1699 St-François-du-Lac.
3. *Charlotte-Josèphe* n 02 b 06-06-1700 St-François-du-Lac m 1723 Pierre CHAPDELAINE.
4. *Michel* n ... m 1723 Madeleine RITCHOT.
5. *Anonyme féminin* n vers 1703 s 27-07-1709 St-François-du-Lac (6 ans).
6. *Marie-Claude* n ... s 09-06-1717 St-François-du-Lac.

Figure 4. *Page from Jetté's* Dictionnaire Généalogique des Familles du Québec des Origines à 1730, *page 918.*

The fourth part gives information concerning the family (see example D). Children are listed chronologically with their date and place of births and baptisms, spouse and year of marriage and date and place of death and burial. Additional information may be provided.

The final part that may be given is ascendancy information (see example E). Even numbers are males and odd numbers are females. For example:

2. is the father of the person named.

3. is the mother of the person named.

4. is the father of 2.

5. is the mother of 2.

6. is the father of 3.

7. is the father of 3.

Additional information is sometimes given on the ascendancy chart. By going back and forth through families, one is able to trace several generations.

Research Strategy

Look at the entry for Charles Pimpare (see example F). Note that Charles has a dit name, Tourangeau. Looking at the information within the parentheses, one sees that the parents of Charles, Pierre and Anne Chaqueneau, were both deceased at the time of Charles's marriage, as indicated by the cross symbol. Following the parentheses, one finds that Charles was of the parish of St-Symphorien, of the city (v., *ville*), department division (*ar., arrondissement*), and archdiocese (*archev., archevêché*) of Tours, Touraine, also called Indre-et-Loire. Charles was twenty-seven years old in 1724; he was a soldier in the *compagnie de la Lignery.* Later, he was a weaver.

Now look at the next entry for Louis Pinard (see example A). In parentheses are the names of his parents, Jean and Marguerite Gaigneur. Following the parentheses we see that Louis was baptized on 12 July 1643 at Ste-Marguerite, which was in the city (v., *ville),* the department division (*ar., arrondissement*), and diocese (*ev., évêché*) of LaRochelle, Aunis, also known as Charente-Maritme. Louis was buried 12 January 1695 at Batiscan, and was the brother of Marie who married Dominique Gareau. In the census of 1666 and 1667, Louis was at Cap-de-la-Madeleine as a master surgeon. In the 1681 census he was at Champlain. On 8 September 1647 he was living at Quebec. In brackets, one will notice [DBC 1 563, AG-LaR]. By looking on p. xxiv, one finds that *DBC* is the abbreviation for the *Dictionnaire biographique du Canada* and *AG-LaR* is the abbreviation for Archange Godbout's, *Familles venues de LaRochelle en Canada,* two sources Jetté used.

Now continue to the next line. The second part gives information concerning the marriage (see example B). The symbol 🌳 indicates that this was a first marriage. The marriage took place 29 October 1658 at Trois Rivières, prior to which a marriage contract had been signed on 11 June 1657 with the notary, Ameau. The first wife of Louis Pinard was Marie-Madeleine Hertel (see example C). Looking within the parentheses one learns that her parents were Jacques and Marie Marguerie. Marie-Madeleine died at Champlain sometime between the census of 1667 and the census of 25 November 1680.

Looking at examples H and G, one learns that Louis Pinard's second wife was Marie Ursule Pepin. They married 30 Nov 1680 at Champlain after having signed a marriage contract on 25 Nov 1680 with the notary, Adhemar. Following Ursule's name, Jetté indicates that she was the widow of Nicolas Geoffrey.

The family of Louis Pinard and his first wife, Marie-Madeleine Hertel, are listed in chronological order (see example D). There are six children, Marie-Francoise, Claude, Louis, Marguerite, Marie-Angelique, and Madeleine. Louis also had six children with his second wife, Marie-Ursule Pepin (see example I). These children were Antoine, Louis, Michel, Guillaume, Marie-Ursule, and Jean-Baptiste. Looking back at example D, one sees that the first child of this marriage, Marie-Francoise was born on the 15th and baptized on the 16th of November 1664 at Trois Rivières. Marie-Francoise married Martin Giguere in 1682. The month and day will be found in the separate entry for Martin Giguere and Marie-Francoise Pinard. Now look at child number 2, Claude. His exact birth or baptism date are not known. He was born about 1667. One also learns he was fourteen years old in the census of 1681. In 1694 he married Marie-Francoise Gamelin. The last item notes that he signed an *engagement* contract to go to the West on 23 August 1691.

As stated previously, different kinds of information can be located (see example J). Look at Jean, the second child of Jean Pilote and Marie-Francoise Gaudry on the sample page. Jean was born on the 5th at Lauzon and baptized on 13 October 1681 at L'Islet. In 1710 he married Catherine Brassard. He fathered a child, but the mother of that child is unknown. The child's name was Ludovic and was baptized at

Useful Vocabulary Words

anonyme—anonymous, unnamed
annule—annulled
ans—years
après—after
arrivera, arrive—arrived
avant—before
avec—with
brulé/brulée par accident—burned by accident
cité—city, town
confirme—confirmed
déposé—deposited
habitant/habitante—settler
héritier/héritière—heir
jumeau, jumelleau—twin (male, female)
enfant natural (natural child)—illegitimate child
engagé—engagement
engageur—person who hires another
entre—between
femme—wife
fin—end
frère—brother
inconnue—unknown
mère—mother
noyé/noyée—drowned
paroisse—parish
père—father
puis—later
soeur—sister
tué/tuée par—killed by
vers—about
veuf, veuve—widow, widower

Tadoussac on the Saguenay on 25 July 1709. More information about the Jean Pilote and Catherine Brassard family can be found in his own entry. This is the only place information on Ludovic is found. Additional information is also given for child 13 and 14, Charles and Jacques of this same family. They were twins *(jumeau)*.

Look at the final section of the entry for Louis Pinard (see example E). This provides the ascendance information for Louis Pinard. The "2" indicates that Jean Pinard is the father of Louis Pinard. He was from the city and department of Cognac in the diocese of Saintes, Saintonge, also known as Charente. He was an upper class merchant. He married 21 August 1618 at Ste-Marguerite de La Rochelle and signed his marriage contract 21 April with the notary Combault. The "3" refers to the wife of Jean Pinard and the mother of Louis Pinard. These are the same two people as in example A. Refer again to the ascendancy chart. You can see that 4 and 5 are the parents of 2. Researchers will notice that this is the same Ahnentafel numbering system used in genealogy. The merchant, Louis Pinard and Gabrielle Mesnard are the father and mother of Jean Pinard. The numbers 6 and 7 refer to the parents of 3. Jean Gaigneur and Guillemette Raynier are the father and mother of Marguerite Gaigneur.

Now look at Claude Pinard (see example K). His parents are Louis Pinard and Marie-Madeleine Hertel (see examples A and C). Claude is child 2 in their family. (See example D.) In his own entry additional information is given. One learns he was a surgeon. By going back between names within a family one is able to seek out additional information and trace back several generations.

Special Problems

If a woman was remarried, one will not find her death or burial information (if known) with her first husband's listing. It will be recorded with her last marriage. Birth and baptism information will be found with her parents and/or her first marriage. To find all the information for a woman, follow her through her parents and all her marriages.

Most importantly, there is no information given for anyone beyond the 1730 cut-off date. Even though a family is included, any births, marriages, or deaths after 1730 are not included. Research will have to continue elsewhere.

A second book, Dictionnaire généalogique des Familles du Québec des origines a 1730: Corrections et Additions, Les Presses de l'Université de Montréal, 1996 is also available.

Remember that Jetté's *Dictionnaire* is a secondary source, and all information should be verified through the use of primary sources.

Although it takes time to learn and use, Jetté's *Dictionnaire* is an invaluable source of information and should not be neglected by the French-Canadian genealogist.

Chapter Ten

Le Fichier Histor, Fichier des Mariages Catholiques et Non Catholiques du Québec 1731-1825

by René Jetté

By Patricia Keeney Geyh

After he completed his *Dictionnaire Génealogique des Familles du Québec des Origines à 1730* in 1990, René Jetté faced the problem of making available to genealogists and historians many thousands of his file cards filled with information that postdated his dictionary. His solution to this problem was to photocopy these cards and create a book. *Le Fichier Histor, Fichier des Mariages Catholiques et Non Catholiques du Québec 1731-1825* is bound in forty-four volumes that are organized into four series. These volumes are copies of 135,000 handwritten file cards, organized on 33,500 pages, four cards to a page. Abbreviations and symbols used in this set appear on the facing page.

The first series, "A," is made up of 26 volumes and contains the Catholic marriages of most the counties of Quebec, with the exception of those entries that can be found in the other three series.

The next series, "B," in 15 volumes, encompasses the marriages of non-Catholics of the nineteenth century, with the exception of those in Montreal or in Quebec City. This series also includes the Catholic marriages of the counties of Beauce, Beauharnois, Bonaventure,

A	Acadien	A. G.	Ange-Gardien
A. Lor	Ancienne-Lorette	Ach	Achigan
Arg	Argenteuil	b	baptême
B. Febvre	Baie-du-Febvre	B. S. Paul	Baie-Saint-Paul
Bce	Beauce	Béc	Bécancour
Bellevue	Sainte-Anne-de-Bellevue	Bmont	Beaumont
Bout Ile	Sainte-Anne-de-Bellevue	Bport	Beauport
Bpré	Beaupré	B'ville	Boucherville
c	cultivateur	C. C.	Christ Church
C. Santé	Cap-Santé	capt mil	capitaine de milice
Ch. R.	Château-Richer	Ccoeur	Contrecoeur
Chguay	Châteauguay	Chsbrg	Charlesbourg
ct	contrat de mariage	cord	cordonnier
d	décès	D	dictionnaire Drouin
Dbault	Deschambault	Dr'ville	Drummondville
Éboul	Éboulements	f	feu, feue
F	fiche existante	Gent	Gentilly
Grond	Grondines	I. J.	Ile Jésus
I. O.	Ile d'Orléans	j	journalier
J. Lor	Jeune-Lorette	Kam	Kamouraska
LaDur	La Durantaye	Lap	Laprairie
LaPrés	La Présentation	Long	Longueuil
Lotb	Lotbinière	L'ville	Louiseville
men	menuisier	n	naissance
Mask	Maskinongé	men	menuisier
Mtl	Montréal	Neuv	Neuville
P. Riv.	Petite-Rivière	Pte	Pointe
Qué	Québec	rem	remariage
R. O.	Rivière-Ouelle	Riv. Pr.	Rivière-des-Prairies
s	sépulture	S. Ant	Saint-Antoine
S. Aug	Saint-Augustin	S. Ben	Saint-Benoit
S. Const	Saint-Constant	S. Eust	Saint-Eustache
S. Frs	Saint-François	S. Gab	Saint-Gabriel
S. Genev	Sainte-Geneviève	S. Joach	Saint-Joachim
S. Nic	Saint-Nicolas	S. Phil	Saint-Philippe
S. Th de Mont	Montmagny	S. V. Paul	Saint-Vincent-de-Paul
Sault Réc	Sault-au-Récollet	sgr	seigneur
Soul	Soulanges	t	témoin, township
T. Riv.	Trois-Rivières	Var	Varennes
Verch	Verchères	T	dictionnaire Tanguay
Tbonne	Terrebonne	Vaud	Vaudreuil
Yam	Yamaska	Yamach	Yamachiche

Principal abbreviations used in Jetté's, Le Fichier Histor, Fichier des Mariages Catholiques et non Catholiques du Québec 1731-1825.

Champlain, Charlevoix, Drummond, Gaspe, Huntingdon, Iberville, Iles-de-la-Madeleine, Ile d'Orleans, Maskinonge, Napierville, Nicolet, Outaouais, Richelieu, Rimouski, Rouville, Saint-Hyancinthe, Saint-Jean, Saint-Maurice, Temiscouata, Trois Rivières, Vercheres and Yamaska.

Series "C," made up of two volumes, abstracts the nineteenth century non-Catholic marriages for Montreal and of Quebec City. It also contains the Catholic marriages of the French settlements of the West in the eighteenth century.

Series "D," titled *Unique,* has only one volume containing the marriages of the Gaspe and of New Brunswick up to 1825 and the baptisms and burials of this region before 1800.

Within each series the cards are filed alphabetically by the surname of the men. They are then filed in the following order:

- Surname of wife
- Year of marriage
- First name of wife
- First name of husband

Other sources, including contracts of marriage, have been extracted and the following information may then be found on a file card:

- The date and the parish of the act of marriage
- The date of the contract of marriage and the name of the notary
- The names of the bride and groom
- The names of the parents and/or the names of the previous spouse, if appropriate
- The death of any of the parents who died before the marriage
- The ages of the bride and of the groom
- Their places of residence
- Their professions

Figure 5. Entry from Volume 1 of Series A.

These volumes are the working files of Jetté and his co-workers and most are handwritten. There are some problems dealing with this resource: the handwriting is sometimes difficult to read, the abbreviations are hard to decipher, and the corrections are unclear. Nonetheless, this is a valuable tool for French-Canadian family historians.

Figure 5 records the marriage of Aube - St Onge, Pierre. The lower case "j" that follows indicates that this man was a *journalier,* i.e., day worker. Beneath his name, in parentheses, are the names of his parents, Pierre and Josephte Gibeau. As is always the case in French-Canadian genealogies, the surname of the father, Pierre, is the same as the child, i.e., Aube *dit* St Onge. It is therefore not repeated when listing the father. Also in parentheses is the name of the mother, Josephte Gibeau. The "F" before her name, which should be lower case, means that at the time of her son's marriage she was dead. Under the name of the parents, and in brackets, the "X16" indicates that there was a remarriage by Pierre in 1816 to Marg.

Charbonneau. The "x" is a symbol for marriage. The "F" following the end bracket shows that a record of this second marriage is also on file in this series. Next is the name of the bride, Charpentier, M. Genevieve. Her parents are Joseph, now dead, and Catherine Plante. Joseph had been a day worker.

Figure 6 records the marriage of Aube dit Aubert, Jean-Charles, son of Charles Aube and the dead Marie Ann Gariepy. Jean-Charles married Therese Mandeville in 1771 and this marriage is noted

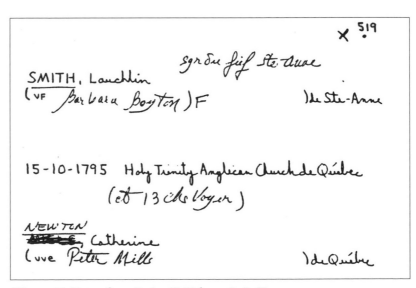

Figure 6. Entry from Volume 1 of Series A.

elsewhere in this file. Jean Charles was married on 14 July 1738 at St Francois, on Ile Jesus. In parentheses there is a reference to the contract of marriage made on 12 of July of 1738 by Notary Coron. Finally, the bride is Marie Genevieve Daze, daughter of Paul Charles Daze, captain in the militia, and Jeanne Chartrand.

The next example, figure 7, is from Series "C" volume 2, L-Z. This series contains many non-Catholic marriages. Protestant records frequently omit the names of the parents of the couple being married, and this is evident here. In this example the upper case "X" on each record and the numbers, 529, have no apparent significance. In the record, note that Lauchlin Smith was a seigneur of the fief of Ste Anne. In that same record it is stated that this information can

Figure 7. Entry from Series C, Volume 2, L-Z.

59

be found in the contract of marriage dated 13 October 1795, written by Notary Charles Voyer. The same marriage record shows that Lauchlin was the widower of Barbara Boyton and that the bride, Catherine Newton, was the widow of Peter Mills. The wedding took place at Holy Trinity Anglican Church of Quebec.

Le Fichier Histor, Fichier des Mariages Catholiques et Non Catholiques du Québec 1731-1825 can be found in libraries in Canada and particularly in the Salle Gagnon of the Bibliotheque Central in Montreal, Quebec. This collection is in a few libraries in the United States.

Chapter Eleven

Dictionnaire National des Canadiens Francais 1608-1760 "The Red Books"

By Patricia Keeney Geyh

The Institut Génealogique Drouin has produced a three volume set, traditionally bound in red, called *The Dictionnaire National des Canadiens Francais* (hereafter referred to as "The Red Books"). The first two volumes are a listing of people married in New France from 1608 to 1760. These marriages are placed in alphabetical order by name of the groom. The names used are the original family names. *Dit* names and other name variations are indicated within the original name. Volume three is a biographical record of many outstanding Québecois (residents of Quebec).

Overview

There is a simple pattern to follow when reading the entries in these volumes, even if the researcher does not know French. Each entry is divided into three sections. The first section pertains to the groom, the second pertains to the bride, and the third section gives the place and date of the marriage. Vertical lines separate these sections. These vertical lines do not appear in The Red Books.

The first column, which is in the section for the groom, shows in capital letters the groom's family surname. In that same column, in lower case and slightly indented, are the dit names and variant spellings used by individual men. In that same column in smaller fine print are any referrals being made to the third volume. Other miscellaneous information may appear in this column.

The second column, in the section for the groom, includes the given name of the groom. Below his given name appears the given name of his father and his mother's maiden name. It is assumed that the father's surname is the same as his son's. Other information regarding the parent may appear.

The second section includes the maiden name of the bride and the names of her parents. It is assumed that the father's surname is the same as the maiden of the daughter. The page number in this section indicates the page in The Red Books on which marriage information about her parents appears.

The third section names the place and date of the marriage. Sometimes, rather than listing a place, the name of a notary is given. This occurs when the marriage record has not been found, but the contract of marriage is available. Using the name of the notary, it is possible to find the original contract of marriage. The originals of these documents are located at the various Quebec government archives. Microfilms of most are available through the Family History Library in Salt Lake City and the various associated Family History Centers throughout the world.

Using The Red Books

Figure 8 shows the entries for Jean Cauchon dit Laverdiere and his father René. In this record it can be seen that Jean Cauchon dit Laverdiere married Jeanne Dubeau at St. Jean, Ile de Orleans, on 25 November 1710. Jean's parents were René and Anne Langlois. Jeanne's parents were Pierre and Marie Madeleine Alaire. For the marriage information about Pierre and Marie Madeleine, turn to page 425.

By looking at the entry for parents' marriages one is able to go back several generations. As you can see in the example, Jean's father René used the spelling "Cochon" for his surname. He sometimes used the dit name Laverdiere. René's parents were René and Charlotte

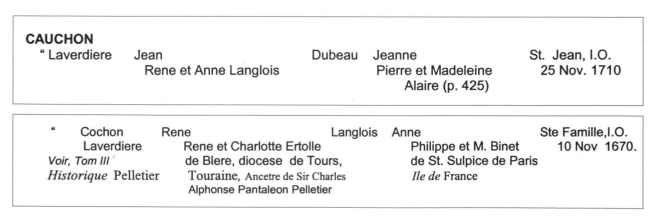

Figure 8. Entries for Jean Cauchon dit Laverdiere (top), and his father Rene Cauchon dit Laverdiere.

Ertolle, who were from Blere, diocese de Tours, Touraine, France. René is the ancestor of Sir Charles Alphonse Pantaleon Pelletier. The researcher is instructed to look at Volume III under the name Pelletier, for more information.

René married Anne Langlois, the daughter of Phillip and Marie Binet of the parish of St. Sulpice, Paris, Ile de France.

René and Anne were married on 10 November 1670 at Ste. Famille, Ile de Orlean.

One of the advantages of using this set of marriage record extracts is that, in most cases, the researcher can trace the family back to a specific location in France.

Chapter Twelve

Repertoire Alphabetique des Mariages des Canadiens-Francais 1760-1935 "The Blue Books"

By Patricia Keeney Geyh

The *Répertoire Alphabetique Des Mariages Des Canadiens Francais 1760-1935*, compiled by Les Services Généalogiques Claude Drouin (commonly known as "The Blue Books") is a continuation of the Institute Drouin's *Dictionnaire National Des Canadiens Francais 1608-1760* (commonly known as "The Red Books"). Although designed as an index, these volumes are useful on their own.

There are a total of 113 volumes in this monumental series, of which forty-nine provide information about the men *(hommes)*. The same information has been re-sorted by the maiden names of the women (femmes) and published in the remaining sixty-four books. These 113 volumes are also on microfilm but are somewhat more difficult to use in this format because it is necessary to roll the microfilm back and forth on the reader to get to the appropriate page. The *Third Cardex Drouin supplement,* an addition to the 113 volumes, will be discussed later in this chapter.

The collection and publication of all this data began in the 1940s, when The Drouin Institute microfilmed all the vital records at the various courthouses in Quebec. These records covered the period from the 1600s to 1935, and were predominantly the second copy of the church records that were required to be sent to the courthouses each year. The staff then extracted marriage data from these films. The information extracted for the years up to 1760 was published and can be found in The Red Books in many libraries throughout North America. The extractions of the records after 1760 were bound in the 113 volumes discussed in this chapter. These extractions, along with the *Third Cardex Drouin Supplement*, were used by the Institute staff as an index to these microfilms.

It is important to note that The Blue Books and the *Cardex* index only the marriages in the civil records. The civil records, however, include births, marriages and deaths. It is necessary, therefore, to locate the marriage of a couple in the civil records and then browse through these records for births and deaths.

The Blue Books usually organize the information on each page in the same format as The Red Books. The pages are a bit difficult to read, however, because they appear to be a copy of an early dot-matrix printout. These volumes, initially work sheets for the Institute, were not prepared for formal publication. Therefore one sees corrections and additions throughout the work, and the format sometimes varies. The data is more compressed than in The Red Books but can be easily understood.

Many abbreviations are used throughout this series. A few examples are:

Adamsv	Adamsville	**pre**	Pierre
Fr	Francois	**vf**	widower
Jb	Jean-Baptiste	**vve**	widow
Jean b	Jean Baptiste	**X**	Xavier
Jos	Joseph		

Each volume of The Blue Books is divided into two sections. Volume 2 of the men, for example, covers the name Audy through Beaudry. The first 470 pages cover the records for those names from the years 1760 to 1880. The remainder of the book starts over with the name Audy and covers the names Audy through Beaudry from 1880 to 1935. This system is also found in the women's records.

As you refer to the sample on the following page (figure 9) from the first section (1760-1880) of Volume 15 of The Blue Books for men, you will note that the first column to the left gives the surname of the groom in lower case type. The second column cites a *dit* name or spelling variation for a particular entry, if one is known to exist. The third column provides the first name of the groom, and on the line below, slightly indented, are the names of the groom's parents. Should this be the second marriage of either the bride or groom, the name of the first spouse will be given and not the name of the parents. Column four provides the surname of the bride. Column five gives the first name of the bride and, on the

```
uouvilla    georger              durablond   elina                  ste-anne la pérade
            gilbert-paquat sophia            david-perreault adélaide 22 nout 1893

"           "                    durablond   m.-emma                ste-anne la pérade
            léandre-lepine flora            david-perreault adélaide 12 janv.1892

"           "                    tessier     aglaée                 ste-anne la pérade
            pr.-tessier adélaide            omer-langlois soline  3 nov.   1885

"           gilbert              paquet      sophia                 grondines
            jos.-rivard thérèse             jos.-chavigny de la ### 11 juil. 1853
                                                chevrotière gertrude

"           honoré               daveau      eléonore               st-nicolas
            ls.-demers m.anne              frs xavier-paquet anast. 16 nov. 1841

"           "                    huard       henr.                  st-nicolas
            vf deveau eléonore             chs.-lambert jos.     3 juin   1851

"           hubert-alexis        douville    adélaide               st-casimir
            alexis-tessier agathe          olivier-vallée adélaide 27 fév.  1854

"           irénée               tessier     albertine              3 rivières
            elzéar-evoy jne                jos.-/ douville elmire 12 sept. 1896

"           isaie                martin      m.-alize               st-casimir
            david-audette madel.           ed.-rivard m.jos.     25 mai    1857

"           jean-bte             anderson    m.                     n.-dame qué.
            jn bte-fréchette judith        vve morisset etienne  6 aout    1844

"           "                    coté        délima                 st-ferdinand még.
            ls.-mc coffrey mary            ls.-navigny sod       12 fév.   1866

"           " -bte               frichette   julie                  st-nicolas
            vf simoneau véronique          ls.-coté m.anne       25 fév.   1811

"           " -bte               miller      m.                     n.-dame qué.
            jn bte-anderson m.             ferd.-st hilaire hélena 25 sept. 1871

" doville   john                 o'flaherty  nellie                 cathédrale mtl
            robert-morgan  may             will.-jodoin aldina   17 sept.  1927

"           jean-bte             simoneau    m.-véronique           st-nicolas
            chs.-charest genev.    &       pr gabriel-demers m.anne 22 aout 1803

"           joachim-télesphore   lefebvre    m.-georgiana           ste-anne la pérade
            joachim-durablon adélaide       chs.uldoric-douville 29 janv.  1867
                                                m.zéphise

"           joseph               archambault madel.                 st-hyac. paroisse
            vf touche lafleur marg.        jn bte-allard m.lse   27 aout   1810

"           "                    catz        cordélie               st-hilaire rouv.
            eusèbe-desjardins julie        paul-petit angèle     6 juil.   1868

"           "                    dufrene     odélisa                st-alban
            vf grégoire desneiges          jn.-chartré marg.     28 oct.   1862

" dauville  "                    dupont      jos.                   st-nicolas
            jos.-bergeron m.ursule         jn.-bergeron m.lse    7 fév.    1763

"           " -chs.              gamme       victoria               beloeil
            jos.-caty cordélia             guill.-berger virg.   31 juil.  1894
```

Figure 9. A portion of a page in "The Blue Books," Vol. 15, First Section, 1760-1880.

line below, slightly indented, appear the names of the parents of the bride. Column six states the place at which the marriage occurred and beneath it is the date of the marriage. In all columns a ditto mark is used if the entry is the same as the one in the line above.

Figure 9 is from the first part of Volume 15, which includes men with the surnames of Douville. In the fourth entry on this sample page the marriage of Gilbert Douville is recorded. In column one is a ditto mark referring to the surname "douville," which appears at the top of the column. Column two is empty. Column three provides the first name, "gilbert" and on the line below, slightly indented, are the names of Gilbert's parents, "jos." and "therese rivard." Note that only the first name of the father is given, it being assumed that his surname is the same as that of Gilbert. Also observe the "jos.", the abbreviation for Joseph. The next column gives the surname of the bride, "paquet." Column five states that the bride's first name is "sophie." Indented on the line below are the names of her parents, "jos." and "gertrude chavigay de la chevrotiere," it being assumed that Sophie's surname is Paquet. The last column to the right states that the wedding took place at Grondines. Below it is the date of the wedding, 11 July 1853.

Further down the page the entry for John Douville gives his dit name as "doville," and still further down this page a Joseph Douville has the name variation "dauville."

Also observe that, although this page is from the first part of the volume that supposedly covers the years 1760-1880, there are several entries dated after 1880. It is important, therefore, to check both sections of a given volume when searching for a particular marriage record.

Figure 10 on the following page is also from Volume 15, but this time from the second section covering the dates 1880 through 1935. Here the surname is capitalized the first time it appears in column one. After that entry, the surname is always repeated, but written entirely in lower case with no ditto marks. Beneath a given surname a number sometimes appears. This number refers to the films of the original courthouse records filmed by the Drouin Institute. These numbers may appear in the first part of each volume, but rarely. At times dit names or spelling variations are given, but seldom in this section of the volume. The rest of the page is formatted as in the first part.

Look at the entry for Pierre Douville. His parents are listed as Louis Douville and Rosalie Marquis. He married Anna Charbonneau, the daughter of Pierre Charbonneau and Marie Brault. They were married at St. Vincent, in Adamsville, on 8 February 1897. This sample page clearly demonstrates how the staff of the Drouin Institute wrote in additions and corrections.

In addition to The Red Books and The Blue Books, the Institut Drouin developed the Third Cardex Supplement. This index provides access to even more names in the civil records. It has not been published in book form but is available on 32 reels of film sorted in alphabetical order by the names of the men.

The Repertoires Alphabetique des Mariages des Canadiens-Francais 1760-1935 (The Blue Books) and the *Third Cardex Supplement* are very difficult to find. They can be located at some of the French-Canadian libraries in the eastern part of the United States, and in the libraries in Quebec. The Salle Gagnon in the Central Library of Montreal (located at 1210 Rue Sherbrooke East, Montreal) has them in its huge collection of books and films dealing with Canadian and French-Canadian research.

DOUVILLE-PHILIAS

douville p	philias	ouellet	m.-marcelline	st-édouard	
	damase-vallée sophie		ls-coulombe luce	24 fév.	1879
douville	philias	guertin	m.-euphémie-myrsa	st-casimir qué	
	elzéar-douville célina		eugène-laganière demerise	17 juin	1913
douville	pierre	charbonneau	anna	st-vincent adamsv.	
	ls-marquis rosalie		pre-brault marie	8 fév.	1897
douville	pierre	charbonneau	anna	st-vincent ferrier	
	ls-marquis rosalie		pre-brault marie	8 fév.	1897
douville	raoul	bélanger	marie	st-thuribe qué	
	elzéar-lemay octavie		ulric-coté virginie	22 juin	1909
douville	roger	gendron	simone	st-thuribe porta.	
	raoul-bélanger maria		henri-vallée délia	14 juil.	1937
douville	roland	gendron	gertrude	st-casimir qué	
	ths-douville ombéline		félix-alphonsine douville	10 juin	1935
douville	rosaire	gosselin	dolorès	st-alban qué	
	chs-langlois mérilda		wilbrod-julien marie	9 juil.	1932
douville	solomon	folley	marie-césarée	st-casimir	
	damase-vallée sophie		daniel-leboeuf célina	23 nov.	1885
DOUVILLE	THOMAS (JOS.=THS)	DOUVILLE	M.-HOMBELINE		
douville	thomas	douville	m.-lse	st-casimir	
	léandre-lépine flora		edmond-tardif arsélie	30 janv.	1894
douville	trefflé	douville	m.-eugénie	st-casimir	
	david-grandbois célanire		eusèbe-ricard aurélie	20 juil.	1880
douville	trefflé	désailliers	marie-philomène	st-casimir	
	jos.-gervais marie		pre-trottier adélaide	12 fév.	1878
douville	valérien	trottier	thérèse	st-thuribe	
	raoul-bélanger maria		henri-delisl hedwidge	21 oct.	1937
douville	wilbrod	fréchette	m.-lse	st-casimir	
	adolphe-grandbois arsélie		clair-lacoursière delima	2 av.	1894
douville	wilbrod	leduc	victoria	st-casimir qué	
	vf fréchette m.-lse		vve jeffrey lépine	12 mai	1937
douville	willie	boisvert	m.-joséphine-aline	st-thuribe qué.	
	damase-boisvert cléophée		pre-mc donald donalda	22 avril	1925
"	XAVIER → Denis Douville	CHEVRIER	BRIGITTE		
DIVAN	john	coughlan	mary	chatam st-michel	
3106	- de black point		-	31 mai	1870
DOVIS	john	lalonde	séphirine	curran	
	pre-lorrain marie		jos.-coté angèle	20 fév.	1832
doris	moise	monnette	mélina	n.-d.g. hull	
	pre-coupal marie		ferdinand-sarrasin henriette	29 sept.	1888

Figure 10. A portion of a page in "The Blue Books," Vol. 15, Second Section, 1880-1935.

C h a p t e r   T h i r t e e n

Répertoire des actes de baptême mariage sépulture et des recensements du Québec ancien

By Linda K. Boyea

The *Index of Acts of Baptism, Marriage, Burial and Censuses of Old Quebec: Research Program in Historical Demography,* also known as PRDH, was a university study begun in 1966 with government financial help. This work was published by the University of Montreal under the direction of Hubert Charbonneau and Jacques Légaré. With the use of computers, information from 300,000 church records, census records, and other documents has been compiled into forty-seven volumes. These volumes include some 2 million names sorted by government area, (Quebec, Trois-Rivières, Montreal), by parish, and by last name. The information is presented in chronological order. It covers the French Period to 1765, and offers a unique record of a people.

Overview

The results of the university study were published over a period of time and are divided into a forty-seven volume set made up of five sections:

Volumes 1-7 (before 1700), 250,000 names

Volumes 1-5 record the information by parish. They extract information from 32,000 records of fifty-one parishes. All baptisms of the parish are listed together in chronological

order, followed by all the marriages and all burials. Each parish is individually indexed.
Volume 6 has the names from the seventeenth century censuses and other documents that supplement the parish registers. (Confirmation lists, marriage annulments, etc.)
Volume 7 is the alphabetical index of surnames in volumes 1-6.

Volumes 8-17 (1700-1729), 425,000 names

Volumes 8-15 extract information from 62,000 records from the registers of eighty-four parishes.
Volume 8 also contains the 1716 census of Quebec.
Volume 11 has the 1700 Mont-Louis census.
Volumes 8 and *13* contain hospital lists.
Volumes 16 and *17* are the alphabetical index of surnames in volumes 8-15.

Volumes 18-30 (1730-1749), 600,000 names

Volumes 18-28 extract information from 86,000 records of 106 parishes. Gaps in church records are filled from civil documents.
Volume 18 contains the 1744 census of Quebec and Quebec hospital lists.
Volume 24 contains Montreal hospital lists.
Volumes 29-30 are the alphabetical index of surnames in volumes 18-28.

Volumes 31-45 (1750-1765), 675,000 names

Volumes 31-42 extract information from 116,000 records of 117 parishes.
Volume 31 also contains the Quebec hospitals lists.
Volume 37 contains the Montreal hospitals lists.
Volumes 43-45 are the alphabetical index of surnames for volumes 31-45.

Volumes 46-47

Volume 46 has additional items from parish registers and the archives of the Archdiocese of Quebec, 1700-1765.
Volume 47 contains the partial censuses before the fall of Quebec.

The inside cover in the front of each volume not only shows the location of all the parishes but also lists each parish under the appropriate government area. (Quebec/Trois-Rivières/Montreal) The inside back cover lists the contents of each volume in the current set and of all previously printed volumes.

Although the format is the same throughout the entire forty-seven volumes, there are some differences between the first set and the rest. Professions and locations are listed by a code number in the first set, and must be interpreted by using the Appendices provided in Volumes 1-7. The other volumes include this information within the individual document.

Using The *Répertoire*

If the researcher knows the parish his ancestors lived in, the fastest way to access the information provided is to go directly to the parish in the proper time frame and consult the parish index for the name, the type of event (baptism, marriage, burial), and the date. Since the recorded events are listed in chronological order, it is then a simple matter to find the proper event on the document pages for that parish.

If the parish is not known, the researcher must consult the general index of the proper set. This is much more time consuming, and can be quite frustrating if the ancestor in question has a common name. However, the general index is well arranged and easy to use.

Using the Parish Records

Within each set of volumes, the parishes are presented by government area. Those of the Quebec area are first, followed by those of the Trois-Rivières area, and then those of the Montreal area. Knowing that an ancestor came from "around Montreal," for instance, would eliminate the need to research many other parishes.

Within each individual volume, the parishes are printed in numerical order by the parish code, not alphabetically by parish name. For example, in Volume 13, the records for Ile-Dupas (071), come before Berthier (073). The top of each page of individual documents (the excerpts from the original records), clearly shows which parish and what type of record is being viewed. See the following example.

M	391	NOTRE-DAME-DE-MONTREAL	Mariages
document code	parish code	parish name or place	type of document

Each individual document in the *Répertoire* consists of a heading and a document proper. The document heading consists of this symbol ☐ followed by the date, which is recorded in "International order": Year, Month, Day. The codes for baptisms and burials precede the symbol. Two dates may be listed, but the document is indexed under the baptism or burial date, not under the birth or death date. Some documents—very few—list a source to the left. If more than one event happened the same day, a sequence number (§) is given to the right of the date.

CODES for document heading:

B : date of baptism   TIRÉ DE B : Burial taken from baptism
D : date of death   TIRÉ DE S : Baptism taken from burial
N : date of birth   O : date of provisional baptism
S : date of burial

DATE INTERPOLEE=date inferred from surrounding certificates
§ sequence number: blank is first; #1 is second on that date, etc.

The document proper duplicates the names, first and last, of all persons, living or dead that are mentioned in the original record: the principal parties, their spouses, parents, and the witnesses. The probands—the principal person(s) in the original record—are given the referral numbers of 01 and 02. All other persons are listed and numbered in the order in which they are mentioned in the original record. Whenever possible, the record also lists the sex, age, marital status, occupation, kinship, place of origin, and place of residence. Family names are duplicated exactly as written in the original document, however, the first names are written in their modern form.

```
CODES for document proper:
Marital Status:    C=single, M=married, V =widowed, S =separated
Presence:          D=deceased, P=present, A=absent
Sex:               M=male, F=female, I=unknown
Age:               ANS = years, MOIS = month
Misc:              C.P.=of the parish to which the document belongs
                   c:=degree of relationship, (marriage contracts only)
                   h:=number of days hospitalized
                   o:=place of origin, (vol.-7, see appendix 2)
                   p:=profession, (vol. 1-7, see appendix 1)
                   r:=place of residence
                   s:=signature; s:OUI, s:NON
                   _ _ _ _ _ =separates different families living in a household (census)
                   •=Commentary inserted at the end of the entry
```

In the example below—the only marriage that took place this day—the names of the probands, **Pierre Suraut** and **Marie Agnes Ledoux**, are in bold print. Pierre is #01, and Marie-Agnes is #02. Following them are the names of those mentioned in the original record in the order they were mentioned.

01 PIERRE/SURAUT		r:C.P	s:NON	20 ANS	C P M
02 MARIE AGNES/LEDOUX		r:C.P.	s:NON	16 ANS	C P F
03 HILAIRE/SURAUT	EPOUX DE 04	PERE DE 01	M D M		
04 LOUISE/PARADIS	EPOUSE DE 03	MERE DE O1	VPF		
05 NICOLAS/LEDOUX p:MAITRE MENUISIER	EPOUX DE 06	PERE DE 02	V P M		
06 MARIE AGNES/BONNEDEAU	EPOUSE DE 05	MERE DE 02	M D F		
07 DENIS/LECOURT		BEAUFRERE DE 01	P M		
08 CHARLES/BARRE			P M		
09 MICHEL/BARRE			P M		
10 /PRIAT p:VICAIRE	R:VILLE-MARIE		C P M		

According to this document, Pierre was a resident of the parish, (r:C.P.) and could not write, (s:NON). He was a single male, (C) (M), 20 years old.

Number 05, Nicolas Ledoux, the father of the bride, (pere de 02), was a master carpenter by trade, (p: MAITRE MENUISER). He was a widower, (V), and was present at the event, (P). His wife, #06, (EPOUSE DE 05), had died. (D).

The fact that Denis Lecourt, #07, is listed as a brother-in-law to Pierre (BEAU-FRERE DE 01) indicates that Pierre has a sister who was already married. But the original record does not indicate whether Denis himself was married or not as there is no code in the proper column. There is also nothing in this document to explain who Charles and Michel Barre (08 and 09) were or why they were present at this wedding.

The last name on the document is that of the curate (p: VICAIRE), who resides, (r:), at Ville Marie (Montreal).

Using the General Index of Names (volumes 7, 16-17, 29-30, 43-45)

In the general index the last name is centered in the column in bold print, and it is written as it was spelled in the original record. The first names are listed beneath the last name to the left with the information about the event to the right (see example below.) If more than one event took place on the same day, a sequence number is given. (No number is the first event; §1 is the second event, etc.) The referral number in this index correlates to the same person/number as found in the document in the parish records.

In the index example below, the referral number of 01 shows that Pierre is the proband (husband) in the document. The lack of a sequence number indicates that this was the only marriage (M), performed in this parish (391) on that date, (18 May 1723). The researcher will find the parish records in volume 13. In the box following the example are the codes for documents as they are listed in the general index and found on the page headings of individual documents.

SURAUT

	Document Code	Parish Code	Date of document	Sequence number §	Referral Number	Volume Number
Hilaire	M	391	1713-09-24		05	13
	M	391	1723-05-18		03	13
Pierre	M	391	1723-05-18		01	13

Document Codes	Additional Codes for Vol. 1-6, 46
B : baptism	A : recantation
M : marriage	C : confirmation
R : census-households	H : hospital sick list
((Menage) are numbered	L : list of migrants
S :burial	N : marriage contract
	Z : marriage annulment
	NOT : Notary
	JSJ Journal des Jesuites certificates

Research Strategy

There are two different approaches to using the information found in the *Répertoire*. Using the parish indexes or the General Index volumes to find references to a particular name and then reviewing each reference is an excellent way to find the individual being researched, his parents, children, and siblings. One can obtain many birth, baptism, marriage, and death dates and places that would otherwise be difficult to obtain. From the marriage documents especially, ancestors can be easily traced backwards or forward through each time period. Since the Family History Library has microfilmed baptism, marriage, and burial church documents through 1876, once the parish is known, it is easy to order the correct film at a Family History Center and view the original record.

Ignoring the indexes and researching the parish documents, the hospital lists, and the census lists is a second approach to the *Répertoire*. The demographics provided by the censuses and the chronological listing of events by parish and hospital list give insights into the community as it existed over time. These demographics answer many questions, but may cause the researcher to ask many more: Who was friends with whom? Why was a particular person present at the marriage? the burial? Why would someone be missing? Why were there substantial numbers of deaths clustered together? Etc.

The two approaches can be used together with great success. Comparing several previous and subsequent documents to the one that lists the ancestor in question can often show interactions between the ancestor and his neighbors, placing him within the life of the community.

Special Problems

Since many of the participants in the events of the earlier time periods were unable to write, last names were written in the original record as the person who wrote it thought it should be spelled. The person who read the original certificate for PRDH may also have misinterpreted the handwriting. The researcher sometimes needs to examine several variations of last names to find the correct ancestor. The example of SURAUT used above was also spelled SURAU, SURAULT, AND SUREAU in the Index. This is not a serious problem in most cases, but it should be anticipated. Knowing how French is pronounced would also aid the researcher in determining which spelling to pursue.

Furthermore, although this *Répertoire* is based on a substantial number of parish records and other documents, the researcher should not consider this index to be all-inclusive. As in all secondary sources, there are errors and omissions.

Because this large work is an actual extraction of information from original records, it is tempting for the genealogist to stop at this point, record the information as given, and assume he has done thorough research. Again, it is important to remember that the *Répertoire* is a secondary source, meant to direct you to the location of the primary source.

Although the entire set of forty-seven volumes is available at the Wisconsin Historical Library in Madison, WI, only a few research centers and libraries have it in their collections.

Additional Information

Originally this work was to encompass all the parish records and other miscellaneous documents of the population of Quebec up to 1850. In fact, the 400,000 documents from the last half of the eighteenth century were transcribed on tape, but it is doubtful that this additional information will ever be published in book form.

In 1997, a CD-ROM set, *RAB du PRDH*, was produced. It included the information from the forty-seven-volume set, corrections to this information, and additional information up to 1799. The CD-ROM set offers an easy search method for finding the name being researched. Since the additional information on the CD-ROM set includes records from the time period when many residents moved within Quebec and on to the United States, it is of great value to researchers.

Within two years the data available on the CD-ROM set was made available on a website in both French and English. It can be used in a free, though limited, version or through a paid subscription. This website will be discussed in the next chapter.

As in any index of this magnitude, errors and omissions can be expected. It is probable that updates and corrections to the CD-ROM set will be produced in the future. The website, by its very nature, allows corrections to be made on a yearly basis.

As the CD-ROM set and the website become more accessible to the researcher, it is possible that the original forty-seven-volume set will be neglected. However, one of the main advantages of the printed work is visibly seeing the chronological layout of events and the entire parish overview: viewing the sequential records shows the relationship of the people within a parish.

Undoubtedly this work is an invaluable source of information, not only about an individual ancestor, but also about the lives and times of an interesting and resourceful people.

Programme de researche en demographie historique (PRDH) Internet Database

By Linda K. Boyea

In 1966 the Research Program in Historical Demography (PRDH) at the University of Montreal began the monumental task of recording births, marriages, deaths, and other biographic and demographic information about the population of Quebec since the beginning of French colonization in the 1600s. Information through 1765 was originally published in a forty-seven-volume set titled: *Répertoire des Actes de Baptême Mariage Sépulture et des Recensements du Québec Ancien, (Programme de recherche en démographie historique)*. This set has been an excellent source for those genealogists able to find it. Detailed instructions on using the set are described in the previous chapter.

In 1997 a CD-ROM set, *RAB du PRDH*, was produced that included the original information from the forty-seven-volume set, corrections to this information, and additional information that covered the years up to 1799. This CD-ROM set is still available for purchase in both a French and an English version. By 1999, the data available on the CD-ROM set was also available on a website <http://www.genealogie.umontreal.ca/en/main.htm>. (The site address as listed is for the English version, but PRDH is also available in French.)

The Website

Before attempting to find ancestors in the database, it is useful to take a tour of the site and to read the background information provided by PRDH. The various pages, accessed by clicking on the links on the left of the home page, include the following (not in this order):

- An explanation of the sources of the information in the database. The great majority of information came from the parish registers; however, other primary and secondary sources were used. Each individual record found in the parish registers is called a "certificate." (The information from the certificates was extracted by PRDH.)
- A complete list of the parishes by full name, giving the abbreviated name that is used as a place name or that is listed as the source in the database.
- Links to a map to find the location of a parish.
- Parish information, including the history of, and the format used, for record keeping as well as statistics on the number of certificates by type and year, for a given parish.
- Facts on immigration from Old France to New France.
- Naming patterns and name variations including statistics on both first and last names.
- Links to other related sites.
- Subscription information. The website allows both public (free) access or paid subscription to the database. Free access only allows a name search of the database. The search will produce a list of references to the certificates, (baptism, marriage, etc.) allowing the researcher to determine if information on a particular ancestor is available in the database.

Accessing the Database by Subscription

On the homepage the researcher clicks on "Data" which appears on the left side of the screen. The information in the database is presented in three distinct but interlinked sections:

1. A Repertory of Vital Events, 1621-1799
2. A Genealogical Dictionary of Families, 1621-1765
3. A Repertory of Couples and Filial Relations, 1621-1799.

The first section, "A Repertory of Vital Events, 1621-1799," is an index and link to the information that was originally transcribed from baptismal, marriage, and burial certificates from the Catholic parishes as well as from census records, marriage contracts, and confirmations prior to 1800. Other sources were used to fill in information gaps. A complete explanation of the sources used can be obtained from the home page.

In this section a search of the database can be done by individual name, by the name of a couple, or by parish name. This request can be modified by the role, e.g., subject of the event, spouse of subject, father of subject, mother of subject. The search can also be limited by the parish, the time period, and/or by the type of event, e.g., baptism, marriage, etc.

This search produces a list of events in chronological order. Dates in PRDH are listed by year, month, and day. Clicking on the date next to an event in the list will display the information that was extracted from the original certificate. This display of information is called a "document."

Date	Type	Parish	Role	Sex	Name	First name
1795-02-09	m	St-Constant	Subject	m	BISSON	LOUIS
1795-06-01	b	Sault-au-Récollet	Subject	m	BISSON	LOUIS JOSEPH
1795-07-05	b	St-Constant	Father	m	BISSON	LOUIS
1795-12-23	b	St-Constant	Subject	m	BISSON	LOUIS
1795-12-23	b	St-Constant	Father	m	BISSON	LOUIS

Number of references : 5   Back to the search page   Navigation principles

To see how many hits you have used from your current subscription.

Example of a list requested by individual, Louis Bisson, limited by time period and parish.

Date	Type	Parish	Sex	Name	First name
1795-02-03	s	St-Constant	f	BOYER	JOSEPHE
1795-02-03	b	St-Constant	m	AUDELIN	GEDEON
1795-02-06	b	St-Constant	f	LONGTIN	SCHOLASTIQUE
1795-02-07	b	St-Constant	m	DEMERS	AUGUSTIN
1795-02-08	b	St-Constant	f	LEMIRE	CHARLOTTE
1795-02-09	m	St-Constant	m	BISSON	LOUIS

Number of references : 6   Back to the search page   Navigation principles

To see how many hits you have used from your current subscription.

Example of a list requested by parish, St-Constant, limited by time period.

"Certificate," "Mariage," and "St-Constant" at the upper left indicate that this document contains the extracted information from the marriage certificate in the parish register of St-Constant. The abbreviations used in the document are listed below but can also be found by clicking on the phrase, "About the M.S. and Pr. Variables," at the bottom of the document. Clicking on the word, "glossary," gives an explanation of terms used by PRDH.

When viewing this document on the website, the names LOUIS BISSON and JOSEPHE CIRCE are in blue, as is the word, "Couple," at the upper right. These are links to documents found in the next two sections of the database. Clicking on either name will produce a document

M.S. (Marital Status):	Pr. (Presence):
c= single	p= present
m= married	a= absent
v= widow/ widower	d= deceased
s= separated	v= alive

		Couple					**№** 347719

ꟿᴀʀɪᴀɢᴇ
St-Constant
1795-02-09

Rank	Name	Age	M.S.	Pr.	Sex
01	**LOUIS BISSON** Residence : ST-CONSTANT	---	c	p	m
02	**JOSEPHE CIRCE** Residence : ST-CONSTANT	---	c	p	f
03	**FRANCOIS BISSON** FATHER OF 01	---	---	d	m
04	**ARCHANGE DUPUIS** MOTHER OF 01	---	---	---	f
05	**JOSEPH CIRCE** FATHER OF 02	---	---	---	m
06	**MARIE LEMIEUX** MOTHER OF 02 Residence : ST-CONSTANT	---	---	---	f
07	**ALEXIS BISSON** ONCLE PATERNEL OF 01	---	---	p	m
08	**ANTOINE BISSON** BROTHER OF 01	---	---	p	m
09	**HIPPOLYTE LONGTIN** BROTHER-IN-LAW OR STEPBROTHER OF 02	---	---	p	m

Back to the **search page**   **Glossary**   Navigation **principles**

To see how many hits you have used from your   **About the M.S., Pr. and Age variables**
current subscription.

Example of a document, marriage of Louis Bisson, 1795-02-09, obtained by clicking on the date, 1789-04-20, in either list above.

titled "Individu," which gives any information known about that person: parents, marriage/s, birth date and place, etc. Clicking on the word "Couple" produces a document (titled "Couple") that lists them and any children who married before 1799.

The documents created from the certificates (baptism, marriage, etc.) originally published in the forty-seven-volume set include all individuals that were present at that event. However the documents generated by the more recent information, 1766-1799, only list individuals who are specifically mentioned as having a relationship to the principal/s in that event. The lists and the documents found in this database can be printed, but the researcher should remember that this is a copyrighted site.

According to PRDH, by using the information from the baptismal, marriage, and burial certificates from the Catholic parish registers to establish individual and family relationships, they have created a "reconstruction of the population of Quebec from the beginnings of French colonization in the seventeenth century." This reconstruction forms the basis of the second and third sections. The documents found in these two sections, titled: "Individu," "Couple," and "Family," correspond to the Individual Records and Family Group Sheets used by most researchers.

A search requested for an individual in the second section, "A Genealogical Dictionary of Families, 1621-1765," displays the birth events showing the father as well as the child. A family request lists both spouses for marriage events. Clicking on the name in the list of birth events produces the "Individu" document that gives personal information for the person chosen (dates of vital events, parents, spouses, etc.). Clicking on the word "Family" displays a document that shows children born of that couple, with the date and place of all known births, marriages, and deaths up to 1765.

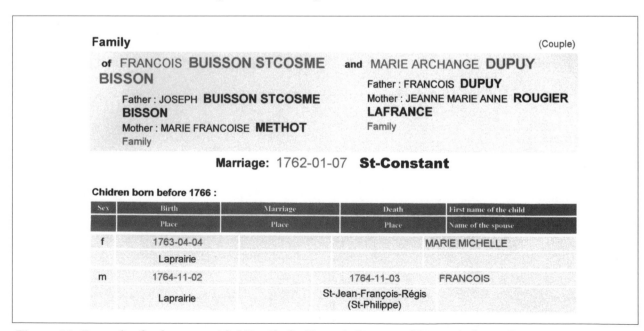

Figure 11. Example of a document titled Family for Francois Bisson and Marie Archange Dupuy.

Figure 11 shows a document that has several links. Clicking on any date will take the researcher to the document titled *Certificate,* which is PRDH's extraction from the original source. Clicking on the person's name will give a document titled "Individu." The word "Couple" will link to the couple's document. Most significant, clicking on the word "Family" under the names of the couple's parents will take the researcher back one more generation to the family document for that set of parents.

The third and last section, "A Repertory of Couples and Filial Relations, 1621-1799," includes data that link each spouse with his or her parents, and to any other spouses. It also links them to their married children. The names of both spouses must be provided to request a search. Only one reference will appear if this couple is in the database. Clicking on the word "union" will produce the document titled "Couple."

In figure 12 we see a document where the date links to a document titled "Certificate." The word "Family" links to the document titled "Family" for Francois and Archange. The word "Couple" links to the document titled "Couple" for the spouses, children, and parents.

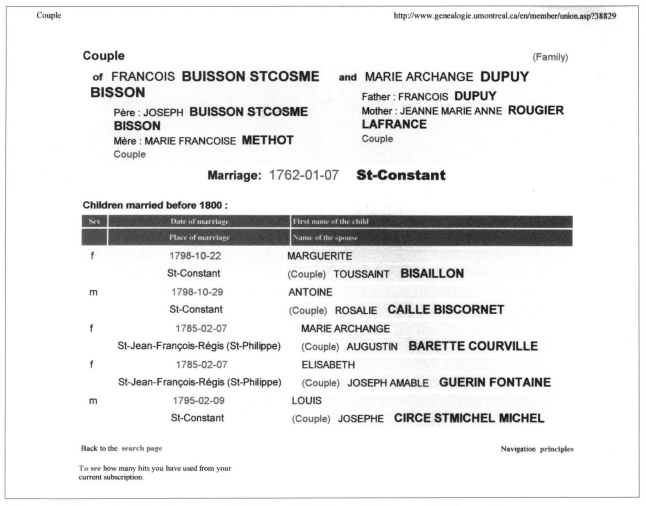

Figure 12. *Example of the document titled "Couple" for Francois Bisson and Archange Dupuy.*

The document shown in figure 12 (Couple) should be compared to the document shown in figure 11 (Family). Both concern Francois Bisson and Archange Dupuy. The "Family" document that is generated though the second section, "A Genealogical Dictionary of Families, 1621-1765," includes only children born before 1765. The "Couple" document is from the third section, "A Repertory of Couples and Filial Relations, 1621-1799," and includes only children married before 1799. The children listed on the document titled "Couple" are not listed on the document titled "Family." This is because they were born after the cutoff date of 1765. To obtain the birth and/or burial information for these other six children, the researcher would need to find the documents titled "Certificate" for those events by searching the first section, "A Repertory of Vital Events, 1621-1799."

Summary

Because it is so easy to link forward and backward to access all pertinent records for an individual or family in the third section, "A Repertory of Couples and Filial Relations, 1621-1799," it may be tempting for the researcher who knows the marriage information to use this one only, and neglect the other two sections. But, as shown above, it is possible to find individuals in the database who have documents titled "Certificate" but are not linked into a family or couple relationship. The researcher will thus benefit by using all three sections.

In addition, a researcher can get an overview of a parish by requesting a parish search for a specific time frame within the first section, "A Repertory of Vital Events, 1621-1799." This is probably one area where the forty-seven-volume set has an advantage over this website. On the website, a chronological list of events within a parish includes only the subject of the event. In the book, the researcher can see the interplay of families in a parish because several documents, complete with all the participants, are right next to one another on the printed page.

Subscriptions and Hits

For a modest fee a subscriber to the PRDH website can purchase a number of "hits" varying from 150 to 10,000. The more hits purchased, the lower the cost per hit. There is no time limit attached to the subscription, and each subscription is complete within itself. That is, if a person purchases a 150-hit subscription, uses up 100 hits and decides to purchase another 150-hit subscription, the two subscriptions are not added together. The original subscription is used up before the new one begins.

Because individuals and events are linked throughout the database, it is difficult for the subscriber to determine how hits are actually counted. Although a hit is charged each time a new page of information is accessed, some documents actually use multiple hits. The researcher who tries to ascertain the system behind the hit is wasting time and energy. However, one way to minimize hits is to narrow a search as much as possible. For example, a request for all the Joseph Boyers in the entire database produced a list of 387 records. The same request from 1750-1799

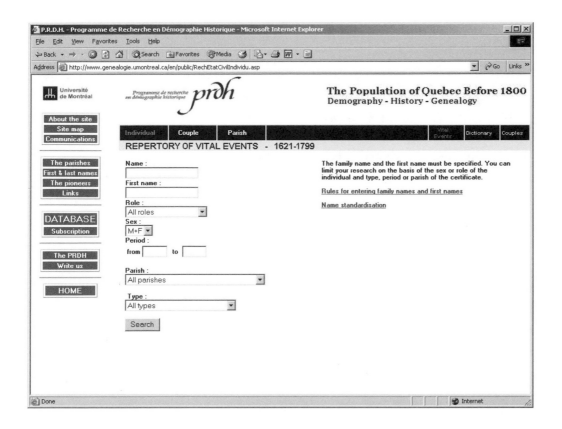

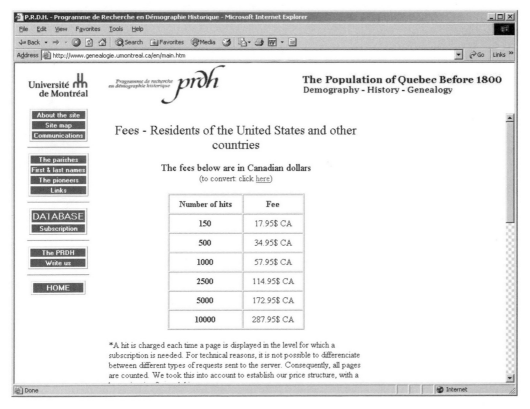

produced 319 records. Redefining the request further to the years 1785-1799 produced 108 records. With twenty records listed on a page, the subscriber would need only six hits to view the redefined list instead of twenty hits to view the list of 387 records.

Most Internet browsers will change the color of visited links. This can be a great help in working with the PRDH website. Whenever a particular record is accessed in one section, the link changes color. If this same record appears on a list in another section or in a document, the link will also appear in the new color. This not only reveals the correct relationship, but it also reduces the chance of repeatedly hitting on the same record. This color change is only true within one session using the website. When one returns to the site at a different time the colors may no longer be differentiated.

Dealing with Name Variations

To simplify confusion with names in using the database, PRDH has done the following:
- Last names are standardized for indexing purposes, but the computer will recognize all variations found in the original records and convert them to the standard form. However, no accents, hyphens, or blank spaces are used, and the computer will not recognize any names that include these items.
- First names are standardized in their modern form. The computer will not recognize any other spelling. Unfortunately, there is no list of first names for the researcher to refer to when in doubt. In addition, the modern form may differ significantly from the original. For example, even though the name, Hippolyte, is found in many records in this database, the name, Paul, might be substituted for it.
- Names can only have one element. To find Jean Pierre, either Jean or Pierre must be used. If Jean is used, all Jeans and all compound names containing Jean will appear in a list.
- Records can be accessed by either the family name or a dit name.

Praises, Problems, and Promises

In the original records children are recorded in the parish registers by their baptismal dates and not their birth dates. Most repertoires also use the baptismal date. PRDH uses the birth date. Since baptisms were generally performed the same day or within a couple days of birth, this should not cause problems for the researcher who wishes to confirm the information by viewing a copy of the actual record.

Because this website is easy to use and because the documents produced are so professional looking, it is easy for the researcher to forget that this is a secondary source of genealogical information. Considering the mass of information collected and connected, errors undoubtedly exist. However, the documents in this database all show their sources, and genealogists are usually able to verify the information found here by researching the original record.

This database is a work in progress. Although there is no intention at present to extend the information beyond 1799, additions and corrections to the existing information continue. The webmaster recognizes the existence of errors and will correct them if provided with proper evidence. The correction, however, is not instantaneous. Changing information that is linked to other information is time-consuming and meticulous work. Additions and corrections will only be done once or twice a year.

Will this site still exist years from now? While guarantees of longevity on the Internet are hard to make, the future of PRDH looks bright. The webmaster for this site is confident that this database will be in existence indefinitely. It is a university research project and is generating enough money to be financially self-sufficient.

The on-going PRDH project has already spanned many years. From the initial collecting of the information to the publishing of the forty-seven-volume set to the production of the CD-ROM set to the creation of the website, this tremendous undertaking continues to yield wonderful results.

C h a p t e r   F i f t e e n

French-Canadian Genealogies

By Patricia Keeney Geyh

Genealogists tracing their roots in French Canada soon learn that the basis for their research is going to be marriage records, rather than census records, as is true in the United States. Having the maiden names of the brides and the maiden names of the mothers of the brides and the grooms means that the skeleton of a family can be set up relatively quickly.

Overview

Entire French-Canadian genealogies have been based completely on marriage records. These tomes may include, in one book, the genealogies of many families but are frequently only records of families living in a given area. They are limited in scope, but valuable when used within these limits.

These genealogies can also be most puzzling to the uninitiated. Figure 13 shows a page from *Généalogie des Familles Originaires des Comtes de Montmagny- L'Islet-Bellechasse*. In that text genealogies are listed in alphabetical order by surname of the family. The reproduced page from this book is the one on which the Martin family genealogy begins. The following discussion will refer to this page.

Codes and Symbols: Translating the Genealogies

The information on the Martin family begins with a brief discussion, in italics, of Joachim Martin, the immigrant into French Canada. Translated, it reads:

MARTIN

Joachim Martin, fils de Jacques Martin et de Luce Chabot, d'Estrée,
::ché de La Rochelle, France, se marie à Québec, le 5 novembre 1662
(contrat Audouart N.P. 17 oct.) à Marie Chalifour, fille de Paul Chali-
:ur et de Jacquette Archambault. En secondes noces, à Québec, le
:5 juin 1669 (contrat Vachon N.P. 27 mai) il épouse Anne Petit, fille
:e Pierre Petit et de Catherine Desnoyers, de St-Germain L'Auxerre, de
Paris. Il fut inhumé à St-Pierre, Ile d'Orléans, le 30 juin 1790.

1-Joachim	5-11-1662	Marie Chalifour	N.D.Québec	
"	16-6-1669	Anne Petit	N.D.Québec	2
2-M.-Anne	12-2-1691	Pierre Roy-Desj.	S.Pierre I.O.	
Marguerite	30-1-1692	Jean Jollet	C.Jacob	
"	9-2-1705	Jacques Picoron	S.Pierre I.O.	
Angélique	12-1-1696	Pierre Chantal	S.Pierre I.O.	
"	26-11-1710	Pierre Châtigny	S.Pierre I.O.	
Catherine	11-2-1697	J.B. Labourlière	S.Pierre I.O.	
Louis	12-10-1700	Louise Ratté	S.Pierre I.O.	3
Jean-Bte	25-2-1710	Marie Genest	S.Pierre I.O.	
M.-Charlotte	25-2-1710	Louis Dufresne	S.Pierre I.O.	
"	14-10-1725	Pierre Ratté	N.D.Québec	
François	25-11-1710	M.-Françoise Autin	R.-Ouelle	4
3-Ursule	14-2-1724	Pierre Chouinard	S.Anne Poc.	
Pierre	13-5-1725	Françoise Lebel	C.Jeanneau	5
Thérèse	7-1-1733	Joseph Vaillancourt	Islet	
Jean	25-7-1737	M.-Anne Boucher	Islet	6
Charlotte	10-10-1740	François Rochefort	Islet	
4-Ch.-François	9-1-1734	Angélique Pelletier	Kamouraska	7
Joseph	21-11-1740	Rosalie Pelletier	S.Roch A.	8
Louis	23-11-1740	M.-Josette Bérubé	R.-Ouelle	9
Ignace	21-11-1741	Marguerite Albert	S.Anne Poc.	10
M.-Josette	17-11-1742	François Michaud	C.Jeanneau	
Pierre	16-8-1745	Geneviève Patry	S.Pierre S.	11
M.-Thérèse	18-2-1747	Charles Pelletier	S.Anne Poc.	
Jean	23-8-1750	Josette Michaud	C.J. Dionne	12
5-Geneviève	25-8-1749	Claude Bonhomme	S.Anne Poc.	
Françoise	12-1-1750	Joseph Forgues	S.Anne Poc.	
Marg.-Ursule	11-5-1751	Pierre Sergerie	S.Anne Poc.	
Pierre	5-1-1757	Josette Gagnon	C.J. Dionne	13
"	8-6-1761	M.-Anne Gagnon	R.-Ouelle	14
Joachim	26-4-1762	Marguerite Hudon	R.-Ouelle	15
6-Ursule	18-2-1767	Julien Chouinard	C.Dupont	

91

Figure 13. A page from Généalogie des Familles Originaires des Comtes de Montmagny- L'Islet-Bellechasse.

Joachim Martin, son of Jacques Martin and of Luce Chabot, of Estree diocese of La Rochelle,
France, married in Quebec, the 5 November 1662 (as recorded in the marriage contract written
by Notary Audouart on 17 Oct) to Marie Chalifour, the daughter of Paul Chalifour and of
Jacquette Archambault. The second marriage, in Quebec, on the 16 of June 1669 (as recorded
by a contract written by Vachon on 27 May) he married Anne Petit, daughter of Pierre Petit and
of Catherine Desnoyers, of St.-Germain L'Auxerre, de Paris. He was buried at St. Pierre, Ile
d'Orleans, the 30th of June 1790.

Beneath this paragraph about Joachim is the genealogy which gives information about
all Joachim's descendants to the extent that this information was known in this area.

The first column at the left contains numbers, which are the numbers identifying the families (by family-number). The next column gives the first name of the Martin whose marriage is being recorded. The third column is the date of the marriage; the fourth is the name of the spouse; the fifth is the place of the marriage and the sixth column gives the identifying number of the parents (parent-number).

How does this work? Look at the family-number 2 in the left-hand column. It can be seen that eight people with the surname of Martin belong to family number 2. They are M. Ann, Marguerite, Angelique, Catherine, Louis, Jean-Bte, M. Charlotte, and Francois. These are all brothers and sisters. Who are their parents? Look to the right at the parent-numbers in column six. Up towards the top is found parent-number 2. It is opposite the record of the marriage of Joachim Martin to Anne Petit. Therefore Joachim and Anne (parent-number 2) are the parents of those listed as part of family-number 2.

Try it again. Look at family-number three in the left column. It can be seen that five people with the surname of Martin belong to family-number 3. They are Ursule, Pierre, Therese, Jean, and Charlotte. Who are their parents? Look in column six and find parent-number 3. Number 3 is opposite the marriage record of Louis Martin and Louise Ratte; therefore they are the parents of the five Martins listed in the left column as family-number 3.

Using this system, it is possible to go backwards or forwards in ascending or descending order. Look at the parent-number in column six to find the number of a couple. Then look for that same number in the family-number column to the left. Once the parent-number and family-number have been matched up, the children are located.

There are more things to observe when using this sort of genealogy. Look once again at column six showing the parent-numbers. Every couple does not have a parent-number. Does this mean that none of these couples had any children? No it does not. It indicates that those putting together this genealogy did not have any information one way or the other. These couples may not have had children, but they probably did. The children, however, may have been born and may have lived in some other area of Quebec. This genealogy, then, will contain no more information about the descendants of these couples.

Look at column three, which gives first names of the Martins whose marriages are recorded. Notice that some of the names are repeated using ditto marks. This indicates that the same person was married more than once. It could possibly mean that there were two people of the same first name in the same nuclear family, but this is unlikely. Be alert, however.

Column three gives the dates of marriage of the couples listed. The dates are given in the fashion found in many places in Europe, which is day, month, year. For example, 7-1-1828 would be the 7th of January 1828. Since it is easy for an American to record these dates inaccurately, genealogists are encouraged to spell out the month of the year when writing a date.

Research Strategy

It is possible to trace back several generations using the following system:

Look at the last Martin listed on this page. It is Ursule who married Julien Chouinard on the 18th of February 1767. Looking at the left hand column for the family-number, one finds that Ursule is part of family-number 6.

Look for the parents of Ursule by searching for number 6 as a parent-number in column six. The parent-number 6 is placed opposite the record of the marriage of Jean Martin and M. Anne Boucher, who were married in Islet on the 25th of July 1737. These then are the parents of Ursule.

Go back another generation. Who are the parents of Ursule's father, Jean Martin? Look to the left column next to Jean's name for the family-number. Jean is part of family-number 3 along with his brothers and sisters Ursule, Pierre, Therese and Charlotte.

Look for Jean's parents by searching for number 3 as a parent-number in column six. The parents are Louis Martin and Louise Ratte, who were married at St. Pierre on the Isle d'Orleans on the 12th of October 1700. Louis and Louise are the parents of Jean.

Now go back still another generation. Who are the parents of Louis Martin, father of Jean? Look to the left column for the family-number. Louis is part of family-number 2 along with his brothers and sisters listed there.

Louis's parents may be found by looking for number 2 in the right-hand column, which gives the parent-number. Number 2 is placed opposite the marriage of Joachim Martin and Anne Petit, who were married in Notre Dame de Québec on the 16th of June 1669. Joachim and Anne are the parents of Louis.

Looking in the left-hand column for the family-number for Joachim, one finds number 1. There is no parent given as number 1, but this information is provided in the paragraph introducing the family, which is in italics. Joachim was the immigrant to Quebec.

Using this one page it has been possible to trace this family back five generations.

Summary

This, then, is another method of recording French-Canadian families. Genealogies written in this fashion have advantages and disadvantages. They are quick to read and space saving. On just a few pages one can carry most of the information needed on a research trip. When one finds a new line marrying into the family, these books will often have information about that new family in the same volume.

Some problems do exist, of course. These genealogies do not provide the birth and death records that at one time or another must be obtained. Also they are usually written for a limited geographical area, and therefore, as families move about Quebec, they disappear from these texts.

All told, however, once the French-Canadian genealogist learns how to understand the recording systems used in these works, another door to valuable secondary records is opened.

Chapter Sixteen

French Canadian Families of the North Central States

By Beverly Ploenske LaBelle and Patricia Sarasin Ustine

Compiled by Paul J. Lareau and Elmer Courteau, *French Canadian Families of the North Central States* was published by the Northwest Territory French and Canadian Heritage Institute (since renamed Northwest Territory Canadian and French Heritage Center) in 1980. The introduction to these eight volumes states: "The intent of this work is to gather together the research of members of the Heritage Institute; the records of diverse churches and civil authorities; extracts taken from locally-produced genealogies; and research by the authors. The information is not complete." The data was accepted by the compilers as it came in, and they made no attempt to verify it. The researcher should keep in mind that the information is not documented.

Overview

These volumes contain an alphabetical listing of families by surname. Most of the families in these volumes settled in Minnesota, Wisconsin, North or South Dakota. Also included were some families from Iowa, Upper Michigan, Manitoba, and Saskatchewan. The families that settled in these areas trace their French-Canadian ancestry to Quebec, some ancestry dating back to the 1600s. The known descendants of these families were included even if their surname was no longer French Canadian and their place of residence was elsewhere.

The amount of family information included with each entry varies. Some entries include only the place of marriage, and some include the date of marriage was well as birth or death information. Others may include first communion, confirmation, religious orders, and divorces.

Using the Dictionary

The capitalized surnames listed on the left side of the page are in alphabetical order and underlined. In some instances *dit* names and other spellings of the surname follow in parentheses. The entry for LEBEAU that follows is an example of this system.

LEBEAU (dit BAU, LaBEAU)

*A1--Etienne (of St-Eustache, Paris, Fr.)	Madeleine Lachaussee	A2
A2--Pierre (m-23 May 1724 MON)	Marguerite DeLaunay	A3
A3--Pierre-Etienne (m-3 Aug 1761 ILD)	Francoise Becard	A4
A4--Catherine (m-22 Octo 1787 LOU)	Alexis Beland	
==========		
B1--Jean BAU (See that name)	Etiennette Lore	B2
B2--Mathurin (m-20 Feb 1713 BVL)	Marie LeSueur	B3

Below the surname is a different family group code for each family. The first family group always starts with the letter A and continues through the alphabet. The entry for LEBEAU shows the first family group A and part of the second family group B. The family groups are separated by a double line. The double line indicates another family with the same surname but the relationship to the other families is unknown. If the family groups use up the first alphabet, the other groups within that surname continue with the letters AA, AB, etc. The instructions at the beginning of volume 1 indicate that when an asterisk appears "before the code number of the first ancestor in a given line, this first ancestor was noted as the first known ancestor in the Tanguay dictionary or other French-Canadian source book." See the entry for Etienne LEBEAU.

Following the family group code is the given name along with the date, event, and place of event, if it is known. The entry for Etienne gives the location of St. Eustache, Paris, France, where he was from. Explanations of the abbreviations for events and places may be found in volume 1. The next information given is the maiden name of the spouse if it is known.

The last information given on the right is the code for the children. In the entry for Etienne and Madeleine Lachaussee, their children are listed under A2. A2, on the left side, indicates that Pierre is their son and is the only child given in this entry even though there may be more children. Additional children would also have been placed under A2.

Summary

It is necessary to read "The Introduction" as well as "How To Use This Book," both of which appear in the first volume. The first volume includes a detailed sample of an entry, and the abbreviations for the events, locations and Quebec notaries. Volumes 2 through 7 contain family groups and some maps. The eighth volume contains three pages of Canadian and American Indians. They are listed by their original Indian names or by Christian names without surnames. This volume also contains the acknowledgments and repeats the location and notary abbreviations found in the first volume.

This set of hardcover volumes is available in many genealogical libraries. A microfiche version is also available.

Chapter Seventeen

The French Canadians 1600-1900: An Alphabetized Directory of the People, Places, and Vital Dates

By Linda K. Boyea

The French Canadians, 1600-1900: An Alphabetized Directory of the People, Places, and Vital Dates consists of three volumes. Edited by Noel Montgomery Elliot and published by The Genealogical Research Library in Toronto, each volume has three distinct parts: one-third of the name index (volume one, A-F; volume two, G-M; volume three, N-Z), the entire index of place names, and the entire list of sources. There are over 468,000 entries listed in the three volumes.

People

The name index lists people who are mentioned in primary and secondary sources during the time period 1600-1900, including persons of all ethnic origins living in Quebec during the entire 300-year time period. Also indexed are persons of French descent living in all the Canadian provinces during the last 100 years. This includes some Metis and Acadians.

Not all the people who lived in Quebec during this time are included in this three-volume set; only those found in the sources cited. Many of the early ancestors are undoubtedly missing. In fact, 75 percent of all the entries are from the nineteenth century alone.

Places

The second part of each volume is the Index of Place Names. The name of a community may have changed over time and might not be found on current maps. Sometimes the same place name refers to several political entities. For example, Laprairie is listed and referenced in this index as a parish, a village, a county, a seigneury, and as part of a name of a church, eleven references in all. This index, as a cross-reference of place names found in the records, and as a community locator, is an excellent stand-alone reference for researchers of French Canada.

Sources

The third part of each volume is the List of Sources used in compiling the name index. The entries in the name index were taken from city and town directories, land records, marriage records, and other sources as diverse as *Report of the Commissioner of the Northwest Mounted Police, 1882,* and *The Canada Herd Book, (Pedigrees of Improved Short-Horned Cattle),* vol. 3., 1875, as well as from Tanguay and various censuses. Many libraries have copies of the source materials and some may be available on microfilm. The Genealogical Research Library has copies of every source document and can provide photocopies upon request [20 Toronto Street, Toronto, Canada M5C 2B8 (416) 360-3929, FAX: (416) 360-4348]. The researcher should be aware that this organization is a commercial entity, not to be confused with the Metropolitan Toronto Reference Library on Yonge Street.

Using the Index

Names in the name index are listed alphabetically by surname followed by the first name. Additional identifying information is given, when available, always in the same sequence, followed by the source code: SURNAME, GIVEN NAME, OCCUPATION, DATE/ ACTION, PLACE, (SOURCE):

Example:

Boyer, Louis, living before 1805 in Red River District, (MB7-57)

Boyer, Louis, living in 1861 in Montreal (L'isle), (PQ120-39)

Boyer, Louis, living in 1861 in Lasalle, (PQ134-27)

Boyer, Louis, commissioner, living in 1871 in Montreal, (PQ2-1061)

Boyer, Louis, inn keeper, living in 1871 in St. John's, (PQ2-1449)

The surname is written as it was found in the original record. A careful researcher will check all variations of spelling. If a surname was not given in the original record, the entry will be listed under "Unknown." If the given name listed is a nickname, it will be enclosed in quotation marks or parentheses.

The information about the occupations is not always available. In the example above, the first three entries do not contain this identifying information because it was not included in the original source. A description or title, such as Jr., or Miss, may be included in this space.

Problems

This index is not for the novice researcher. Although only five entries for the name "Louis" were listed in the example above, nineteen are listed in the index. Because neither parents' nor children's names are given, the researcher has no clue as to which Louis is the one sought. Unless the researcher already has some basic information on the correct Louis, an unrealistic amount of time would be needed to find and search the source given for each entry. For an experienced researcher who has exhausted all conventional sources, this index may be of greater value.

It must also be remembered that this is only an index, not an extraction. To determine if the information listed is of value, one must research the original record.

Additional Information

The Genealogical Research Library has also published two other sets of indexes for researching in Canada.

- *The Atlantic Canadians, 1600-1900,* contains over 500,000 name entries from Nova Scotia, New Brunswick, Newfoundland, Labrador, Prince Edward Islands, the Magdalen Islands, and the French islands of St-Pierre and Miquelon. It includes information from census records for the Acadians before and during the expulsion, and those covering the return of many Acadians after the expulsion. Also included are names from island-wide directories for Newfoundland for 1871 and 1908. The layout is much the same as in *The French Canadians, 1600-1900.*

- *The Central Canadians, 1600-1900,* contains over 500,000 name entries from Ontario and Manitoba. As in the other two sets, a wide range of sources, from censuses to farmers records, were used to create this name index.

An Annotated Bibliography of French-Canadian Research Sources

By Joyce Soltis Banachowski

French-Canadian genealogists soon realize how fortunate they are to have a large number of secondary and microfilmed primary sources available. A lack of knowledge of the French language is a hindrance, and may cause English-speaking researchers to feel intimidated, but with time researchers will become adept at extracting this information. In addition to the many sources discussed in this section of the book, there is a great amount of information in other secondary sources about the lives, times, and environment of early French Canadians.

The following annotated bibliography includes books that may help to add insight and information about ancestors and open new areas to investigate. Some are in French, but don't let that keep you from using them. After a reasonable amount of effort, most researchers can extract all the information they want and, from this, find the original document.

For example, to find additional information about an ancestor who participated in the fur trade, look at an inventory of fur trade agreements in *Rapport de l'Archiviste de la Province de Québec (RAPQ)* (see the entry on p. 107). An item in the inventory may give the date of the engagement, the name of the person and to whom he was contracted, the location where he was sent, and the notary who wrote the contract. Already this is more information than would be found in a *dictionnaire*. The original document on microfilm or at the archives in Quebec would take much more expertise in reading French and transcribing the handwriting and abbreviations used by the notary.

Below are many more sources available to you, which are usually found at archival centers, state historical societies, major libraries, university libraries, or city libraries. If they are not readily available to you, keep them in mind when you are traveling to other locations to do research.

Sets of Books

1. Auger, Roland, *French Canadian and Acadian Genealogical Review*, 9 vols. (Québec: Centre Québecois des Recherches Genealogiques, 1968-1981). Although this is a quarterly periodical, it deserves mention. It provides an abundance of genealogical and historical information on the French regime and Acadia. (English)

2. *Le Bulletin des Recherches Historiques*, 70 volumes, 1895-1968; Roy, Pierre-Georges, director, vols. 1-54; Roy, Antoine, director, vols. 55-70. This is just what the name implies: historical research. It includes articles of historical and genealogical interest of French Canada. It pulls articles from a number of sources—e.g., various archives, seminary records, judicial records, ecclesiastical documents, judgments and deliberations, and private collections. There are many articles on individuals, most of them of the French regime. There is a table of contents at the end of each volume, and a two-volume index for the years 1895-1925. Going through these volumes can be tedious but is often well worth the effort. Some articles of interest to French-Canadian genealogy are listed below, loosely translated into English. (French)

Vol. 8, 1902	Licenses of the Medical Bureau of Canada 1788-1848, pp. 175-209
Vol. 11, 1905	Passengers of the Rubis who were Patients of Hôtel Dieu, pp. 299-309
Vol. 11, 1905	Abjurations at Quebec in 1665, pp. 26-27
Vol. 19, 1913	Church Wardens of Notre Dame, Villemarie, 1657-1913, pp. 276-284
Vol. 20, 1914	Surgeons of Montreal in the 17th century, pp. 252-256
Vol. 24, 1918	Land surveyors of Montreal during the French regime, pp. 303-307
Vol. 24, 1918	List of pilots at Trinity House, Quebec, 1805-1846, pp. 148-160; 185-192; 215-224; 245-253
Vol. 27, 1921	Surgeons and doctors of Montreal, pp. 41-46; 75-79; 325-327
Vol. 27, 1921	Habitants of the city of Quebec 1769-1770, pp. 81-88; 119-125
Vol. 27, 1921	Habitants of the city of Quebec 1770-1771, pp. 218-224; 247-252
Vol. 28, 1922	Surgeons and doctors of Montreal during the French regime, pp. 247-251
Vol. 30, 1924	Surgeons of Hôtel Dieu, Montreal, p. 400
Vol. 31, 1925	List of surgeons and druggists during the French regime, pp. 166-170
Vol. 32, 1926	List of *huissiers*, pp. 79-92
Vol. 32, 1926	List coming to Canada from Dieppe, pp. 682-688

Vol. 32, 1926	Those who lost homes in the fire of 1721 at Montreal, pp. 586-608
Vol. 33, 1927	Colonists of Montreal from 1642 to 1667, pp. 170-192; 224-239; 312-320; 379-384; 433-448; 467-482; 538-548; 613-625; 650-652
Vol. 34, 1928	Interpreters at Montreal during the French regime, pp. 140-150
Vol. 34, 1928	Surgeons of Montreal during the French regime, pp. 580-582
Vol. 34, 1928	Passengers on *l'Elephant* in 1718, pp. 759-760
Vol. 35, 1929	Recruit of 1659 for Montreal, pp. 671-678
Vol. 35, 1929	Sundial, hourglass and clockmakers during the French regime, pp. 325-330
Vol. 36, 1930	Gold and silver smiths and jewelers of the French regime, pp. 30-32
Vol. 36, 1930	List of Officers of Justice in New France, pp. 151-157
Vol. 36, 1930	Acadians at Quebec in 1757, pp. 50-64; 105-128; 169-175
Vol. 37, 1931	Passengers on *l'Elephant,* May 1729, pp. 61-62
Vol. 38, 1932	1686 Census of Acadia, pp. 677-696; 721-734
Vol. 38, 1932	List of surgeons, doctors, and druggists during the French regime, pp. 515-522
Vol. 39, 1933	Land surveyors of Upper and Lower Canada 1764-1867, pp. 723-738
Vol. 39, 1933	List of Protestant housekeepers in Montreal 1764, p. 158
Vol. 45, 1939	Women who came to Canada in 1639, pp. 3-15
Vol. 45, 1939	Girls who came to marry 1649-1653, pp. 257-270
Vol. 46, 1940	Women who came to Canada 1654-1657, pp. 338-350
Vol. 47, 1941	Women who came to Canada 1658-1661, pp. 96-115
Vol. 61, 1955	The Swiss in Canada, pp. 51-70
Vol. 63, 1957	Protestants in Canada Before 1760, pp. 5-33

3. *Cadastres Abreges* (Land Survey Register Summary) *des Seigneuries Appartenant a la Couronne*, 1 vol.; *Cadastres Abreges des Seigneuries du District Québec*, 2 vols.; *Cadastres Abreges des Seigneuries du District Móntreal*, 3 vols.; *Cadastres Abreges des Seigneuries du District des Trois Rivières*, 1 vol. (Stewart Derbishire and George Desbarats, Québec: 1863). As a result of the Seigneurial Act of 1854 and its amendments, a land survey was taken of the seigneuries and fiefs of Quebec. The survey was started in 1854 and completed in 1862.

All seven volumes are organized much the same. Each seigneury is numbered in an Index at the beginning of each volume. The proprietor is listed in the Index in the Quebec, Montreal, and Trois-Rivières volumes. In the la Couronne volume, this information is given with a brief history of the seigneury before each seigneurial survey. Each volume is then divided into the individual seigneurial surveys. The introductory page of each gives the number of the survey, the name of the seigneury being surveyed, the proprietor of the seigneury, the date of the survey and the person who took the survey. The next page lists the concessions of that particular seigneury.

The seigneurial survey register summary is in chart form, making it easier to read although it is in French. The information found on the chart includes the name of the *censitaire*; the extent of the concession or of land owned by frontage, depth, and area; the value of buildings and improvements for agricultural use; and the rent that was to be paid by the *censitaire*. A summary of the total value of the seigneury is given at the end of each survey.

The names of the *censitaires* are not arranged alphabetically nor is there an index of names provided. Once you have learned the seigneury or location of an ancestor, it is then necessary to peruse the list within that particular survey to locate him.

4. *The Canadian Centenary Series*. This is a series of books, each written by a different author, an expert in his or her own field. All were published by McClelland and Stewart Limited, Toronto and New York. All these books, written in English, are documented with endnotes, a bibliography, and index. The authors and titles in this series of interest to the French-Canadian genealogist are:

Eccles, W. J., *Canada Under Louis XIV, 1663-1701*, 1964
Miquelon, Dale, *New France, 1701-1744*, 1989
Neatby, Hilda, *Quebec: The Revolutionary Age, 1760-1791*, 1966
Ouellet, Fernand, *Lower Canada, 1791-1840*, 1980
Rich, E.E., *The Fur Trade and the Northwest to 1857*,
Stanley, G.F.G., *New France: The Last Phase, 1744-1760*, 1968
Trudel, Marcel, *The Beginnings of New France, 1524-1663*, 1973

5. *The Canadian History Series*. This is a series of books written by different authors. All were published by Doubleday and Company, Inc., New York. All are written in English. Interesting and readable accounts of the French regime and Canada, they are a good place to start to gain a background on the French in Canada.
Costain, Thomas B., *The White and the Gold: The French Regime in Canada*, 1954.
Raddall, Thomas H., *The Path of Destiny from the British Conquest to Home Rule 1763-1850*, 1957.
Rutledge, Joseph Lister, *Century of Conflict: The Struggle Between the French and British in Colonial America*, 1956.

6. *CIHM Canadiana Monographs Collection*, Canadian Institute of Historical Reproductions, Ottawa. This is a collection on microfiche of over 70,000 books and periodicals documenting the development of Canada from mid-16th century to 1900. Some are in French, others are in English.

A separate bibliography of the CIHM Collection, in both French and English, is titled *Genealogy and Local History to 1900*, compiled by J. Brian Gilchrist and Clifford Duxbury

Collier, Ottawa, 1995. The bibliography is organized by name, locality, or general subject. There is also a "Register-*Registre*" section that gives a brief summary of each source. Some libraries such as the Wisconsin Historical Society in Madison, Wisconsin, have copies of the bibliography only.

The CIHM collection is presently available in the United States at the Library of Congress, Boston Public Library, the Pacific Consortium c/o the University of Washington, Seattle, and the University of Maine, Orono; in Quebec at the Bibliotheque Nationale du Québec, McGill University, Universite de Móntreal, Universite de Sherbrooke, Universite du Québec à Móntreal, and Universite Laval; in Ontario at the Carleton University, Lakehead University, Metropolitan Toronto Reference Library, National Archives of Ontario, National Library of Canada, North York Public Library, Queen's University, Trent University, University of Guelph, University of Ottawa, University of Toronto, University of Waterloo, University of Western Ontario, University of Windsor and York University; in Nova Scotia at the Acadia University and Dalhousie University; in New Brunswick at Mount Allison University, Universite de Moncton, and the University of New Brunswick; in Newfoundland at Memorial University; in Saskatchewan at the University of Regina and University of Saskatchewan; in Alberta at Stoney Tribal Association, University of Alberta, University of Calgary and University of Lethbridge; and in British Columbia at the University of British Columbia, University of Northern British Columbia, and University of Victoria.

7. *Collectif de'Archives de la Province de Québec (Collection of the Archives of Quebec)*. This is a collection of indexes of many sources in French-Canadian research. Most of them are usually shelved together as a complete set. The indexed documents in this collection are housed at the National Archives of Quebec or the Palais de Justice. The monumental compilation was the work of Pierre-Georges Roy, archivist, of the Quebec National Archives. Most of the volumes included in the collection are noted below. (French)

A. *Inventaire des Concessions en fief et seigneurie fois et hommages et aveux et Dénombrements conserve aux Archives de la Province de Québec*, 6 vols. (Beauceville: L'Eclaireur limitee, 1927). These volumes are organized by seigneuries. Within each seigneury, the acts are arranged chronologically. Volumes 1-5 contain acts of concession, declarations, acts of *foi et hommage, vente, contracts of marriage, sentence de'adjudication, enumerations, process verbal, ordonnances, pièce détachée,* and ratifications. Volume 6 contains a table of fiefs, seigneuries, and arriere-fiefs. This volume is arranged alphabetically with references back to the first five volumes. In volume 6 there is a table of premiers (first) seigneuries of New France with the name of the fief or seigneury and date of concession listed alphabetically. In addition, there is an alphabetical name index with references to volumes 1-5. Page numbers are at the back of volume 6.

B. *Inventaire d'une Collection de Pièces Judiciaires, Notariales, etc. etc. Conserves aux Archives Judiciaires de Québec*, 2 vols. (Beauceville: La Compagnie de l'Éclaireur, 1917). This includes criminal procedures, complaints, ordinances, and concessions, etc. It is organized chronologically for the years 1638-1859. Each item includes the date and a brief description with names of those involved. In volume 2 you will find a list of *"Inventaires conserved aux Archives Judiciairies à Québec"* and a list of forty-four notaries and the number of *feuillets* (papers) in their possession.

C. *Inventaire des Contrats de Mariage du Régime Francais Conserves aux Archives Judiciaries de Québec, Québec*, 1937-1938. This list is arranged alphabetically by the names of both the bride and the groom. Besides the names of the bride and groom, the name of the notary and the date of the contract are given.

D. *Inventaire des Registres de l'État Civil Conserves aux Archives Judiciaires*, 1 vol. (Beauceville: L'Eclaireur Limitée, 1921). This is an index of the civil registers of the province of Quebec. Some of the events found here could be birth, marriage, and death, acts of the religious, and responsibilities of civil officers of state. Names of institutions (churches, seigneuries, hospitals) are indexed at the end of this volume.

E. *Inventaire des Proces-Verbaux des Grands Voyers Conserves aux Archives de la Province de Québec*, 6 vols. (Beauceville: L'Eclaireur Limitée, 1923). These volumes are arranged chronologically, covering the years 1667-1840. Volume 6 is a *repertoire* of legal statements of the *grand voyers*, parish by parish. The parishes are arranged alphabetically; the acts are arranged chronologically under each parish.

F. *Inventaire des Ordonnances des Intendants de la Nouvelle France Conserves aux Archives Provincials de Québec*, 4 vols. (Beauceville: L'Eclaireur, 1919). The ordinances are arranged chronologically. Volume 4 contains the same information but it is organized differently by intendant. Within these, items are arranged chronologically.

G. *Ordonnances, Commissions, etc. etc., des Gouverneurs et Intendant de la Nouvelle France 1639-1706*, 2 vols. (Beauceville: L'Eclaireur, 1924). This is an index of the ordinances of the governors and intendants of New France. There is a table of contents for both volumes at the end of volume 2.

H. *Index des Jugements et Délibérations du Conseil Souverain de 1663 a 1716*, 1 vol. (Quebec, 1940). In this alphabetical index by surname, the volume number and page numbers are given.

I. *Inventaire des Insinuations du Conseil Souverain de la Nouvelle France*, 1 vol. (Beauceville: L'Eclaireur Limitée, 1921). It is arranged chronologically for the period of the French regime, 1663-1758. The date, a brief explanation of the case, the type of record, and the parties involved are generally included. Most are between the conseil souverain and the king. A name index is at the back.

J. *Inventaire des Jugements et Délibérations du Conseil Supérieur de la Nouvelle France de 1717-1760*, 5 vols. (Beauceville: L'Eclaireur, 1934). These are arranged chronologically. After the date is a statement of the issue or problem and who is involved.

K. *Lettres de Noblesse, Genealogies, Erections de Comtes et Baronnies Insinuees par la Conseil Souverain de la Nouvelle-France*, 2 vols., (L'Eclaireur: Beauceville, 1920). *Lettres* are grouped by family name, but the family groups are not necessarily alphabetical. There is a table of contents and a name index at the end of volume 2.

L. *Inventaire des Insinuations de la Prévôté de Québec*, 3 vols. (Beauceville: L'Eclaireur, 1936). These are arranged alphabetically by name. Information includes type of record, date, name of the notary or priest, and location. Volume 3 also has an *"Inventaire des Insinuations du Régime Militaire à Québec"* and an appendix, *"Quelque Insinuations de la Prévôté de Québec."* These insinuations are preserved at the Archives Judiciaries (Palais de Justice) of Quebec.

M. *Inventaire des Testaments, Donations et Inventaires du Régime Francais Conserves aus Archives Judiciairies de Québec*, 3 vols. (Quebec, 1941). Volume 1 is arranged alphabetically by name. The information given is the type of document *(testament, inventaire, donation, donation mutuelle)*, the date and the name of the notary. Volume 2 contains an index of the *testaments* (wills) and olographes conserved at the Archives Judicaires de Québec. This information includes the name, occupation, spouse, type of record, and date. The appendix of Volume 3 includes transcriptions of *don mutuels, testaments*, and *inventaires* of prominent men of New France.

N. *Inventaire de Pieces sur la Coté de Labrador Conserves aux Archives de Province de Québec*, 2 vols., 1940 and 1942. It includes *concessions, brevets de confirmation, aveux et dénombrements* etc., and some notarial acts. The lists of published pieces by volume are found at the back of volume 2.

8. *Collection de Manuscrits Contenant Lettres, Memoires et Autres Documents Historiques Relatifs à la Nouvelle-France*, 4 vols. (Québec: Impremie A Coté et Cie, vol. 1, 1883; vols. 2-3, 1884; and vol. 4, 1885). The four volumes contain partial or complete documents that

pertain to the history of New France. There is a table of contents at the end of each volume. (French)

9. De Jordy, G. A., *Généalogies des Principales Familles du Richelieu*, 2 vols. (Arthabaska: L'Imprimerie d'Arthabaska, Inc., 1927). These volumes are organized alphabetically by surname of families who settled in the Richelieu valley. (French)

10. *Dictionary of Canadian Biography*, 5 vols. (Toronto: University of Toronto Press, 1966-1969). Each volume is arranged by time period, 1000-1700; 1701-1740; 1741-1770; 1771-1800; and 1801-1820. Articles within each volume are arranged alphabetically, followed by biographical information about the person. The author of the article and the sources used for the article are given. (English)

11. *Inventaire des Greffes des Notaries du Régime Francais*, 27 vols. (Québec: Archives de la Province de Québec, 1943-1976). It is an index of the *greffes* of a number of notaries. This collection was the work of Antoine Roy, archivist, and covers the 17th and 18th centuries. Each act listed provides the date of the act, the type of notary act, and a brief description with the people involved named. The collection is organized by the name of the notary and the location where he practiced. Within each notary's collection, the acts are arranged chronologically. Volumes 1-8 are not indexed. Volumes 9-27 are indexed by name. The notaries whose *greffes* are indexed are noted below. Most of the original documents are on microfilm. (French)

Adhemar, Antoine: Vol. V, VI, XXVII

Ameau, Severin: Vol. XI, XXVI

Auber, Claude: Vol. I

Audouart, Guillaume: Vol. I

Badeau, Francois: Vol. I

Bancheron, Henry: Vol. I

Barette, Guillaume: Vol. XXI

Basset, Benigne: Vol. I

Becquet, Romain: Vol. II, III.

Bermen, Laurent: Vol. I

Boujonnier, Flour: Vol. XXVII

Bourdon, Jacques: Vol. X

Bourgine, Hilaire: Vol. XI

Bouron, Jean-Henry: Vol. XXIII

Cabazie, Pierre: Vol. X

Caron, Joseph: Vol. XXVI

Chambalon, Louis: Vol. XVIII, XIX, XX

Chorel de Saint-Romain, René: Vol. XVI

Closse, Raphael-Lambert: Vol. I

Comparet, Francois: Vol. XIV

Coron, Francois: Vol. XXIII

Cusson, Jean: Vol. XXVI

David, Jacques: Vol. XII

Demeromont, Louis: Vol. XXVI

Desmarets, Charles D.: Vol. XXIII

Duquet, Pierre: Vol. II

Filion, Michel: Vol. II

Fleuricourt, Jean-Baptiste: Vol. XIII

Frerot (de la Chenaye), Thomas: Vol. X, XXVII

Gaschet, René: Vol. XVI

Gatineau (Gastineau-Duplessis), Nicolas: Vol. I, XXVII

Gaudron de Chevremont, Charles-René: Vol. XII

Genaple, Francois: Vol. VII

Gloria, Jean: Vol. II

Godet, Rolland: Vol. I

Gourdeau de Beaulieu, Jacques: Vol. II

Guillet de Chaumont, Nicolas-Augustin: Vol. XVI

Guitet, Jean: Vol. I

Herlin, Claude: Vol. II

Jacob, Etienne: Vol. VII

Jacob, Joseph: Vol. VII

Janneau, Etienne: Vol. XIV

Janvrin Dufresne, Jean-Baptiste: Vol. XXIV

LaRiviere, Hilaire-Bernard: Vol. VIII

LaRue, Guillaume de: Vol. XXVI

Laurent, sieur de Portail, Louis: Vol. XXVI

La Tousche, Jacques: Vol. XXVI

Lecomte, Jean: Vol. VIII

Lecoustre, Claude: Vol. I

Lepailleur, Francois: Vol. XXV

LeSieur, Charle: Vol. XXVII

Lespinasse, Jean de: Vol. I

Louet, Jean-Claude: Vol. X

Maugue, Claude: Vol. IX

Metru, Nicolas: Vol. VIII

Michon, Abel: Vol. XXII

Moreau, Michel: Vol. X

Mouchy, Nicolas de: Vol. II

Petit, Pierre: Vol. XXVII

Peuvret de Mesnu, Jean-Baptiste: Vol: II

Pilliamet, Phil.-P.: Vol. XXIII

Piraube, Martial: Vol. I

Porlier, C.J.: Vol. XV

Pottier, Jean-Baptiste: Vol. XI

Poulin, Pierre: Vol. XXVI

Rageot, Gilles: Vol. III, IV

Raimbault, Joseph-Charles: Vol. XXI

Roy dit Chatellerault, Michel: Vol. XXVI

Rouer de Villeray, Louis: Vol. I

Rousselot, Pierre: Vol. XXIII

Saint-Pere, Jean de: Vol. II

Sainguinet, Simon (father): Vol. XIII

Senet, Nicolas: Vol. XVII

Souste, Andre: Vol. XXIV

Tailhandier, Marien: Vol. VIII

Tetro, Jean-Baptiste: Vol. XIII

Tronquet, Guillaume: Vol. I

Trotain dit Saint-Seurin, Francois: Vol. XXVII

Vachon, Paul: Vol. II

Veron de Grandmesnil, Etienne: Vol. XXVII

Verreau, Barthelemy: Vol. XXII

12. *Jugements et Délibèrations du Conseil Souverain de la Nouvelle France*, 6 vols. Vol. 1-4, Imprimerie A. Coté et Cie, Québec, 1885, 1886, 1887, and 1888 respectively; vols. 5-6, Imprimerie Joseph Dussault, Québec, 1889 and 1891. This is a collection of deliberations and decisions made by the sovereign council during the French regime between 1663 and 1716. It is arranged chronologically and the names of those who were sitting on Council are given. The case is presented and the decision, if any, is given. A case might have been carried to another date if there was a need to gather other information, witnesses or investigation. Therefore, you may have to search further than one date for the same litigation. The date is followed by a brief summation of the subject of the case, often with names of the litigants. Each volume has a table of contents, arranged chronologically, at the back of the book. The collection is in French. The six volumes and the years they cover are as follows:

Vol. 1   18 Sep 1663—29 Oct 1675

Vol. 2   15 June 1676—1 Jan 1686

Vol. 3   7 Jan 1686—19 Dec 1695

Vol. 4	9 Jan 1696—22 Dec 1704
Vol. 5	2 Jan 1705—23 Dec 1709
Vol. 6	7 Jan 1710—22 Dec 1716

13. Laforest, Thomas J., *Our French Canadian Ancestors*, 30 vols. (Palm Harbor, FL: LISI Press, 1983-1998). This is a collection of biographies of early inhabitants of New France. They are translations of biographies from *Nos Ancetres* by Father Gerard Lebel. The biographies provide a picture of what the lives of our ancestors was like. Laforest has added vignettes of life in New France from *The Life of New France 1663-1760*. There is a name index at the back of each volume. (English)

14. *Minnesota History*, Collections of the Minnesota Historical Society, Minnesota Historical Society, St. Paul, Minnesota. Some of the following topics may be of interest to the French-Canadian genealogist:

Vol. 1	Early French explorers
Vol. 2	Early French forts
Vol. 6	Voyageurs
Vol. 8	The Red River Settlement
Vol. 9	History of Duluth
Vol. 9	History and lumbering in the St. Croix Valley
Vol. 10	Radisson and Groseilliers
Vol. 14	Lahontan in Minnesota (includes maps)
Vol. 19	Fur trade of the western Great Lakes
Vol. 19	Supplies for the Nicolet Expedition 1838
Vol. 21	A legal case at Grand Portage
Vol. 22	Hudson Bay Company posts in Minnesota

15. Parkman, Francis, *France and England in North America*, (a series). (Boston: Little, Brown and Company, 1897-1927). The titles in the series are:

A Half Century of Conflict, 2 vols., 1903

Count Frontenac and New France Under Louis XIV, 1 vol., 1904, 1927

LaSalle and the Discovery of the Great West, 1 vol., 1903

Montcalm and Wolfe, 2 vols. 1899

Pioneers of France in the New World, 1 vol., 1901

The Jesuits in North America, 1 vol. 1893

The Old Regime in Canada, 1 vol., 1904, 1927

For a long time, this has been the authority on the history of French Canada. His works are footnoted and indexed. (English)

16. *Pioneer Collections: Report of the Pioneer Society of the State of Michigan* (Lansing, MI: Pioneer Society of the State of Michigan, published annually beginning in 1878). The following topics may be of interest to the French-Canadian genealogist:

Vol. 2	French settlement
Vol. 3	Detroit in 1796
Vol. 4	Old French traditions
Vol. 5	Kaskaskia
Vol. 10	Petition of inhabitants of Detroit
Vol. 10	Survey of the settlement of Detroit
Vol. 12	1884 census
Vol. 13	Old French carts
Vol. 28	Fort St. Joseph and mission church at Mackinac
Vol. 29	Fort Pontchartrain
Vol. 32	Jesuits in Michigan
Vol. 33	Jesuit missionaries
Vol. 33	List of those coming to Detroit in 1706
Vol. 33	Cadillac papers
Vol. 34	Cadillac papers
Vol. 34	Lands granted at Detroit
Vol. 34	Old Fort St. Joseph
Vol. 40	Documents relating to Detroit

17. Prévost, Robert, *Portraits de familles pionnières*, 5 vols. (Montréal: Libre Expression, 1993-1997). These five volumes provide biographies of principal families of the French regime. The volumes are interspersed with photos of churches, homes, monuments, mills, etc., related to the surnames included. Each volume is indexed, and volume 5 includes a listing of the surnames covered in each of the preceding volumes. (French)

18. *Rapport de l'Archiviste de la Province de Québec (RAPQ)*, published between 1920 and 1982 under the editorship of Antoine Roy. Each volume is organized by year. These volumes are a printed collection of materials found in the Archives of Quebec. Volume 1964 has an index for volumes 1920-1964. The following may be of special interest to the French-Canadian genealogist (French):

Vol. 1920-1921	Organization of parishes in 1721, pp. 262-380
Vol. 1920-1921	List of colonists in the 1653 Recruit, pp. 309-320
Vol. 1921-1922	*Congés** 1681-1737, pp. 189-225
Vol. 1922-1923	*Congés** 1739-1752, pp. 192-265
Vol. 1923-1924	Bourguignon emigrants to Canada, pp. 394-399
Vol. 1929-1930	*Engagements*** 1670-1745, pp. 191-466

Vol. 1930-1931	*Engagements*** 1746-1752, pp. 353-453
Vol. 1931-1932	*Engagements*** 1753-1758, pp. 243-365
Vol. 1932-1933	*Engagements*** 1758-1778, pp. 245-304
Vol. 1946-1947	*Engagements*** 1778-1788, pp. 301-369
Vol. 1942-1943	*Engagements*** 1788-1797, pp. 261-397
Vol. 1943-1944	*Engagements*** 1798-1801, pp. 335-444
Vol. 1944-1945	*Engagements*** 1802-1804, pp. 307-401
Vol. 1945-1946	*Engagements*** 1805-1821, pp. 225-340
Vol. 1935-1936	1666 Census Quebec City, pp. 1-154
Vol. 1941-1942	1731 Census Seigneury of Montreal, pp. 3-176
Vol. 1939-1940	1744 Census Quebec City, pp. 1-154
Vol. 1946-1947	1760-1762 Census Trois Rivières, pp. 3-53
Vol. 1925-1926	1762 Quebec Census, pp. 1-143
Vol. 1936-1937	1765 Census Montreal and Trois Rivières, pp. 1-121
Vol. 1948-1949	Church Census for Quebec City for 1792, 1795, 1798, and 1805, pp. 3-250
Vol. 1949-1951	Military Records 1641-1760, pp. 261-527
Vol. 1955-1957	Military Records 1641-1760, pp. 225-252
Vol. 1951-1953	Testimonies for Freedom to Marry 1757-1763, pp. 3-159
Vol. 1951-1953	Ancestors of the 17th century: *Abrancourt-Avisse*, pp. 449- 544
Vol. 1953-1955	Ancestors of the 17th century: *Babea-Besquet*, pp. 445-536
Vol. 1955-1957	Ancestors of the 17th century: *Bedard-Bissonet*, pp. 379-489
Vol. 1957-1959	Ancestors of the 17th century: *Bissot-Bonneau*, pp. 383-440
Vol. 1959-1960	Ancestors of the 17th century: *Bonnedeau-Bousquet*, pp. 277-353
Vol. 1965-1966	Ancestors of the 17th century: *Bouteillu-Brassard*, pp. 147-181
Vol. 1970-1971	*"Familles Venues de la Rochelle en Canada,"* pp. 129-367
Vol. 1975	*"Veilles Families de France en Nouvelle France"*
Vol. 1973	*"Les Terres de L'Ille d'Orleans"*
Vol. 1949-1951	*"Les Terres de la Ste Famille,"* pp. 149-260
Vol. 1951-1953	*"Les Terres de St. Jean,"* pp. 303-368
Vol. 1953-1955	*"Les Terres de St. Pierre,"* pp. 3-69
Vol. 1975	An inventory of cases in various courts in New France, pp. 3-50
Vol. 1975	Inventory of the *prévôté**** of Quebec, pp. 53-413

* *congés*—fur trade licenses

** *engagements*—fur trade contracts

***prévôté— royal court of Quebec

19. The *Reports of the Public Archives of Canada* are sometimes called *Report of Canadian Archives*, (1883-1884); *Canadian Archives*, (1899); *Report Concerning Canadian Archives*,

(1904); *Report of the Work of the Public Archives,* (1912-1915); or *Report of the Public Archives,* (1918-1923), Ottawa. This is a yearly report of holdings of the Archives of Canada, first published in 1882, and it is still issuing yearly reports. Just as its name indicates, it has a variety of articles on collections in the Canadian Archives, both French and English. Many of the archive reports contain synopses of collections of the French period—letters, dispatches, decrees, memorials, petitions, minutes, warrants, ordinances to and from the king, the *conseil de marine,* the governor generals, the intendants, the *conseils souverein* and *supérieur,* etc. Although the original documents may be in French, the archive reports are in English. Much information can be extracted from the synopses themselves. These archive reports are available at archival centers, historical societies, university libraries, and public libraries. Some libraries have a better collection of the *Archive Reports* than others.

If one is interested in locating the actual document, the identifying title, the series letter, the folio number, and the number of pages in the document are indicated. The documents, for the most part, have been microfilmed and are available at archival centers, university libraries, and large public libraries which specialize in French-Canadian history.

Following are some volumes of *The Reports of the Public Archives of Canada* one might consider when doing French-Canadian genealogical research:

1883	Synopsis of documents between France and New France
1884	Abstracts of *Acts of fealty and hommage*
1885	Presbyterian parish of Montreal (Oct 1766-Sep 1787) Includes a number of French-Canadian names.
1887	Synopsis of general correspondence
1895	Voyages of Radisson
1899	(Supplement) Synopsis of "Collection of Moreau Mery" *(Souverain Conseil)*
1899	(Supplement) Synopsis of despatches to and from the king, the *Conseil de Marine,* registers of governor-generals and intendants and sovereign and superior councils.
1899	(Supplement) Translation of letters of Madeleine de Vercheres
1904	(Appendix G) Documents of Bigot, Vergor, and Villeray
1904	(Appendix J) List of men wounded or killed in 1837-1838
1904	(Appendix K) Summary of documents in Paris (Letters, Dispatches, decrees, ordinances, grants, of the king) There is an index for this group of documents.
1905	1752 Census of Sieur de La Roque (Acadia)
1905	Genealogies of the families of the Island of Orleans
1905	Acadian genealogy and notes
1912	(Appendix O) Patent of Nobility to Robert Giffard
1913	Ordinances after the English conquest

1914-1915	(Appendix C) Ordinances of the governor and Council 1768-1791
1918	(Appendix B) Ordinances and Documents Issued by Military Governors (Conquest- Aug 1764)
1918	(Appendix B) Notes of Census Trois Rivières, 1760
1923	Synopsis of miscellaneous documents
1928	Account of Trade—Northwest Company
1939	List of partners, clerks and interpreters of the Northwest Fur Trade Company
1939	Hudson Bay Company
1940	Militia regulations under the French regime

20. *Records of Our History*. All four volumes are published by the Public Archives of Canada, Ottawa and are translated into English. This series traces the development of Canada through its documents. The subject matter is arranged by themes. Each section has a short introduction and copies or extracts of documents. Captions explain each document.

Bolotenko, George, *A Future Defined: Canada from 1849 to 1873*, 1992

Vachon, Andre, *Dreams of Empire: Canada Before 1700*, 1982

Vachon, Andre, *Taking Root: Canada from 1700 to 1760*, 1985

Wilson, Bruce G., *Colonial Identities: Canada from 1760 to 1815*, 1988

21. Robert, Normand, *Nos Origines en France: des Débuts à 1825*, 13 vols. (Montréal: Archiv Histo, 1984-1998). This set will help locate the parish and village of origin of immigrant ancestors to French Canada. There is a surname index in each volume. The years below indicate year of publication. (French)

Vol. 1	Béarn et Gasgogne, 1984
Vol. 2	Guyenne et Périgord, 1985
Vol. 3	Angoumois et Saintonge, 1987
Vol. 4	Aunis, 1988
Vol. 5	Poitou, 1989
Vol. 6	Comtat-Venaissin, Comté de Foix, Dauphine, Languedoc, Lyonnais, Provence, Roussillon et Savoie, 1990
Vol. 7	Normandie et Perche, 1991
Vol. 8	Auvergne, Berry, Bourbonnais, Limousin, Marche et Nivernois, 1992
Vol. 9	Alsace, Bourgogne, Champagne, Franche-Comté et Lorraine, 1993
Vol. 10	Anjou, Maine, Orléanais et Touraine, 1994
Vol. 11	Île de France, 1995
Vol. 12	Artois, Flandre et Picardie, 1996
Vol. 13	Bretagne, 1998

22. Sulte, Benjamin, *Histoire des Canadiens Francais 1608-1880*, 8 volumes, Wilson & Cie, editors, Montreal, 1882. Although these are in French, there are censuses and lists of *habitants* that can be understood by the English reader.

Vol. 1	First colonists to New France
Vol. 2	Members of the Company of One Hundred Associates
Vol. 2	Families established 1636-1639
Vol. 2	Chart of those who migrated to New France, 1608-1642
Vol. 2	The habitants of Trois Rivières when it was established in 1634
Vol. 3	Colonists who came to New France, 1646-1648
Vol. 3	Chart of those who came to New France, 1641-1654
Vol. 4	Militia recruited by René Robineau in 1657
Vol. 4	Militia of Montreal the first day it was organized, 1663
Vol. 4	1666 and 1667 Quebec Census
Vol. 4	1671 Acadian Census
Vol. 5	1681 Quebec Census
Vol. 6	1686 Acadian Census
Vol. 6	Clergy who came to New France
Vol. 7	Concessions of land made between 1672 and 1700

23. *Transactions and Proceedings of La Société Royal de Canada*, Series I, vols. 1-12 (1882/1883-1894); Series II, vols. 1-12 (1895-1906); Series III, vols. 1-57 (1907-1963), Jos. Hope and Son, Ottawa. Each volume within each series is organized the same—proceedings, general business, appendixes (mostly reports), and transactions. The transactions section contains articles on a number of Canadian topics. It is divided into four sections. Section I covers French literature, history and archaeology of Canada, and is written in French. Section II contains articles on the history, literature, and archaeology of Canada and is written in English. Sections III and IV contain articles on mathematics, physical and chemical science, geography, geology, biology, and metallurgy. Sections I and II of Transactions contain the articles of interest to us. The pages of each volume are not numbered consecutively. Each section within the Transactions begins its own numbering system. (Each section begins with page number 1.) This can be confusing. There is a general index to the first and second series. Some libraries have these volumes on microfilm. Some articles which may be of interest to those researching French-Canadian family history are listed.

Series	Volume	Section	Article
1	1 (1883)	1	*Premiers seigneurs du Canada, 1634–1664*, pp. 131-137
1	2 (1884)	2	The making of Canada, pp. 1-15
1	4 (1886)	2	Local government in Lower Canada, pp. 43-56

2	8 (1902)	1	Regiment Carignan, pp. 25-95
2	9 (1903)	1	Intendants of New France, pp. 65-107
2	11 (1905)	2	Origin of the French Canadians, pp. 99-119
3	4 (1910)	1	*Les Bretons en Canada,* pp. 45-56
3	5 (1911)	1	*Coureur du bois á lac Superior* 1660, pp. 249-266
3	7 (1913)	1	*Les colons de Montréal, 1642-1657,* pp. 3-65
3	10 (1916)	1	*Les tribunaux and officers de Justice à Montréal, Le Prévôté de Québec 1648- 1760,* pp. 273-338
3	11 (1917)	1	*Arrets, edits, ordonnances, mandements et règle ments de archives palais justice,* pp. 147-174
3	12 (1918)	1	(continuation of above) p. 209
3	15 (1921)	1	*1741 recensement de Montréal,* pp. 1-61
3	29 (1935)	1	Gold and silversmiths of old Quebec, pp. 113-125
3	35 (1941)	1	Canadian potters, pp. 13-21
3	42 (1948)	2	Early Canadian history of 15th & 16th centuries, p. 31
3	48 (1954)	2	French settlements west of Lake Superior, p. 107

24. Thwaites, Reuben, editor, *Jesuit Relations and Allied Documents.* 71 vols., plus an index in vols. 72-73, Cleveland. *The Jesuit Relations* is a collection of letters and reports by various Jesuit missionaries in New France that were sent back to their superiors in France. It was first published in France because the information drew interest and was a means of promoting the Jesuit society. Thwaites had the collection translated and published in these 71 volumes. Each volume is published in both French and English. Thwaites also added notes and comments at the end of each volume. At times, details were exaggerated or omitted. These reports were edited and published in France and used to promote the religious, political, and financial interests of the Jesuits.

25. *Wisconsin Historical Collections.* (Wisconsin Historical Society, Madison). Some topics of interest to the French-Canadian genealogist that can be found in these volumes appear below:

Vol. 10	Fur trader's journal, 1803-1804
Vol. 16	The French Regime in Wisconsin, 1634-1727
Vol. 17	The French Regime in Wisconsin, 1727-1748
Vol. 17	Fur trade
Vol. 18	Fur trade
Vol. 18	French Regime in Wisconsin, 1743-1760
Vol. 18	Mackinac Register of Marriages, 1725-1821
Vol. 19	Mackinac Register of Baptisms and Interments, 1695-1821

Vol. 19   Fur trade

Vol. 19   Journal of Francois Victor Malhiot, 1804-1805

Vol. 20   Fur trade

Demographic Studies

Demographic studies have become important to genealogists because not only do they give an analysis of the population in a specific location, they provide detailed information about the lives of our ancestors. Often in these studies, records of ancestors are used to provide evidence to support the conclusions the authors make. Not only do we find ancestors named, but we learn interesting or colorful information about them. Additional information often appears in footnotes or endnotes as well as in the general text.

26. Chénier, Rémi, *Québec: A French Colonial Town in America, 1660-1690* (Ottawa: Environment Canada, Parks Service, 1991). This is a well-documented study of the administration, construction, appearance, and population of Quebec. It contains an extensive bibliography but there is no index. (English)

27. Dechéne, Louise, *Habitants and Merchants in Seventeenth Century Montreal* (Montreal: McGill-Queens University Press, 1992). This is an extensive demographic study of the population of Montreal. It is well documented with explanatory notes. There is no index. (English)

28. Desloges, Yvon, *A Tenant's Town: Quebec in the 18th Century* (Ottawa: Environment Canada, Parks Service, 1991). This is also available in French under the title, *Une ville de locataire: Québec au XVIII siècle*. It includes annotated endnotes and a bibliography. There is no index. (English)

29. Greer, Allan, *Peasant, Lord, and Merchant: Rural Society in Three Quebec Parishes 1740-1840* (Toronto: University of Toronto Press, 1991). This is a study of the economy of the rural parishes of Sorel, St. Ours, and St. Denis. It is well documented with explanatory notes. An appendix has comparison graphs. An index is included. (English)

Origins of Our Ancestors

Once researchers have traced their ancestry to the immigrant ancestors, they become anxious to locate them in France or in whatever country they were born. Here are some sources to help trace ancestors to their place of origin.

30. Auger, Abbé Leon, *Vendéens au Canada aux 17 et 18 siècles*, Abbe-Leon Auger, 1990. This is an alphabetical, biographical listing of settlers in New France from the department of Vendee. Organized by parish. (French)

31. Fournier, Marcel, *Dictionnaire Biographique des Bretons en Nouvelle-France 1600-1765*, Archives Nationale du Québec,1981. This is an alphabetical, biographical listing of immigrants to New France from Bretagne (Brittany). Following each biography, in parentheses, is a code to identify the source of this information. (French)

32. Fournier, Marcel, *Les Européens au Canada des origines à 1765* (Montréal: Éditions du Fleuve, 1989). This is an alphabetical, biographical listing of Europeans (English, German, Irish, Scots, Swiss, Belgians, Luxembourgers, Austro-Hungarians, Italians, Spanish, Portuguese, and Hollanders) who went to Canada before 1765. Sources for this information are noted. (French)

33. Godbout, Archange, *Émigration Rochelaise en Nouvelle-France* (Archives Nationales du Québec, 1970). This is an alphabetical, biographical listing of those who emigrated from La Rochelle. Each item includes the names of their children and biographical information on their children as well. (French)

34. Godbout, Archange, *Origine des Familles Canadiennes Francaises* (Montréal: Editions Elysée, 1979). This book is organized by city or town, then by parish within that town, and finally by individual or family surname. The information included varies. In addition to the individual's name, it could include birth and/or baptism information, parents' names, and marriage and burial information. The information included was extracted by Godbout from French civil records. It includes a surname index. (French)

35. Larin, Robert, *La Contribution du Haut-Poitou au peuplement de la Nouvelle-France* (Moncton: editions d'acadie, 1994). This is an alphabetical, biographical listing of the immigrant to New France from Haut-Poitou. It is organized by regions (Loudunais, Chatelleraudais, region of Poitiers, the city of Poitiers, Montmorillonnais, Civraisien, region of East Thouet, Niortais, the city of Niort, and other smaller regions), then by towns within each region. Sources for this information are noted. (French)

36. Robert, Normand, and Thibault, Michel, *Catalogue des immigrants catholiques des Îles Britanniques avant 1825/ Catalog of Catholic immigrants from the British Isles before 1825* (Montréal: Archiv-Histo, 1988). This is an alphabetical listing within each country—England, Scotland, Wales, and the Channel Islands and Ireland. The name of the person, his/her parents, and date, place and spouse's name are usually given. Most of it is in both French and English.

37. Trudel, Marcel, *Catalogue des immigrants, 1632-1662*, (Montréal: Hurtubise, 1983). This is an alphabetical, biographical listing organized by year from 1632 to 1662. (French)
See also Robert, Normand, number 21.

History and Daily Life of New France

A good genealogist should learn about the political, economic, and social history of the time and location of his or her ancestors. There is an abundance of secondary sources giving an overview of the history and daily lives of the settlers of New France. A brief list follows.

38. Eccles, W.J., *Essays on New France* (Toronto: Oxford University Press, 1987). Eccles presents a series of essays on Parkman, the role of the church, social welfare, the western frontier, the fur trade, the military, the Battle of Quebec, the impact of the French on North America and the role of American colonies on foreign policy of the 18th century. They are in English and there are endnotes.

39. Eccles, W.J., *The French in North America 1500-1783* (East Lansing, MI: Michigan State University Press, 1998). This book is footnoted and contains a bibliographical essay and index.

40. Kingsford, William, *The History of Canada*, 15 vols. (Toronto & London, New York: AMS, 1887, 1968). This is a chronological history of Canada. (English)

41. Moogk, Peter N., *La Nouvelle France: The Making of French Canada—A Cultural History* (East Lansing, MI: Michigan State University Press, 2000). This is one of the recent social histories of New France. It is a history of the culture of the common man as seen through the records he left. It has an index and is well documented with endnotes. (English)

42. Wrong, George M., *The Rise and Fall of New France*, 2 vols. (New York: Octagon Books, 1970). Volume 1 includes the establishment of New France as well as life in New France. Volume 2 covers the conflict between the English and the French. Each volume has a bibliography for each chapter. An index appears in volume 2. (English)

See also Parkman, Francis, number 15.
See also Sulte, Benjamin, number 22.

Captives

During the 17th and early 18th centuries, continuous war waged between England and France. Indian tribes allied themselves with either the French or the English. In North America, these wars often took the form of raids on each other's settlements. Many settlers were killed, and the French and Indians often took survivors to Canada. Some captive settlers stayed with their Indian captors and were often adopted into their tribes. Captive Indians lived among the French, were baptized into the Catholic faith, and took French names. Some of the captives were repatriated back to New England; many others remained in Canada and were assimilated into the French population. Many books have been written by and about individuals or individual families and their experiences. Two of the best-known repositories of these are in the Edward E. Ayer Collection at the Newberry Library in Chicago and at the Wisconsin Historical Society Library in Madison. Many other libraries have good collections as well. Those listed below help to identify many individuals who were taken from New England and other American colonies into Canada.

43. Baker, Alice, *True Stories of New England Captives* (Cambridge: E. A Hall & Co., 1897; reprint, Bowie, Maryland: Heritage Books). This is the first book to study the fate of the captives taken to Canada. A name index is included.

44. Coleman, Emma Lewis, *New England Captives Carried to Canada: Between 1677 and 1760 During the French and Indian Wars*, 2 vols. (Portland, Maine: Southworth Press, 1925; reprint, Bowie, Maryland: Heritage Books, 1989). These two volumes contain background information on the wars, treatment of the captives, the redemption attempts, and the raids on various New England settlements. Most important it includes the names of captives taken to Canada and traces what happened to them. A name index is included. (English)

45. Fournier, Marcel, *De la Nouvelle-Angleterre à la Nouvelle-France* (Montréal: Société Généalogique Canadienne-Francaise, 1992). The first part provides information on the various French and Indian wars, statistics on the Anglo-Americans in New France, the Indian missions, and a timeline of this period. The second part is an alphabetical biographical listing of New Englanders who went, or were taken, to New France. (French; but with little effort, English-speaking readers will find the biographical listing easy to understand.)

46. Vaughn, Alden T., and Clark, Edward W., editors, *Puritans Among the Indians: Accounts of Captivity and Redemption, 1676-1724* (Cambridge, Massachusetts and London, England: Belknap Press, 1981). This book is an anthology of the stories of the captives Mary Rowalandson, Quentin Stockwell, John Gyles, Hannah Swarton, Hannah Dustan, John Williams and Elizabeth Hanson. (English)

Grosse Ile

Grosse Ile was the reception and inspection center for immigrant ships entering Canada. In May 1847, one of these ships, the *Syria*, anchored with typhus aboard. This led to a large epidemic, which broke out at Grosse Ile and spread into Quebec. Many, especially Irish immigrants, died and are buried there. Their surviving children were often adopted into families in Quebec. The sources listed in this section are in English.

47. Charbonneau, Andre and Sevigny, Andre, *1847 Grosse Île: A Record of Daily Events* (Parks Canada: Canadian Heritage, 1997). It is written in chronicle form and is easily read. Newspapers are the source of much of the information presented. It includes tables of daily arrival and departure of ships.

48. O'Gallagher, Marianna and Rose Masson Dompierre, *Eyewitness Grosse Isle 1847* (Sainte Foy: Carraig Books, 1995). The story of Grosse Ile is presented through the letters of pastors who served there during the epidemic. Burial registers of the various churches are included.

49. O'Gallagher, Marianna, *Grosse Ile: Gateway to Canada 1832-1937* (Quebec: Carriage Books, 1984). This book tells the story of Grosse Ile from its inception to its conclusion. Of most importance to the genealogist is the appendix, which provides a list of the children who were orphaned, their place of origin, the names of their parents, and the name of the person who adopted them.

Huguenots in New France

When the Reformation took place in France during the sixteenth and seventeenth centurie, the result was a number of violent outbreaks and wars with the king vacillating between a policy of tolerance and one of intolerance. In New France, ordinances required that everyone be of the Catholic faith. Many Huguenots, especially from La Rochelle, were strongly involved in trade with New France. The restrictions forced most Huguenots in New France to abjure their religion.

50. Annett, Kenneth Hugh, *Huguenot Influence in Quebec*. This is a history of Huguenots in Quebec. (English)

51. Baird, Charles W., *Huguenot Emigration to America* (Baltimore, MD: Genealogical Publishing Co., 1985). (English)

52. Bedard, Marc Andre, *Les Protestants en Nouvelle France*, Cahiers d'Histoire no. 31 (Québec: La Societe de Historique de Québec, 1978). This volume provides information on the Protestants and their influence in New France. Although much of the book would require a reader adept at reading French, the appendix, which provides a listing of the 477 Protestants in New France, is easily understood by the English reader. (French)

53. Harrison, Michael, editor, *Canada's Huguenot Heritage* (Toronto: Huguenot Society of Canada, 1987). This is a collection of articles by different authors. It covers a variety of

topics from the background of Huguenots in Europe to Huguenots in Canadian trade and canal building. (English)

54. Reamon, G. Elmore, *The Trail of the Huguenots in Europe, the United States, South Africa, and Canada* (Baltimore, MD: Genealogical Publishing Company, 1986). (English)

55. Reamon, G. Elmore, *The Trail of the Black Walnut* (Toronto: McClelland & Stewart Limited, 1957). This book follows Huguenot migration through the United States into Canada. The appendixes include many lists of early settlers and identifies the first locations and dates of settlement in Upper Canada. (English)

56. Weiss, Charles, *History of French Protestant Refugees* (Edinburgh and London: William Blackwood & Sons, 1854). (English)

Rebellion of 1837-1838

In 1837-1838, under the leadership of Louis-Joseph Papineau, a revolt broke out in Lower Canada. These rebels who called themselves patriots were hoping for an independent nation. Their attempt failed and most of those who took part were forced to flee. Nearly one hundred were brought to trial. Twelve were condemned to death and hanged. Fifty-eight were sent as prisoners to New South Wales in Australia. The remainder were imprisoned or exiled.

57. Borthwick, Rev. J. Douglas, *Montreal Prison: A.D. 1784 to A.D. 1886* (Montreal: A. Feriard, Bookseller, Publisher, 1886). A history of the prison is presented as well as information on the patriots who were imprisoned there. (English)

58. Cahill, Jack, *Forgotten Patriots: Canadian Rebels on Australia's Convict Shores* (Toronto: Robin Brass Studio, 1998). This book provides the stories of French and English rebels who were tried, convicted, and sent to Australia, their lives there, and their return to Canada. Appendixes include lists of those who were transported to Australia, information on the Hunters' Lodges, letters, and newspaper extracts. There are endnotes, a bibliography, and an index. (English)

59. Ducharme, Leon (Leandre), *Journal of a Political Exile in Australia*, trans. George Mackaness (Sydney: Australian Historical Monograph, 1944). This is a journal kept by one of the prisoners sent to Australia. It primarily describes the voyage to and from Australia. (English)

60. Greer, Allan, *The Patriots and the People: The Rebellion of 1837 in Rural Lower Canada* (Toronto: University of Toronto Press, 1996). This book is a social history of the participants and events of the Rebellion of 1837. Footnoted with an index. (English)

61. LePailleur, Francois-Maurice, *Land of a Thousand Sorrows*, trans. F. Murray Greenwood (Vancouver: University of British Columbia Press, 1980). This is the Australian prison journal for the years 1840-1842. It contains the list of prisoners who were transported to Australia. (English)

62. Prieur, Francois-Xavier, *Notes of a Convict of 1838*, trans. George Mackaness (Sydney: D.S. Ford Printers, 1949). This is an account of Prieur from the point of embarkation to his life as a prisoner in Australia. He includes a list of all those brought to trial and the judgement that was rendered.

63. *Report of the State Trials, Before a General Court Martial Held at Montreal in 1838-1839; Exhibiting a Complete History of the Late Rebellion in Lower Canada*, 2 vols. (Montreal, 1839). This is a complete account of the trials and rebellion. (English)

64. Schull, Joseph, *Rebellion: The Rising in French Canada 1837* (Toronto: Macmillan Canada, 1996). This readable history of the Rebellion of 1837. It is indexed, and has a bibliography and endnotes. (English)

65. Sexton, Robert, *HMS Buffalo* (Adelaid: Australasian Maritime Historical Society, 1984). This book describes the ship and conditions on board the ship that took the French-Canadian prisoners to the penal colony in Australia. (English)

The Frontier

From the very beginning of New France, the French were interested in the midwestern and western part of North America. Furs were found there. Fur and military posts and forts were established there. Wars with the English were fought there. Early explorers and *voyageurs* traveled along the waterways and routes found there.

66. Alvord, Clarence Walworth, *Cahokia Records 1778-1790* and *Kaskaskia Records 1778-1790*, Collections of the Illinois State Historical Library, vols. 4 and 5, (Virginia Series, vols. 1 and 2), Illinois State Historical Library, 1909. This collection of historical records has not been published earlier. A list of the documents and an index are included. (English)

67. Balesi, Charles J., *The Time of the French in the Heart of North America: 1673-1818* (Alliance Francaise Chicago, 1991). This is a history of the French in middle America on both sides of the Mississippi River during the colonial period. There are endnotes after each chapter, a bibliography, and an index. (English)

68. Belting, Natalia Maree, *Kaskaskia Under the French Regime* (New Orleans: Polyanthos, 1975). As the title states, this is a history of Kaskaskia. Within the text, there are many names of French Canadians. The book is well documented and has an index and bibliography as well as an appendix, which contains extracts from the parish records and notes on the census of 1752. (English)

69. Birk, Douglas A., ed., *John Sayer's Snake River Journal, 1804-1805* (Minneapolis, MN: Institute for Minnesota Archeology, Inc., 1989). For many years this unsigned diary of a Canadian fur trader for the Northwest Company was thought to be that of Thomas Connor. Douglas provides very convincing evidence that it is the diary of John Sayer. (English)

70. Briggs, Elizabeth and Anne Morton. *Biographical Resources at the Hudson Bay Company Archives,* vol. 1 (Winnipeg: Westgarth, 1996). This guide is a must for anyone who intends to do research at the Hudson Bay Archives in Winnipeg, Manitoba. It provides samples of types of material available and guides the researcher through the many record series available.

71. Brown, Margaret Kimball and Lawrie Cena Dean, eds., *The Village of Chartres in Colonial Illinois 1720-1765* (New Orleans: Polyanthos, 1977; published for La Compagnie des Amis de Fort de Chartres). This book contains transcriptions in French and translations in English of church records for St. Anne and for the Chapel of the Visitation, and English translations of land records and some notarial records from the Randolph County Archives. There is a name index at the back.

72. Burton, C.M., comp., *Cadillac's Village or Detroit Under Cadillac with List of Property Owners and A History of the Settlement 1701-1710* (1896; reprint, Detroit: Detroit Society for Genealogical Research, Inc., 1999). This book is exactly as stated. (English with an index)

73. Crowder, Lola Frazer, *Early Kaskaskia, Illinois Newspapers 1814-1832* (Galveston: Frontier Press, 1994). This book contains excerpts from seven early-19th century newspapers of western Illinois. (English)

74. Denissen, Fr. Christian, *Genealogy of the French Families of the Detroit River Region 1701-1936*, 2 vols. (Detroit: Detroit Society for Genealogical Research, 1976, 1987). The title indicates the contents of these volumes. There is an explanation as to how to use the genealogy and abbreviations used, at the beginning of volume 1. Volume 2 includes a name index. (English)

75. Fairbault-Beaugrand, Marthe, *La population des forts francais d'Amérique*, 2 vols. (Montréal: Editions Bergeron, 1982, 1984). The organization within these volumes is by the name of the fort. Within these locations are alphabetical listings for marriage, baptism, and burial information. Volume 2 includes the censuses for 1723, 1726, and 1727 for the Arkansas post. Not all of the French forts or posts are included. A name index is located at the end of each volume. They are in French but should pose little problem for the English reader.

76. Gilman, Carolyn, *The Grand Portage Story* (St. Paul: Minnesota Historical Society Press, 1992). This book is the story of the fur trade along the northern shore of Lake Superior. There are endnotes, a bibliography, and an index. (English)

77. Gilman, Carolyn, *Where Two Worlds Meet: The Great Lakes Fur Trade* (St. Paul: Minnesota Historical Society, 1982). This book provides the story of the fur trade in the Great Lakes region with many photos, illustrations, and segments of documents to enhance it. It includes endnotes and a bibliography. (English)

78. Hanson, James, FASG, "The Origin of the Roc/Rock Family of Prairie du Chien and Wabasha: Frontier Genealogy among the Voyageurs" *The Genealogist* 1 no. 1 (Spring 1997): 3-36. James Hanson, a recognized authority on the early settlers and voyageurs of Prairie du Chien, Wisconsin, provides an excellent example of research into voyageurs.

79. Hennepin, Louis, *Father Louis Hennepin's Description of Louisiana: By Canoe to the Upper Mississippi in 1680* (University of Minnesota Press, 1938). Hennepin's voyage begins near Niagara Falls, moves on through Lake Michigan, and progresses into the Illinois country, along the upper Mississippi. He also describes the manners and customs of the Indians he meets. (English translation by Marion E. Cross)

80. Innis, Harold A., *The Fur Trade in Canada* (Toronto: University of Toronto Press, 1984). Originally published in 1930, this comprehensive study of the fur trade is still considered one of the leading authorities on the fur trade. It is well documented, and has an extensive bibliography. (English)

81. Jury, Wilfrid and Elsie McLeod Jury, *Sainte-Marie Among the Hurons* (Toronto: Oxford University Press, 1954). This book provides a history of Sainte-Marie, now in Ontario, from 1639 when it was founded until 1649 when it was destroyed. (English)

82. Kellogg, Louise Phelps, editor, *Early Narratives of the Northwest: 1634-1699* (New York: Barnes & Noble, Inc., 1917, 1967). The narratives are of the discovery and exploratory periods of the French. The book is footnoted and has an index. (English)

83. Kellogg, Louise Phelps, *The French Regime in Wisconsin and the Northwest* (New York: Cooper Square Publishers, Inc., 1968). This book covers the history of the French in Wisconsin from its discovery and exploration to the end of the French regime. It is footnoted and has an index. (English)

84. Kent, Timothy J., *Ft. Pontchartrain at Detroit: A Guide to the Daily Lives of Fur Trade and Military Personnel, Settlers and Missionaries at French Posts*, 2 vols. (Michigan: Silver Fox Enterprises, Ossineke, 2001). This monumental set covers in great detail all aspects of life in a French post. It shows a tremendous amount of research and knowledge on the part of the author. Historians, archaeologists, and genealogists will find this work both interesting and informative. It is indexed and has an extensive bibliography. (English)

85. Lande, Lawrence M., *The Development of the Voyageur Contract (1686-1821)* (Montreal: Lawrence Lande Foundation for Canadian Historical Research, McGill University, 1989). This compilation traces the changes in the voyageurs' contracts over a period of more than 100 years. The contracts included are from the Lande collection. The book includes a description of the voyageur, photocopies of voyageur contracts, and summaries of information extracted from voyageur contracts. This book is generally restricted to library use only because there were only a limited number published. (English)

86. *Mapping the French Empire in North America* (Chicago: Newberry Library, 1991). This catalog was prepared by David Buisseret for the Seventh Annual Conference of the French Colonial Historical Society. It provides an explanation for each of the maps on display. A bibliography is included. (English)

87. Munnick, Harriet Duncan, comp., *Catholic Church Records of the Pacific Northwest: St. Paul, Oregon 1839-1898*, vols. 1, 2, and 3 (bound as one book), (Portland: Binford & Mort, Thomas Binford, Publisher, 1979). This book includes English translations of French church records for St. Paul, Oregon, which were found in the Fort Vancouver Register. An index follows each of the volumes of records. Following the church registers and their indexes are two sections titled "Illustrations" and "Annotations." "Illustrations" includes photos of early pioneers, and "Annotations" includes additional information. An index is also included.

88. Munnick, Harriet Duncan, comp., *Catholic Church Records of the Pacific Northwest: Vancouver, vol 1 and 2, and Stellamaris Mission* [bound as one book] (St. Paul, Oregon: French Prairie Press, 1972). This book includes English translations of French church records. Following the church registers are sections titled "Index," "Illustrations," "Annotations," and also a bibliography. The "Illustrations" section includes photos of early pioneers, and the "Annotations" section provides additional information that appear in the church records.

89. Normandeau-Jones, Lea, *French Forts in New France...(North America)* (Toronto: Heritage Productions, 1998). This book provides a short history of French forts, a brief description of the French forts, some maps, and a listing of the military personnel at Fort Normandeau. (English)

90. Ross, Hamilton Nelson, *La Pointe: Village Outpost on Madeleine Island* (Madison: Wisconsin Historical Society, 2000). This is the story of Lapointe located on Madeleine Island, north of Ashland, Wisconsin, on the southwestern part of Lake Superior. It covers the creation of the region, native and French interests, and its history through the 19th century. It provides an English-Ojibway glossary, a bibliography of primary and secondary sources, and an index. Well-footnoted. (English)

91. Scanlan Peter L., *Prairie du Chien: French, British, American* (Menasha, WI: George Bants Publishing, 1937). This book describes the people and events that helped to settle and develop Prairie du Chien. An appendix provides a list of those from the region who received licenses from the French and English. There are endnotes and an index. (English)

92. Severance, Frank, *An Old Frontier of France: The Niagara Region and Adjacent Lakes under French Control*, 2 vols. (Frank H. Severance, 1917; reprinted Bowie, MD: Heritage Books, 1998). These two volumes describe events in the Niagara region in what is now New York and Canada. Volume 1 covers the period of time between the beginning of the 17th century and concludes about 1750. Volume 2 continues through the period of conflict between the French and English and includes a list of the French commandants on the Niagara before the English conquest, genealogical notes of the Joncaire-Chabert family as well as an index. (English)

93. Voorhis, Ernest, comp., *Historic Forts and Trading Posts of the French Regime and of the English Fur Trading Companies* (Ottawa: Department of the Interior, 1930). More than 600 forts are listed. Information which is provided for each fort is its location, sometimes a brief history of the fort, and other pertinent information about the fort. A bibliography and sectional maps are included. (English)

French-Canadian Migrations to the United States

By the mid 1800s, there were large migrations of French Canadians into the Eastern Townships of Quebec, into New England, and into the Midwest and Western North America seeking jobs and free or cheap land.

94. Albert, Felix, *Immigrant Odyssey: A French-Canadian Habitant in New England* (Orono: University of Maine Press, 1991). This is the story of a farmer from Quebec who

went to Lowell, Massachusetts, in the 1880s. This autobiographical account was first published in 1909 under the title *Histoire d'un enfant pauvre*. Both the French and English accounts appear in this book.

95. Chartier, Armand, *The Franco-Americans of New England: A History* (Manchester and Worcester: ACA Assurance and Institut Francais of Assumption College, 2000). As the title indicates, this is a history of the Franco-American existence in New England from 1860 to the 1990s. The book has an extensive bibliography and an index. (English)

96. Quintal, Claire, editor, *Steeples and Smokestacks: A Collection of essays on The Franco-American Experience in New England* (Worcester: Institut Francais, Assumption College, 1996). Among the topics covered in this collection of essays are emigration, settlement of Franco-American communities, religion, education, journalism, literature, and folklore within those communities. (English)

Miscellaneous

97. Anderson, Karen, *Chain Her By One Foot: The subjugation of women in seventeenth-century New France* (London and New York: Routledge, 1991). This book looks at French-Canadian women and Indian women during the 17th century. (English)

98. Auger, Roland J., *La Recrue de 1653* (Montréal: Société Généalogique Canadienne-Francaise, 1955). This book is a history of the Recruit of 1653 for Montreal. Besides a listing of the recruits, there is a biographical sketch of each of the recruits who actually came to Montreal and transcriptions of notarial records and documents pertaining to these recruits. The lists and biographical sections are usable to the English reader. The historical account would require someone adept at reading French. (French)

99. Beauregard, Denis, *Dictionnaire généalogique de nos origines*, 2 vols. and a supplement to volume 1 (Vol. 1, 1608-1730, Vol. 2, 1731-1799), (Quebec: Productions FrancoGéne, Ste. Julie, 1998). Volume 1 and the supplement to volume 1 are a complement to Jetté. They are done in the same format. The page and column before the surname is the location that the surname is found in Jetté. The author provides corrections and additions to what is available in Jetté. He includes the sources for these corrections and/or additions. The author provides two additional sections to volume 1. One is entitled "Speculations and Errors." Here the researcher will find educated guesses that are not yet confirmed and errors that are repeated as they were because no correction is yet available. The last section of this volume is "Search Trails." The purpose of this section is to encourage researchers to locate additional lines. Volume 2 follows the same format as volume 1 but covers the years beyond Jetté which have been done in other genealogical sources such

as Tanguay and Drouin. There is an English version that includes the introduction translated into English. (French)

100. Bosher, J.F., *Men and Ships in the Canada Trade, 1660-1760* (Ottawa: Parks Service, Environment Canada, 1992). This is a biographical dictionary of men involved in trade between Canada and Europe. It includes an introduction on the background of the trade and the sources consulted. The biographical dictionary is followed by a "dictionary of ships" used in the trade. This section provides information on the time the ships sailed, the cargoes carried, the names of commanding officers and owners, and damages incurred. (English)

101. Bouchard, Leon, *Morts Tragiques et Violentes au Canada*, 2 vols. These volumes are an alphabetical, biographical listing of those in New France who had tragic or violent deaths (by freezing, drowning, fires, Indian attacks, battles, accidents, etc.) in the 17th and 18th centuries. Sources for the biographical information are given. Appendixes in volume two include a graph of the births and deaths of the 17th and 18th centuries and a listing of mothers presumed dead as a result of childbirth. This chart includes the spouse's name, the date of burial of the mother, the child's name and the child's date of baptism. A bibliography and two indexes, by name and by location, are included. (Although in French, these volumes are usable by the English reader.)

102. Boulet, Viateur, *1608-1760 Les Transporteurs de Nos Ancetres* (Laval-des-Rapids, 1998). This book is organized by the name of the ship and the date. It provides the name of the owner and the captain of the ship and a list of the passengers who were on board. (French)

103. Boyer, Raymond, *Les Crimes et Les Châtiments au Canada Francais du XVII au XX Siècle* (Montréal: Le Cercle du Livre de France, 1966). This book touches on one aspect of the life of one's ancestors—crime and punishment. The book is organized by the type of crime and by the punishment. It is filled with well-documented examples. The table of contents is at the back, as well as a name index and a topic index. The non-French reader will need assistance in translating, but it is well worth the effort. (French)

104. Cahall, Raymond Du bois, *The Sovereign Council of New France* (New York: Columbia University, 1915; reprint, Pawtucket: Quintin Publications, 1998). This book provides information on the history, organization, procedures, functions and achievements of the Sovereign Council. The last section which describes the achievements of the Council includes a great deal of information on the lives of the inhabitants of New France. The book contains a bibliography. (English)

105. De Marce, Virginia Easley, *German Military Settlers in Canada after the American Revolution,* Joy Reisinger, Sparta, Wisconsin. This book provides an alphabetical listing of the Germans who remained in Canada following the American Revolution. Military and biographical information is provided for each. The researcher will also find background information on the various German regiments in Canada, an extensive bibliography of other sources, and a name index. (English)

106. Dumont, Micheline, Michele Jean, Marie Lavigne, and Jennifer Stoddart, (The Clio Collective) *Quebec Women: A History,* trans. Roger Gannon and Rosalind Gill (Quebec: The Women's Press, 1987). This is a history of women in Quebec from the 17th century to 1940. It includes many examples of actual ancestors. There are endnotes and a bibliography after each chapter.

107. Faillon, Etienne Michel, *Histoire Colonie Francaise en Canada,* 3 vols. (Villemarie: Bibliotheque Paroissiale, 1865-1866). These three volumes cover the period from exploration to the 1680s. The three volumes have marginal notes and endnotes. Of particular interest, the endnotes in the second volume include the roll of the Recruit of 1653 and information on the first chapel of Ste Anne de Beaupre. (French)

108. Fournier, Marcel, dir., *Les origines familiales des pionniers du Québec ancien (1621-1865)* (Fédération québécoise des sociétés de généalogie, 2001). This is an alphabetical catalog of the men and women who came to Quebec between 1621 and 1865. It provides basic biographic information for the immigrant and his/her parents and cites the sources for the information given. It states whether the immigrant is married, but it does not always state his/her spouse. (French, but can be handled by the English reader.)

109. Godbout, P. Archange, *Les Passagers du Saint-André: La Recrue de 1659* (Montréal: Publication de la Société Généalogique Canadienne-Francaise—no. 5, 1964). This book provides an account of the voyage followed by an alphabetical biographical listing of the passengers recruited for Montreal in 1659. More extensive notes are provided for the Cardinal, Charbonneau, Courtemanche, Cuillerier, Goyette, Masta, Mathieu, Roy, and Trudeau families. (French, but the biographical sections are usable by the English reader.)

110. Jaenen, Cornelius J., *The Role of the Church in New France* (Toronto, New York: McGraw-Hill Ryerson Limites, 1976). This is an analysis of the part the church played in New France during the exploratory and the colonization periods. It has endnotes, a bibliography, and an index. (English)

111. Langlois, Michel, *Dictionnaire Biographique Des Ancêtres Québécois (1608-1700)*, 4 vols. (Sillery, Québec: La Maison Des Ancêtres, 1998-2001). These volumes are a biographical dictionary of both men and women of the 17th century. (volume 1: A-C; volume 2: D-I; volume 3: J-M; volume 4: N-Z.) They are arranged alphabetically by surname, followed by the ancestor's birth and death date. This is followed by a biographical sketch of the ancestor and a specific listing of sources. If a notarial source is stated, the notary's name and the exact date of the notarial record are given. Following each letter of the alphabet is a section containing signatures of the ancestors who appear in the preceding letter division. (French)

112. Magnuson, Roger, *Education in New France* (Montreal: McGill-Queen's University Press, 1992). This book provides a history of elementary education of boys and girls, secondary, vocational, and professional education, and mission and seminary schools for the Indians. There are endnotes, a bibliography, and an index. (English)

113. Montagne, Madame Pierre, *Tourouvre et Les Juchereau* (Québec: Société Canadienne de Généalogie, 1965). This book includes background information on the town of Tourouvre in Perche and the origin of many of the Percheron emigrants to French Canada in the 17th century. Of special interest to the genealogist are transcriptions or summaries of the *engagement* contracts and other notarial records of these ancestors. (French)

114. Montagne, Pierre and Francoise, *Ils sont venus de Tourouvre. Les registres de catholicité concernant les Canadiens 1589-1713* (Montréal: Societe genealogique Canadienne-Francaise, 1989). This book contains photocopies and their transcriptions of the church records of Tourouvre, France. (French, but usable to the English reader.)

115. Moogk, Peter N., *Building a House in New France: An Account of the Perplexities of Client and Craftsmen in Early Canada* (Toronto: McClelland and Stewart, 1977). This is an account of one aspect of life in New France from Newfoundland to the Great Lakes. Examples are given throughout. This book is well documented with endnotes for each chapter. A bibliography and index are also provided. (English)

116. Neering, Rosemary and Stan Garrod, *Life in New France* (Fitzhenry and Whiteside, Ltd., 1976).

117. Paquette, B.C., *Old French Papers* (Montreal: Payette Radio Limited, 1966). This is a collection of a variety of documents and articles. They include maps of old Montreal and Missilimakinak (Michilmackinac), plans of buildings in New France, information and pictures of models of ships who brought some of the early explorers to New France, a tax

list of habitants and the amounts they were assessed for fortifications, a confirmation list for 24 Aug 1660 at Montreal, excerpts from the Montreal register, and ship armaments. Some are in French and others in English.

118. Pepin, Jean-Pierre-Yves, *Généalogies familiales: Nos historiques ancêtres les plus remarquables* (Longueuil, Québec: Les Editions historiques et généalogiques Pepin, 1999). This volume contains a variety of information about our ancestors during the French regime—reproductions of drawings of events in their lives, photos of monuments and plaques, photos or drawings of personalities, diverse documents, coats of arms of cities and regions with surnames of ancestors who migrated from there, and historic notices. Historic notices includes individuals who were not included in Drouin's *Dictionnaire National Canadiens Francais 1608-1760*. Some are handwritten and others are in the typed format found in Drouin. (French)

119. Proulx, Gilles, *Between France and New France: Life Aboard the Tall Sailing Ships* (Toronto: Dundurn Press Limited, 1984). This book gives a picture of maritime traffic, conditions of the Atlantic crossing and life aboard the ships, primarily during the 18th century. The appendix includes a listing of the king's ships in New France from 1713 to 1760. It is well documented, includes an index. (English)

120. Robeson, Virginia R., ed., *Documents in Canadian History: New France 1713-1760*, Ontario Institute for Studies in Education curriculum, Series 23. These documents or excerpts of documents are organized under the following topics: Colonial Policy and New France, The Administration of New France, The Seigneurial Regime and Agriculture, Trade and Industry, Towns in New France, and Daily Life in New France. (Translated into English)

121. Roy, Pierre Georges, *L'Ile D'Orleans* or *The Isle of Orleans* (Québec: Ls. A. Proulx, 1928; reprinted, Pawtucket: Quintin Publications) It contains a variety of articles pertaining to the Ile D'Orleans. The table of contents is located at the back of the book. (Available in both French and English.)

122. Séguin, Robert-Lionel, *La Sorcellerie au Canada du XVI au XIX siècle* (Ducharme, Montréal, 1961). This book discusses sorcery in New France and Canada. Examples are explained. One would need to be adept at reading French.

123. Séguin, Robert-Lionel, *La Vie libertine en Nouvelle-France au dix-septième siècle*, 2 vols. (Lemeac, Montréal, 1972). These volumes about the "Free spirited Women" of New France are organized by the following topics: public women, daily life, matrimonial life, the repression, and historic and social implications. Many examples are given, and footnotes

provide genealogical information. These volumes would be usable to those adept at reading and translating French.

124. Silvey, Father Antoine, S.J., *Letters from America,* trans. Ivy Alice Dickson (Belleville, Ontario: Mika Publishing Company, 1980). This is a collection of 89 letters, on various topics, written between 1709-1710 from New France. These letters are believed to have been written by the Jesuit, Father Antoine Silvey. The preface provides an explanation of the conclusion that the letters were written by Father Silvey and an explanation as to why the letters were not published sooner. There are endnotes provided by the compiler.

125. Trudel, Marcel, *Atlas de la nouvelle-francaise/An Atlas of New France* (Québec: Les presses de l'universite Laval, 1973). This is a collection of historic maps of New France from before New France, the 16th, 17th, and 18th centuries in New France, the Fall of New France, the settlement of the St. Lawrence, and the cities and towns of New France. (Explanations in French and English.)

126. Trudel, Marcel, *Dictionnaire des esclaves et de leurs propriétaires au Canada francais* (Hurtubise, Québec: Cahiers du Québec, 1994). This is an alphabetical listing of slaves—Indian, Metis, and Negro—in French Canada. It is organized by region in part one and by proprietor in part two. (French, but should be a problem to the English reader.)

127. Winks, Robin W., *The Blacks in Canada: A History* (Montreal: McGill-Queens University Press, 1971). This book provides a history of blacks in Canada. One chapter is devoted to slavery in New France. It is well documented and has an index. (English)

Finding Aids

128. Fortin, Francine, *Guide des registres d'état civil du Québec: Catholiques, protestants et autres denominations* or *Guide to Quebec's Parishes and Civil Registers: Catholic, Protestant and Other Denominations, 1621-1993* (Pointe Claire: Quebec Family History Society, 1993). This guide is organized alphabetically by towns or toponyms (locality or region), then by counties. At the end is a listing of usual toponyms and the actual town name. (French and English)

129. Mennie-de Varennes, Kathleen, *Bibliographie annotee d'ouvrages généalogiques au Canada* or *Annotated Bibliography of Genealogical Works in Canada*, 2 vols. (Canada: Fitzhenry & Whiteside, in association with the National Library of Canada and the Canadian Government Publishing Centre, Supply and Services). This is primarily a compilation of bibliographical and genealogical sources provide information on three or more generations. The bulk of the sources noted are of Canadian works, but some from other

countries are noted if the author found them in Canadian libraries. The volumes are organized by surname and parish. (Introduction is in French and English; the sources listed are in the language they were written.)

130. White, Jeanne Sauve, *Guide to Quebec Catholic Parishes and Published Parish Marriage Records* (Baltimore: Clearfield, 1998). This book is intended to help a researcher locate the parish in a county, the archives where records may be located and the availability of published marriage records of his Catholic ancestors. The letters "L" and "R" after a parish name indicate that the marriages of that parish are in the Loiselle Marriage Index and the Rivest Marriage Index respectively. (English)

Chapter Nineteen

The Periodical Source Index (PERSI)

by Francele Sherburne, SSND, and Joyce Soltis Banachowski

T*he Periodical Source Index,* better known as *PERSI,* is a comprehensive index to sur- names and places found in articles published in American and Canadian genealogical periodicals and in some foreign journals. The Allen County Public Library at Fort Wayne, Indiana, is responsible for assembling this monumental and valuable work.

Volumes 1 through 12 cover periodical articles from 1847 to 1985. Yearly supplements from 1986 have been added.

PERSI is divided into five sections or classifications. The articles within *PERSI* are fur- ther divided into twenty-two categories which the editors have chosen to call "record types." These record types will be discussed later.

The five sections are:.

1. U.S. Places: One needs to know the state or the state and county of research inter- est. The states are arranged alphabetically by abbreviation, then by county within each state, and finally by the twenty-two record types.

2. Canadian Places: Listings are alphabetical by province, then by the twenty-two record types.

3. Other Foreign Places: The alphabetical listing is by country, then in some cases, by smaller political divisions. Then the listings are by the twenty-two record types.

4. Research Methodology: This section contains a listing of "how to" articles grouped in the twenty-two record types.

5. Families: This is an alphabetical listing by surname of families discussed in articles. It includes articles on individual families, cemeteries where all who are buried have the same surname, a single record about an individual or between individuals, and family Bible records. Family surname journals, queries, ancestor charts and group sheets are not included. This section is not divided into the twenty-two record types.

All sections of this massive index are used in much the same fashion. The simplest to use is "Families." For example when using the Family Records Section, locate the appropriate surname. This surname is followed by a slash and then the title of the article. This in turn is followed by a four-letter abbreviation of the name of the journal in which this article is found as well as the volume, number, month, and year of publication.

TITLE OF ARTICLE	JOURNAL	VOL	NUM	MON	YEAR
JEANEAUX/ SOLOMON JUNEAUX 1846 Land Cert	WIGN	37	2	SEP	1990

As indicated before, there are twenty-two record types (categories of articles) found in the first four sections. The term "record types" can be confusing, leading the searcher to believe that this is an index to records such as probate or birth records. It is not; it is an index to articles about such records. Keep in mind, therefore, when reading these pages, that a record type is a category of article found in a publication. For the convenience of the readers, information about these record types is here quoted from the introduction to *PERSI*.

1. Biography. Includes articles that do not fit neatly into other categories. Will include names with some significant data such as date and place.

2. Cemetery. Includes cemetery inscriptions or lists of cemeteries. Family cemeteries where all burials are for persons of the same name are indexed by that surname in the families section.

3. Census. Includes all local, state, and federal schedules. Also includes statistical abstracts as well as other census schedules such as mortality, slave, agricultural, etc. Indexes to same and lists of inhabitants are included if no biographical information is provided.

4. Church. Includes all records related to a church, such as marriages, baptisms, burials, rosters, lists, history, minister diaries, and histories of individual religious sects. Church cemeteries are listed under cemeteries.

PERiodical Source Index
12/19/97 pg 17

FAMILY RECORDS	TITLE OF ARTICLE	JOURNAL	VOL	NUM	MON	YEAR
	BAKER/Mary Baker letter, Eng. and NY, 1845	NDNG	1	5	Spr	1980
	BAKER/Oscar Baker bio., Modoc co., CA	CAMC		5		1983
	BAKER/Squire Baker, Wattisfield, Eng.	ENCO	17	4	Nov	1955
	BAKER/Thomas Baker arms grant, Eng., 1649	ENGT	22	2		1906
	BAKER/Title abstract; Baker & Hess families, OR	ORCT	11	4	Sum	1971
	BAKER/Weaver & Baker families, AR	ARCQ	30	2	Sum	1984
	BAKER/Wm. Dawson-Mary Spearcy-Nancy Baker Rush	ORGF	33	2	Dec	1983
	BALCARRES/Lindsay (Balcarres) notes, peerage Gr.Br	ENGT	2	S		1885
	BALDWIN/Abraham Baldwin, GA patriot	GAHQ	3	4	Dec	1919
	BALDWIN/Abraham Baldwin, GA statesman & educator	GAHQ	11	2	Jun	1927
	BALDWIN/Abraham Baldwin,GA Yankee,old man congress	GAHQ	56	1	Spr	1972
	BALDWIN/Canon Baldwin obit., Ontario, 1908	CNYP				1909
	BALDWIN/Charles Baldwin, Greene co., NY	NYGC	2	1	Spr	1978
	BALDWIN/Emma Baldwin Gleaves, 1976 obit., AR	ARCQ	21	4	Win	1977
	BALDWIN/James Baldwin obit., 1950, Dutchess co.,NY	NYDY	35			1950
	BALDWIN/M.B. Baldwin memoriam, Modoc co., CA	CAMC		4		1982
	BALDWIN/Milo Fannin Baldwin, Allegany co., NY	NYCU	4	8	Aug	1973
	BALDWIN/N. Baldwin, fundamentalist movement, UT	UTHQ	47	1	Win	1979
	BALDWIN/Noah Baldwin bio., Sullivan co., TN	VAWB		12	Sep	1945
	BALDWIN/Richard Bladwin arms grant, Eng., 1663	ENGT	22	3		1906
	BALDWIN/Virgil Baldwin mems., CO River freighting	UTHQ	32	2	Spr	1964
	BALES/Joseph Bales obit., Ontario, 1829-1910	CNYP				1911
	BALES/Minnie Westenhaver Bales, Pickaway co., OH	OHPQ	24	3	Sum	1982

A page from PERSI

5. Court. Includes all court records which cannot be placed in another category, or court records of a mixed nature; e.g., freeman, justices of the peace records, chancery, divorce, jury lists, name changes, legislative acts, etc.

6. Deeds. Includes records of deeds, deed abstracts, or indexes to same.

7. Directories. Includes many types of directories such as city, county, business, and rural.

8. History. Includes histories of towns, counties, states, industry, social movements, etc.

9. Institutions. Includes records of state institutions, jails, orphanages, hospitals, county homes, mental facilities, etc.

10. Land. Includes records concerning land and land transfer that are not deeds or deed indexes.

11. Maps. Includes pictorially represented maps.

12. Military. Includes all traditional military records, such as pension, service, muster, bounty land, regimental histories, CSA and GAR records. Includes 1890 Union Army veterans' census schedules as well.

13. Naturalizations. Includes naturalization records and indexes, passports, declaration of intent, visas, and oaths of allegiance.

14. Obituaries. Includes records that are obituaries or indexes to same. Death notices may be included.

15. Other. A general category that includes records that do not fit any of the other classifications. These records are frequently lists.

16. Passenger Lists. Includes passenger lists or indexes of same, officers and crews, and histories of specific ships. These are indexed by location of the port of entry.

17. Probate. Includes estate records, inventories, administrations, wills when listed with other probate records, guardianships, orphan court records, etc.

18. School. Includes class rosters, school censuses, alumni lists, teacher's diaries, payrolls, board of education minutes, etc.

19. Tax. Includes all types of taxes and assessments at all levels of government and all geographic locations: real, person, etc.

20. Vital Records. Includes births, deaths, marriages, mortuary and funeral home records, bastardies, etc. May include death notices. Divorces are indexed under court records.

21. Voter. Includes lists of voters, tabulated results of elections, slates of candidates, poll taxes, Great Registers, etc.

22. Will. Includes only records that are wills, indexes, or abstracts of same. The date used for an individual's will is the date of probate.

RECORD TYPE	TITLE OF ARTICLE	JOURNAL	VOL	NUM	MON	YEAR
Probate	Understanding Probate Records	ALVL	17	3	Mar	1983

The Research Methodology Section will help you to consider other areas of research. Locate the record type desired. This is again followed by the title of the article, the four-letter abbreviation for the journal and the volume, number, month, and year of the publication.

In the Places Sections, look under the U.S. Place (by state and county), Canadian Place (by Province) or foreign places (by country name other than Canada). Just as the previous sample, in the U.S. Places Section, the state and county columns are followed by record type, title of article, four-letter journal abbreviation, volume, number, month, and year of publication. Canadian Places and Foreign Places are organized in the same manner.

STATE	COUNTY	RECORD TYPE	TITLE OF ARTICLE	JOURNAL	VOL	NUM	MON	YEAR
NY	Osweg	History	Fort Ontario	DARM	119	10	Dec	1985

It is important to understand what you will not find in *PERSI*. *PERSI* does not index every subject appearing in any individual article. It does not index family surname journals, newsletters, queries, ancestor charts, or book reviews. It does not include page numbers of articles.

After locating the article of interest, the next task is to locate the complete name of the journal in which it is located. Appendix A at the back of each volume lists the four letter code for each journal along with the full name of the publication.

To find a copy of the article, check in nearby libraries. If it is not found there, remember that all these publications are housed at the Allen County Public Library, P.O. Box 2270, Fort Wayne, Indiana 46801, and they will copy and mail an article for a fee.

PERSI is now available on CD-ROM. The hardcover volumes are condensed into one index covering over a million records in more than 5,000 periodicals. Its obvious advantage over the hardcover volumes is that there is only one index, one search, and the ability to limit the search electronically.

Primary Sources

Primary records are those generated at the time of the event: church records, civil registration, census, etc. Microfilm copies or photocopies of these records are also considered primary sources as long as they are pictures of the original record or entry. These primary documents are considered the most valid sources for the genealogist and are the records that confirm the information obtained from other sources.

This does not mean that there are no errors found in primary sources. Human nature being what it is, there may be errors in any record. The transcription of such documents, however, creates a new opportunity for error; the genealogist's copy of the transcription lends itself to even more mistakes.

The census, both in the United States and Canada, although a primary source of information, is very prone to error. This is because the person answering the door is very likely the one who provides the information to the census taker. If that information giver is not accurate, then the census entry is inaccurate. Also the census taker may be writing down what s/he thinks is being said to her/him by someone speaking with an unfamiliar accent.

When finding that several primary documents contradict one another, the search is on for still other records that will establish the truth. At times there is no record that establishes the truth. In this case the genealogist must weigh the evidence and make the hard decision. This decision and its rationale should be explained in the genealogist's records.

French-Canadian church records are the most valuable primary records available to genealogists. Most of the Roman Catholic records are still in existence and on microfilm; in the French tradition, they provide a wealth of information. Until well into the twentieth century all priests, ministers, rabbi's, etc., were required, annually, to provide the courthouse with an exact copy of the church records from the past year. These copies served as the civil records. Since these civil records are much less available than the church records, they are less used.

Protestant records are more difficult to locate and tend to have less information in them than the Roman Catholic records. Many of the secondary sources are beginning to include them, and as this practice expands it will make researching Protestant records much easier. Protestant ministers as well as Roman Catholic priests were required annually to turn in copies of their records to the civil authorities. Since this is the case, it is worthwhile to search and find the nearest repository for films of these records.

Whenever possible it is advisable to make a photocopy of these primary documents. At the Family History Library in Salt Lake City, Utah, it is currently possible to copy these records directly to a CD.

The chapters in this section discuss church records, civil registration, notary records, and census records. It is important to stress that the number of pages devoted to discussion of a given set of primary documents is in no way indicative of its relative merit.

Chapter Twenty

French-Canadian Church Records

By Patricia Keeney Geyh

The most significant primary source of information available to French-Canadian genealogists researching Quebec ancestors is the huge quantity of easily accessible Roman Catholic church records. The vast majority of the records from the 1600s through the 1920s are still in existence and have been microfilmed. Those after the early twentieth century have not been filmed as yet. Since most French Canadians were and are Roman Catholic, this information is invaluable.

Tanguay, Jetté, and editors of the various published genealogies and repertoires extracted much of the information found in their works from the pages of the various Roman Catholic church registers. No matter how conscientious those people and their staffs were, many errors entered their work. Often, as a matter of policy, much information was omitted. It is essential, therefore, that the genealogist confirm all data obtained by finding the primary source from which the secondary information was extracted. In most cases this means searching through the church registers.

Roman Catholic Church Records

These church records have been made in duplicate since 1621 and have been written, like those in France, according to the royal ordinance of Villers-Cotterets issued in 1539[1]. In Quebec the original of the church record stayed in the parish itself, and the copy was sent to the courthouse at the end of each year. The original church records through most of the 1870s have been microfilmed by The Church of Jesus Christ of Latter-day Saints and are available through the church's family history centers throughout the world and through its

Family History Library in Salt Lake City, Utah. Copies of these films are available in many repositories in Quebec also.

Roman Catholic church records for the period of the 1870s into the 1920s are also on film and available in Quebec at various archives and at the Gagnon Room of the Montreal Central Library.

The vast majority of Roman Catholic church records are written in French. Major exceptions to this seem to occur in areas where English-speaking people settled. In such areas records are sometimes in English. A few priests used Latin. The French records, although written in paragraph form, tend to follow a strict format and after a period of time the non-French-speaking researcher can read them with relative ease. A difficulty with these records is that usually the date is spelled out rather than appearing in Arabic numerals. A translation guide to dates is provided in the appendix of this book, as is a list of French words which will be of use to the researcher.

In the following chapter there are photocopies of baptismal, marriage, and burial records as they are written in French. These records have then been transcribed on the computer, and following that they have been translated.

Baptism Records

Records of baptism often include the date of birth of the child as well as the date of the baptism. Some records do not include the birth date, but French-Canadian children were usually baptized within a day or two of their birth. The records also include the names of the parents, giving the maiden name of the mother, and the name of the parish in which the family resided if they were not from the parish of baptism. The occupation of the father is frequently provided. The names of the sponsors are also listed and may include their relationship with the family or other identifying information. For example the record might indicate that the sponsors were the grandparents of the child.

Marriage Records

Marriage records include the date and place of marriage, the names of the bride and groom, and the name of the parish from which they came. The parents' names are given, as is their place of residence, if different than the place of marriage. Witnesses are named and frequently their relationship to one or another of the married couple is stated. Occupations of various members of the group may be noted. In the records of the immigrants to French Canada, the place of origin in France is frequently cited. All women are identified by their maiden names.

Burial Records

Burial records include the name of the deceased and the date and place of burial. They sometimes include the date and place of death, the age of the deceased and the name of the spouse. The names of parents of deceased children are sometimes given. Women are identified by their maiden names.

Additional Information about Roman Catholic Church Records in Quebec

- The signatures at the end of each record are noteworthy. Each participant is asked to sign the document. If s/he cannot write, the priest indicates this fact. These signatures may be used to help verify the identity of individuals.
- Confirmation records may sometimes be found.
- Illegitimate births are identified.
- Sometimes a parish history appears in the records.
- Abjurations (renunciations of Protestant faith) are indicated.
- Divorces might be listed.
- Separations and annulments are indicated.

When baptism, marriage, and burial records are entered in the registers in chronological order, the researcher is provided with an excellent means of following the history of the family. Not only can the births, marriages, and burials be seen in context, but the friends and relatives of the family may be identified as they serve as sponsors and witnesses.

Some church registers are indexed. These indexes are sometimes at the end or the beginning of each volume and may cover several years. At other times the indexes are in separate volumes. These indexes are a valuable tool for genealogists, but there is an important caveat. Many times these lists are incomplete. Even if a name is not found in an index, be sure to check the records themselves.

Many little glitches may occur when researching microfilmed records. It is important to remember that some of the records may have been filmed out of order. This happened rarely, but it did occur. Also, if a church was served by a neighboring priest for a time, the church records generated by him may have been taken to his home parish.

Check the date of founding of a parish. If the records being searched for predate the existence of the parish, check to see where the parishioners attended church before the formation of the new parish.

Non–Catholic Church Records

Non-Catholic records pose a difficult problem for the genealogist researching French-Canadian roots. This is because there are very few published indexes, extractions, etc., from non-Catholic church records. The National Archives of Quebec has been continuously adding new data to the *Loiselle Quebec Marriage Index*, and these additions include extractions from a large number of non-Catholic church registers. Other than this, there does not seem to be any province-wide, organized extraction or indexing program. While extractions of records of individual parishes may have been published, finding this published information involves searching card catalogs and bibliographies, writing letters, and a great deal of determination.

Anglican Church Records

The Anglican Church is known by several names, usually dependent on the location of the parishes. In England it is the Church of England; in Ireland it is the Church of Ireland; in the Northern Hemisphere it is known as the Anglican Church or the Episcopalian Church.

There are two Anglican dioceses in the province of Quebec. They are the Montreal Diocese and the Quebec Diocese. In addition, three other dioceses headquartered outside of the province include part of Quebec in their diocesan boundaries. They are the Diocese of Ottawa, the Diocese of Moosonee, and the Diocese of the Arctic.[2] (See address list at end of this book.)

Those Anglican registers predating 1875 are generally found in the diocesan archives. Those postdating 1875 are usually found in the parish. When a church closes, its records go to the diocese. Some Anglican church records are on microfilm.

The United Church of Canada

On 10 June 1925 the following denominations joined together to form the United Church of Canada: the Methodist Church of Canada, about half of the Presbyterians, the Congregational Union, and the United Church of Western Canada.[3]

Most United Church records are kept at the parish level. If a church closes, the registers are sent to the United Church Centre. The records for all of Quebec, except the Gaspe, are kept there. Some of the records from the Gaspe are kept at Pine Hill Divinity Hall. The addresses for these archives are:

United Church Centre, 3480 Decarie Boulevard, Montréal, PQ H4A 3J5 Canada
Pine Hill Divinity Hall, Franklin Street, Halifax, NS B3H 3S5, Canada

A Guide to Research in the United Church of Canada Archives, published by the Ontario Genealogical Society is an essential reference tool for those whose ancestors' records may be found in the United Church.

Baptist

Baptist church records are usually kept in the home parish. The Canadian Baptist Archives are kept at McMaster University Archives in Hamilton, Ontario. No research is done by the staff and a daily fee is charged for researching onsite. Records of the Baptist Church in Atlantic Canada are housed at Acadia University Archives in Wolfville, Nova Scotia.

McMaster University Archives, 1280 Main St. West, Hamilton, Ontario, L8C4L8.

Presbyterian

Presbyterian church records are usually maintained in the original parish. Those in archives will be found in the archives of the United Church or in the Presbyterian Church of Canada Archives.

There are many other smaller denominations in Canada. Researchers looking for their ancestors in one of these parishes should check *The Directory of Canadian Archives,* Ottawa, Canadian Council of Archives, 1990. It lists most church and denominational archives along with their addresses and gives some idea of their holdings.

1. "Genealogy through marriage records." *French Canadian and Acadian Genealogical Review.* vol. 2, no 1. p. 5.

2. Baxter, Angus. *In Search of Your Canadian Roots.* Genealogical Publishing Company, 1994. p. 305-6.

3. Douglas, Althea. *Here Be Dragons! Navigating the Hazards Found in Canadian Family Research: A Guide for Genealogists with Some Uncommon Useful Knowledge.* Toronto: Ontario Genealogical Society, 1996.

Chapter Twenty-one

French-Canadian Church Records Transcribed and Translated

*By Joyce Soltis Banachowski and Linda K. Boyea
with additional help by Patricia Keeney Geyh*

In order to provide French-Canadian genealogists with examples of church records to study, photocopies of original records from the 1800s, the 1700s and the 1600s are presented in this chapter. One baptism record, one marriage record and one death record is provided for each of these three centuries—and each is transcribed and translated.

The examples that follow are records of the Roman Catholic Church only. We do this for two reasons. First, the vast majority of French Canadians were Roman Catholic, so examples should logically be from that church. These records were usually written in French. A very small number were written in Latin. Second, most of the ministers of other faiths wrote their records in English, thereby eliminating the need for transcription and translation.

Using the original church records, most of which have been microfilmed and are available through the Family History Library in Salt Lake City, Utah, and its branches worldwide, requires patience and determination. Non-French speaking genealogists must decipher handwriting written years ago and in a foreign tongue. It can be done but it will take time at first.

The information in most French-Canadian church records is written in one or more paragraphs, and is not entered on a form. The text, however, is written in a standardized format, making it easier for the researcher to quickly identify the information. Usually the paragraph begins with the date, and is followed by the type of sacrament being administered. The name(s) of the person(s) receiving the sacrament generally follows, e.g. the child being baptized, or the bride and groom, or the person being buried. In addition, witnesses are listed, along with the name of the priest. The relationship of the witnesses to the person receiving the sacrament is also sometimes given. Depending on the type of sacrament being recorded, other information may be provided as well.

Many times the name(s) of the person(s) receiving the sacrament is also written in the margin, making it easier to locate the desired record as the genealogist scans the records. Sometimes there is an index to the names of the people receiving the sacrament. These indexes may appear at the beginning of a volume or at the end. At other times there is a master index to many volumes in a given church. The researcher should

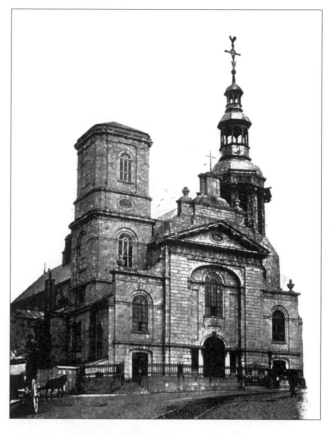

search these resources first, but, if a name is not in the index, s/he should be sure to check the original records themselves. Be aware that there are many errors in these indexes.

Capitalization in these records is haphazard. Sometimes a surname is capitalized, sometimes not. Sometimes a first name is capitalized, sometimes not. Sometimes a place name is capitalized, sometimes not. Do not try to impose English patterns on these old French records.

Punctuation is equally inconsistent and sometimes completely absent.

Dictionaries, if they existed at all, were not widely available in early French Canada. This is obvious in reading church records. The same word may be spelled many different ways in a given record; surnames are often spelled in many different ways in the same paragraph. Not only are there differences in spelling but individual priests often developed their own system of abbreviations.

In order to read the handwriting of a particular priest it may be necessary to compare his formation of a given letter with his handwriting in a previous record. It is possible that only by noting how this one man actually formed his letters can a researcher decipher his handwriting.

Signatures of person(s) receiving the sacrament, and the witnesses who were able to sign, are found, along with the signature of the priest, at the end of the record. Frequently the witnesses' relationship to the person receiving the sacrament is cited. Not only are these signatures an excellent genealogical resource, but they also provide a means of identifying the individual(s) when he/she sign his/her names in other documents.

The transcriptions that follow may contain errors. Several people familiar with these records have checked the transcriptions, but, since some of the handwriting is difficult to read, it is impossible to guarantee that they are completely free of errors.

Since genealogists work backward, from the present to the past, the church records are presented from the 1800s, then the 1700s, and finally the 1600s. In addition to following the format of good genealogy, placing the records in this order helps the twenty-first-century researcher, who must go from the more familiar handwriting of the nineteenth century, to the much less familiar style of the seventeenth century.

French-Canadian Church Records of the 1800s

Baptism Record of the church of St. Pierre Les Becquets for Joseph Grandiose Michel

Family History Library Film # 1031897

Transcription

Margin: B.2 Joseph Grandiose Michel

Le huit Janvier, mil huit cent soixante
seize, Nous, prétre, vicaire soussigné, avons
baptisé Joseph Gandiose, né ce jour du
legitime mariage de Wilbrod Michel,
cultivateur et de Clarisse St Pierre, de cette
paroisse. Parrain : Jeoffroi St. Pierre;
marraine: Elmire Tepin, laquelle a
déclaré ne savoir signe ainsi que le père
le parrain a signé ainsi nous.

Jeoffroi de St. Pierre
E.M. Brunel Ptre. Vic.

Translation

Margin: B.2 (i.e. baptism #2) Joseph Grandiose Michel

The eighth of January one thousand eight hundred
seventy six, our undersigned priest vicar has
baptized Joseph Gandiose, born this day of
the legitimate marriage of Wilbrod Michel,
farmer and of Clarisse St Pierre of this
parish. Godfather : Jeoffroi St. Pierre;
godmother: Elmire Tepin, who has
declared that she cannot sign. and also the father
the god father has signed below.

Jeoffroi de St. Pierre
E.M. Brunel, Priest, Vicar

French-Canadian Church Records of the 1800s

Marriage Record of the Church of St. Isidore for Remi Coté and Catherine Poupart

Family History Library # 1290053

Transcription

Margin: M 1[1] Rémi Côté et Catherine Poupart Veuve Bouchard

Le quinze Janvier mil huit cent cinquante
cinq, oú la dispence de deux bans de mariage
accordée par Monseigneur de Sydonie et la publi[2]
-cation du troisième ban faite aux prônes
des messes Paroissiales de celieu et de Chateau
-gay Entre Rémi Coté fils majeur d'Ignace
Côté +[3]et de défunte Ursule Quesnel de-
Chateaugay d'une part et Catherine -

Notes

[1]The M 1 in the margin indicates that this was the first marriage performed in the parish in this calendar year.

[2] Notice publication is split over two lines. The hyphen is placed at the beginning of the second line.

[3] Note the cross in the original document further indicating that Ursule Quesnel is dead.

Poupart veuve mijneure de Julien
Bouchard de cette Paroisse d'autre part
Ne s'étant découvert aucun empêchement-
canonique Nous curé de cette Paroisse soussigné avons reçue des époux leur mutuel
consentement de mariage en présence
d'Ignace Coté, Alexis Poupart Maxime
Coté et Pierre Bourdeau qui tous ont
déclaré ne savoir signer.

J.N.Trudel ᴾᵗʳᵉ

Translation

Margin: M 1 (i.e. Marriage #1) Rémi Côté and Catherine Poupart widow Bouchard

The fifteenth of January one thousand eight hundred fifty
five, with the dispensation of two bans of marriage
granted by Monseigneur de Sydonie and the
publication of the third ban made at the homilies
at parish masses here and of Chateaugay
between Rémi Coté son, of legal age, of Ignace
Côté + and of deceased Ursule Quesnel of
Chateaugay, of the first part, and Catherine
Poupart, widow, of legal age, of Julien
Bouchard of this parish, of the other part
Not finding any impediment
of the church, we the curé of this parish
signed below, had received of the spouses their mutual
consent of marriage in the presence
of Ignace Coté, Alexis Poupart, Maxime
Coté and Pierre Bourdeau who all have
declared they were not able to sign

J.N. Trudelᴾʳⁱᵉˢᵗ

French-Canadian Church Records of the 1800s
Burial Record of the Church of St. Isidore for Julien Bouchard
Family History Library Film #1290053

Transcription

Margin: S 18 Julien Bouchard

Le quinze Juin mil huit cent cinquante quatre
par nous prêtre soussigné a été inhumé dans le
cimetiere de ce lieu Julien Bouchard cultivateur
époux de Catherine Poupart décédé en cette paroisse
depuis deux jours agé de vingt trois ans ont été prescence
Jean Baptiste Gregoire et Alexis Ménard qui n'ont signer

J. N. Trudel [Ptre]

Translation

Margin: S 18 (i.e. Death #18) Julien Bouchard

The fifteenth of June, one thousand eight hundred and fifty-four
by us the priest signed below has buried in the
cemetery of this place Julien Bouchard, farmer,
spouse of Catherine Poupart, died in this parish
two days ago, age of twenty-three years, in the presence of
Jean Baptiste Gregoire and Alexis Menard who were unable to sign.

J.N. Trudel [Priest]

French-Canadian Church Records of the 1700s

Baptism of the church of St Anges Lachine for Cathering Brou dit Freniere Pomenville

Montreal Archives Film #46

Transcription

Margin: B de Cather, fille de Freniere Pomenville

L'an mil Sept cent Soixante Trois et Le sept d' aout je Soussigné ai baptisé
catherine née aujourhui fille legitime de françois brou dit freniere pomenville et d'agathe
Sarrazin Le parrain a eté ignace bonhomme et la marrainne angelique bourbonnois
qui n'ont sçû signer

Delagarde prtre

Translation

Margin: B (i.e. Baptism) of Catherine daughter of Freniere Pomenville

The year one thousand seven hundred sixty three, the seventh of August, I, the undersigned have baptized
Catherine, born today, legitimate daughter of Francois Brou dit Freniere Pomenville and of Agatha
Sarrazin. The godfather was Ignace Bonhomme and the godmother Angelique Bourbonnois
do not know how to sign

Delagarde priest

French-Canadian Church Records of the 1700s

Marriage Record from the Church of St. Anges Lachine for Antoine Picard and Catherine Caron

Montreal Archives Film #46

Transcription

Margin: M Antoine Picard Catherine Caron

L'an mil sept cent trénte un et le huit^e Jan^{er} aprés
avon fait trois publication de ban de mariage aux trônes
des messes parroissiales le premier, le dimanche 31e decemb^r. le
2.^{d} le Jour suivant 1er Janvier, et le 3e le dimanche 7e du ce
mois et ne s'etant trouvé aucun Empechement Je prétre
missionaire soussigné ai recû le mutuel Consentement de
mariage par paroles de parti et ai donné la benediction nuptiale
selon les ceremonies de nôtre meré la Ste Eglise a antonie
picard age de trente un an files de deffunt gabriel picard et de
marie magdélainé rapin les pere et mere de cette parroisse
et a Catherine Caron agée de vingt huit ans fille de S^r
Vital caron cap^{ne} de milice de cette par^{se} et de marie
pertuis les pere et mere. en pres de marie magdelaine
rapin la mére du et marié Joseph picard son frére ^{de} Jean Chenier

et Jean rapin les oncles et de Sr Vital caron pére de la
mariée de bap. Caron son frére de bap. Pominville son Beaufrére
de charles tessier son cousin et de plusieurs autre parent et
amis desquels marie mag^{de} picard Jean chenie Jean
rapin ont signér

Note the use of superscripts by this priest as well as the indiscriminate use of capital- ization.

Mari madailene Rapen

Ch. Texier

Jean baptiste Rapin   jean chenie

Joseph Sauvé   Bernard St Germin

Anthoiene Rapin

Translation

Margin: M (I.E. Marriage) Antoine Picard and Catherine Caron

The year one thousand seven hundred thirty one and the eighth of January after
having done three publications of bans of marriage at the homily
of the parish masses: the first on the Sunday December 31st .the
2nd on the day following, 1st January, and the 3rd the Sunday the 7th of this
month and not finding any impediments, I the priest,
missionary, signed below, having received the mutual consent of
marriage by the vows of the parties and have given the nuptial benediction
according to the ceremonies of our Holy Mother Church to Antoine
Picard, age of thirty one years, son of the deceased Gabriel Picard and of
Marie Magdelaine Rapin the father and mother, of this parish
and to Catherine Caron age of twenty eight years, daughter of S^r
Vital Caron, captain of the militia, of this parish and Marie
Pertuis, the father and mother. In the presence of Marie Magdelaine
Rapin, the mother of the groom, and Joseph Picard, his brother, of Jean Chenier
and Jean Rapin his uncles, and of Sr Vital Caron, father of the
bride, of Bap. (Baptiste) Caron, her brother, of Bap.(Baptiste) Pominville, brother-in-law
of Charles Tessier, cousin and many other relatives and
friends with whom Marie Magdelaine Picard, Jean Chenie and Jean
Rapin have signed.

Mari madailene rapen

Ch. Texier

Jean baptiste Rapin   jean chenie

Joseph Sauvé   Bernard St Germin

Anthoiene Rapin

French-Canadian Church Records of the 1700s

Burial Record from the Church of St. Pierre Les Becquets for Claire Apoline Viola

Family History Library Film # 1031893

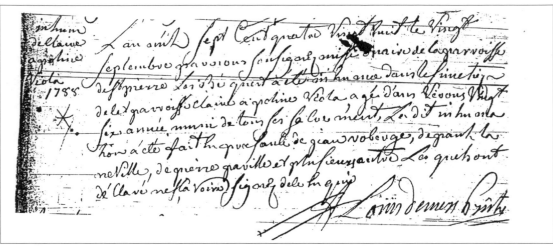

Transcription

Margin: inhume de Claire Apoline Viola 1788

Lan mil Sept Cent quatre Vingt huit le Vingt
Septembre par nous Sousignez missionaire de la parroisse
de St pierre Les Bé quest à été inhume dans le Cimetier
de les parroisse claire apoline Viola, agé d'ans Virons Vingt
Six année muni de tous les Sacrement, La dit inhuma
tion[4] à été fait En presance de Jean roberge, de paul la
neVille, de pierre graville et plusieurs autre Les quels ont
dé Claré ne sÇasvoir signez de le Enquis

F. Loüis Demers Prêtre

Note

[4] Notice that the word *inhumation* is split over two lines, without the use of a hyphen.

Translation

Margin: burial of Claire Apoline Viola 1788

The year one thousand seven hundred eighty-eight, the twentieth of
September by us the undersigned missionary of the parish
of St Pierre Les Béquest was buried in the cemetery
of this parish, Claire Apoline Viola, age of about twenty-
six years, armed with all the sacraments; this burial
was in the presence of Jean Roberge, of Paul La
Neville, of Pierre Graville and many others who have
declared they are not able to sign.

F. Loüis Demers Priest

French-Canadian Church Records of the 1600s
Baptismal Record from the Church of the Cathedral
of Notre Dame de Montreal for Francoise Hunaut
Family History Library Film # 375840

Transcription

Margin: <u>46</u> Francoise hunaut

Le 5e Jour de Decembre 1667

A este[5] Baptisée Francoise fille-de
Toussainet hunaut habitant et de
Marie-Lorgueil sa femme, Le Parrin-
Mathurin Rouillier habitant la marrine-
Marie-Grandin femme-de-Jacgues Picot
dit la Brie-habitant.`

Translation

Margin: <u>46</u> Francoise Hunaut

The 5th Day of December 1667

Was baptized Francoise daughter of
Toussaint Hunaut habitant and of
Marie-Lorgueil his wife, The Godfather,
Mathurin Roullier habitant, the godmother,
Marie Grandin, wife-of-Jacques Picot
known as la Brie habitant.

Note

[5] *A este* seems the best transcription of these words written by the priest in the 1600's.

French-Canadian Church Records of the 1600s

Marriage Record of the Church of Notre Dame of Montreal for Pierre Peré and Denise Le Maistre

Family History Library Film # 0375840

Transcription

Margin: M 3. Pierre Peré and Denise Lemaistre

Le 26me Janvier 1660⁶

A este ' fait et solemnisé le mariage de Pierre
Peras fils de deffunct Pierre Et Jeanne Laniel
avec Denise le maistre fille de Denys Et de
C'este Catherine deharme tous deux de cette paroisse
Le trois bans ayant este ' publies auparavant. le
mariage fet en presence de Dam^{lle} Jeanne Mance
administratrice de l'hospital Jacques LeMoyne
Marchant, Louys Chartier Chirigien et plus^{re} (plusieurs)
au amys communs des parties.

Translation

Margin: M 3. (i.e. marriage # 3) Pierre Peré and Denise Lemaistre

The 26th January 1660

Was made and solemnized the marriage of Pierre
Peras son of the deceased Pierre and Jeanne Laniel
With Denise Lemaistre daughter of Denys and of
this Catherine Deharme all two of this parish
The three bans having been published previously. The
marriage was in the presence of Mademoiselle Jeanne Mance
administrator of the hospital, Jacques LeMoyne
merchant, Louys Chartier, surgeon and many
of the friends in common of the parties

> **Note**
>
> ⁶ In many of the 17th century records the date precedes the document and are not included as part of it. Often the month or year are not given at all, so the researcher has to look back at previous records to locate this information.

French-Canadian Church Records of the 1600s
Burial Record of the Church of Notre Dame de Montreal for Joseph des Autels
Family History Library Film # 0375840

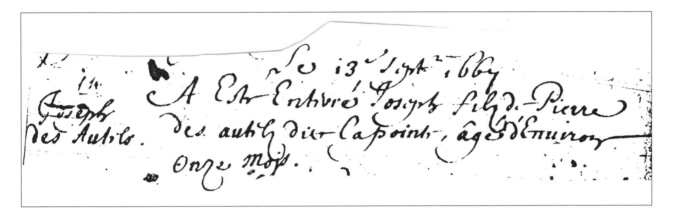

Transcription

Margin: 14 Joseph des Autels

Le 13' Sept^{re} 1667

A Esté Enterré[7] Joseph fils de Pierre
des autels dit la point, âgé d'Environ
onze Mojs.

> **Note**
>
> [7] This word is unclear in this record. In other records by this priest it is clearly *enterré*

Translation

Margin: 14 (i.e. burial #14) Joseph des Autels (Desantels)

The 13th of September 1667
Was buried Joseph son of Pierre
Desautels dit LaPoint, age about
11 months.

Civil Registration in the Province of Quebec

By Patricia Keeney Geyh

Until the late 1900s, church registers in Quebec served as civil and vital records in that province. Throughout the years a second copy of church records, from all denominations, was sent annually to the appropriate courthouse. During the 1940s the vital record collections in courthouses throughout Quebec were filmed by the Institut Généalogique Drouin. These civil records should be an exact copy of the church records. Humanity being what it is, however, there are sometimes a few differences.

Some of the variations could be simple copying errors made while duplicating the original register. Also, through time, corrections and additions have been made. Although these changes should have been recorded in both places, it sometimes happened that only the courthouse or only the church recorded the change.

There is a real advantage to having these two sets of records. They serve as insurance against loss and fire. Records from the courthouse may cover registers that are missing in the parish. The parish may have records that were burned or lost in the courthouse.

Accessing this information can be done by referring to the three sets of records created by the Drouin Institute especially for that purpose. The first is titled *Dictionnaire National des Canadiens Francais 1608-1760*, commonly known as *The Red Books*. The second set is titled *Répertoire Alphabetique des Mariages des Canadiens Francais, 1760-1935*, commonly known as *The Blue Books*. The *Third Cardex Drouin Supplement* is the final index to names found in the vital records. Finding the extraction of a particular marriage record in one of these sets of indexes will provide the researcher with the name of the parish and the date of the marriage. It might even provide the number of the roll of film needed, using Drouin's numbering system. More detailed information about these indexes may be found in the Secondary Sources section of this book.

The indexes listed above include only marriage records. It is important to recognize, however, that when turning to the Civil Registration itself, birth and death records are also included.

If the film number is not provided it is necessary to refer to one of six volumes of *Inventaire des 2365 microfilms du Fonds Drouin* by Jean-Pierre-Yves Pepin. The volumes and their contents are:

Volume 1   This is of little value to the genealogist since it merely lists the volume numbers used by the Institute with no reference to what is contained in them.

Volume 2   This volume, and volume 3, is where the researcher turns when looking for the film number of a given church. The names of Quebec communities are given in alphabetical order. This volume covers A-M. Under the name of a given community are the names of the churches within that community whose records have been filmed. The numbers of the films are provided.

Volume 3   This volume is the same as Volume 2, except that communities from N-Z are listed.

Volume 4   This volume lists the records from various locations in Acadia, Ontario, and the United States that are filmed in this collection and the film numbers for the appropriate dates.

Volume 5   Although notarial records are not the main feature of this collection, a good many have been filmed. This catalogue gives the name of the notary and the film number on which his records may be found.

Volume 6   This volume lists the rolls of film in this collection in numerical order and provides the name of the churches whose records appear on a given roll and the dates covered.

When looking at records on one of the reels of microfilm it will be noted that to the left is a narrow strip that gives the name of the record being looked at and the date.

Unfortunately this collection is not readily available. It can be found in some libraries in Quebec and elsewhere in Canada and in a very few libraries in the United States. The Salle Gagnon of the Bibliothèque Centrale de Montréal, 1210 Rue Sherbrooke East, is a remarkable place for French-Canadian researchers and has all of these resources.

Following is a list of places where this collection can be found:

Bibliotheque Centrale du Montréal
Salle Gagnon
1210 Sherbrooke East
Montréal, QC H2L IL9

Société Généalogique Canadienne Francaise
3440 Davidson
Montréal, QC H1W 225
ph. 514-527-1010

Le Club de Généalogie
CP 21021
Succ. Jacques-Cartier
Longueuil, QC J4J 5J4

Societé de Généalogie et d'Archives de Rimouski
110 de l'Erêche est
Rimouski, QC G5L IX9

Chapter Twenty-three

Canadian Census Records

By Joyce Soltis Banachowski and Patricia Keeney Geyh

Most French-Canadian genealogists tend to avoid using Canadian Census records and concentrate more on the use of the various indexes and church records that are available in abundance. This is certainly the most efficient way of tracing a French-Canadian ancestor. It is important to note, however, that many census records do exist as early as 1659, and these records provide a great deal of information about the lives of people in past generations.

The Canadian Censuses, especially those of 1851 and later, are useful as stepping stones into other records. Information on them is particularly valuable when researching land records and church records.

For example, in Ontario the land records are not filed by the name of the grantor or grantee, as in the United States. They are filed by land description. In the 1851 and 1861 censuses, the land description is included in each entry in the Agricultural Schedule. In the 1871 census the land description is included in Schedule Four, which is called "Cultivated Lands, Products, Plants and Fruits." In 1901 the land description is in the Schedule of Public Lands and Buildings, which is Schedule Two.

Many Canadian censuses since 1851 list the religion of the individuals being counted. This information should be extracted most carefully, especially for non-Catholics. Many Protestant groups broke off and formed new branches of the same religion and then at times re-formed to found still a different group. It is necessary to get into the right denomination in order to locate the correct church records.

Three Census Formats

Censuses tend to fall into one of three different formats. Some are nominal and name everyone in the household. Some are head of household and name only the head of the household and sometimes provide other information. Others are aggregate and provide only statistical summaries.

Census Records Differ Through History

Inasmuch as the Confederation of Canada was not established until 1867, there are many differences between censuses taken in various parts of Canada before that date. Those taken prior to 1851 are especially diversified. Some were for an entire province. Others enumerated people in a particular town or area. Some were taken by seigneurs and included only those on the particular seigneury. Others were church censuses.

Throughout most of the French Regime (1608-1759) annual censuses were mandated. Some of these still exist. During the early years of the English regime, places such as Ontario were also required to produce an annual census, usually on a township level. Some of these are still extant.

The 1851 and 1861 schedules, although taken before the Confederation, are very similar. The 1851 census was actually taken in 1852. David P. Gagan, associate professor of history at McMaster University, wrote an article titled "Enumerator's Instructions for the Census of Canada, 1852 and 1861," appearing in *Histoire Sociale-Social History,* Vol 7, #14, pp. 355-365, November 1974. In this article he commented that the 1851 census was rather badly done, because the population tended to be suspicious of the census, believing that it would increase their taxes.

Later Censuses Organized by Registration Districts

To access the 1851, 1861, 1871, 1881, 1891, and 1901 Canadian censuses, one must know the registration district. Be aware that, as populations grew, there were changes in district boundaries, meaning that names of districts sometimes changed from one census year to the next.

Catalogue of Census Returns on Microfilm, 1666-1891, by Thomas A. Hillman, Ottawa, Canadian Government Publishing Centre and the addendum, *Catalogue of Census Returns on Microfilm, 1901* are the catalogues used to access most Canadian Census Records. The 1851 through 1901 records are sorted by registration district.

Indexes Usually Not Available

There is not a Canada-wide series of indexes to the various census records. There are, however, some indexes done by organizations and individuals for specific areas. It is important to check resources for a given locality to see if indexes are available.

The Date of the Schedule and The Census Day

In the 1851, 1861, 1871, 1881, 1891 and 1901 censuses, "The Date of the Schedule" is noted on each page of the census itself. This date is the actual date that the enumerator took the information from the family. "The Census Day," on the other hand, is the official date from which the census taker should have computed ages and other such information. For example, if a person was born after The Census Day but before the Date of the Schedule, s/he should not appear on the census.

Count People in Their Usual Place of Abode

Beginning in 1871, the year of the first Canadian Census after Confederation, it was mandated that people be counted in their usual (or "official") residences, regardless of where they were on the day of the census. Those who had no set place of abode were listed wherever they were found.

Place Names Change

When researching French-Canadian ancestors it is easy to be confused by changes in place names. Governmental units of all sizes have changed names throughout history. Using provincial gazetteers is one way to trace these changes. Some of the major name changes affecting census research in French Canada are as follows:

Ontario
1620-1791	called Quebec
1791-1841	called Upper Canada
1841-1867	called Canada West
1867-present	called Ontario

Prince Edward Island
1603-1763	called Ile St. Jean
1763-1799	called St. John's Island
1799-present	called Prince Edward Island

Quebec
1620-1791	called Quebec or New France
1791-1841	called Lower Canada
1841-1867	called Canada East
1867-present	called Quebec

Learn to Decipher Handwriting

Some census records or census abstracts have been published in books. Others are available in manuscript form. Some of the manuscripts have been transferred to microfilm. When using the primary census records, whether in manuscript form or on microfilm, one should be prepared for the fact that they are all handwritten. Patience may be required to read them. Also know that all early French schedules up through 1851 list women by their maiden names. That woman living with Grandfather, who is the head of the household, is probably his wife. As with all research, a little creative thinking may help. Names may be misspelled. Dit names may be used. Sometimes the only certain way to identify a family is to confirm that the children have the correct names and ages.

Additional Census Information in Appendixes

A comprehensive chart that appears in Appendix D lists all the census records known to the authors for Ontario, Quebec, New Brunswick, Nova Scotia, Newfoundland, and Prince Edward Island, excluding all statistical summaries. Areas outside of Quebec are included because many Québecois migrated in and out of these regions.

The chart gives a separate listing for Acadian census records, although what was known as Acadia is now part of Nova Scotia and New Brunswick. Records from Cape Breton, formerly known as Isle Royale, have been noted, although that portion of Canada is now part of the province of Nova Scotia. Ontario schedules have been included—even though this is not considered a French-Canadian area—because of the French settlements in this province and since it was a major emigration route from Quebec to the United States. French settlements in the United States and in the western part of Canada have not been included, though censuses do exist for these areas.

Pre-1851 census records for Ontario are quite incomplete. Although an annual census was to be taken in those early days by township, few have survived. The chart lists those from Augusta Township in Granville County and York (now Toronto), in the Home District. Researchers should be sure to check each individual area of interest to find if a census for a particular township still exists.

The chart includes the year of the census and the area(s) enumerated. Various types of censuses and census substitutes are indicated. These include nominal censuses (everyone in the household is named), head of family censuses, church censuses, seigneurial censuses, poll tax rolls, and listings of principal settlers, landholders, and inhabitants. When known, census indexes are noted.

Appendix D is a summary of the information found on each of the censuses listed on the chart. This summary provides the place of the enumeration, type of census, and a description of the information to be found within each schedule. *The Census Day*, where appropriate, is given at the end of each summary.

Numbers in brackets for each entry indicate the repository or publication in which this record may be found. These sources, identified by their number, follow immediately after the summary and are listed as Appendix E.

Although much effort has been expended to include all extant censuses for the six provinces, some are bound to have been overlooked. Those who know of other census records that are available are urged to notify the French-Canadian Acadian Genealogical Society, Box 414, Hales Corners, WI. 53130. This information will be published in that organization's quarterly, and will be included in revisions of this book.

At the time of publication of this book, Canadian Census records later than 1901 were not available for public examination.

For further information:

1991 Census Handbook. Ottawa: Statistics Canada, 1991.

Census of the Canadas: 1851-2. Quebec: John Lovell, 1853.

Census of Canada, 1870-71. Ottawa: I.B. Taylor, 1873.

Census of Canada, 1880-81. Ottawa: Maclean, Roger & Co., 1882.

Census of Canada, 1890-91. Ottawa: S.E. Dawson, 1893.

Crowder, Norman Kenneth. *Indexes to Ontario Census Records: An Inventory.* Ontario: Crowder Enterprises, 1988.

Corbett, Michel and Patricia Kennedy. *Census and Related Records, Recensements et documentation, Finding Aid #30.* Ottawa: National Archives of Canada, 1992.

Fourth Census of Canada. 1901, Vol. 1. Population. Ottawa: S.E. Dawson, 1902.

Gagan, David P. "Enumerator's Instructions for the Census of Canada 1852 and 1861," *Histoire Sociale-Social History,* vol 7, no. 4 (November 1974): 355-365.

Hillman, Thomas A. *Catalogue of Census Returns on Microfilm, 1901.* Ottawa: Canadian Government Publishing Center, 1993.

Hillman, Thomas A. *Catalogue of Census Returns on Microfilm, 1666-1891.* Ottawa: Canadian Government Publishing Center, 1987.

Jonasson, Eric. "Pre-1851 Census Records of Ontario, " *Genealogical Journal,* vol. 13, no. 2 (Summer 1984).

Jonasson, Eric. *The Canadian Genealogical Handbook, Second Edition.* Winnipeg: Wheatfield Press, 1978.

Langton, John. *The Census of 1861.* Quebec: Henter Rose & Company, 1864.

Department of Agriculture. "Census Branch." *Manual Containing "The Census Act", and the Instructions to Officers Employed in the Taking of the First Census of Canada, (1871).* Ottawa: Brown Chamberlin, 1871.

Merriman, Brenda Dougall. "Census Returns," *Genealogy in Ontario: Searching the Records, Third Edition.* Toronto: Ontario Genealogical Society, 1996.

Trudel, Marcel. *La Population du Canada en 1663.* Montréal: Fides, 1986.

Trudel, Marcel. *La Population du Canada en 1666, Recensement Reconstitue.* Quebec: Septentrion, Sillary, 1995. (See page 301 for more information.)

Chapter Twenty-four

Notarial Records

By Joyce Soltis Banachowski

Notaries were public officers who were responsible for writing legal documents, usually between individuals. In the process, they also often served the role of advisor to both parties. Notaries began to practice in France near the end of the fourteenth century. Their activities varied, however, from province to province. At first they were important only to nobility, but by the fifteenth century they were important to everyone. By the sixteenth century, notaries were available throughout all France. There were apostolic or religious notaries who were responsible for acts involving the church. *Tabellions*, royal notaries, and seigneurial notaries wrote acts for individuals. Tabellions were public scribes who would prepare legal agreements and later, register their papers with a notary. They wrote notarial acts and made copies of them. Royal notaries were appointed by the king, or one of his representatives, and could write acts throughout the kingdom, while seigneurial notaries could write acts only for their seigneury. By the end of the sixteenth century, tabellions had evolved into royal notaries.

Notarial System Became Official in 1663

When New France was founded, handshakes sealed the first agreements. Later, clerks made handwritten agreements, and court scribes or judge's assistants kept court proceedings. These scribes were known as *greffiers* and acted as notaries. New France began to officially use the French notarial system in 1663.

In 1678, during the French Regime, Louis XIV forbade lawyers to practice in New France. As a result, people had to represent themselves in court. By prohibiting lawyers, he hoped to avoid lengthy trials. As a result notaries became extremely important. They had the responsibility to draw up all documents between individuals and to act as mediators. They were familiar with legal issues, and some were experts in contract law.

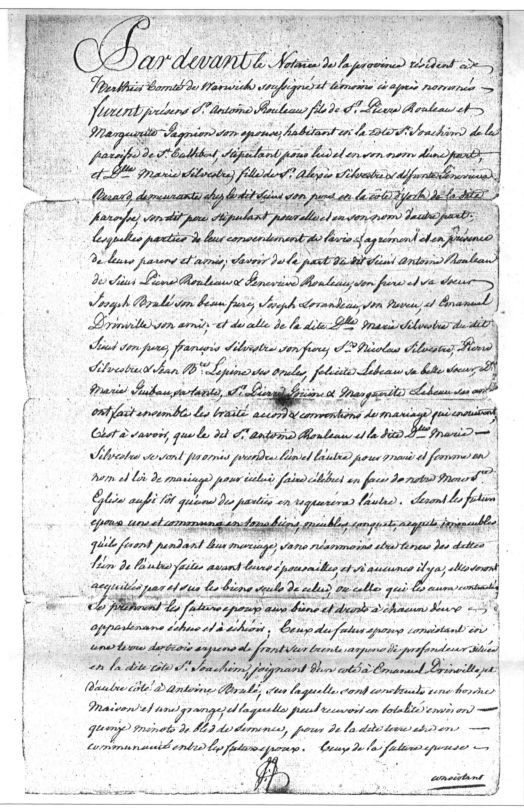

Page 1 of a privately owned marriage contract between Antoine Rouleau and Marie Silvestre 23 January 1796.

Responsibilities of the Notary

As the colony grew, notaries became an integral part of the daily lives of the people. They made marriage contracts; they made inventories of the deceased; they wrote up individual wills and powers of attorney; they wrote contracts for the construction of private, government, and religious buildings; they wrote the agreements for the hiring of individuals as apprentices, for *voyageurs* in the fur trade, and for artisans. They wrote agreements between buyer and seller, between tenant and owner, between partners, between employer and worker, and between parents and children. They were present for auctions, for the purchase and sale of land, land concessions, and the transfer of lands. The notary served the inhabitants of French Canada from the time they married to after they died. As a result, four to five million notarial records covering the lives of the inhabitants of Quebec are located in various archival centers in Quebec.

Royal Notaries and Seigneurial Notaries

There were two types of notaries who recorded transactions in New France. The first, the royal notary, received his appointment from the king or the king's intendant. He had the right to practice throughout the entire area of New France. Royal notaries were centered in Quebec, Montreal, and Trois Rivières. The second, the seigneurial notary, was appointed by the seigneur or local landholder. He could only act within the domain of his seigneury.

In both cases, the notary's job was to prepare and witness all legal transactions or acts, to keep a written record of their transactions, to preserve copies of these, and to collect a fee for his services. The amount paid to the seigneurial notary was half of that paid to the royal notary.

In 1669, the *Conseil Souverain* and the *Intendant* began to make notary appointments, not only royal, but seigneurial as well. Gradually seigneurial notaries became royal notaries until seigneurial notaries disappeared altogether.

Notarial System Spread Throughout Area Controlled by France

The notarial system existed wherever France extended its control in the New World. Priests and military officers were allowed to write up acts and agreements if no notary was present. These then were filed with a regular notary as soon as it was possible. These private acts, *les actes sous seing privé*, are a part of notarial files. Notarial records exist for Acadia, Louisiana, the fur trade outposts of Michilmackinac and Grand Portage, at posts and settlements in the present-day states of Illinois, Indiana, Michigan, Minnesota and Wisconsin, and French settlements in western Canada.

Rules Established for Notaries

By the eighteenth century, it became obvious that the ways of drawing documents and preserving them would have to be organized. In 1717 regulations concerning duties and records of notaries were laid out, but they were generally ignored. In 1724, widows of notaries were to deliver their deceased husband's documents to a clerk in their jurisdiction. In 1732, Verrier presented to the king a report of the defects in some notarial acts, making them invalid (e.g., a notary's signature was missing or the date or other signatures were missing.) On 6 May 1733, the king responded with the first notarial code in Canada. It included statements on the defects. Duties and fines were set for those not observing the proper formalities.

Soon the profession itself established rules to be followed. Notaries were to be twenty-five years of age, literate, male, of good moral character, and possibly have some knowledge of law although legal knowledge was not considered absolutely necessary. Most colonial notaries learned their trade from others or by using acts prepared by their predecessors as guides. The result was the evolution of a pattern for different types of documents generally following the same format. Notaries kept a copy of the original act they created. Another copy went to the participating parties. As official copies they did not have to be proven in or out of court. Notaries were not called into court as witnesses—the document was enough. When the notary died, his acts were to be transferred to another notary or placed in an archives. Notaries were poorly paid, and as a result, most had other jobs or responsibilities.

When the English took control after the French and Indian War there appeared a danger that the practice would be lost. After the surrender of Montreal in 1760, it was agreed the practice of using notarial acts would continue in the colony. In 1763 the French system was abolished legally, but in 1764, the English gave Quebec citizens the right to use their language, and keep their religion, property, and civil rights (*coutume de Paris*) which included royal decrees and ordinances. For this reason there were few differences before 1760 and after 1760. The Quebec Act in 1774 preserved the legal system and the role of the notary. During the English regime, they became known as *notaire public*.

Notaries Assigned Throughout New France

During the French regime, the notaries of Quebec, Montreal, and Trois Rivières also had representatives in posts and settlements which were under the control of the governor of New France. La Salle set up Jacques Métairie as notary at Fort Frontenac; La Salle later took Métairie with him in the same capacity when he went into Louisiana, Arkansas, and Illinois. In 1672, the notary, Pierre Duquet, accompanied an expedition into the Ohio Valley. When Lamothe-Cadillac founded Detroit, he drew up land grants and contracts himself. In 1706 a secretary of Lamothe-Cadillac drew up a marriage contract. Later Etienne Véron de Grandmesnil became Lamothe-Cadillac's secretary and drew up acts. On 22 May 1734, the Intendant officially appointed Robert Navarre as notary of Detroit. Jean-Baptiste Campeau succeeded him on 17 June 1758. In 1734, the Intendant also appointed Léonard Billeron as notary of Kaskaskia, province of Louisiana. On 6 April 1754, the last notarial position appointed in the west was at Michilimackinac when an old soldier of the garrison,

Francois-Louis Cardin, was appointed notary.

In Acadia and the East notaries appear from the beginning of settlement. Although some notarial records of the frontier, Louisiana, and Acadia have been lost, there are still a number which exist from those areas.

Guides to Locate Specific Acts

Notaries were required to provide two guides for locating their acts—the repertoire and the index. The repertoire was a catalog organized by date, the number of the act, and a short description of it. The index was a table organized by year and the first letter of the surname. In the index one could find the act number, the parties involved, and the type of notarial act. Unfortunately, not all of these guides are available. Some have been lost, and some notaries were negligent in keeping one or both of them. Many of those in existence have been published.

All acts were handwritten in a specific format. The spelling, language, and writing reflect the individual and the period during which the acts were written. Not only did each notary have his own unique style of handwriting, but each also had his own system of short-hand abbreviations. These factors make it quite difficult to read, transcribe, and translate. Rather than translate, it may be more practical to learn to abstract information from the notarial records; otherwise one would need to hire a translator or know old French to go into notarial records.

Assistance in Reading Old French Script

There are three booklets by Marcel Lafortune titled *Initiation à la paléographie franco-canadienne, Les écritures des notaires aux XVIIe et XVIII siècles: The Méthode Collectione*, Société de recherche historique Archiv-Histo Inc., Montréal, 1982, 1983, 1988. They are a guide to the evolution of letters and to the reading of the old French script. Samples of some seventeenth and eighteenth century notarial records are also provided. (Volume 1 includes part of the records of Antoine Adhemar, Benigne Basset, Romain Becquet, Jean-Baptiste Daguilhe; Volume 2 includes samples from Guillaume Audouart, Cyr de Monmerqué, Daniel Normandin, Gilles Rageot and Volume 3 includes samples from Guillaume Baret). All the booklets are in French and can be used as an aid in recognizing the formation of letters in old French.

Types of Notarial Acts

Besides providing genealogical information (name, occupations, relationships, places of birth), notarial records can provide many details about the lives of the ancestors and show them as an active part of the community. Notarial records can also provide a picture of the social and economic world in which these people lived and worked. In spite of the inherent difficulties, notarial records are one of the richest sources of information for French-Canadian researchers.

Numerous kinds of notarial records exist. Although marriage contracts, donations and inventories might be of the most interest to genealogists, other kinds of notarial acts should not be neglected.

Mariage contrats—Marriage contracts are one of the most widely used notarial acts. They can be helpful in establishing a marriage when no marriage record is available. The signing of the marriage contract was an important part of the marriage celebration. Usually completed a day or so prior to the marriage ceremony, the contract included the names of the couple, their parent's names, their places of birth, occupations, witnesses, sometimes their ages, and the terms of the contract. It might establish co-ownership between spouses. Contracts varied according to what was brought to the marriage by both parties. And remember, a marriage contract did not always mean that a marriage took place; it was possible to break or annul a marriage contract. A marriage contract was often linked with a donation.

Following is a list of terms may be included in the conditions of the marriage contract. They will prove helpful in understanding the marriage contract.

acquêts—Real estate not held by inheritance. Property that was acquired by gift or purchase before co-ownership.

conquit—Property which is acquired during co-ownership. One half belongs to the wife.

don (donation) mutuelle—Gift that the husband or wife makes to the survivor. (See donations.)

dowry—What is brought to the marriage by the wife and is given to the husband to be used during his life. Dowries were also given to the convent when girls entered religious orders.

douaire or jointure—Money a husband gave his wife at the time of marriage. It was to be used during her life.

douaire coutumier—One half the property of a husband was given to his wife.

douaire préfet—A predetermined agreement as to property distribution.

préciput-prefuance legacy—Property the survivor got before the estate was divided according to the law of the times.

Donation—A gift a person freely makes of his property, often in return for stated conditions.

donation à cause de mort—This was made before leaving on a long trip or military expedition, or venturing into the wilderness in the fur trade. Property was given only if the donor did not return. The act was no longer valid after his/her return.

donation entre vif or donation avant décèes—Property rights could be given up when one is alive in exchange for advantages. At retiring age (usually in the 50s), a parent might give himself/herself over to one who was to inherit. It included the obligations of the heir. If there were other children, it included the obligation of the heir toward siblings at home, the care of parents, and conditions and obligations, pres-

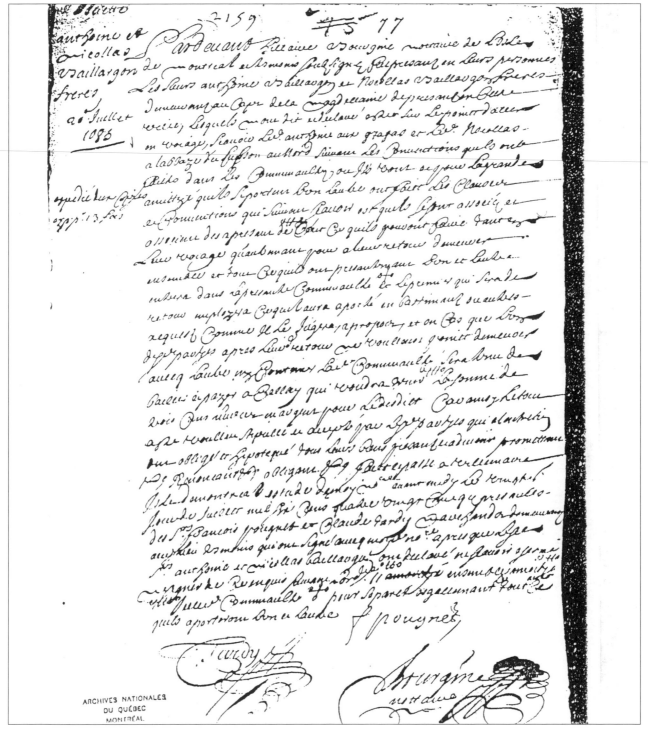

An engagement for Antoine and Nicollas Baillargeon 20 July 1685 by the notary Hilaire Bourgine. National Archives of Quebec, Montreal microfilm #2103.

ent and future. It could put conditions of marriage on the heir, and it could restrict the heir from selling or transfering land.

donation viagre—The donor retains the use of the donation during his/her lifetime.

mutual donations inter vivos—This was made between spouses when they had no heir. The last survivor would inherited.

Inventaire—This was an inventory drawn up to protect the property of minors or heirs. An inventory was taken after the death of a spouse, often prior to the survivor's remarriage. The inventory was a complete listing of possessions—land, buildings, goods, and property. The goods and property are listed with an appraiser's value. Often the date of death, circumstances of death, name, age, and civil status of heirs is included. With a notarial inventory one generally gets a description of clothes, furniture, cooking utensils, linens, foodstuffs, stores of fuel, farm tools and equipment, crops, farm animals, house and outer buildings, land and land usage, debts and claims, personal papers, and letters. It is the best source to show material ownership and the economic position of the inhabitants of French Canada in the seventeenth through the nineteenth centuries.

Accords, Obligations, or Contrats—Agreements or settlements regarding almost anything. These were prepared at the request of the parties involved. The notary works for both parties, helping them to reach a fair and balanced agreement.

Achat—These are acts regarding the purchase of property. (See *Vente* and substitute the word "achat" for vente.)

Acte—Almost any official document.

Acte a ete redige—An act of restitution.

Arrêté de compte—The record of a judgement.

Bail—This was a lease (rent) on land or buildings. Most of the people of the French period were tenants. In the Parchemin data bank (see page 178) there are about 11,400 notarial acts of Montreal that are leases.

bail à ferme—To lease a farm.

bail d'une maison—To lease a house.

bail emphytcotique—The right to lease a sizable property.

Cession—A transfer or assignment of property.

cession d'une terre—A transfer of land.

cession de biens meubles et immeubles—A transfer of furniture and contents.

cession de travaux de defrichement—A transfer of work of clearing land.

Concession—A general term meaning giving of land grants
billet de concession—Certificate of a grant to a settler.
contrat de concession—Given once a settler proved he was serious about establishing residency. The most desirable land was along a riverbank.
deuxiéme concession or rang—The concession of a piece of land granted behind the first concession.
troisiéme rang—The concession of land behind the *deuxiéme rang*.

Constitution—The establishment or settlement of something.
constitution de rente—Setting the rent.

Convention—A covenant or agreement.

Curatelle—A representative for an absent person.

Declaration—A statement acknowledging an act that took place in the past

Engagement—Labor contract or an agreement to take an apprentice or to hire a person for a specified job. It included name, wages, terms of employment, and the responsibilites and obligations of employer and employee. A large number of engagements were for the fur trade.
Brevet d'apprentissage—An apprenticeship warrant or commission.

Indenture—A contract of servitude, usually for three years.

Marché—A business agreement or contract between two or more people.
marché de construction—A building contract; a building contract specified what was to be constructed, the size, quantity and type of materials to be used, and the cost. Contractors, carpenters, roofers, and masons were involved in these contracts. A description of the building was often given.
marché de maconnerie—A contract concerning stonework or masonry.
marché de pairment de gages—An agreement concerning payroll wages.
marché en bloc—a building contract for a fixed total price.
marché les clefs à la main—A building contract to complete a house ready for occupancy.

Obligation—An agreement between two or more stating the amount of money borrowed and conditions for repayment; a lien to be satisfied; a bond.

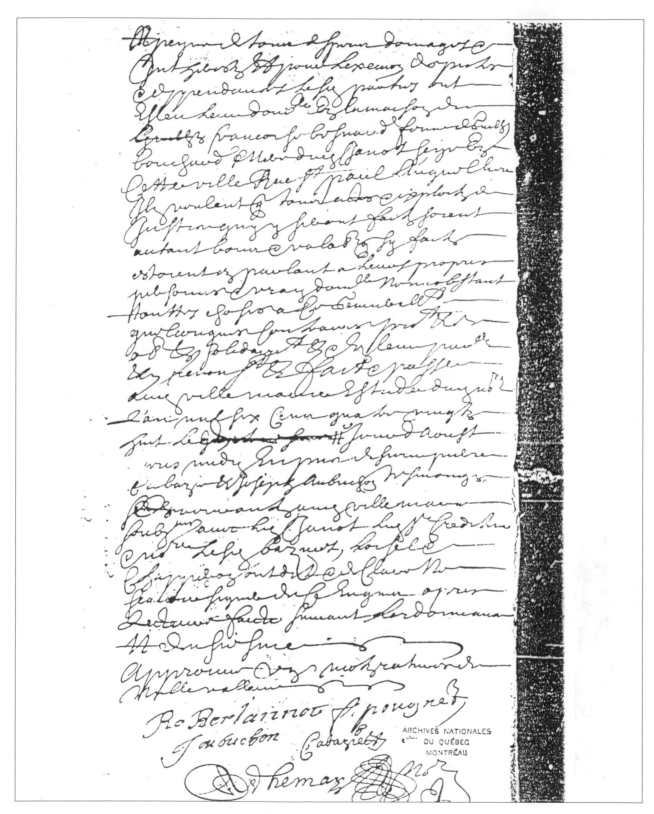

Part of an obligation of Antoine Bazinet to Loyse Janot, 2 August 1688 by notary, Antoine Adhemar. National Archives of Quebec, Montreal. Microfilm #4634.

Partage—Sharing or partition; usually the division of land among heirs.

partage d'un restant terre—The sharing of left-over land.

partage de'une maison—The sharing of a house.

partage de biens meubles et immeubles—The division of goods (personal property and real estate).

Pension—Establishing room and board (often for the elderly).

Proces-verbaux—An official statement.

proces-verbaux de liberté—A statement proving someone was free, e.g. a statement that a spouse had died elsewhere—in France, in a battle, etc.—allowing the other to remarry.

Procuration—This is when one gives or receives the Power of Attorney.

Quittance—A discharge from a debt or obligation; a quit claim.

quittance géneralé et réciproque—Giving up something in exchange for something else.

Ratification—A statement made by a second person accepting a decision.

Remise—To return, or give back.

Remise d'une concession—The return of property.

Remise de 882 livres—The return of that sum of money.

Renonciation—The surrender of a claim.

Renonciation d'heritage—Giving up one's inheritance. Children might give up a part or all of their share of an inheritance and give it to a mother who might need it.

Requête—A petition.

Société—Partnership or association.

Testament—A will. Testaments were not used very often in New France. When they were used, it was generally for religious endowments or because there were no living heirs. By law the division of inheritance was predetermined. The English were more likely to use wills than the French.

testament olographe—A written will.

testament orale—An oral will.

Transport—To transfer.

transport de droits successifs mobiliets et immobiliers—The transfer of right to property.

transport d'une somme d'argent—The transfer of a sum of money.

Tutelle—Papers regarding the guardianship of a child or children. They were designed to protect the inheritance and rights of orphaned or semi-orphaned children. Much genealogical information can be found here.

Vente—Acts regarding the sale of property.

vente d'une concession—The sale of land.

vente d'une continuation de terre—The sale of adjacent land.

vente de droits et pretentions—The sale of rights and claims.

vente de droits—The sale of rights to something.

vente d'un morceau—The sale of a parcel of land.

vente d'un emplacement—The sale of a site, business, or farm.

vente à rente—Selling the rental of a property (yearly income, stock, funds).

vente d'une maison—The sale of a house.

vente de meubles—The sale of personal property.

vente portant constitution de rente—The selling of rights to rental property.

vente de terre—The sale of land.

vente de la juste moitie—The sale of 1/2 of an equal share.

Parchemin

Four to five million notarial records have been located in nine regional archives. In order to be able to use this information more quickly and efficiently, a project, *Parchemin*, was instituted. It is a joint project under the efforts of the Societe de Recherche Historique Archiv-Histo, the Archives Nationales du Québec, and the Chambre des Notaires du Québec. In 1981, it was organized to produce a national data bank with the goal to index and abstract all notarial records from 1635 to 1885.

The data bank currently includes records of the French regime to the end of 1775.

Only these extracts are presently available for research by genealogists. This is an on-going project and will continue for many years. The data bank includes notarial acts of Quebec only. It does not include notarial records from other provincial or outside locations.

The extracts from the French regime now available and can be accessed by name and by 119 other divisions including occupation, place, date, type of notarial act, or pew rent, a combination of occupation with date and/or place, just to name a few.

Information obtained in the Parchemin data banks is the name of the notary, the date of the document, and a short abstract of the act. Witnesses to the original document are not included. Names are spelled as they appear in the document. Therefore, it is necessary to search all spellings as well as dit names. After obtaining the abstract, the researcher may want a photocopy of the entire document. These documents are available on microfilm at many archival centers in Canada or the United States or through the Family History Library in Salt Lake City, Utah.

It is currently planned to place the entire data bank on the Internet for a fee. At the time of publication, a sampling of approximately 30,000 acts was available on the Internet at <http://www.cdnq.org>. Use of this website is free.

Presently the Parchemin data banks for the French Regime, 1635-1775, are available at: the following places:

Archives Nationales du Québec—Montréal
535 Rue Viger Est
Móntreal, Québec H2L 2P3

Archives Nationales du Québec—Québec
1210, Avenue du Seminaire
Case postale 10450
Ste-Foy, Québec G1V 4N1

Service des bibliothèque Bibliothèque Alain-Grandbois
4300, boulevard Samson
Laval, Québec H7V 3Z4

Bibliothèque Montarville-Boucher de la Bruere
501, chemin du Lac
Boucherville, Québec J4B 6V6

Bibliothèque municipale de Jonquiere
2850, place Davis
Jonquiere, Québec G7S 2C5

Bibliothèque municipale de Longueuil
Centre culturel Jacques Ferron
100, rue St-Laurent ouest
Longueuil, Québec J4K 1M1

Bibliothèque municipale de Móntreal Centrale—Salle de Gagnon
1210, rue Sherbrooke est
Montréal, Québec H2L 1L9

Bibliothèque municipale de Saint-Eustache
80, boulevard Arthur-Sauve
Saint-Eustache, Québec J7R 2H7

Bibliothèque municipale de Terrebonne
885, Placc Ile des Moulins
Terrebonne, Québec J6W 4N7

Centre d'archives du Seminaire de St-Hyacinthe
655, rue Girouard est
St-Hyacinthe, Québec

Centre d'information documentaire Comte Saint Germain
545, rue des Écoles
Drummondville, Québec J2B 1J6

Centre regional d'archives de Lanaudiere
270, boulevard l'Ange-Gardien
L'Assomption, Québec

Société franco-ontarienne d'histoire et de généalogie
300, chemin Montréal
Co-Cathedrale de la Nativite B.H.V.M.
Cornwall, Ontario

Société généalogique canadienne-francais
3300, boul. Rosemont, suite 110
Móntreal, Québec

Société d'histoirie du Lac-St-Jean
54, rue St-Joseph sud
Alma, Québec

American Canadian Genealogical Society
4 Elm Street
Manchester, N.H. 03108

Centre d'études Canadiennes
35, avenue Montaigne
Paris, France 7500

Université de Montréal
Bibliothèque des sciences sociales
Pavillon Bronfmann
3000, rue Jean-Brillant
Montréal, Québec H3T 3J7
(student use only)

Université du Québec à Móntreal
Bibliothèque centrale
Pavillon Hubert-Aquin
case postale 8889, succ.
Montréal, Québec H3C 3P3
(student use only)

Bibliography

Asselin, Fleurette and Tanguay, Jean-Marie. *Transcriptions d'actes notaries* (Collection *Je lis mes ancêtres*). 25 tomes. Le Club de Généalogie du Longueuil Inc., 1994-1995.

Auger, Roland J. "Inventory of the Notaries' Registries Under the French Régime." *French Canadian and Acadian Genealogical Review,* 4 (Spring 1972): 3-6.

Chartrand, René. *Early Notaries of Canada.* Polyanthos, New Orleans, 1977.

Contrats de Mariages notaries de Montréal 1642-1840. Société Généalogique de Lanaudiere, Joliette, Québec, 1993.

De Ville, Winston. *The Loppinot Papers 1687-1710: Genealogical Abstracts of the Earliest Notarial Records for the Province of Acadia,* Ville Platte, Louisiana, 1991.

"Diverse Notary Acts 1609-1760." *Rapport de L'Archiviste de Province de Québec* 51 (1973): 1-67.

Dulong, John P., "The Notarial Acts of Quebec: Their Genealogical Value and Use." *National Genealogical Society Quarterly* 82 (March 1994): 5-16.

Fauteux, Aegidius, "Trois Actes du Tabellionage de Dieppe." *Bulletin des Recherches de Historique* 37 (1931): 268-273.

Inventaire des Greffes des Notaires du Régime Francais, 27 vols., Archives de la Province du Québec, 1943-1976.

Lawrence, Roger, "How To Translate A French Notarial Document." *American-Canadian Genealogist* 14 (Spring 1988): 60-63.

Leveille, Pierrette Gilbert, *Repertoire des greffes des notaires*, 3 vols., Société de généalogie de Québec, nos. 46, 50, 57, Québec, 1985, 1986, 1988.

"Marriage Contract Inventory of the French Regime (Quebec)." *French Canadian and Acadian Genealogical Review* 4 (Summer 1972): 65-67.

"Les Notaires au Canada sous de Régime Francais." *Rapport L'Archiviste de la Province de Québec.* 1921-1922, Louis-A Proulx, Publisher, 1922: 1-58.

Léveillé, Pierrette Gilbert. *Répertoire des greffes des notaires,* 3 vols., Société de généalogie de Québec, nos. 46, 50, 57, Québec, 1985, 1986, 1988.

Paquet, Lucie. "The Notarial Profession." *The Archivist* (May/June 1989): 16-17.

Pellerin, J.P. "Types of Early Notarial Records." *Connecticut Maple Leaf* 3 (Winter 1988): 349.

Roy, Joseph, Edmond. "The Notariate in the Western Settlements: Mississippi, Acadia, Ile Royale and Newfoundland." *French Canadian and Acadian Genealogical Review* 4 (Winter 1972): 198-207.

Roy, Pierre-Georges. *Inventaire d'une collection de Pièces Judiciaires, Notarials, etc. etc. Conserves aux Archives Judiciaires de Québec*, 2 vols, 1917.

Roy, Pierre-Georges. *Inventaire des contrats de mariage du régime francais conserves aux Archives judiciares de Québec,* 4 or 6 vols., Québec, Archives de la Province du Québec, 1937-1938.

Roy, Pierre-Georges. *Inventaire des testaments, donations et inventaires du Régime francais conserves aux Archives judiciaires de Québec*, 3 vols. Québec, Archives de la province du Québec, 1941.

Roy, Pierre-Georges. "Les Notaires au Canada," *Le Rapport de l'Archiviste de la Province de Québec*, 1921-1922: 1-58.

"Wills, Acts of Donations and Inventories Under the French Regime in the District of Quebec." *French Canadian and Acadian Genealogical Review* 5, nos. 1-2 (1975): 3-23.

Specialized Areas of Research

From fur traders to the Internet, French Canadian research covers it all. Explore the chapters in this section and discover how to find out if one of your grandmothers was a daughter of the king. Perhaps you want to learn more about your porkeater grandfather. Was another ancestor a soldier in the French or British military? What are some of the important things to consider when searching the Internet?

The following section covers information about all of the above and gives the genealogist insight into the specialized research needed to successfully trace the paths of the *voyageur, fille du roi,* or military man.

Chapter Twenty-five

Les Filles du Roi—The King's Daughters

By Linda K. Boyea

Ah, to claim a little royal blood! Although most genealogists are looking for the truth about their ancestors and not searching for that connection to someone famous, a hint of royalty might bring a tiny smile to any researcher's face. Alas, although most French-Canadian researchers can find at least one *fille du roi* among the ancestors, this term does not denote descent from Louis XIV of France. The term *Les filles du roi* refers to the women who came to New France between 1663 and 1673 with the express purpose of marrying and raising families. The king provided these women with transportation, lodging, clothing, and a chest that contained needles, thread, and miscellaneous supplies. Most importantly, he promised them a dowry. The dowry offered ranged from 30 to 50 to 100 livres depending on the year she emigrated and whether she married an officer. In French society of that day, the father provided the dowry, hence the sobriquet "Daughters of the King."

To best understand the phenomenon of *les filles du roi* it is necessary to know that originally the people who came to New France did not come as permanent settlers but rather to procure the furs and other wealth that could be found there for the king of France. However, the growth of population in the English colonies (New England), and the threat this posed to the French, caused the king and his advisors to encourage permanent settlement of New France. (In 1663, according to one demographer, the population of New France was estimated to be 2,500 whereas the population of New England was around 80,000.) Although there were families in New France at this time, including wives and daughters, women were in very short supply. The king realized the immediate need to increase population rapidly through immigration and the need to encourage the permanent settlement of the men already there.

Why would a young woman be willing to leave her home and undertake such a journey to marry a stranger? Although some *filles du roi* had additional funds and possessions, the majority of these women were poor. Many were orphans and a few were widows. Without a dowry they would find it difficult to marry or even to enter a convent. They would likely experience poverty and often be forced to live on the streets. The king's offer, with all the hazards and uncertainties it entailed, may have been their only real choice.

The women were chosen based on their age, assumed ability to bear children, and their overall health. After the first arrivals in 1663, the request was made to send women who were from the countryside and better able to adjust to the climate and the hard work than city-raised women. Parish priests in France were asked to help recruit healthy village girls.

It is estimated that over 770 *filles du roi* came to New France. The names and information about these women were determined through marriage contracts that list the dowry, and from inference because of their association with known *filles du roi,* or from the years they appeared in official records. Statistics regarding these women—how many arrived each year, which province in France they came from, and personal information about a substantial number of the *filles du roi*—may be found in the books and articles listed in the bibliography. Additional information may be found in the many other books written about these women, and on the Internet, particularly through the historical information sites about Quebec.

Three *Filles du Roi* Sources Published Prior to 2001

Although the information available on an individual *fille du roi* in each of the books in the bibliography is similar, a researcher may want to consult all three texts. In some cases significant details are found in one book and not the other. The best place for the English speaking/reading researcher to start is with *The King's Daughters* by Joy Reisinger and Elmer Courteau. With the English information as a guide, it is easy to review the other two books and to note the differences.

For example, in *The King's Daughters*, the entry for Marguerite Tenard lists her parish as St-Pierre de Milly-la-Forêt en Gastinais, in the archdiocese of Sens. It names her parents, Barthelemi Tenard and Jeanne Govin, also mentioning that her father has died. It is not clear from the wording in this book whether the mother is also dead. Also included is the date and place of her marriage to Charles Boyer: 23 November 1666 at Montreal. The book also states that she died before 29 October 1678 at Laprairie.

The entry in *Les Filles du Roi en Nouvelle-France* by Silvio Dumas adds the information that Marguerite was born in 1633, giving the place as the village of Milly, Ile-de-France, but it does not give the parish. It is still unclear from the wording in this entry if both parents are dead, but definitely Barthelemi has died. Along with the date and place of the marriage of Marguerite and Charles, it names the notary for the marriage contract as Basset; it states that there is no mention in the marriage contract regarding the king's dowry.

The entry in *Les Filles du roi au XVIIe siècle* by Yves Landry concurs that the parish, St-Pierre, is in the village of Milly-la Forêt in Gastinais, in the archdiocese of Sens, and that it is indeed in the province of Île-de-France. It clearly lists both parents as deceased. In addition, this entry limits the time of Marguerite's death to between 16 February 1678 and 29 October 1678. It further adds that Charles, who was born around 1631 and died after 24 July 1703, was a *habitant*, and that neither of them could sign. Also included is the information that Charles and Marguerite established a home at Laprairie and that they had six children.

Using all three sources, the researcher has obtained significant information: Marguerite's year and place of birth, the names of her parents, the parish in France where she was baptized, the date and place of marriage, and the name of the notary, the number of children she had, birth and death information on her husband, where she lived and died, and the approximate date of her death.

Additional Information

There is even more information about these women to be found in these books. Some entries may include information on second or third marriages (if any), the amount of the dowry she received from the king and/or other sources, names and/or baptismal dates for her children, and the exact date and place of her death. The researcher may find information on her behavior or that of her spouse and/or comments about their financial or social status.

Example #1: Catherine Gateau (Gasteau).

In addition to the type of information found in the example of Marguerite Tenard, the entries on Catherine Gateau state that she signed, but then annulled, a marriage contract with Abraham Albert (11 October 1671). She then signed and annulled another marriage contract, this time with Vivien Jean (2 November 1671). However she and Jean changed their minds and revalidated the marriage contract on 19 November 1671. The marriage ceremony took place on November 29th and Catherine brought a dowry of 350 livres to the marriage. This included fifty livres from the king. Catherine and Jean had nine children.

This additional information gives life to the ancestor. Try to imagine debarking a ship and facing unknown numbers of strange men all looking at you with the intention of marriage. This must have been daunting. What affected her decision? Was it her dowry or her personality that gave her the courage to annul the marriage contract? Catherine was not the only *fille du roi* to sign and then annul a marriage contract. There are over 100 instances of this listed in *The King's Daughters*. One woman, Catherine Le Roux, signed and then annulled one marriage contract only to marry the first man's brother.

There is an additional note on Catherine Gateau in *Les Filles du Roi en Nouvelle-France* which states that Tanguay had erred when he wrote that Catherine's husband was Jean Jean, son of Vivien Jean and Isabel Drouet. According to the marriage contract of 29 November 1671, Vivien Jean is the son of Vivien Jean and Suzanne Ayrault. This note did not appear in the other two books.

Example #2: Marie Riviere

Marie married Jean Ratier *dit* Du Buisson on 16 February 1672. According to *The King's Daughters*, in 1679, Jean was sentenced to hang. However, the executioner had died. Jean was given the choice of becoming the new executioner or waiting until a new one was found. Of course, he took the job.

This story is not mentioned in *Les Filles du Roi en Nouvelle-France*. But a different one is. In 1695, Marie and her daughter Charlotte were tried for possession of stolen goods. They were sentenced to be whipped in public by the executioner, Jean Ratier, who was Marie's husband and the father of Charlotte.

Neither story is mentioned in *Les Filles du roi au XVIIe siècle*.

A Fille du Roi Source Published in 2001

The two-volume set titled *King's Daughters and Founding Mothers: The Filles du Roi, 1663-1673,* by Peter J. Gagné, published In 2001, needs special mention. It is written in English and it includes substantially more information on most of the women than the other sources. This extra information includes baptisms and deaths of the children, places where the family lived, and additional information about the husbands.

For example, the biographical sketch of Marguerite Tenard states that her first two children, Marie and Joseph, were baptized in Montreal (24 August 1667 and 07 January 1669). Then the family moved to Laprairie when the remaining children were baptized: Antoine (10 April 1671), Jean-Baptiste (18 August 1673), Marguerite (06 July 1675), Louise (16 January 1678).

In addition, this entry contains biographical information on her husband, Charles Boyer, including his birthplace in France, the names of his parents, the date he left France, the ship he sailed on, the date he arrived at Quebec City, and the name of the woman he married after Marguerite died.

One interesting difference between this entry on Marguerite and the information obtained from the three books previously mentioned concerns her birth. Here it states that she was born *about* 1633 instead of *in* 1633.

Some women who are barely mentioned in the other sources have several paragraphs written about them, their husbands and/or their children—all in English!

Problems and Pitfalls

It is possible to find a woman listed as a *fille du roi* in one book or article and not in the others. Researchers varied on the criteria used to determine whether to include the woman in the list and may have found different sources for the information. In *King's Daughters and Founding Mothers: The Filles du Roi, 1663-1673,* the author identifies thirty-six women who were previously thought to be *filles du roi* and he gives compelling reasons for their exclusion from the list.

As in all secondary sources, the possibility of error exists. Some of the information on the women in the books mentioned in this article was obtained from the books by Tanguay and Jetté, which are themselves secondary sources. Both of the books are written in French, and *King's Daughters and Founding Mothers: The Filles du Roi, 1663-1673* lists the notary for the marriage contract, when known; and *The King's Daughters* includes many footnotes. It may be difficult, however, for a researcher to find and interpret the original documents used by the authors in these books, and it is reasonable to assume that the information contained within is accurate. It must still be remembered that these books and articles on *les filles du roi* are secondary sources.

Summary

The individual entries not only add a human dimension to the female ancestor(s) being researched, but in most instances they take the researcher back another generation into France. However, it is not necessary to have a *fille du roi* as an ancestor to enjoy reading about them. The information found in these sources gives the reader greater insight into the women and the times they lived. The additional information and the demographic tables in *Les Filles du Roi en Nouvelle-France* and in *Les Filles du roi au XVIIe siècle* are a wealth of information for those who can read French. The article mentioned in the Bibliography, "Les filles du roi— Mothers of the Nation" by Mary-Jean Chaput and Donald P. Chaput, provides the English-only reader with some of the statistical information found in *Les Filles du roi au XVIIe siècle.* It is well worth the reading. *King's Daughters and Founding Mothers: The Filles du Roi, 1663-1673* also contains background information, a transcription and translation of two marriage contracts, and an informative demographic chart.

The decision by Louis XIV to implement the policy involving the *filles du roi* to populate New France was indeed successful. By 1672 the population of New France had increased to around 6,700. Although the increase was caused not only by the courageous *filles du roi* and the children they bore, but also by the increase of men who emigrated during these years, the credit was largely due to these women. Thomas J. Laforest says it best in his article "The King's Daughters" (see bibliography): "Without exaggeration it can be said that these women created a nation, from which millions of us have peopled both Canada and the United States."

Bibliography

Chaput, Mary-Jean and Donald P. Chaput. "Les filles du roi —Mothers of the Nation," *American-Canadian Genealogist* 85, vol 26, number 3.

Dumas, Silvio. *Les fille du roi en Nouvelle-France.* Québec: Societé Historique de Québec, 1972.

Gagné, Peter J. *King's Daughters and Founding Mothers: The Filles do Roi, 1663-1673.* 2 vols. Pawtucket, Rhode Island: Quintin Publications, 2001.

Laforest, Thomas J. "The King's Daughters," *Heritage Quest* 22 (May/June 1989): 7-12. republished, *Je Me Souviens* 23, no. 1 (Spring 2000): 15-25.

Landry, Yves. *Orphelines en France—Pionnieres au Canada—Les filles du roi au XVIIe siècle.* Ottawa: Lémeac Éditeur Inc., 1992.

Reisinger, Joy and Elmer Courteau. *The King's Daughters.* rev. ed. Dexter, Michigan: Thomson-Shore, 1988.

Chapter Twenty-six

Finding Fur Trading Ancestors

By Francele Sherburne, SSND

Fur trading in the North Atlantic was initiated by coastal Indians who bartered for European goods with early French fishermen. When reports of the wealth to be had in furs arrived in France, the vast territory to be known as New France beckoned adventurers who were only too ready to leave the political, economic, and religious turmoil of their country.

Background Information

Simple bartering clusters at Quebec and Montreal eventually developed into companies that dispatched their traders westward in huge canoes, until French posts dotted major northern and central waterways across the continent.

When the British defeated the French in 1763, French control of the trade ended. The British and their company subsequently directed the fur trade, with French *voyageurs* continuing in service. Ultimately, with shifts in political history, Americans acquired the substance of the trade. By the mid-nineteenth century the traffic lost its eminence, because of animal depletion, lack of demand, and a major social and cultural change in the Indian population.

The Challenge of Research

The number and mobility of the people involved in this commerce—boatmen, trappers, traders, partners, clerks, notaries, bankers (not to mention families brought along or sired on the way), coupled with the vast spread of the business—will challenge anyone searching for his or her ancestors. The extensive scatter of records to be located, and the mesh of information to be made with them, demand a different and difficult kind of work.

Catholic Church Records

Catholic Church records made in the French settlements that sprang up along the trade routes contain ample and precise data entered by the missionaries. With the early records however, language becomes a problem for the researcher. *Dit* names were often spelled phonetically. One priest might enter the family name with one spelling, another priest at another time or place might spell it differently. Names sometimes changed, even among related families or from generation to generation. Here, as always, it is important to make sure that you are tracking the same individual throughout. (See Chapter 3)

Church records at a given settlement, moreover, were not always complete. At times, the circuit missionary took the registry with him and left it at his base of operations.

The mobility of the Catholic fur trade employee adds a further problem of identification/location. He may have been married at one site, have had a child baptized there, two years later another child baptized three hundred miles distant, and a third perhaps a thousand miles away, depending on his labor contract. He himself could conceivably have retired to Quebec and eventually have been buried there. Microfilms of some Catholic Church records may be searched at the Family History Library in Salt Lake City, Utah, and its associated Family History Centers throughout the world. Some Catholic dioceses, like those in Milwaukee, for example, have also had all their records microfilmed and made available. Others, like Green Bay, have not. A fair number have not been transferred to diocesan archives; for example, records for Little Chute, Wisconsin, in the Green Bay Diocese, still remain in the parish. Without doubt, fur trader ancestry research will demand a geographical crisscross hunt and much resourcefulness.

Notarial Records

When the fur traders moved to the "up country," they brought with them the French notarial system and their own notaries. These men drafted a range of notarial acts, not merely witnessed signatures as notaries public in the United States do today. Of interest to the fur trade researcher is the labor *engagement*, the contract between trading companies and men heading for parts west to trap and trade with the Indians. One special kind of *engagement* was the contract signed by an individual voyageur with the fur trading company to take a load of supplies to the West where he would "winter in" and then return with a load of furs in the late spring or early summer.

Notaries kept their own files, some of which have been lost. Those extant can be found in various archives. The Parchemin Project (see page 178) has prepared indexes of notarial documents. To read them, in complete or summarized form, one needs a rudimentary knowledge of old French—at least enough to spot the desired data—and the ability to decipher a unique notarial script. Specialized abbreviations that appear from time to time will also need decoding.

Though marriage contracts yield the most information in regard to families, *engagement* contracts sometimes hold the only leads for searchers whose families settled in the Great Lakes, Mississippi, or Gulf areas.

A Northwest Company engagement contract for Constant Longtin of St. Pierre de La Prairie on 19 August 1814. On the bottom is a notation for another engagé, Louis Fournier of La Tortue, middle boatman—same engagement. He was advanced ten piastres. Fort William Resource Center, Thunder Bay, Ontario.

U.S. Customs Records

U.S. Customs records may be of use in pinpointing the whereabouts of a relative within a conjectured span of time. These records will postdate the establishment of the Federal Customs Service in 1789. Initially, Michilimackinac, long the primary locus for east-west traffic on the upper Great Lakes, was designated as the sole port of entry for this region. In 1863, when Mackinac was for a time made a port of delivery, Sault Ste. Marie, Michigan, became the port of entry for customs. The Bayliss Public Library in Sault Ste. Marie now houses what remains of the extensive but incomplete Fort Mackinac customs records.

Another significant resource for customs material lies in the Burton Historical Collection in the Detroit Public Library. Inquiries about customs records from other trading posts along the shores of the Great Lakes may be made at their respective state historical society libraries.

Although later customs documents reflect the growing diversity of commerce in the nineteenth century, the early Montreal trade is well represented. Of value to the researcher whose ancestor is cited somewhere as a voyageur to the West, are manifests for entire canoe brigades. Later records likewise yield detailed information which includes dates, signatures of vessel masters, names of consignees, and lists of crews and passengers.

Account Books

Account books are another fertile source of trader surnames. They help the researcher put the individual or family into an appropriate time frame in a particular place. Of value are not only the records of pelts seasonally delivered and sold, but also the transactions with

License issued to Augustus Grignon, 21 October 1840. Grignon, Lawe and Porlier Papers, Wisconsin Historical Society, Madison, WI: Microfilm #P84-381.

Lists of engagés to Augustin Grignon, son of Pierre Grignon. Law and Porlier Papers Microfilm #P84-381. Wisconsin State Historical Society, Madison.

the area businessmen who sold supplies at the post, especially when pieced together with other records. Bruce M. White's *The Fur Trade in Minnesota: An Introductory Guide to Archive and Manuscript Sources* is an excellent source for this and other topics. It describes repositories in both Canada and the United States and is therefore useful for more than Minnesota research.

Land Records

Land claims sometimes had to be reestablished when borderlines shifted and governments changed hands. The United States government, for example, sent commissioners to interview landholders, requiring proof of ownership if notarial records were non-existent. Holders had to state that the land was theirs, from whom it had been obtained or through whom it had descended, and for how long it had been cultivated. This kind of information must be treated with caution, for much of it was hearsay, inaccurate through transmission. It is to be remembered that at times the landholder had a vested interest in giving the "right" answers. The Gendex Corporation markets a computerized version of Phillip W. Mc

Mullin's index to land grants and claims titled *Grass Roots of America. American State Papers: Public Lands (1789 – 1837)*.

Native American Records

Indian records may be useful to any Canadian or American who has a strain of Indian blood. Frequently white traders married into a tribe to further their businesses. At the time of the Indian treaties—the first half of the nineteenth century—a tribe sometimes gave their white-Indian offspring ("mixed bloods" or "metis") a small part of the treaty money or a small parcel of land. Those of mixed blood would later be obliged to establish their claims before a government commission in much the same way as described earlier. Indian records tend to deal with a single family and can cover several generations, serving as a bridge to information found elsewhere. Canadian records relating to Indian Affairs are in the Public Land Records Archives, Ottawa. Inventories and records of Native Americans lie in the National Archives and Records Administration, Washington, D.C. Ever expanding sources of Native American records are scattered around the United States and Canada in the archives of states, provinces, churches, tribes, universities, and fur trade companies.

Summary

This brief survey of mechanisms for locating fur trading ancestors—church registries, account books, notarial files, customs house records, land claims, Indian records—makes it clear that this kind of research is labor intensive, broad scope research. A beginner who ventures into it will need ingenuity and perseverance.

Bibliography—Courtesy of James L. Hansen, FASG, State Historical Society of Wisconsin

Brown, Jennifer S.H. *Strangers in Blood: Fur Trade Company Families in Indian Country*. Vancouver, 1980.

Chittenden, Hiram M. *The American Fur Trade of the Far West*. New York, 1935; Reprint, Lincoln, Nebraska, 1986.

Golman, Rhoda R. "The Fur Trade in the Upper Mississippi Valley, 1630-1850" in *Wisconsin Magazine of History*, v. 58 no. 1 (Autumn 1974): 3-18. A good brief introduction to the subject.

Lavender, David. *The Fist in the Wilderness*. New York, 1964.

Phillips, Paul C. *The Fur Trade*. Norman, Oklahoma, 1961. 2 vols.

Van Kirk, Sylvia. *"Many Tender Ties": Women in Fur-Trade Society in Western Canada, 1670-1870*. Winnipeg, 1980.

Chapter Twenty-seven

Military Records

By Karen Vincent Humiston

Of the many reference works, handbooks, and secondary sources available to the French-Canadian genealogist, relatively few touch on the subject of military records. This omission is largely due to the difficulty of obtaining such records from the French and British periods. It is certainly not an indication that French Canadians did not participate in the military. The history of New France and Canada is one of frequent conflict, whether with the Iroquois, the Dutch, the British, or the Americans. Indeed, it is safe to say that anyone of French-Canadian descent can count soldiers among his or her ancestors. This universality of military participation should make it a topic of interest to any researcher who wants to understand more fully the lives and experiences of those ancestors. While the records may be scattered and difficult to obtain, it is well worth the trouble to seek them out. Fortunately, in most cases one need not wade through the archives of several nations in search of obscure primary sources. Much of this work has already been done in several recently published secondary sources. Using these it is possible to go back directly to the primary sources.

Any study of military records requires at least a passing knowledge of the historical context. This chapter will proceed, therefore, in a more or less chronological fashion through the different wars and conflicts, looking at the types of records produced. First, however, an important distinction must be made between the two types of military service in what is now Canada: the militia and the regular, full-time troops.

Militia Service

The concept of a militia has become a foreign one to twenty-first century Americans. In the early years of United States, and until recently in Canada, the militia, a part-time locally organized military force, was an integral part of the national defense. Its purpose was to provide local defense in case of an emergency and to support the regular troops when broader conflicts necessitated their assistance. Perhaps the closest analogy in the United States today would be the National Guard. During most of the French and British regimes, however, service in the militia was compulsory for all able-bodied men between the ages of sixteen and sixty. The troops from each parish or neighborhood were organized into a company, the basic unit of the local militia. Each company was required to meet once a month for drills and exercises. At least once a year the dozen or so companies that formed a battalion were summoned for a week of more intensive training. Except in cases of unusual hardship, every man was required to provide his own weapon.

The commanding officer of a militia company was the captain. Like his subordinate officers, the lieutenant and the ensign, he was usually chosen from among the local *habitants*. The *capitaine de milice* assumed an important role and status in the community in addition to his military responsibilities. In times of peace, he was called on to organize his men for various public work projects, such as repairing roads or bridges. The captain's superior officers were the colonel, lieutenant colonel, and majors, who commanded at the battalion level. These officers were typically drawn from the well-connected and moneyed classes, usually from France. Most of the latter returned to France upon completion of their tours of duty.

Few records exist of service in the militia during the French Regime, and those that do are usually limited to officers. The captain, for instance, is often referred to by his title in church or notarial records. The records are somewhat better during the British period. Since militia service was unpaid and compulsory for all, nominal rolls were rarely kept in peacetime. It was during times of war or regional conflicts that a paper trail was most likely to be created, especially if a militia company was called to service with the regular troops. Some troop or officer lists have been published for particular conflicts, and these will be discussed below.

Manuscript collections are another valuable source for militia research. One such collection held by the Archives du Séminaire de Trois-Rivières, contains such documents as letters, muster lists, and financial papers. A guide to this collection was published in 1995 titled *Guide de recherche sur la Milice, 1713-1965* (ed. Chantale Caron, Joane Pellerin, and Suzanne Girard).

Official Military Forces

Prior to 1870, Canada's only official military forces were French or British. There were three different types of regular troops during the French Regime: the Carignan-Salieres Regiment, the *Troupes de la Marine*, and the regular army soldiers from France brought over to fight in the last French and Indian War.

In the early years of New France, every settler was, of necessity, a soldier. The French were in frequent conflict with their rivals in North America, the Dutch and the English. An even greater threat came from the Five Nations of the Iroquois Confederation. The Iroquois were allies of the Dutch, and later, the English, and were formidable warriors. For much of the seventeenth century the habitants were subjected to frequent guerrilla attacks and raids from their Native American adversaries. They were harassed, terrorized, and murdered to such an extent that by 1660, the very survival of New France was seriously in question.

While every man, woman, and older child had to be constantly prepared for self-defense, it was not until 1651, under the orders of Governor d'Ailleboust, that the first militia was organized near Trois-Rivières. This organized militia was no match for the Iroquois. In 1661, Pierre Boucher went to France to beg Louis XIV for military assistance. Four years later, the king finally decided to protect his economic interests in the colony by sending troops. The Carignan-Saliéres Regiment consisted of over a thousand men in twenty companies, who had fought in several European conflicts.

Transporting an entire regiment to North America was a daunting task—it had never been done before. When the troops arrived at last in New France in 1665, they were greeted with joy and gratitude by the war-weary settlers. The twenty companies of the Carignan Regiment were joined by four other detached companies brought from the West Indies by the Marquis de Tracy.

Carignan-Salieres Regiment

Some accounts of the Carignan-Salieres Regiment paint them as heroes and saints, and their history as an uninterrupted series of glorious victories. In reality, they had the usual quota of saints and sinners, with a lot of average men in between. They suffered through several fiascoes and ordeals as a result of the incompetent leadership of the new governor, Daniel de Remy, Sieur de Courcelle. Courcelle, like many who came after him, was confident in his European military training. He disdained the advice of the Canadians, who had learned the art of guerilla-style warfare from their Indian allies. European combat methods simply did not work in the wilderness of New France and the English colonies and inevitably led to disaster. By 1668 saner heads prevailed and the regiment was able to achieve a victory over the Dutch and the Iroquois, securing a peace that lasted nearly twenty years.

At this point, soldiers from the Carignan-Salieres Regiment and the four other companies of soldiers under Marquis Tracy were offered land in New France as an incentive to stay on and strengthen the colony. Over 400 men chose to accept the offer and did not return to France. Most French Canadians are descended from one or more of these soldiers. In their genealogical works Jetté and Tanguay (see appropriate chapters in this book) usually indicate if an individual belonged to the Carignan—Salieres Regiment, and the company to which he was attached. More complete lists can be found in *Lost in Canada*, Vols. 8-10 (August 1982 to May 1984, ed. Joy Reisinger) or in *The Good Regiment: The Carignan-Saliéres Regiment in Canada, 1663-1668*, by Jack Verney (Montreal: McGill-Queen's

University Press, 1991). The latter book is an especially thorough and fascinating account of this regiment's story and is highly recommended.

After the departure of the Carignan-Salieres Regiment, King Louis XIV established a compulsory militia in New France, in much the same form that it would assume for the next two hundred years. The men of the French militia, although amateurs, came to be well known for their skill at wilderness fighting and for their stamina and endurance. Muster rolls from this period do not exist, but since service was compulsory, it can assumed that one's ancestors belonged to the militia. This was the sole military force until 1683, when renewed hostilities with the Iroquois and the English required support from full time troops. At this time a permanent force of *Troupes de la Marine* were dispatched to Canada.

Les Troupes de la Marine

The marines were French troops under the jurisdiction of the navy. Initially, all of the officers were from France, although eventually Canadians were given commissions as well. Like the Carignan-Salieres Regiment before them, the marines came to recognize and value the expertise of the French Canadians in wilderness warfare, and adopted many of their methods. Although most of them returned to France when their term of service was completed, some chose to marry and stay in Canada.

There are several research options open to genealogists searching for officers in the *Troupes de la Marine*. A doctoral dissertation by Jay Cassel, entitled *The Troupes de la Marine in Canada, 1683-1760: Men and Material* (University of Toronto, 1987) provides an in-depth look at the marines' service in North America. One of Cassel's appendixes, "Officers of the Troupes de la Marine in Canada," is printed in the quarterly *Michigan's Habitant Heritage*, vol. 16, nos. 3 and 4. These articles provide an alphabetical list of marine officers, along with their birth and death dates, and the dates they entered and left service.

The Archives Nationales du Québec has a large microfilm collection of materials found in French Archives. Of particular interest is the Archives Nationales, France, *Fonds des Colonies,* series D2C, see pp. 118-120 and 186-187; series D2D, see pp. 190-191; and series D2A, pp.192-194.

The Alphabet Laffilard is also helpful, according to Dr. John DuLong in his article, "Genealogical Research among the Military Records of New France: An Update" (*Michigan's Habitant Heritage*, vol.15, no. 1).

French Regular Army Troops in the Last French and Indian War

The third type of official military force under the French Regime was the regular troops sent to defend Canada in the last French and Indian War. This war in North America was actually an extension of a much larger military conflict in Europe, the Seven Years War. These regular army troops fought with the Troupes de la Marine and the Canadian militia, but they disdained their tactics. The officers, in particular, looked down on the Canadian officers, regarding them as mere provincials. In 1663, France lost Canada to the British.

British Troops Replace the French

From this point on, the regular troops from France were replaced by troops from England. It was less likely that these soldiers would have married into French-Canadian society due to the differences in culture and religion, but it did happen occasionally. The records for British military forces serving in Canada may be found in the National Archives of Canada in Record Group 8 and in the Public Record Office at Kew, just outside of London, England. These earlier records are more likely to include officers than enlisted men.

American Revolution

The first test of the British military in Canada came with the American Revolution. The British expected their new Canadian subjects to come to the defense of their government and defy the rebels to the south. Others, both in Quebec and the thirteen lower British colonies, hoped that those in Quebec would join in the revolution and throw off British rule.

There was a long history of antipathy between the settlers of New France and those of New England. Also there was the passage of the Quebec Act in which the British promised freedom of religion to Catholics and a continuation of the church's role in community life. Consequently the majority of Canadians remained loyal to the British.

There were some, of course, who joined the American forces.

When the American army was defeated in Canada and forced to retreat to the lower colonies, enough French Canadians stayed with the rebels to form two regiments: the First Canadian under James Livingston and the Second Canadian under Moses Hazen. Livingston's regiment eventually merged with that of Moses Hazen. In addition to these two regiments, many French Canadians fought with the Americans in companies scattered throughout the colonies. Dr. Virginia Easley Demarce performed a valuable service to genealogists when she searched through the many scattered and obscure records to find 2,500 Canadians who served the American cause. Among these more than 750 were officially mustered. These individuals are listed, along with a very helpful overview of their role in the conflict, in her book, *Canadian Participants in the American Revolution: An Index* (1980).

German Mercenaries

Another group of people that played a part in the American Revolution and ended up marrying into Canadian families was the German soldiers who were sent to support the British against the American rebels. Although many were not actually from Hesse, they have become known in North American as Hessians. After the war many were offered, and accepted, land in Canada as a reward for their services. An excellent place to begin research on Hessian ancestors is *German Military Settlers in Canada after the Revolution* (1984) by Virginia DeMarce.

American Loyalists

The American Loyalists were another group that greatly impacted Canada both during and after the Revolution. Those in the thirteen colonies who sided with the British were often driven from their homes and forced to flee to the north as refugees. There are many sources for Loyalist research—too numerous to list here. A good starting point would be to check the subject section of the Family History Library Catalog for "American Loyalists." The papers of Sir Frederick Haldimand are also an excellent manuscript source for such details as muster rolls, lists of disbanded troops, and lists of prisoners of war. An index to the Haldimand papers is available.

Militia Under the British

After the American Revolution, the British government re-established the militias in Canada in much the same form as under the French. These companies were called upon when hostilities again broke out between the British and the Americans in the War of 1812. Luc Lépine's *Lower Canada's Militia Officers, 1812-1815,* provides a wealth of information on the officers of the militia who served in this war. Another listing of militia members in the War of 1812 can be found in the *Index de Miliciens, 1812-1814.* This card index, which includes enlisted men as well as officers, has been filmed and is available on microfiche (#6334280) through LDS Family History Centers.

In 1830, a law took effect that reorganized the militia, revoking all previous commissions and starting afresh. Using this convenient starting point, Denis Racine has produced an excellent resource for the genealogist, entitled *Répertoire des officiers de milice du Bas-Canada, 1830 - 1848* (Société de généalogie de Québec, 1986). This work begins with an overview of the history of the militia in Canada. It then goes on to list officers according to their local battalions, and provides the dates of their commissions, along with such details as transfers or retirements. Lesser offices, such as quartermaster, paymaster, and surgeon, are also included. The years covered by Racine's book are particularly significant because they include the *Patriote* Rebellion of 1837-1838. Racine concludes his book with a chapter listing those officers who were disciplined for insubordination in the Rebellion. Although the historical sections may be daunting to those who cannot read French, the main body of the book that lists the officers can be easily negotiated by any reader. This book provides a thorough index.

Summary

This chapter is not intended as an exhaustive overview of French-Canadian military records. The military experiences of French Canadians were too many and varied to be listed here in full. Some other possible areas of interest may include the Fenian Invasion, the American Civil War, and the regular Canadian army formed after the Confederation in 1868.

Bibliography—Compiled by Joyce Soltis Banachowski

Back, Francis and René Chartrand. "Canadian Militia, 1750-1760." *Military Collector and Historian* 36, no. 1 (Spring 1984):19-21. Company of Military Historians, Washington, D.C.

Bonin, "Jolicour" Charles. *Memoir of a French and Indian War Soldier.* Bowie, Maryland: Heritage Books, 1993.

Caron, Chantale, Joane Pellerin, and Suzanne Girard. *Guide de Recherche Sur la Milice, 1713-1965.* 1995.

Cassel, Jay. *The Troupes de la Marine in Canada, 1683-1760: Men and Material.* Doctoral Dissertation, University of Toronto, 1987.

Courteau, Elmer. "The Carignan Regiment," *Lost In Canada,* Vols 8-10, 1982-1984.

Chartrand, René. *The French Army in the American War of Independence.* London: Osprey Publishing, 1991.

Chartrand, René. *The French Soldier in Colonial America.* Ottawa: Museum Restoration Service, 1984.

Chartrand, René. *Louis XIV's Army.* London: Osprey Publishing Ltd., 1988.

De Bonnault, Claude. *"Notes pour servir à L'éstablissement d'une liste des capitaines de milice au Canada sous le régime francais"* Bulletin des Recherches Historiques, Vol. 56, 1950 pp 259-272.

DeMarce, Virginia. *The Settlement of Former German Auxiliary Troops in Canada after the American Revolution.* Joy Reisinger, Sparta, WI. 1984.

DeMarce, Virginia. *Canadian Participants in the American Revolution: An Index.* Joy Reisinger, Sparta, WI 1980.

DeMarce, Virginia, "An Annotated List of 317 German Soldiers Remaining in Canada" *Lost in Canada* 8 (1982).

DeVille, Winston, *French Troops in the Mississippi Valley and on the Gulf Coast, 1745.* Ville Platte, LA., 1986.

DuLong, John P. "Genealogical Research Among the Military Records of New France: An Update" *Michigan Habitant Heritage*, vol. 15, no. 1 (January 1994): 5-9 (Journal of the French-Canadian Heritage Society of Michigan).

Dunnigan, Brian Leigh. "The British Army at Mackinac, 1812-1815." *Reports in Mackinac History and Archeology* 7. Mackinac Island State Park Commission, 1980.

Fryer, Mary Beacock. *More Battlefields of Canada*. Toronto: Dundurn Press, 1993.

Fryer, Mary Beacock, and Lieutenant Colonel William A. Smy C.D. "Rolls of the Provincial (Loyalist) Corps, Canadian Command American Revolutionary Period." *Dundern Canadian Historical Document Series: Publication 1*. Toronto: Dundern Press, Ltd 1981.

Gallup, Andrew and Donald F. Shaffer. *La Marine: The French Colonial Soldier in Canada: 1745-1761*. Bowie, Maryland: Heritage Books, 1992.

Jonasson, Eric. *Canadian Veterans of the War of 1812*. Winnipeg: Wheatfield Press, 1981.

Lanctot, Gustav, editor. "Canadian Militia Regulations Under the French Regime and Early British Rule, 1651-1777. *Dominion of Canada Report of Public Archives 1940*. pp. 7-22. Ottawa: Edmond Cloutier, 1941.

LéPine, Luc. *Les Officiers de Milice du Bas-Canada, 1812-1815*. Montréal: Société Généalogique Canadienne-Francaise, 1996.

"La Milice Canadienne-Francaise à Québec en 1775," *Bulletin des Recherches Historiques*, vol. 11, nos. 8 and 9 (August and September 1905): 227-242, and 257-269.

Manders, Eric I. And René Chartrand. "Lower Canada Select Embodied Militia Battalions 1812-1815," *Military Collector and Historian*, vol. 26, no. 2, Summer 1974, pp. 127. Company of Military Historians, Washington, D.C.

McBarron Jr., H. Charles, and René Chartrand. "The Quebec Militia 1775-1776," *Military Collector and Historian*, vol. 23, no. 2 (Summer 1971): 45-47. (Company of Military Historians, Washington, D.C.).

Nicolai, Martin I. "A Different Kind of Courage: The French Military and the Canadian Irregular Soldier During the Seven Year's War," *Canadian Historical Review*, vol. 70, no. 1 (1989): 53-73. (University of Toronto Press, Toronto).

Proulx, Gilles. *The Garrison of Québec 1748-1759.* Ottawa: National Historic Sites, Parks Service, Environment Canada, 1991.

Racine, Denis. *Répertoire des Officiers de milice du Bas-Canada, 1830-1848.* Société de Généalogie de Québec, 1986.

Racine, Denis. *Répertoire des Officiers de Milice du Bas-Canada La Milice Sédentaire ou Non Active (1846-1868),* no. 88. Québec: Société de généalogie de Québec, 2000.

Reuter, Claus. *Brunswick Troops in North America, 1776-1783.* Bowie, Maryland: Heritage Books, Inc., 1999.

Spring, Ted. "The French Marines 1754-1761," *Sketchbook 66,* vol. 2. Osseo, Minnesota: Track of the Wolf, Inc., 1991.

Spring, Ted. "The Women of the French War Era," 1750-1769," *Sketchbook 56,* vol. 5. Osseo, Minnesota: Track of the Wolf, Inc., 1991.

Stanley, George F.G. *Canada's Soldiers: The Military History of an Unmilitary People.* Toronto: McMillan of Canada, 1974.

Sulte, Benjamin. "Troupes du Canada 1670-1687." *Memoires de la Société Royale du Canada,* vol. 14, Series 3, Section 1, (May 1920): 1-21.

Todish, Timothy J. *America's First First World War: The French and Indian War, 1754-1763.* Ogden, Utah: Eagle's View Publishing Co., 1988.

Valois, Jack, editor. "War of 1812, Veteran of Military Service with the Canadian Forces," *Connecticut Maple Leaf,* vol. 1, nos. 1-3 (June 1983, December 1983, June 1984). (French-Canadian Genealogical Society of Connecticut, Rocky Hill, Connecticut).

Verney, Jack. *The Good Regiment.* Montreal: McGill-Queens University Press, 1998.

Chapter Twenty-eight

Genealogy and the Internet

By Patricia Keeney Geyh

The genealogical community has been set on its ear by the Internet. Researchers are browsing through hundreds of websites searching for that one elusive piece of information to extend a family line. There is a lot of information floating through cyberspace, and researchers should be encouraged to use it.

Many secondary sources are available online. Entire books are reproduced. Historical background information is plentiful. Extractions from, and indexes to, many primary records can be found. The genealogist planning a research trip to an archives or library can save time by searching the library or archive catalog online before beginning the trip.

Some of the most enthusiastically used sources are those that provide the means to communicate with others who are researching the same family. Queries can be placed that may be answered from anywhere in the world. With the wide use of scanners pictures can be exchanged with far-flung family members. Remember, except for the pictures, these are all secondary sources.

At this time, few primary records have been put online. However these are becoming increasingly available. The entire body of the U.S. Population Census Records through 1930 is accessible. Many of the original federal land grants are already there. Some genealogists are putting images of primary documents online and a careful search is necessary to find them.

Other information is available including maps and translation services. The maps may take the researcher down to the tiniest village in Quebec. The translation of a short passage in French can shed light on a valuable French-Canadian document.

All of this amazing array of information must be accepted with certain warnings. Websites appear and disappear and change their addresses. Keep searching. Persistence pays off.

Also remember that this secondary information, as with all secondary sources, must be verified with primary data. Further research is always necessary. Even with primary data it is best to have two or more sources for a given fact.

One should always be careful when sharing information. If data was received from someone else, it is only courteous to obtain permission from that person before forwarding it. It is particularly important not to include information about those who are living unless their permission has been obtained. Some genealogy programs allow the researcher to block specific information. It is extremely important that the information being disseminated has been checked carefully for accuracy. Don't perpetuate error.

Most websites are free, but some require a membership or user fee.

Space does not allow a listing of all current websites relating to French Canada. There are, however, some that should be mentioned. They all provide links to other sites of importance.

http://www.ancestry.com Offers a wide variety of free and subscription-based information for family historians. There is a growing collection of Canadian and French-Canadian data.

http://www.cyndislist.com This is a source for thousands of hyperlinks to websites all over the world.

http://www.familysearch.org This is the site for the Family History Library.

http://www.fcgw.org This is the website of the French-Canadian/Acadian Genealogical Society of Wisconsin

http://www.rootsweb.com The oldest and largest free online community for genealogists. The site contains extensive interactive guides and numerous research tools for tracing family histories.

By the very nature of the Internet it is easy for errors to be transmitted around the world with lightning speed. If a citation is not given for a specific piece of data, see if it can be obtained from the person disseminating the information.

Appendix
Table of Contents

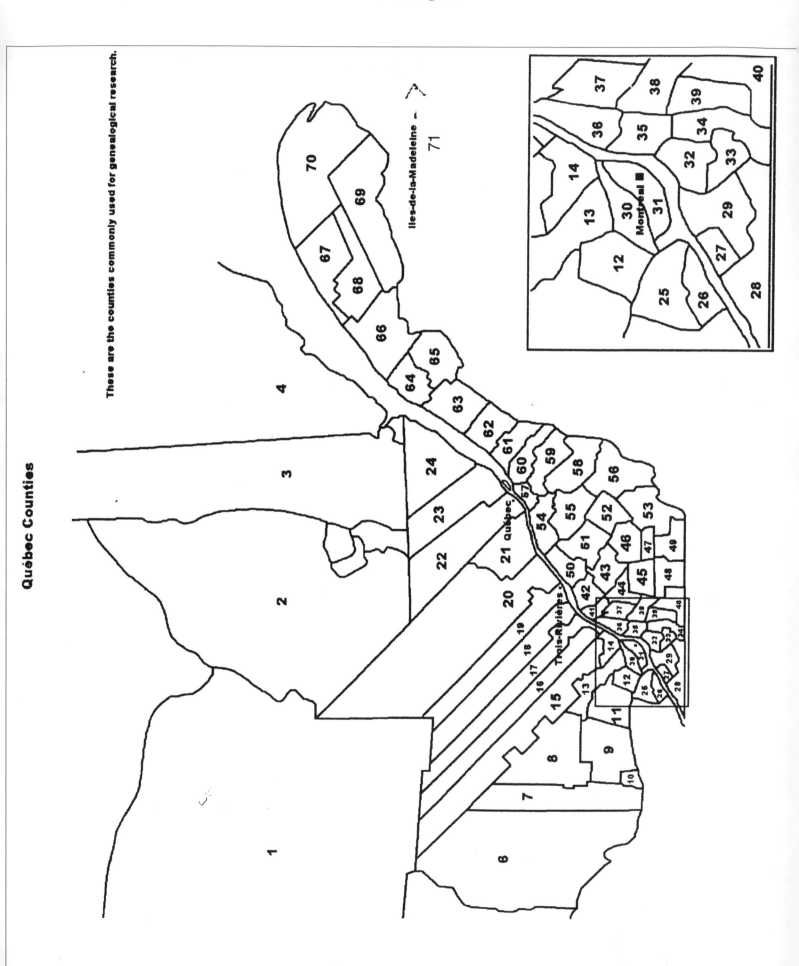

French-Canadian Sources: A Guide for Genealogists

Map of Quebec

By Beverly Ploenske LaBelle

The map on the facing page shows the counties in Canada that are useful for genealogical research. Since the government in Quebec is not necessarily based on a state and county structure, most maps do not show the county lines. Even when traveling in Quebec the counties are not as well defined as they are in the United States. The boundaries in Quebec today are different for judicial districts, administrative regions and electoral units. The county boundaries are helpful in searching for early church records of vital statistics and secondary sources.

Numerical Order of Quebec Counties

Number	County
1	Abitibi
2	Lac Saint Jean
3	Chicoutimi
4	Saguenay
5	Temiscamingue
6	Pontiac
7	Gatineau
8	Labelle
9	Papineau
10	Hull
11	Argenteuil
12	Deux-Montagnes
13	Terrebonne
14	L'Assomption
15	Montcalm
16	Joliette
17	Berthier
18	Maskinonge
19	St-Maurice
20	Champlain
21	Portneuf
22	Québec
23	Montmorency
24	Charlevoix
25	Vaudreuil
26	Soulanges
27	Beauharnois

28 . . . . .Huntingdon
29 . . . . .Chateauguay
30 . . . . .Ile-Jesus (Laval)
31 . . . . .Ile-de-Montréal
(Jacques-Cartier, Hochelaga)
32 . . . . .Laprairie
33 . . . . .Napierville
34 . . . . .St-Jean
35 . . . . .Chambly
36 . . . . .Vercheres
37 . . . . .St-Hyacinthe
38 . . . . .Rouville
39 . . . . .Iberville
40 . . . . .Missisquoi
41 . . . . .Richelieu
42 . . . . .Yamaska
43 . . . . .Drummond
44 . . . . .Bagot
45 . . . . .Shefford
46 . . . . .Richmond
47 . . . . .Sherbrooke
48 . . . . .Brome
49 . . . . .Stanstead
50 . . . . .Nicolet
51 . . . . .Arthabaska
52 . . . . .Wolfe
53 . . . . .Compton
54 . . . . .Lotbiniere
55 . . . . .Megantic
56 . . . . .Frontenac
57 . . . . .Levis
58 . . . . .Beauce
59 . . . . .Dorchester
60 . . . . .Bellechasse
61 . . . . .Montmagny
62 . . . . .L'Islet
63 . . . . .Kamouraska

64 . . . . .Riviere-du-Loup
65 . . . . .Temiscouata
66 . . . . .Rimouski
67 . . . . .Matane
68 . . . . .Matapedia
69 . . . . .Bonaventure
70 . . . . .Gaspe
71 . . . . .Iles-de-la-Madeleine
(Magdalen Islands)

Alphabetical Order of Québec Counties

French Vocabulary: Words and Phrases

By Joyce Soltis Banachowski

The following list of words and phrases is meant to aid in doing genealogical research. In different centuries or regions, words have had different meanings and sometimes different spellings. For example, the French-Canadian words for "godfather" and "godmother" have had numerous spellings throughout the seventeenth, eighteenth and nineteenth centuries—none of which are consistent with a particular time period or location. The differences in spelling seem to be by individual preference of the priests who wrote them. (Godfather: *parain, parein, parrain, parraine, parrein, parrin;* Godmother: *maraine, marainne, mareine, mareinee, marraine, marrainne, marrein, marreine, marrenine, marreinne, marrin*). This listing includes some words and phrases encountered in French-Canadian and Acadian research in censuses; birth, marriage and death records; seigneurial, court, and notarial inventaires and records; and in general reading. By no means is this a complete listing. Remember l' before a word often serves as an article (e.g. l'ancien or ancien). Abbreviations used: m—masculine / f—feminine; s—singular / p—plural; sl.—slang; obs.—obsolete.

This list of French-Canadian words and phrases has been compiled over years of research. Some of these words or phrases are now obsolete and will not be found in a modern dictionary. Various spellings of the same word are given. Some have the "correct" diacritical marks and others do not. Most of these have been copied directly out of documents and publications during years of research. Some, of course, come from dictionaries.

A

à—to, for

aagé/aagés(s/p)—age, ages

abandon—cession, surrender

abandon de terres—transfer of land

abandons—claims for insurance when property or ships were lost.

abandons de biens—bankruptcy reports

abattus ou vendus pour l'abattoir ou exportation—killed or sold for slaughter or exportation

abcès, abèes—abscess

abjure—to recant, to renounce (in New France, to give up Protestant faith)

aboiteau—Acadian method of reclaiming land from the sea by the building of dikes whereby the water was allowed to drain out at low tide

accord—an agreement

accordé—accord, granted

accouchement—child birth

accusé—the accused; defendant

acensements—system by which land was granted in New France

acheter—to buy; a popular expression for giving birth

acquit, l'acquit—release or discharge (of a debt)

acte—almost any official document (e.g., deed, bill, notarial record, etc.)

acte à ete redige—act of restitution

acte octroyé—an act to grant or concede

acte de renonciation—surrender of claims

actuellement—now

acusée—accused

adoptif, adoptive—adopted

affermée—leased or rented

affiches—posters, bills

afin de—in order to

affinité—relationship (through marriage)

afin que—so that

agê/âgé/âgée (m/f)—age, one's age

agé—aged

age au jour anniversaire de naissance suivant—age on birthday coming up

agricole—agricultural; agriculture

agriculteur-one who farms land or raises animals for use as food

aide-de-poste—assistant to a post master

aieux—ancestors, forbears; grandparents

aiguilles—needles

aiguillettes—small needles

aîné, aine—elder; eldest (it could be used to distinguish between a father and a son or an older brother and a younger brother with the same name.)

à-la-gaumine—a public declaration of marriage; in the eighteenth century, when a couple was refused the right to marriage, they would openly claim during mass that they were taking each other as husband and wife

a la naissance—at birth

a la toiture—to the roof

aliénés—unsound mind

allant à l'école—going to school

alors—then (that time)

amandes—almonds

amelioré/ameliorée (m/f)—improved (as in improved land)

ami/amie (m/f)—friend

Amiraute—Admiralty Court

à moitié—half

an, ans—year, years

ancien—old, former

ancien chirurgien-major—former head surgeon

ancien compagnie or l'ancien compagnie—see ancien société

ancien gouverneur—former governor

ancien lieutenant de la marine—former marine lieutenant

ancien marguillers—those who already had served as churchwardens and now were involved as advisors for their parishes

ancien régime—before 1789 (the French Revolution) in France

l'ancien société—creation of the government in which they believed public funds should not be used to set up colonies. Colonization was limited to those directly involved with the fur trade. (e.g., Compagnie de Canada, Compaigne de la Nouvelle France, Compaigne de Conde, Compaigne de Champlain, Compaigne de Rouen, or Compaigne de St. Malo)

angine—quinsy (a disease of the throat)

anglais—English

Angleterre—England

animaux—animals; livestock

animaux de race—pure-bred stock

animaux vendus dans l'année—livestock sold during the year

animaux vivants—livestock

annedda—Indian name for juniper from which they taught the explorers and voyageurs to make a brew to combat scurvy

année, annee/années (s/p)—year

annuellement—annually

anonyme—child born, but no other information; anonymous; unnamed

anse—bay, cove

anspessade—lance corporal

ante—before

août—August

apercer historique—historic overview

appellation—to name, to challenge, to appeal

appendice—appendix

apothicaire—apothecary, pharmacist

après or d'après—after

après-midi—afternoon

apprenti—apprentice, novice

aquet—common property of a married couple

arbitrage—arbitration

arbre—tree

arbres plantés—trees planted

archdiacre—archdeacon

archevèque—archbishop

archer—bowman, archer; guard

architecte—architect

architecte du roi—official who served as Deputy Overseer of Highways in Quebec

ardoise—slate

argent—silver, silver money

argentier—treasurer (old meaning); silverware cabinet

armateur—privateer, ship owner: business manager

armée—army, forces, troops

armes—weapons (guns)

armes à feu—wounds; guns

armurier-gunsmith

arpent—a unit of land measurement, equal to .845 acres (about 5/6 acre) or .342 hectares

arpenter—to survey

arpents de terre en valeur—arpents of cultivated land

arpenteur—land surveyor

ârret—decree to order to stop

arrêt/arrêts (s/p)—suspension, stoppage, judgement, arrest

arrêté, arrêté—decree, order, decision; stopped

arrêt de compte—record of a judgment

arrêt du roi—royal decree

arrière-fief—a sub-seigneury; a seigneury conceded within a larger seigneury. It was held from the seigneur of the larger seigneury rather than from the king (often no larger than a square arpent).

arquebusier—gunsmith who repaired guns and manufactured bullets

arthrite—arthritis

artisan—craftsman, tradesman

assassinés—murdered

assesseurs au conseil—assistant judges at the council

assignation—writ, subpoena

assigné/assignée (m/f)—appointee

asiles—asylums; places of refuge, homes, shelters

asiles d'alienes—lunatic asylums

assolement—rotation of crops

à temps—in time

à titre de ferme et moissons de grains—lease contract made with tenant farmers indicating the flat rate payable in grain (usually a third)

à titre de ferme et moitié de tous grains—a share cropper's lease with payment of half the grain

auberges—inns, public houses, taverns

aubergiste—bar keeper; innkeeper

au carqan—a means of execution practiced by the Hurons in the early French period: the victim was attached by an iron collar to a pole and left to be killed by other Indians or whatever

aucun—not any, none, no one

au-dessus, audessus—over (e.g., over a given age); above (location, eg. au-dessus la riviere—above the river)

au-dessous, audessous—below or under (e.g., under a given age)

auditeur—listener

au feu—fire

auges de bough—wooden troughs used to catch maple sap

augmentation—the extension of 10-40 arpents of land to an original homestead made by a seigneur as a favor to a hard working colonist

l'augmentation—enlargement

aujourd 'hui, or aujourd huy—today

aumône, l'aumône—relief, welfare, alms, paupers

aumönier—chaplain

aune—unit of measurement; an ell; about one yard

au rez-de chaussée—on the ground floor

aussi—also, too, as; and so

auteur—author

l'automne—autumn

autre, autres—other

avaloir avec un portefais cheine—cupboard of oak

avance—advance (as an advance in wages)

avance d'hoirie—advance on an inheritance which would eventually be returned to the parent's estate

avant—before, previously

avant—in the fur trade, the foreman who stood in the front of the canoe and directed the passage of the canoe

avant hier—day before yesterday

avant-poste—outpost

avant-propos—preface, introduction

avant que—before

avant-toit—eaves

avant-veille—two days before

avec—with

avec moy j'ay—with me/I

aveu et dénombrement—a list of the holdings (buildings, cleared land, and livestock) and dues which were charged within a seigneury; description and accounting of amount of cens and rents due to a seigneur; an enumeration or census.

aveugle, aveugles—blind

avocat—barrister, counsel, lawyer

avoine—oats

avortement—abortion; miscarriage

avril—April

ayant—to have

ayant droit—beneficiary

ayeul—grandfather

ayeule—grandmother

B

bacoté—a lean to

baie—bay

bail/baux (s/p)—lease

bail emphytcotique—right to lease a sizable property

bail à loyer—lease a house, furniture, etc.

bail à loyer d'une maison—lease a house

baillage—name of lower court

bailleurs—ballots, votes

bailli—a judge in the baillage

balises—poles or trees placed at intervals to mark the course of a road or ice road or bridge in winter

ban—proclamation affecting the city

banalité, banality—a charge which a seigneur levied for a service (i.e., use of flour mill or sawmill)

banc—bench

banc d'église—pew

banc d'oeuvre—special pew in the church which was occupied by the church warden (marguilliers), usually located against the wall opposite the pulpit and at right angles to the rest of the pews

banlieue—area extending about one lieue (2.5 miles) from the city and subject to laws (ban) affecting the city; suburb

bannissement—banishment

banquier—banker

baptême—baptism

baptisé/baptisée (m/f)—baptized

barbier/barbiers (s/p)—barber/barbers

bardeau—wood shingle

baril/barils (s/p)—dry measure equal to about 180 livres

baril—liquid measure equal to twenty gallons; barrel

barrique/barriques (s/p)—hogshead (an early measure of volume, cask or barrel equal to 60-140 gallons), a keg; one barrique was equal to 1/4 of a tonneau or barrel or 210 litres; also known as a pipe

barque—small boat using both oars and sails

barque Pontee—decked ship of 25-30 tons, 2-3 masts, used for unloading ships at Quebec and for supply and trade boats up and down the river

bas, les bas—socks

bas/basse (m/f)—lower

bas Canada—lower Canada; Quebec

bas de soie—silk socks

bassins—troughs for crushing and mixing lime, used by masons

batârd—a ten-man canoe

bateau or bateaux—an open boat, sharp at both ends, flat-bottomed, of various sizes for rowing or sailing, generally with a crew of five men

bateau de barque—a dinghy; used by larger vessels as a lifeboat

bateau plat—a flatboat used for transporting troops and supplies during the Indian Wars

batelier/bateliers (s/p)—ferryman, boatman, bargeman/ferrymen, boatmen/bargemen

bâtiments—buildings; boats, structures

batises—poles which were placed along roadways to mark the way (used especially in winter)

bâtisse saisis—seized building

batiste toile—sheer, finely woven cloth of linen

battelée—a boat load

battu et fletri de verges—form of punishment when a person was birched and branded (whipped and branded with the shape of the fleur-de-lis)

baux a ferme—land lease

bazils—weighted leg irons

beaudets—cradles, children's bed

beau-fils—stepson; son-in-law

beau-frère—brother-in-law; stepbrother

beau-père—father-in-law; stepfather

bêche—spade

bêcheur—a digger (occupation)

bedeau—verger, lay person who is caretaker of the interior of the church

beignets—fritters; a kind of deep fried doughnut sprinkled with sugar

belle-fille—step daughter; daughter-in-law

belle-mère—mother-in-law; step mother

belle-soeur—sister-in-law; step sister

bénéfice—benefits, profit, gain, advantage

berger—shepherd

berlines—larger carrioles carrying more passengers

berlôt—sleigh with wooden runners and sides on it

besace—small bag containing personal belongings worn on the waistband by Acadian women

besoin—want, wants (because he needs); need, necessity

bessons/bessonnes (m/f)—twins

bétail/bestiaux (s/p)—livestock, cattle

bête—animal, beast

bêtes a cornes—horned animal; cattle or oxen, neat cattle

bette, blette raves—mangel wurtzel and other beets

betteraves—beets

beurre—butter

beurre de ménage—homemade butter

bidon à lait—milk churn

bienfaiteur de l'église—church benefactor

bien—good

bién-fonds, biéns-fonds—real property (land and buildings)

bien que—although

biens—goods, wealth

biens de communauté—property (moveable wealth and land purchased) acquired by a married couple after the couple's marriage

biens immeubles—real property

biens immobiliers—real estate

biens meubles—personal property; movable assets

bière—beer

bijouterie—jewelry

bijoutier—jeweler

billet—bill; permit; ticket; letter

billet de concession—certificate of concession

bique—nanny goat, female goat

bis—brown

blanc—white

blanchisseur—washes and irons clothes; launderer

blanchisseuse—laundress, washerwoman

blé—wheat

blé d'automne—fall wheat

blé d'inde—corn

blé d'inde en épi—ear of corn

blé de turguie—originally corn or coarse millet

blé du printemps—spring wheat

blé noir—buckwheat

blé sarrasin—buckwheat

bled froment—fermenting wheat; yeast

bless, blessures, or blesser—wound, wounds

blessé—wounded

bleu—blue

bleuets—blueberries

boeuf/boeufs—bull/bulls, steer; ox/oxen

boeufs de traval—working oxen

bois—wood, timber

bois de calumet—dogwood used for the stems of smoking pipes during the French regime

bois de construction—lumber

boisseau/boisseaux—bushel/bushels (one boisseau=fifteen ares)

boisson/boissons—drink, beverage; drinking; drunkenness

boivel—young bull or steer

bon/bonne (m/f)—good

bons—name given to notes issued by private merchants and not the government in the eighteenth century. They were commonly used until 1830.

bonhomme—a simple, good-natured man

bonnetier/bonnetière (m/f)—stocking maker, hosier; maker and seller of lingerie and knitting objects

bosse—the hump of the buffalo

bosses à peindre—paint brushes (for an artist)

botte—bunches; bales

bottin—a directory

boucher—butcher

boucherie—butcher shop; slaughter house

bouchon—a bunch of branches hanging over the door of a roadside inn indicating that it was a place that sold liquor

boudin—blood sausage

boue—billy goat, male goat

bouillon—a common drink of New France. It was a mash of wheat or corn, fermented, diluted with water and allowed to age in a cask

boulanger—baker

boulangerie, la boulangerie—bakery; bakehouse

bourg—market town

bourgeois—middle class, townsman

bourgeois du congé—the merchant who provided the permit and had a share in the returns of the fur trade

bourgeoisie—wealthiest of the middle class and found only in cities and towns

bourgeois-rentiers—gentlemen of private means

bourreau—executioner, hangman

bourrelier—harness maker

bouteille/bouteilles (s/p)—bottle/bottles

bouteiller—bottle maker or bottler

boutons, les boutons—buttons

boutonnier—person who slips in a piece of cloth to permit insertion of a button, button-hole maker

bouts or les bouts—the avant and gouvernail

bouveau/bouveaux (s/p)—young ox/oxen

braconnier—poacher

brasses—linear measure equal to the span of the arms

brasseur—brewer

brayages—a social event of flax beating

brayet—short pair of canvas trousers which had soft leather inserts at the seat and knee. They were adopted from the Indians by the coureurs de bois.

brebis—sheep

brevet—patent, certificate, warrant

breveté—patented

brigade—3 or 4 canoes traveling together

brigantine—a ship larger than a schooner, but less than 100 tons

briquetier—brick maker

briqueteur—brick layer

brossiers—brush and broom makers

brouette—wheelbarrow

bru—daughter-in-law

brulé par accident—burned by accident

brûlures—burns and scalds

brûleurs de coke—coke burners

brun—brown, dark

bûcheron/bûcherons (s/p)—wood chopper/choppers

C

cabane (1)—term used in French-Canadian records to indicate type of crude cabin with no floor or fireplace, made of trees sharpened on one end and stuck in the ground. Thatch and bark were used for the roof and to fill in the gaps. It would provide enough storage for supplies and a chest and would house a settler when he first came until a better building on cleared land could be constructed.

cabane (2)—an alcove usually nailed to the wall where parents slept

cabane d'écorce—type of primitive chapel made of

medium-sized branches or trunks, driven into the ground to form walls filled in with clay, with a roof of pliable branches bent to form a vault and covered with bark. The door was a sheet of bark or cloth; hut, shanty

cabaret—tavern; place which served drinks and often times food

cabaretier—tavern keeper

le cabinet—sleeping room

cabinet au cuisine—kitchen

cabotage—coasting trade; coasting vessel

caboteur—coasting vessel

cabriolet—(gig) a light, two-wheeled carriage with a folding hood

cabrouet—simple, open carriage consisting of a backless seat attached to a shaft on wheels

cadet des troupes—young gentleman in training to be an officer

cahiers—notebook; paper covered book

caisse—chest, trunk

cajeux—a form of water transpotation for heavy goods (pieces of cedar wood would be bound together so they could be fitted with sails); They were also used as fire ships off the Quebec shores in the Seven Years War. They were loaded with flaming logs and left to float with the current or tide.

calèche—light, horse drawn buggy

calfateur—man who caulks planks on a ship

caline—kind of indoor bonnet worn by Acadian women on the top of their heads and coming down the side covering their ears

calomnie—slander

camarade de voyage—travel companion

canard—a duck

canivets—small knife

canonnier—gunner

canot du maître—(Montreal Canoe) large canoe used on Great Lakes and large rivers from Montreal to outposts and back; Approximately forty feet in length with a fourteen-man crew

canot du nord—(North canoe) canoe used in smaller streams or lakes primarily west of Grand Portage; Approximately twenty-five feet in length with an eight man crew

cantor—involved in the chuch choir

capine—a kind of Acadian bonnet made of white unbleached or printed cotton

caporal—corporal

capot or capote—a greatcoat with a hood made from a blanket; used by nearly all traders and voyageurs; hooded overcoat

captaine—captain

captaine de côte—a literate habitant of standing who drew up the muster for the militia, acted as intermediary between the intendant and the rural population and organized labor for public works

captaine de milice—captain of the parish militia who was appointed by the governor. (He was the civil and military authority on the parish level. He represented the governor and intendant to the population, and saw to it that decrees were announced and posted.)

captaine de vaisseau—ship's captain

captaine reformé—discharged captain, retired captain

captivité—captivity

cardeur—carder

cardeur de laine—wool carder

cardonier—someone who works with wool

Carignan Salières Regiment—a regiment of twenty companies sent from France to New France between 1665-1668 to protect the colonists from the Indians

cariole, carriole—a boxlike Canadian sleigh for carrying one or two passengers; a kind of dogsled used by fur traders in the Northwest

carotte/carottes (s/p)—carrot/carrots

carqan—form of punishment in which a person was placed in an iron collar attached to a pole with weights attached to his feet

carrefour—crossroads

carrier/carriers (s/p)—quarryman

carrière—quarry

carriole—light cart

carrossiers—carriage and wagon makers

carrot—a solid bundle of tobacco leaves laid together lengthwise, compressed and wrapped in a cloth, tightly bound with cord

carte—map; ticket, bill of fare, playing card

car tel est notre plaisir—for that is our wish

casaque—short gown or jacket

cask—a medium to large barrel of any measure

casseaux—birch bark containers

cassettes—chests containing personal belongings

cassonade—moist or brown sugar

castor—beaver skins; beaver

castoreum—a liquid from the glands of beaver used in perfume making and baiting traps

castor gras—(greasy beaver); beaver fur after it was worn by the Indians for two to three years. It was more valuable than castor sec.

castor sec—(dry beaver) the beaver fur as it came from the animal

catalognes—costume worn by colonists of New France resembling those worn in the Basque country

cautionnement—bail, security

cavale—mare

cavalier—horseman

cave—cellar

ce, cet, cette—this

ceinture—belt; sash

cela—that; that thing

celle-ci (f)—this one, this person

celui, ceux—that, those

celui-ci (m)—this one, this person

cens—a token cash payment levied on *rotures* (see entry in this appendix) paid to a seigneur

cens et rente—annual payment in money or produce given to a seigneur

censitaire—the person who paid a cens for a roture or concession

censives—land held by a censitaire

cent—hundred

Cent Associés—refers to the Company of 100 Associates

centième—hundredth

cerevisia—barley beer (see bouillon)

cerisier—cherry tree; cherry wood

ceinture fléchée—bright colored sash with an arrow weave, worn by voyageurs

cerises—cherries

certificat de liberté—written evidence of freedom, (eg. affidavit proving a husband or wife was dead and the spouse was free to remarry)

cession—transfer; assignment of property

cession d'une terre—transfer of land

c'est cela—that's it

cette—for this

ceux, celui—that, those

ceux-ci—this one

chacun—each, every one

chafaux—platforms for drying fish

chaffetier—teamster

chaise/chaises (s/p)—chair/chairs

chale/chales (s/p)—shawl/shawls

chaloupe—flat-bottomed cargo boat propelled with sails and oars

chaloupe biscayne—small boat used on small rivers for hunting and fishing (smaller than a charoy)

chaloupe de grave—boat that can be beached; small boat often times used to go between a ship and shore

chaloupiers—boatmen

chambre—room; court

chambre au cuisine—dining room

champ—field

chandelier—candlestick maker

chanoine—canon; priests who were not allowed to teach or become parish priests. They were to pray and in some cases become missionaries.

chanson—song

chantre—singer; choir member

chanvre—hemp

chapeaux de castor—beaver hat

chapelier—hatter; hat maker

chapelle—chapel

chapitre—Bishop's advisory council

charbon—coal, charcoal

charbon de bois—charcoal

charbon de terre—coal

charbonnier—coal man; charcoal burner

charlot—wagon, cart

charoy—boat used for hunting and fishing on the St. Lawrence

chaque—each, every

chariot—wagon

charivari, chivari—way in which a community showed its disapproval of a marriage—one which was legal but considered distasteful (e.g., an old man marrying a very young woman or a marriage of a widow too soon after her husband's death); the neighbors would gather, creating a great amount of noise and insults. They might be bought off with liquor or money for a celebration. During the English regime, the practice began to change to a good-natured celebration.

charpentier—carpenter

charpentier de gros—see charpentier des grosses oeuvre

charpentier de grosses oeuvre—contractor, builder

charpentier de navire—ship builder, ship carpenter

charretier—wagoner, carter; teamster

charrettes—carts

charron—wheelwright; wheel maker

charroyeur—carter, transporter

charrue—plow

chasseurs—hunters

Château St. Louis—place in Quebec where the governor-general stayed; meeting place of the Council Sovereign

châtiments—punishments

la chaudière—large copper pot; boiler

chaudé—a white wine imported from Poitou, France

chaudron—copper cauldron

chaudronnier—tinsmith, brazier, coppersmith, tinker, pot maker

chaufournier—lime burner

chaussée—road, pavement

chaussons—bed socks

chaussures—footwear

chelin—unit of currency similar to the English shilling, one chelin equals about twenty sous

chemins de communication—roads to give access to farms not fronting on royal roads

chemins de fer—steam railway

chemins de moulin—roads built at the order of a seigneur

chemins du roi—royal roads (main highways)

chemins royaux et de poste—See chemins du roi

chemise—shirt (could be worn by men or women); underwear shirt

chemise e corps—an article of clothing worn under a woman's other clothing during the day and as a night shirt for sleeping

chêne—oak

chenet—andiron

cheval/chevaux (s/p)—horse/horses

cheval-de-bois—a kind of punishment, a person would have to ride a kind of wooden horse for a designated period of time with weights (6 lbs) hanging from his feet

chevaux de tous ages—horse of any age

chevalier—horseman; mounted fighter; military order (the only one in New France was Chevalier-de-Saint-Louis)

Chevalier-de-Saint Louis—only military order in New France

chèvre—goat

chez—at, in the care of, with, among

chien/chienne (m/f)—dog

chirurgicale—surgery, operation

chirurgien-surgeon

chirurgien-major—head surgeon

chirurgien-du-navire—fleet surgeon

chirurgien de la paroisse—parish surgeon

chivari—See charivari

cholera—cholera

chopine—used for measuring shot or liquor, equal to .98 English pint; half liter measure

chou—cabbage

ci—if

ci-contre—opposite

ci-devant—coming up in the future; to be

cidre—cider

cidre paré—fermented cider

cimetière—cemetery

cincture—belt

cinq—five

cinquante—fifty

cinquantième—fiftieth

cinquième—fifth

cipote—See sipaille

cire—wax

ciseau—chisel; scissors

ciseaux—scissors

ciseleurs—carvers (usually of wood)

cité—city, town

citoyen—citizen, burgess

citron—lemon

citrouille—pumpkin; gourd

cloche—bell; blister

clocher—belfry; steeple

clôture—closing of an account

clôtures—fences; enclosures

clou—boil, festering sore

clou/cloux (s/p)—nail/nails

cloutier—nail and tack maker and dealer

cocher—coachman; carriage driver

cochère—carriage

cochon—pig, hog

cocottes—round or oval lidded pots

code postal—zip code

coeur palpitations—heart palpitations

coffre/coffres (s/p)—chest; cedar chests

coif/coifs (s/p)—woman's head covering; cap

cohéritiers—co-heirs

collié à cheval—horse collar

colombage—half-timbered construction of a building in which the space between the posts in the wooden walls are filled with clay, stone, rubble or other material

colombage bousille—when stone with mud or clay was used to fill the spaces between upright posts in the walls of buildings

colombage pierroté—half-timbered houses

colon—farmer (term used in Quebec)

colporteur—peddler

commandant de la place—governor

commerçant—shopkeeper, merchant, trader, commercial business man

commerçant en gros—wholesale merchant

commerciale—commercial

commis—clerk; (a commis on board a ship is a steward); (in the fur trade, clerks trained to become a bourgeois and possibly a full fledged partner)

commis aux vivres—commissary clerk

commis de traite—in charge of exchange regarding trade and commerce

commissaire-ordonnateur—commissarial official of the colony

commis voyageurs—traveling salesmen

communauté de biens—personal goods; property

compagnie—company

comparant—person appearing in court on a summons

compte—record, report

compte rendu—report; review

comptes—value; account

comté/comtés (s/p)—county/counties

concession—a land grant from the king given through one of his representatves—a company, intendant, seigneur or the church

concierge—hall porter, caretaker

condamné à payer—ordered to pay

confirmé—confirmed

confiseur—confectioner

confrérie—organization of workers whose functions permitted them to hold an annual mass and dinner

congé/congés (s/p)—permission to trade; the French government issued licenses which allowed private merchants to send canoes to the west

congé de traite—trading permits (see congé)

connaisseur—expert

connus—known, understood

conquet—acquired property

consanguin/consanguine (m/f)—blood relation

consanguinité—close blood relationship; consanguinity

conseiller—counsel, adviser

conseiller du roi—royal adviser

Conseil Souverain—organized in 1663 to take the place of the executive council and the court of appeals; Sovereign Council

Conseil Superieur—In 1703 Conseil Souverain changed to Conseil Superieur. It took the place of the provincial Parlement or high judicial court in France. It only had jurisdiction in Canada.

consentement—consent; ascent, agreement

consentment mutuel—mutual consent

conservateur des archives—keeper of the records

consomption—tuberculosis

constitution—establishment; settlement

constructeurs de chaloupes—boat builders

constructeurs de navires—ship and boat builders

contagieux/contagieuse (m/f)—contagious

contrat (ct)—contract

contrat de mariage—an agreement prior to marriage establishing ownership of spousal property during the marriage

contre—against; between

contrebandiers—smugglers

contre-maîtres, contremaître—foreman, overseer; first mate on a ship

contremaîtres charpentiers du roi—king's shipwright foreman

contrevent—shutter

contrôleur—controller

convenable—proper

convention—agreement, treaty

convention de mariage—agreement to marriage

convolé—had an affair

coq—cock, rooster

coqueluche—whooping cough

cordage—rope; rigging

cordelier—Franciscan friar

cordier—rope maker

cordonnier—shoe and boot maker

corps de garde—barracks room

corroyeur—currier, leather worker

cors—corns

corvée, corvées—the responsibility of each inhabitant for building and upkeep of roads

corvette—a sloop of war

côté—a line of settlement along the St. Lawrence River, a tributary, or a road

cotilion, cotillon—a woman's slip made of white cotton

cotte—wool skirt worn by Acadian women

cotuteur—joint guardian

coup de soleil—sunstroke

coups et blessures—assault and battery

coureur de bois—illegal fur traders trading without a license

courrier—courier

cousin—cousin; relative or very close friend

cousin germaine—first cousin

cousins—a kind of small cake made for religious holidays

couteau/couteaux (s/p)—knife/knives

coutelas—a type of knife

coutelier—cutler, one who manufactures, repairs and sells cutlery

Coûtume de Paris—civil law of Paris that was followed in New France

couterier/couturières (s/p)—dressmaker/dressmakers

couvertes, couvertures—covers, blankets

couverture chevauchée—lapped board roof

couvreur—roofer

couvreur d'ardoises—tile (slate) roofer

cramalliere—cream separator

cravate—men's neckwear; tie

cravates de toile—cloth ties

créancier—creditor

créancier hypothicaire—mortgage holder

créateur—founder; inventor

crêpe—thin pancake

crible—winnowing screen; fanning mill

criée/criées (s/p)—auction

crin—coarse hair (horse hair)

cris cardiaque—heart attack

crocheton—an enlarged sickle-like tool used for harvesting peas

crocquecignole—kind of doughnut; cruller

Croix St. André—form of punishment, person was bound to a cross in the shape of an X and both arms and legs would be broken by being struck with an iron rod

croop—croup

cuillier à pot—ladle

cuisinier—cook

cuivre—brass; copper

culasse—men's breeches

culote, culottes—cut off pants; breeches (cut between the knee and the ankle)

culote d'été—summer pants

culte—worship; religion

cultivateur—farmer, raises crops; cultivator (the implement)

curatelle—guardianship

curateur—trustee, guardian

curé—pastor; parish priest

cy-devant gouverneur—former governor

D

d'abord—at first

damas—rich fabric woven with elaborate designs

d'après la loi—according to the law

dame—(title), lady

dame d'honneur—lady in waiting

dartre, dard—sting

de—from, of, by, with, in

débauche—debauchery; indulgence in sensual pleasures

de bois de merisier—of cherry wood

de bon foi—informal verbal agreements which were never registered

de bon matin—early

début—lead, debut

décédé/décedee, decede/decedee (m/f)—died

decembre—December

décés—death

décharge—when packs are removed, and the canoe is hauled or pulled past rapids

décharge—release; acquittal; discharge

déclarant—informant

déclaration/déclaration (s/p)—proclamation, disclosure; a statement acknowledging an act that took place in the past

décrèe—ordered

défaut accordé—judgement accorded

défendeur, deffendeur—defendant

défricher—to reclaim; clear (land)

défricheur—settler, clearer of land

défunt, défunts, deffunct—deceased

de grand matin—early

délai est accordé—delay was granted

délaissement—destitution; desertion

demain—tomorrow

demandeur—person pressing charges

demesne—section of a fief reserved for the exclusive use of the seigneur

demeurant—living; dwelling

demeure—dwelling; living

demiard—approximately one half of an English pint

demi, demy—half

demi-charge—part of a load of a canoe

demi ciel—half measurement

dèmi-frère—half brother

démission—resignation

demoiselle—young lady; maiden

denier—smallest unit of French regime currency, 1 denier equals 1/240 of a livre

dénombrement—enumeration; census

dentelles—lace

dentition—teeth

dent/dents (s/p)—tooth/teeth

dépens—expense, costs

de plus, plus de—more

déposé—deposited

depot—deposit

dépouilles—portions of fat from a buffalo used as a substitute for bread

depte active—present outstanding debts

depts, deptes passive—past debts

depuis—from, since

depuis lors—since then

depuis peu—lately

dernier du dernier—last (of)

derniere récolte—last harvest

dérouine—short trading trips made by winterers to places where Indians brought a number of skins

dés à coudre—thimble

déserter—clearer of land by felling trees

deserteur—deserter

désistement du marché—cancelled the contract or agreement

dessin—drawing, sketch

dessoller ny dessaisonner—to rotate crops (usually wheat followed by a year of peas or oats and the third year it lay fallow)

détin—lead

détroit—strait, channel

deux—two

deuxième—second

devanteau—colored bib apron worn by Acadian women

devis des ouvrages—statement of the work to be done (not a part of the contract)

diacre—deacon

diarrhée—diarrhea

dimanche—Sunday

dinde—turkey hen

dindon—turkey cock

dindons—turkeys

diphtérie—diphtheria

directeur—manager, head, superintendent, principal

directeur-général des vivres—supply master

dis, dix—ten

dispense—dispensation

dit/dite (m/f)—also known as (The French-Canadian used names other than their given surnames. These are known as "dit" names.)

dit jour—said day

divertissant—a native of ...

dix, dis—ten

dixième—tenth

dix-huit—eighteen

dix-huitième—eighteenth

dix-neuf—nineteen

dix-neuvième—nineteenth

dix-sept—seventeen

dix-septième—seventeenth

doire—dowry

domain—section of a seigneury for the personal use of the seigneur

domestique—domestic, household worker, servant; someone employed to the personal service of a family, home or hotel

domestique engagé—hired on a daily basis; generally either a maid or farm hand

domestique jardinier—hired gardener

domicilié—home, domicile, residence

domicilié à—living at

donation—deed of gift; contract where one transfers property prior to death in return for certain stated conditions

donation entre vif—voluntary abandoning of property rights between living persons in return for advantages; deed of a gift between two living persons

donné—lay people who signed agreements to serve God without wages or claims, but they did not take religious vows

don mutuel—agreement between husband and wife which leaves each other heir to their property

doreur—one who covers objects with gold; gilder

dot—dowry

douaire—a widow's dower or a marriage settlement

douaire coutumier—right of a widow to half of the revenue derived from her deceased husband's personal property during her lifetime

douaire préfix—lump sum payment stated in a marriage contract that the widow could claim of her deceased husband's personal property

douzaine, douzaines (s/p)—dozen/dozens

douze—twelve

douzième—twelfth

drap—a woolen cloth; sheet

drap fin—broadcloth

drapier—clothier; cloth seller

draps—sheets

drap du pays—a rough cloth produced by local sheep owners

draps fins—fine sheets

dressoir—sideboard (Acadian word)

drogueries—drugs

droguets de laine—skeins of wool

droit/droits (s/p)—right/rights

droit de banalité—the seigneur had the right to control services by forcing his censitaires to use the bake oven and grist mill on his seigneury

droit de bois de chauffage—Same as droit de coupe de bois

droit casuels—fees for religious services (e.g., baptisms, burials)

droit de coupe de bois—right of the seigneur to gather wood on the land of censitaires; (This right to cut wood applied in the seventeenth century, but was often restricted by the Intendant.)

droit de mouture—the 14th measure of grain a censitaire had to leave for the seigneur when he had his grain ground at the seigneury mill

droit de pêche—the portion of fish caught along the frontage of a seigneury which had to be turned over to the seigneur. (usually the twentieth or eleventh fish)

droit de réel—milling right; See *droit de mouture*

droit de retrait—the right to take over land which had been sold by paying the purchase price within a specified time to the buyer

droit de réunion—right of seigneurs to repossess vacant lots which colonists had vacated (legalized in 1711)

droit de tabellionnage—privilege of seigneurs to decree police regulations, and appoint administers, especially notaries

du fleuve—the river

du matin—this morning

d'un puits—a well

du pain bis—brown bread

du pain bis blanc au poids—white bread made with peas

durant—during

E

eau—water

eau de puits—well water

eau-de-vie—brandy

eaux de foréts—etchings

ebenistes—cabinet and furniture makers

éboulement—landslide

écarlatines—trade blankets of blue, red, or white cloth edged with black stripes

ecclésiastique—clergyman

échange—exchange; an agreement between two or more people to exchange land

écheoir—to fall due; devolve, expire

échue—disappointment

école/écoles (s/p)—school/schools

écolier—student

économiques—economics

ecrasés par des arbres—death by a falling tree

écrivain—writer

écru—unbleached, natural-colored

écu—a crown; a petit écu was a silver coin, one écu equaled four livres in New France, one petit écu equaled three livres, one gros écu equaled six livres (In France, one écu equaled three livres)

écuelle—porringer

écuier—writer

écurie—stable for horses

écuyer, ecuier—squire (lowest title in French hierarchy, hereditary title); riding master

également—equally

église/églises (s/p)—church/churches

élève du seminaire—seminary student

élèves—students

éleveur—cattle breeder, stock raiser

ell/ells (s/p)—unit of measurement; one ell equals 1.188 meters, about one yard

élu/élue (m/f)—the elected members; the elect

emballeurs—packers

embarcations ordinaires ou de plaisir—common or pleasure boats

émigres—emigrants

empêchement—hindrance, impediment

empêchement dirimant—any obstacle which caused a marriage to be null and void

empêchement ecclésiastique—impediment for a religious reason

emplacement—building lot; piece of land or property; site, place, location

employeés aux canaux—canal men

empoisonnements—poison

emptins—form of yeast made from the dregs of beer

en—in

en bois debout ou incultes—standing and downed timber

encanteur—auctioneer

enceinte—defensive walls of a city

en colombage—see *colombage*

encre de Chine—China ink

en culture—in farming, land under cultivation; field crops

en droit—in law

l'endroit—the area

en droiture—when a ship went directly to Quebec and back.

enduit—plaster

en fact—in fact

enfant/enfants (s/p)—child/children

enfant natural—blood son or daughter

enfants du roi—abandoned children who were supported by the crown

enfant trouvé—foundling (often left on the doorstep of a church or religious institution)

enflure—swelling

en foi de quoi—in testimony thereof

en forêt ou inculte—under wood or forest; wild

engagé—one who is hired by contract; imported labor; hired helper under contract; indentured worker

engagement—the contract for the indenture or hiring of someone; The length of time for an indenture was usually three years. Fur trade engagements were usually for a year or two.

engageur—person who hires another by contract

engagé vagabond—in seventeenth century New France, an artisan or tradesman whose contract had expired. At this time the engagé would return to France or take up land in New France and become a habitant. If he remained in Canada and engaged himself for a day, week, or month, he was known as an engagé vagabond. His role was much like that of a laborer or journalier.

enivrant—intoxicating

en plus—extra

en plus de—in addition to

en rapport—bearing (as in trees bearing fruit)

enseigne—ensign

enseigne en pied—first ensign

enseigne des troupes—ensign in the military

enseigne de vaisseau—marine officer; ship's ensign

ensuite—afterwards, in the next place; following

enterrement, enterement—burial, funeral

enterres—buried

entorse—sprain

entre—between

l'entrée—the entrance

entrepreneur—contractor, master builder

entrepreneur de piche—person in charge of a group of fishermen

envers—wrong side; reverse; back

environ—around; about

épices—spices

épicier/épiciers (s/p)—grocer/grocers

épidemié—epidemic

épingles—pins

épluchettes—social event of corn husking

épouse—spouse, wife, bride

époux—spouse, husband, bridegroom

l'équipage—personnel (crew)

l'escadre—fleet

eschevin—city official (like an alderman)

l'esclavage—slavery

esclave/esclaves (s/p)—slave/slaves

espèces—kinds, sorts; hard cash

essains d'abeilles—hives of bees

est—east

et—and

étable—stable for cattle; pig sty

étages—storys, floors

etain—tin, pewter

étamine—twilled woolen fabric having a rough, shaggy surface; a kind of muslin cloth woven by women of Acadia

états civils—civil records

États-Unis—United States

et aux depens %—to the dependents (found at the end of a document)

été—summer

étoffe—any loosely woven woolen cloth

etoffes de ménage—homemade fabrics

l'étoffe du pays—homespun cloth

etoffie foulier verges—yardage of material or stuffing

etoffes fralees par verge—fulled cloth by the yard

étranger—foreigner, stranger (In census reports, it meant visitors or lodgers who were neither blood relatives nor hired employees.)

étude—room for study; office; practice

étudiant/étudiants (s/p)—student/students

étudiants en droit—students at law

étuis de ciseaux—scissors sheath or holder

évêché—diocese

exéc. de haute justice—execution by hanging

l'excecteur de la haute justice—public executioner

executeur des hautes oeuvres—public executioner

F

fabricant—producer, maker; manufacturer

fabricant de voules et de tentes—sail, tent, and awning maker

fabricants de brosses et balais—broom and brush makers

fabricants de poëles, fournaise et grilles—stove, furnace and grate makers

fabricants de pondre et de cartouches—powder and cartridge makers

fabrique—parish council that administered the upkeep of the church, rectory and cemetery

fabrique pour la potasse et la perlosse—place for potash and pearl ash production

facter d'orgues—organ builder

faire—fair, market

faire—to make do; to get

faisance—responsibility of a commitment of a farmer who leased land to obligate himself above and beyond the price of the lease (an old French word)

faiseur—charlatan, quack; maker, doer

faiseur d'avirons—oar maker

faiseurs de Roues—wheelwrights

faiseur de sabots—wooden shoe maker

faiseur de toile—sail maker

famille-souche—founding family

farine—flour; meal

farinier—flour miller

farinier au moulin—flour miller at the mill

fathom—tobacco braided and twisted and measured in terms of length rather than weight

faubourgs—urban extensions; suburbs, outskirts

faucheuses—mowers (farm implement)

la faucille—sickle

faussaire—forger

faux, la faux—scythe

faux—wrong; false

faux monnayeur—counterfeiter

faux saunier/faux saulnier—salt smugglers; those who dealt in illegal trade of salt in France. One of their punishments was banishment to New France for life.

faveroles—beans

fe'—wife

feiullets—papers (e.g., notary records)

femme—wife; married woman; female

femme mariée—woman already married

fendeur de bois—woodsplitter

fer—iron; stuffing, padding

fer blanc—tinplate; tin

ferblantier—tin roofer; tinsmith

ferme—leased farm; farmstead

ferme/fermes (s/p)—post that was farmed out, given or sold to a trader who would then have some control of the prices and regulations of the fur trade; this system was created in order to establish and maintain the price of furs. Those which were farmed out or sold were usually for a period of three years

fermier/fermiers (s/p)—trader or official who was in charge of the ferme, traders who leased posts and therefore, had control of the fur trade in their district. They were sold or farmed out to the highest bidder, usually for a period of three years

fermier—tenant; farmer, raises livestock and or other animals; works land whether he is owner or not

fermière—farmer's wife

ferrailles—junk

ferrier—farrier, shoes horses

fête—holiday; feast day; festival

Fête-Dieu—Corpus Christi

feu/feue (m/f)—deceased

feu—fire

feu de joie—volley fired in honor of the arrival of voyageurs, dignitaries, etc.

fáves—beans

feves—beans

février—February

fiancé/fiancée (m/f)—betrothed

fichier—card-index

fichu/fichus (s/p)—neckerchief; handkerchief

fief—small seigneurie

fièvre—fever

fièvre scarlatine—scarlet fever

fil—thread

fil de chanvre—thread from goat hair (This was an item sent from France to the stores in Quebec and Louisiana in the eighteenth century.)

fil de lin—yarn

fille—daughter; girl

fille aine/aînée/âineè—eldest daughter

fille a marier—girl to be married

filles-de-chambres—chambermaids

filles de joie—Same as fille du roi

filles du roi—King's daughters; women who were brought to New France at the crown's expense to become wives for the men (between the years, 1665–1673)

fils—son; boy

fils aine—eldest son

fils de famille—young men who were sent to New France because of the way they conducted their lives. They were undesirable or an embarrassment to their families

fils unique—only son

fin, la fin—the end

firkin—container holding 66 3/4 lbs. (used for butter)

flakes—trellis like tables used for drying cod

flanelle—flannel

fléau/fléaux (s/p)—flail

flèche—spire

flétrissure—punishment by branding

fleur—flower

fleur-de-lis—symbol of the royal family of France

fleuristes—florist

fleuve—river

flibustier—pirate

flibustier du corsaire—pirate on the ship

flute—large royal merchantman

flux de sang—smallpox

foi appel—irrelevant appeal

foie—liver

foi et hommage—"fealty and hommage"; a statement of vassalage owed by a seigneur to a seigneur of higher order from which he held land or to the king; oath of fealty which was given to a seigneur

foin—hay

foin bottes—baled hay

folie—insanity

fondateur—founder

fondeur/fondeurs (s/p)—smelter, foundryman

fondeur de cloches—bell maker

fondeurs de cuivre—brass founder

forain—foreign, outsider

forestiers—lumbermen

foret/forêt—woodland, forest

forge—forge, blacksmith shop

forgeron—black smith

forgeur d'arquebuses—maker of guns

foscille—scythe

fosses/fossés—ditches

fossoyeur—grave digger

fouet, le fouet—the whip

fouine—fishing spear; pitchfork

foulon—fuller

four—outdoor bake oven usually built of stone and mortar with a shingle roof

fourche—farm tool which was a two to three pronged fork, usually of wood (resembling a forked tree branch)

fourchette—fork (kitchen utensil)

fourrage—fodder

fourrier—quartermaster

fourbisseur—sword cutler

fourniture—supplies; supplying, providing

fourreur—furrier

fourrures—furs

foyers—hearth; fireplace

frais—costs

framboise—raspberry

fromage—cheese

franc—a French regime coin; one franc equals one livre

fregate—frigate up to 400 tons

frene/frêne—ash wood

frere/frère—brother

fricassee—dish of cut up and stewed meat; hash

furoncle—a boil

fusil/fusils (s/p)—gun/guns

fustigation—form of punishment by flogging or whipping

futaine—coarse cotton or flax cloth in one color

G

gabarres—flat bottomed barges used for loading and unloading war ships

gabelle—salt tax in France

gage—pledge

gages—pay, wages

galères, galeres—punishment of hard labor on the galleys

galeries—elevated covered walks; balconies

galette—a kind of sea biscuit; hard thin cake

galons—pants

gan/gants (s/p)—glove/gloves

gantier—glove maker

garçon—young man, boy; bachelor

garçons de comptoirs—bartenders

garçon de service—bus boy

garçon maître—restaurant server

garde—guard

garde des sceaux du conseil superieur—guard of the seal of the Superior Council

garde-magasin—storekeeper

garde-marine—honor guard

garde-marine du roi—king's naval guard

garde-sel—person appointed by the crown to oversee the distribution of salt in New France; these were necessary because there were salt shortages and its importation was regulated.

gardes-malades—hospital attendants; nurses

gardiens—keepers, guards

gardiens de troupeaux—stock herders

geleé—frostbite

gendre/gendres (s/p)—son-in-law/sons-in-law

général—general

genisses—female calf; heifers

gens—persons; men; servants; people

le gens qui trafiquent à la mer—those who make their living from the sea

gens du nord—northmen; canoemen who transported furs from the company's scattered posts across the west

gens-libre—small independent fur traders who would sell their furs to larger companies

geolier, geôlier—guard, jailer

lier—guard, jailer

gibaut—Minke whale

gilet—vest

glace—ice

glans-dis—lead bullet

goélette—schooner

goudrelles, goudrilles—spiles (led the sap from maple trees to the trough)

gouvernail—steersman who attended the helm

gouverneur—governor

graine—seed

graine d'herbe—grass seed

graine de trèfle—clover seed

grains mélés—mixed grains

grand chambre, la grande chambre—parlor

grande bétail—oxen, etc.

grande chodiere de cuivre—large copper boiler

grande chaloupe—boat larger than a bateau and fitted with oars and one or two sails

grand-mère—grandmother

grand-père—grandfather

grand pénitencier—member of the bishop's advisory council who was especially appointed to hear confession

Grand rivière—name given to the St. Lawrence River

grand-vicaire—the bishop's representative

grand voyer—main road surveyor; in charge of construction and repair of roads, bridges and ferries; overseer of highways

grange—barn; See *métairie*

granie de lin—the grain of flax

gratification—reward; gratuity; extra pay

gratte—scraper (farm equipment); a kind of hoe

grave—beach

graveur/graveurs (s/p)—engraver/engravers

greffe—the collected acts of a greffier

greffier—clerk of court, registrar, recorder

greffier chef, greffier en chef—chief clerk; scribe

greffier de l'admiraute—clerk of admiralty court

greffier de la maréchausée—clerk for the police constabulary

grenier—loft, attic; upper loft of the usual Acadian house where children slept, the loom was kept and grain was stored

grenier à foin—hay loft

grese—grease

gros écu—see *écu*

groseille—currant

groseille à maquereau—gooseberry

gross bétail—oxen, cattle, etc.

grosse—coarse

gross verolle—syphillis

guèret—fallow land; land plowed but not sown

guerre—war; warfare, fighting

guerrier—warrior; fighting man

guide—in the fur trade, the person in the head or stern who commanded the brigade

guinguette—a small tavern on the outskirts of a town, usually with a pleasure garden

H

habitant—a resident in New France; a free man; one who was permanently settled and working for himself

habitants qui habitent—habitants who live there

habitation—a small colony or settlement in a deserted uninhabited place; (In seventeenth century New France, it meant the entire seigneury)

habits—clothing; clothes

haché—hatchet, small axe; chopper (kitchen utensil)

hardes—worn or used apparel

haut—high, upper

haut Canada—Upper Canada (Ontario)

haut et puissant—high and powerful

hérésie—heresy

hériter—to inherit

héritier/héritière (m/f)—heir/heiress

hernie—hernia

herse—a farm implement, a wooden triangular or rectangular frame used like a harrow

heure—hour, time

hier—yesterday

histoire—history

hiver—winter

hivernauts—(winterers) experienced voyageurs who wintered at posts in the interiors

hogshead—early measure of volume, cask or barrel equal to 60-140 gallons

homme—male, man; husband

homme de confiance—confidant

homme de l'équipage—ship crew member

hommes de chantier—raftsmen

hommes de guet—watchmen

hôpital—hospital

Hôpital général—hospital

hôpitaux—hospitals

horloges—time pieces (watches, pendulum, hour glasses)

horloger—clock and timepiece maker

hospices divers—various asylums

Hôspitaliere-de-la-Misericorde-de-Jesus—religious nuns who looked after the Hôtel Dieu, Québec (hospital)

hôtel—large house, mansion; hotel, inn

hôtel de ville—town hall

hôtel des ventes—auction mart; auction house

hôtellerie—hotel, inn

hôtel meublée—furnished lodgings

Hôtel Dieu—name of hospital in New France; one in Quebec and one in Montreal

hôteliers—hotel keepers

houblon—hops

houe—hoe; a hook blade hoe

houragans—birch bark containers holding maple sugar (an Indian word, adopted by the French)

houx—hoe

huche—large wooden trough used for kneading bread

Huguenots—followers of Calvin

huissier—an official enforcer, usually a bailiff, sheriff or process server

huissier au conseil superieur—bailiff at a higher court

huissier audiencier—court crier

hussier au bailliage—huissier at a lower court; bailman

huissier geôlier—jailer

huissier royal/royaux—royal guard

huit—eight

huitième—eighth

hulles—oils

hydropisie—dropsy

hypotheque, hypothesque—mortgage

I

ici—here; in this place

idem—ditto; same as previous one

ignolée—celebration of the renewal of the year

il'ajouta—he added

illégalement—illegally

illégitimé—illegitimate

immatricule—registered

immeubles—real estate; property

imprimeur—printer

incapables de lire—unable to read

incapables d'écrire—unable to write

incendie/incendies (s/p)—fire/fires

inculte—uncultivated

indenture—contract of servitude, usually for three years

indigents—paupers

industrielle—industrial

infirme/infirmes (s/p)—disabled, crippled

ingénieur—engineer

inhume/inhumée (m/f)—buried

insomnie—insomnia

instituteur—school master

instruments aratoires—farm implements and machinery

instruments d'agriculture—farm implements

Intendance—administrative building (meeting place of Conseil Souverain/Superieur)

interdict—ruling of the church that forbids members to perform certain church offices (sacraments, burials)

interdit—forbidden, prohibited

interprète—interpreter

inventaire—a listing of goods and their value of the possessions of a person who had died; these were taken to assure the inheritance of children.

inventaire—inventory of a collection (e.g., a listing of the acts of a notary)

inventaires après décès—post mortem inventories

issu—born to; descended; sprung from

ivrogne—drunken; drunkard

ivrognerie—alcoholism

J

jamisse—jaundice

janvier—January

jardin/jardins (s/p)—garden/gardens

jardinier/jardiniers (s/p)—gardener /gardeners

jarretelles, les jarretelles—garters

jaune—yellow

javelier—a farm tool used for cutting grain, much like a cradle scythe

jeu, jeux—gambling

jeudi—Thursday

jeune, l'jeune—young; younger

l'jeune—the young

joaillier—jeweller

jointe—a dry measure, two hands cupped together

joug—yoke

jour/jours (s/p)—day/days

jours-gras—meat days

journalier/journaliers (s/p)—day laborer/laborers, journeyman/journeymen; hired hand

journalier de ferme—farm laborer

journée—daily

jours-gras—meat days

juge/juges—judge/judges

juge d'épée—judge who presided over the maréchausée

juge de paix—justice of the peace

juge prévost—judge in a lower court

juillet—July

juin—June

jumeau, jumeaux /jumelle, jumelles (s/p)/(m/f)—twin/twins

jupe—woman's outer skirt

jupon—woman's inner skirt; petticoat

juré—juror

jurement—swearing

justicier—to punish; to execute

justoucorps—the great coat worn by officers of the French military

L

laboureur—common worker; plowman, farm hand (usually referred to tenant farmers and sharecroppers)

lac—lake

ladite—the aforesaid

l'aine—the elder (used when there are two children of the same name in a family or a parent and a child of the same name.)

lâiné—wool

lainier—of wool, woolen

lait—milk

lait de chaux—lime whitewash

laitiers—dairymen

landier—andiron

langue—language, tongue

langue de boeuf—trowel like tool used by quarrymen

lard—bacon or side pork

la regrette—the deceased

large—wide

largeur—width

league—a distance of about two and one half miles

ledit, lesdits, lesdites, ladite—the aforesaid

législation patents—legislative act granting some right or privilege

légitimé—legitimate

légumes—vegetables

l'jeune, lejeune—the younger (used when there are two children of the same name in a family or a parent and a child by the same name)

le lendemain, lendemain—the day after; the next day

le même—the same

le plus de—the most

lepre—leprosy

le regrette—the late or deceased

lessive, la lessive—wooden mallet used for beating clothes to wash them

lettres de cachet—letters or documents under the king's personal seal

lettres de castor—"beaver bills"; bills of exchange used by merchants; bearers could endorse them and use them as payments in the colony

lettres de grace—royal pardons

letters de marque—permission granted to captains on ships allowing them to seize any enemy vessels

lettre missive—letter sworn to before a sovereign, by which someone could take some action

lettres patents—licensed letters formally transcribed and recorded at the clerk's office of Conseil Souverain, which granted some rights or privileges

leur/leurs (s/p)—their/theirs

la leur, le leurs—theirs

liasse—packet, bundle (used in describing archival material)

libertines—a person who acts without moral restraints; one who is defiant of moral and religious precepts; a free spirit

libraire—bookseller

libre—free, independent; unconfined

lict consistant/consistans—firm bed

lict de plume—feather mattress

lieu—spot, place, location; premises

lieu, lieue—a unit of measurement, a league (about 2.5 miles)

lieu dit—the place called

lieutenant criminal—judge usually appointed by the king for a court of royal jurisdiction

lieutenant-général—judge of the admiralty court

lieutenant-général civil et criminal—judge in a royal court of New France

lieutenant particulier—assistant to the lieutenant-général civil and criminal

lieutenant réformé—discharged lieutenant

lieu de naissance—place of birth

lieux-dits—place names

lin—flax

linge de table—tablecloth

liqueurs—liqueurs; cordials

lit—bed

litotomye or opilation de la pierre—kidney/gall stones

livre—unit of currency in New France

livre—a unit of weight, equal to 489.41 grams or about 1.08 English pounds

livrée—livery; livery servants

locataire/locataires (s/p)—tenant/tenants

lods et ventes—a tax of one-twelfth of the sale price of land that was levied on and given to the seigneur for the sale of the roture out of the direct line of succession

logement—lodgings

logement convenable—proper lodging

longues vues—binoculars

lors—then

loue—rent

Louis—a gold piece bearing the image of the king equal to ten livres

Louis d'argent—a silver coin equal to three livres

Louis d'or—a gold piece equal to twenty-five livres, or equal to an English pound

loupe marins—seals

loutres—otters

loyal—fair, honest

loyer—rent

loyer de la terre et des bâtiments loués—rent of land and buildings leased

lundi—Monday

M

machines à battre—threshing machine

maçon—mason; stone cutter

madriers—heavy planks; beams

magasin/magazin—storehouse, warehouse

mai—May

mais—but, why

maison—house, building, home

maison à la gasparde—process in which the interior of

a house was lined with wooden slats with a clay based plaster spread over them

maison de pension—boarding or lodging house

maître/maîtresse (m/f)—master; expert

maître d'armes—master gunsmith; fencing master

maître de barque—ferry master

maître de camp—military instructor

maître canonier—master gunner

maître de chaloupe—master of a small boat

maître des comptes—accountant

maître constructeur—master builder

maître drapier—specialist in the making of cloth

maître d'ecole—school master

maître d'équipage—boatswain

maître d'hôtel—hotel supervisor; head waiter

maître d'hôtel ordinaire—second level of command

maître marechal—army general

maître merise—wild cherry

maître de musique—music teacher

maître de navire—ship master

maître d'oeuvre—foreman

maître de poste—post master

maître des requetes—expert investigator for trials; magistrate reporting to the state council

maître de vaisseau—boatswain

maître vitrier—person who makes, sells, or installs windows

majeur—of legal age

major des troupes—company major

mal—bad

maladie—illness, disease, sick

maladies de la gorge—diseases of the throat

maladies du foie—liver disease

mal au pied—sore feet

mal caduc—crippled

mal de gorge—sore throat

manacles—handcuffs

manchonniers—furriers

mandement/mandements (s/p)—mandate; authorized command or institution

mangeur du lard—"pork eaters"; novices who managed canoes, carrying goods to outposts and furs back to Montreal, but not further into the wilderness

mangel-wurzel—a variety of beet used primarily for cattle feed

manoeuvre—unskilled workman, laborer on a boat; laborer

manoeuvrier/manoeuvriers (s/p)—skilled tacticians; expert seamen

manouvrier—day laborer

mansard—dormers constructed with heavy wood framing

mansardé—mansard roof; attic, garret

mantelet—shawl

manteaux—short cloak

maraicher—truck farmer

marais—marsh

marbrier—marble cutter, polisher

marchand—merchant; shopkeeper

marchand de bétail—cattle merchant

marchand bourgeois—adviser in trade and commerce

marchand de bouvier—man who hauls or drives cattle to market, but not necessarily a merchant himself

marchand cirier—wax dealer

marchand drapier—clothier, sheet maker

marchand de draps de soie—merchant of silk products

marchand forain—an itinerant merchant; (one who comes only seasonally); peddlers who did not have residential status

marchand de fourrues—fur merchant

marchand en gros—wholesale dealer

marchand habitués—regular merchant

marchand hôtelier—merchant who sells supplies to hotels

marchand mercier—runs a general store

marchand moquignon—merchant dealing in the sale of horses, bulls, etc.

marchand pelletier—fur pelt merchant or trader

marchand poissonnier—fish monger

marchand privilège du roi—priveleged royal merchant

marchand quincailleur—iron work or hardware merchant

marchand de soie—silk merchant

marchand tapissier—one who sells or installs carpets or furniture upholstery

marchand tanneur—leather merchant

marchand de vin—wine merchant

marchand voyageur—traveling salesman or merchant

marché—contract; agreement

marché à la journée—building contract where payment is made by the day

marché les clefs à la main—contract for a completed house ready for occupancy

marché en bloc—contract for constructing a building for a fixed price

marché en tâche—same as marché en bloc

mardi—Tuesday

maréchal—officer in military

maréchal-ferrant—farrier, shoeing smith

maréchaux—farriers

maréchaussée—mounted constabulary; guards who were under a lieutenant; a kind of police force

mareyeur—fish salesman or fish dealer

marguilliers, marguillers—church warden (elected by parishioners)

marguilliers de l'oeuvre—those who took care of the church's construction

marguiller-en-charge—church wardens in charge of secular affairs of the church

mari—husband

mariage—marriage

mariage à la facan du pays—"marriage of the country"; ceremony when a fur trader married an Indian

mariage-à-la-gaumine—see *a-la-gaumine*

marié (m)—married, bridegroom

mariée (f)—married, bride

mariès—married

marin—marine, sailor, seaman

maringouins—mosquitoes

marinier—mariner, marine, naval

marmite—large earthenware or metal cooking pot

marraine, marrein—godmother; *see other spellings listed in the introduction*

marronnier—chestnut tree

marronnier d'Inde—horse chestnut tree

mars—March

marteaux—hammer

marteau à deux mains—sledge hammer

martres—martins

masse—a quantity of merchandise whose weight or amount was determined by usage

masse—sledge hammer

matelot—seaman, sailor

matelot de navire—naval seaman

matelot du vaisseau—naval seaman, but on a smaller ship

matin; du matin—morning; this morning

mauchonnier—one who makes fur-lined muffs

maux de jambes—sore legs

mazamets—wool shirts

médecin—physician, doctor

megisseur—leather worker, prepares leather

megissier—leather worker; leather dresser

mélis—a linen cloth imported from France used as a trade item in the fur trade; also used by the colonists.

le même—the same

même lieu—same location; home

mémère—granny

mémoire/mémoires (s/p)—memoire, memoirs; memorandum; account; statement; explanation of an account; bill; transaction; recollection

ménage—household; family

menu bétail—sheep, goats, etc. (smaller animals)

menusier—joiner, carpenter

menusier en bâtiments—house carpenter

mer—sea

mer de l'ouest—western sea (French fur traders often referred to the western prairies as the western sea)

mercier grossiste—wholesale merchant

mercredi—Wednesday

mercredi des cendres—Ash Wednesday

mère—mother

merluche—dried and lightly salted cod

mésalliance—bad marriage match (e.g., when a man of the upper class marries a commoner)

mesme jour—same day

messager—messenger

messire—lord; master

métairie—used by religious communities to refer to lands they managed themselves or those they farmed out for a fixed amount

métayer—small farmer who paid a portion of his produce as rent, share cropper

meteil—rye and wheat ground together for flour for bread

métier, mestier—craft, trade

métier—a loom

métier à tisser—loom

métiers divers—mechanics

métier libre, métiér libre—free exercise of manual trades without requiring proof of mastery; free and unregulated practice of the trades

métis/métisse (m/f)—mixed Indian and white; half breed

meuble/meubles (s/p)—moveable assets (furniture, clothing, kitchen utensils etc.); personal property

meubles—cabinet ware and furniture

meubliers—cabinet and furniture makers

meule—grindstone, millstone

meunier—miller

meunière—miller's wife

meurtre—murder

mi—half; semi; mid

mi-carème—middle of Lent, mid-Lent

mi-chemin—halfway

miches—large round breads (mainstay of the diet of the eighteenth century habitant)

midi—noon; midday

miel—honey

mil, mille, millier—a thousand

milice—militia

milicien—militiaman

milieux—those paddlers who sat in the middle of the canoe who had little if any experience

militaire—serviceman

millième—thousandth

mineur—under age

mineur—miner

ministre—clergyman

ministres des cultes—clergymen

ministere de la marine—naval administry

minot—a unit of measure equal to 1.107 bushels

minute—minute

minutier—the collection of a notary's acts

mirise—wild cherry

misette—marsh grasses used for cattle pasturage (an Acadian word)

mitaines—mittens

mitasses—a kind of gaiter or leggings made of canvas or skins, worn by the fur traders (adopted from the Indians)

mitoyen/mitoyenne (m/f)—jointly owned

mitoyens—middle; intermediate

mocochs, mocoks, mohuk, mokuk, mocock—birch bark or elm bark vessels which were used for storing maple sugar or other dry food items (Indian word adopted by the early French)

moeurs—morals; manners; customs; habits

moindre—less

moins—less; fewer; under

moiré—type of fabric with a wavy or watered pattern

mois—month

moisson—harvest

moisson de fourage—forage crops

moisson de fourage nourriture d'été—forage crops for summer feeding

moisson de fourage nourriture d'hiver—forage crops for winter feeding

moissonneures—reapers

moitié— half

monde—world

monnaie de carte—card money in New France. Card money was made from playing cards and used for currency. A card could be worth up to 100 livres and had the mark of the intendant's seal on it.

Monseigneur—title of the governor-general of New France

montagne—mountain, hill

montant—flowing in; rising tide; upright of a ladder; post

montres—watches

mort, morte—death

morts d'une chute—death by falling

morts-nés—still-born

mort subite—sudden death

mouce—cabin boy

mouchoirs—handkerchiefs

mouchoirs de fil—lace handkerchiefs

mouleur/mouleurs (s/p)—metal workers, moulder, mold maker

moulin—mill

moulin à cardeur—carding mill

moulin à farine—flour mill

moulin à foulon—fulling mill

moulin à scie—saw mill

moulin banal—obligation of a censitaire to have his corn ground at the seigneur's mill

moulinet—small mill

moulin foulons—fulling mill

moulin pour la fabrique des huiles—mill to manufacture oils

mousquet—musket

mousse—ship's boy

mouton—sheep

moyen—average
muets—dumb (as unable to speak)
mulot—field mouse
musicien—musician
myrtille—blueberry

N

nageurs de barque—oarsmen on a barque
naissance—birth
naissance avant terme—premature birth
nappes—tablecloths
natif—native
naufrage—sinking of a ship; shipwreck
navets—turnips
navigateur—navigator
navire/navires (s/p)—ship/ships
nay—born
ne—no, not; without
né, née—born
ne à l'etranger—foreign born
né au pays—born in the country
né de pèere étranger—foreign born father
né pouvant ni lire ni écrire—cannot read and write
négociant/négociante (m/f)—merchant who went into wholesale or overseas trade (higher in importance than merchant), wholesaler
négociant forain—foreign merchant
neige—snow
neige fondue—sleet
nés dans les douze derniers mois—born within the last twelve months
nettoyer or nettoyeur—clearer of land who gets rid of stumps, brush, etc.
neuf—nine
neuvième—ninth
neveu—nephew
nièce—niece
noble homme—nobleman
noblesse—nobility
noce, noces—wedding
noir, noire—black

nombre—number
nommé, nom/noms (s/p)—name
non—no, not
non données—not given
non en rapport—non-bearing (as in non-bearing trees)
non lieu—no case
non marié/non-mariés (m/f)—unmarried
nord—north
notaire—notary; officer who writes and attends to other public records
notaire royal—royal notary
nourrices—nurses
nourrisseur—stock raiser; dairyman
nourriture—food; breast feeding
nourriture du feu—firewood
nourriture honnête—decent food
nous—we
nouvelle—new
Nouvelle-Ecossé—(New Scotland) Nova Scotia
l'nouvelle société—a private company which believed in free trade and in colonizing. The company, however would own whatever was traded for. (e.g., Compaigne des Cent-Associes)
novembre—November
noyades—drowning
noyé, noyer, se noyer, noyés—drowned; flooded
noyer—walnut wood; walnut tree
noyer tendre—butternut wood
nud en chemise/nue en chemise (m/f)—nude except for a shirt (a form of punishment, a person dressed as such had to kneel in the square and beg forgiveness before the priest and king)
nuit—night
numero—number

O

oates—wild rice
objets de valeur—valuables
obligation—debt, to owe something; an agreement between two or more stating amount of money borrowed and conditions for repayment; a lien to be

satisfied (e.g., It could be owing of pension to feed, house, support or maintain retiring parents.)

occupé, occupée—occupied

octobre—October

octroyé—escrow

oest—male turkey

oeufs—eggs

Officiate—ecclesiastical court

oies—geese

omis—omitted

once—ounce

oncle—uncle

ondoyé/ondoyée (m,f)—baptized privately

onze—eleven

onzième—eleventh

opilation de la pierre—kidney or gall stones; obstruction

orateur sauvage—Indian spokesman

ordonnance/ordonnances (s/p)—law/laws, ordinances

ordonne—ordered

ordre—order; command

l'Ordre de Bon Temps—first social club. It was organized in 1606 by fifteen men. Each took his turn to prepare and serve an elaborate meal.

ordre d'en registrer—order

oreilles—ears

oreillons—mumps

orfèvre—goldsmith; silversmith

orge, l'orge—barley

originaire—native of, originally from

orignal—moose hides (Basque word adopted in Canada at the end of the sixteenth century)

orphelin/orpheline (m/f)—orphan

ou—or

où—where

ouest, l'ouest—west; the west

oui—yes

ours—bears

ouvrier—workman

ouvriers en outils—edge tool makers

ouvriers travaillant la paille—straw worker

P

paiement, payement—payment

pain, le pain—bread

pain bis—brown bread

pain perdu—French toast

paillasse—straw mattress

paires—pair

palais—palace, law court, court house

palette—long handled paddle for sliding loaves of bread in and out of an oven

Panis/Panisse (m/f)—term for an Indian taken as a slave, probably came from the word, Pawnee

des panniers les criades—bum rolls (worn by women under their skirts)

pantalon—trousers

papetiers—paper makers

papiers de noblesse—"Letters Patent of Nobility"; papers which granted a title

par—by, of

paraphe (par)—a mark or symbol which a person used as a signature. (This was often an X.)

par-dessous—under, beneath, underneath

par-dessus—over, above

parent—relative

paroisse—parish

parrain, parrein—godfather; *see introduction to the vocabulary for other spellings*

partage—share; partition

parte de l'équipage—crew member

passeur—ferryman

patates—potatoes

pâtissier—pastry cook

patron de la chaloupe de la flute—skipper on a cargo boat

pâturage—pasture

pâture—pasture; fodder

pauvre—the poor, the needy; pauper; beggar

paveur—paver of streets

payement—see *paiement*

pays—country; land; region

pays d'en haut—term French traders used to designate forest lands of the Northwest above the St.

Lawrence (Detroit was the center); upper country of Canada; interior lands

pays ou provinces du naissance—country or province of birth

peaux de castor—beaver skins

peaux de veaux crues—blown up skins hung on the front of a canoe to protect it from broken ice and winds

pêche—fishing

pêcherie—fishing ground; fishery

pêchers—peach trees

pêches—peaches

pêcheur, pechur—fisherman

péchur, pécheur/pécheresse (m/f)—sinner

peignes—combs

pein, peine—punishment; penalty

pein du carqan—see *carqan*

peintre—painter

pelisse—kind of cape worn by upper-class women

pelissier—person who makes fur garments

pelle—long-handled wooden paddle; shovel

pelle à feu—(the coal shovel) a popular expression for midwife

pelleterie—skins worn as furs

pelletier, pelletière—furrier

pemmican—dried buffalo strips mixed with grease

pénitencier—one who was appointed to hear confessions; see *grand penitencier*

pension—annuity; board and lodging

pensionnaire—pensioner; boarder

pensionnats des jeunes personnes—boarding school for young people, usually students.

pensionnaire perpétuelle—permanent boarder

pensions alimentaires—list of goods or services that children are obligated to provide parents yearly in exchange for receiving land ceded to them by their parents

pépé—grandpa

pépinières—nurseries (garden)

pépiniéristes—nursery men

perche—old French unit of distance, 1 perche equals 18 pieds equals 5.84 meters equals about 6 yards or 18-19 feet

perdu—lost, ruined; wrecked

père—father

père né au pays—father born in Canada

pére originaire—fatherland

perlasse—pearl ash

perron—front entrance stone steps; steps

perruquier—(obs. barber); wig maker; hair dresser

personnes de distinction—people of good breeding

perte, la perte—loss; waste; ruin

peste—plague

petit/petite (m/f)—small, little

petit bêtail—sheep, goats, etc. (smaller animals)

petit corps—a part of the costume of Acadian women, worn tightly over the chemise.

petit écu—see écu

petite chodiere à boire—small drinking dipper

petite école—elementary school

petite-fille—grandchild (granddaughter)

petit fils, petite-fils—grandchild (grandson)

petite vérolle, vérole—smallpox

petite-oies—yards of ribbons used to decorate men's clothing in early New France

pétition—petition; request

petits négociants—dealers and traders

petits pois—green peas

peu—little; not much; few

peut-être, peutre-être—perhaps, maybe

peut-être que non—perhaps not

piastre—Spanish coin accepted in New France

picote, picoté—pox

pièces—In the fur trade, a term applied to each bundle, into which cargo was packed, each weighing about ninety pounds

pièces de bois sur pièces de bois—same as *pièces-sur-pièces*

pièces-sur-pièces—form of wood building construction whereby there was a wall of vertical squared logs and whose corners were flush

pièce tourtière—the contents that went into the tourtière pan. Over the years the cooking dish (tourtière), became synonymous with the contents.

pied—the French foot, equal to about 12.789 English inches

pierre—stone, rock

pierre a calumet—pipestone (used for the bowls of tobacco pipes during the French regime)

pierres d'attente—projecting stones on a building left to help support lateral walls which would be built later

pierre de gré—limestone

pilote—marine pilot

pilote cotier—pilot of a vessel along the coast

pioche, la pioche—pick axe

pinceaux—paint brushes (for house)

pinte—unit of measure, about one U.S quart

pipe—the standard of measurement used by voyageurs on the water, distances covered between rests

pipe—a measure of wine, equal to 126 gallons

pirogue—dug out canoe about forty feet in length, primarily used on the Mississippi. It was adopted by the French from the Indians.

pistole—in the seventeenth century, a gold coin used by the French, Portugese, and Spanish worth about eleven livres; one pistole equals ten livre

place—public square; town; job, situation; place, seat

placet—petition

planche—thin board or plank

plancher—floor

plancher haut—ceiling in a one story building

planches de bois—wood board or plank

planches chevauchées—kind of roofing where boards were overlapped parallel to the eaves

plares—sores

pleurésie—pleurisy

plomb, plonb—lead

plombiers—plumbers

pluie—rain

plus, plus de, de plus—more

plusieurs—several

plus tard—late; later

pluvieux—rainy

pneumonie—pneumonia

les poches—pockets holding a woman's personal belongings, worn under her skirt

poële—long handled pan for making crepes

poêl/poêles (s/p)—stove/stoves; frying pan/pans

poêlier—one who sells or installs stoves

poids—weight

poigne—a unit of dry measure, a handful

poil—hair (of an animal)

poil de chien—of dog hair

poille—stove

poincons—large casks

poire/poires (s/p)—pear/pears

poiriers—pear trees

pois—peas; pulse (green peas, white peas, chick peas, beans)

poisson—fish

poisson doree—pickeral

poisson prépare—prepared fish

poissonnier—fish monger

poissons blanc—white fish

poivre—pepper

pomme—apple

pomme de terre—potato

pommiers—apple trees

pompiers—firemen

pont/ponts (s/p)—bridge/bridges

population de droit—in a census, a person is counted where he is located

population de jure—in a census, a person is counted where he normally resides

port—harbor

portage—the carrying of goods and boats overland in order to continue on some other water system or to bypass natural obstacles such as waterfalls, mountains, etc.

portage collier, collie or tumpline—"portage collar"; a three-inch straps of leather that went over the forehead of a voyageur to carry pieces of goods when on a portage

portant fort—strong and good health

porte—gate; door

portefaix—man who carries loads on his back

porteur des hardes—bearer of old clothing

porteuse—woman who held the child at the christening

portier, portiers (s/p)—door keeper; janitor

posé—stopping places, of varying intervals, on portages

poseurs de sonnettes—bell hangers

possédée—owned

posthume—born after the death of his father

pot—used for measuring wine or other liquids, equal to one tankard or 1/2 U.S. gallon

potage—soup

potasse—potash

pot-au-feu—pot for cooking meat

pot d'etain—pewter tankard

pot-de-vin—bribe; during the French regime, a drink taken to seal an agreement after a contract was made

poteaux-en-tcrre—posts-in-ground style of house (used at outposts)

potier/potière (m/f)—potter

potier d'etain—one who makes and sells pewter products

pouce—a French inch; about 1.06 English inches; 12 pouces equal 1 pied

poudre—gunpowder, powder

poudrerie, la poudrerie—blowing snow

poudrier—powderman

poulain—colt; foal

poule, poulle/poules (s/p)—hen/hens; chicken/chickens

poulet—chicken

poulier—chicken coop

poulle dinde—female turkey

poumons—lungs

pour—on behalf of

pour et contre—pro and con

pour libera—for burial rites

pourquoi—why?

pourvoyeurs de navires—ship chandlers

poutres—beams

pouvant lire et ecrire—can read and write

pouvant lire seulement—can only read

pre—meadow, prairie, grassland

précheur, préchur—preacher

préciput—gave a surviving spouse the right to keep a certain amount prior to the division of the estate

premier, premiére (m/f)—first

prendre feu—to catch fire

prés, prés de, depres—near; almost

présent/presentes (s/p)—witness/witnesses

prêt—loan; pay, already prepaid

prêtre (prtre, ptre)—priest

prêtre (prtre) missionnaire—missionary priest

prêtres seculiers—secular priests

prévôté—royal court in Quebec city; lower court on the Jesuit seigneury

les priant de libérer—pleading, praying, or begging to release

prie-dieu—praying stool, church seat, pew

printemps—spring (the season)

prise—hold, capture

prisé/prisées (s/p)—value; price

prisée et estimeé—estimated price or value

prisée et estimeé à cause de sa vieillece—estimated value because of old age

prisonier, prisonnier—prisoner

privé—private

privee de son cure—without a priest

prix—price, value, cost

prix de gros—wholesale price

prix moyen—average value

procés—trial; hearing; lawsuit

procès-verbal, procès-verbaux—official statement; verbal agreement; a record

prochain—next, neighboring

proche—near

procuration—power of attorney

procurer fiscal—comptroller, inspector general of finance; tax collector

procureur—representative of high courts; solicitor

procureur du roi—king's attorney

procureur-général—attorney general

procuter—attorney general, prosecutor

produit en minots—produce in bushels

produits des champs—field products

professeur—teacher

proffondeur, profondeur—depth (eg. depth of land)

propre/propres (s/p)—personal property; property owned by an individual (e.g. land inherited by either husband or wife)

propriétaire/proprietaires (s/p)—owner/owners

propriétaire de navires—ship owner

propriétaires des terres et emplacements—property owners

propriétés fonciéres—real estate

Provost—court of Quebec set up by the Compagnie des Indes Occidentales in 1666-1667

prûche—a hemlock tree in Quebec; a spruce tree in Acadia

prune—plum

pruniers—plum trees

puchet, pucheux—ladle for maple syrup or soup

puis—after that, besides; later

punition—punishment

pur—pure

putain—slut, whore

Q

quai—wharf

quand—when

quarante—forty

quarantième—fortieth

quartier—district, ward, section

quatorze—fourteen

quatorzième—fourteenth

quatre—four

quatre-vingt—eighty

quatre-vingt-dix—ninety

quatre-vingt-dixième—ninetieth

quatre-vingtième—eightieth

quatrième—fourth

quel/quelle (m/f)—who, what, which

quelque chose—anything, something

quelconque—any

quelque—some; any; however

quel que, quelle que—whoever, whatever

quincaillerie—iron, tin and copper ware

quint—a tax of one-fifth of the sale price of a seigneury (the fifth part of the whole purchase price paid to a seigneur's feudal superior if the seigneur chose to sell his seigneury; However, he was allowed a rabat, which was a reduction of two-thirds, if the money was laid down immediately.)

quintal/quintaux (s/p)—unit of measuring weight equal to 100 kilograms

quinze—fifteen

quinzième—fifteenth

quincaillier—hardware dealer

quittance—discharge from a debt or obligation; a quit claim; remittance

quoi—which, what

R

rabat—a rebate, reduction; see *quint*

racines—field roots

ragouet, ragoût—stew

raisin—grapes

ramoneur—chimney sweep

rapatriés—repatriated; those who were sent back to France

rapporta—reported

rapporteur—reporter; appointed delegate who explained issues to be discussed and recorded votes in the general assembly of New France

raquettes a pres—(prairie shoes) a kind of wooden shoe for horses so they could work in the reclaimed mud of Acadia

rasade—multi colored glass beads used as a trade item in the fur trade

rasoirs—razors

râteau—a farm tool, a rake

rateàux a cheval—horse rakes

ratification—statement made by a second person accepting a decision

rats musqués—muskrat

recensement—census

réception et installation—receiving receipt and inaugurate

récolté, récolte—crops; harvest; harvesting

récoltes des champs—field crops

reconnaissance—recognized

redevances—rental contracts

refroidissement—a cold

régime—regime; form of government

registre—register

registre paroissial—parish register

règlement—regulation

regrattier—huckster; dealer in vegetables, cheese etc.

le regrette—the late or deceased

réhabilité—revalidated

reigle—a mason's rule

reine—queen

reins—kidneys

relieurs—book binders

religieuse—religious person (eg. nun or monk)

remedè—remedy

remise—rebate, remittance; discount; commission; delay

renard—fox

renaud—disc representing 32 points of a compass used by a ship's pilot to note the direction being followed

renchaussage—in French Canada, the process in which soil and straw were packed against the house foundation to protect it from the cold

rendezvous—place of meeting; usually a designated meeting place in the fur trade where voyageurs, partners, Indians, and winterers met to celebrate and exchange goods

rendu—arrived

renonciation—denial

renonciation à un droit—waiver of a right

rente/rentes (s/p)—moneys due; a charge which a seigneur levied for a roture held from him; revenue; unearned income

rente constituée/rentes constituées (s/p)—loan or loans which inhabitants made whereby interest on the loan would be paid annually, but the lender could not demand the principal.

rente-pension—unearned income

rentier/rentiere (m/f)—retired person

renvoyes—those who were returned to France from New France because they were undesirable

répertoire—index; list; catalog (e.g., a list of marriages of a parish)

repondre de—vouch for

reprise—recovery

requérant—requested

requéte—petition; request; appeal

rescripts—letters of exchange

réserve—stock; store

réserve—obligation of a father to leave four-fifths of his personal property to his heirs

residents notables—prominent residents

resiliation d'un bail—cancellation of a lease

rétablissement—restoration

retour—return, exchange

retraite aux malades—hospitals for the sick

retrait seigneurial—the right to expropriate land which had exchanged hands after its sale; the buyer would be reimbursed the full price and costs within 40 days. These occurred in Montreal at the end of the seventeenth century.

retrouvons—we found

réveillon—celebration and special meal prepared after Christmas Eve mass

revesches—rough cloths used as trade items

revocation—repeal; dismissal

rez de chaussée, rez-de-chaussée—ground level

rhingrave—knee breeches worn in New France

rhumatisme—rheumatism

rhum—a kind of drink made from cane-sugar molasses, popular in New France

rhumb de vent—fixed survey line

rive, rivière—river

roi—king

roquille—used for measuring rum, about one-third of a pint

roture—a concession of land which could not be sub-conceded and which was held by a roturier from a seigneur; a concession of land held by a censitaire

roturier—one who held a roture

rouet, rouette—spinning wheel

rouette sans garniture—spinning wheel without the trimmings

rouge—red

rougeole—measles

roulier—wagoner, carrier, in charge of delivering merchandise by wheeled transport

rubans—ribbons

rubéole—measles

ruches d'abeilles—bee hives

rue—street

ruelles or ruettes—lanes or alleys that linked streets

S

sablier—hour-glass

sabotier—maker of wooden shoes

sabots—wooden shoes

sacristain—sexton who cares for the church building, vestments, attends the clergyman, is the bellringer and at times digs graves

sagamité, sagamite—pancake boiled in water; dish of cracked corn porridge eaten with cream and maple sugar; a soup made with corn flour, fish and peas

sage—wise

sage-femme—midwife

saignée—bloodletting

saignement de nez—nosebleeding

saisie—foreclosure, seizure

saison/saisons (s/p)—season/seasons

saleurs de viandes—meat curers; meat packers

salinier—salt vendor

salle à manger—dining room

samedi—Saturday

sans—without

sans moyen—without means

sans quoi—otherwise

sans travail—unemployed

sans valeur—worthless

sapeur-pompier—fireman

sapinette—spruce tree

sarrasin—buckwheat

sarraux, les sarraux—smocks (similar to a shirt but made to slip over other clothes)

saunier—salt maker; salt merchant

sauvage—native, Indian; wild

sauvages allies—Indian allies

savetier—cobbler, shoemaker

savonniers—candle, soap, and tallow makers

savons—soaps

savoyard—chimney sweep

scarlatine—scarlet fever

scie, scier—a saw

scierie—sawmill

scieries; scieurs—sawyers

scieur de long—one who cuts a piece of lumber lengthwise

scieur de planches—sawyer of boards or planks

scorbut—scurvy

secourir—to assist

secours—help, assistance

sculpteur—sculptor, carver

second—second

second maître—petty officer

sécretaire—secretary

sécretaire qui avait la plume—the first secretary who signed the king's name to dispatches

sedilot—chair maker

seigle—rye

seigneur—landlord, nobleman, lord; anyone entitled to an oath of fealty for land held from him; someone who held land directly from a company or the king

seigneurie, seigneury—the land held by a seigneur

seize—sixteen

seizième—sixteenth

sel—salt

sellier—saddler; harness and saddle maker

semaine—week

semaines de travail à gages—weeks of hired labor

senechal—judge of the *sénéchaussée*

senechal du pays—court officer of the region

sénéchaussée—lower court of Montreal jurisdiction

sentence rendue au proces—sentence rendered or given at a trial or hearing

sept—seven

septembre—September

septième—seventh

sépulture—burial

sépulture ecclésiastique—religious burial

serape—a kind of hooking sickle for harvesting peas

sergent—sergeant

sergent royale—official who served writs and made arrests for the royal courts

serge sur fil—kind of fabric made in the colony by MMe. de Repentigny. It was made of the hair of Illinois cattle.

serpe—billhook

serrurier—locksmith

serviteur—servant

serviteur du fort—laborer in the fort

serviteur domestique—serves meals at your table

ses ridaux à couchet tournée—used bed curtains that enclosed the bed

seul—only; alone

seulement—only, even, merely

shagganappie—anything improvised or of inferior quality (Indian word adopted by the French)

shérif—sheriff

si bien que—so that

siècle/siècles (s/p)—century/centuries

signé—signed

signification—legal notice

sipaille—"sea pie"; a one dish meal in which various types of sea food were layered with a thin pastry and cooked for several hours. Sipaille was adopted from the English colonies and was popular in New France along the coastal area. Later on, this dish meant any meats and vegetables layered between pastry. In Wisconsin, it was called cipote and was usually made with venison, rabbit or other wild game.

sirop—syrup

sissobaquet—maple sugar (Indian word adopted by the French)

situé—situated

six, siz—six (six before a consonant; siz before a vowel)

sixième—sixth

société /sociétiés (s/p)—business partnerships or associations of merchants and/or manufacturers set up for their mutual protections and for controlling prices. (See l'ancien sociétiés and l'nouvelle sociétiés); community

société de commerce—business associates

soeur—sister

soie—silk

soir—evening, night

soit—be it so; granted

soixante—sixty

soixante-dix—seventy

soixante-dixième—seventieth

soixante-dix-sept—seventy-seven

soixante-dix-septième—seventy-eventh

soixante-quinze—seventy-five

soixante-quinzième—seventy-fifth

soixantième—sixtieth

solage—in New France, the stone base on which the foundation of a house was laid

soldat—soldier

sole—field alternately planted in different crops

soleil couché—sunset

sols, solz—unit of currency; twenty sols equal one livre

sommation—summons; demand

somme—sum, amount

sonner—to ring

sorcellerie—witchcraft, sorcery

sorcier/sorcière (m/f)—sorcerer, wizard, witch

sorte—type, kind, sort

sorte que—so that

sortie—exit, going out

souche—tree stump

souliers—shoes

souliers de peau—Indian moccasins

souper—supper

soupiraux—vents in a building

sourds—deaf

sous culture—crops under cultivation

sous lieutenant—second lieutenant

sous-louer—sub-let

sou/sous (s/p)—unit of currency, 1 sou equals 12 deniers

sous seing privé—contract or agreement drawn up by an individual rather than a notary (e.g., drawn up by a merchant, priest, etc. with all parties signing)

soussigné—the undersigned

sous-diaconat—sub deacon (this position no longer exists in the church)

sous quelle tenure telle terre est tenure—length of time on the land

sous-soyers—inspectors of roads after the English took control

squadron—in the fur trade, a number of brigades of canoes often totaling thirty to forty canoes

strouds—a kind of cloth fabric used as a trade item

sub-délégue-de-l'intendant—representative of the intendant in civil affairs

subrage—deputy

subrogé—substitute; surrogate

succession—inheritance

sucre—sugar

sucre d'érable—maple sugar

sud—south

sueurs—sweats

suite—the rest; continuation

suivant, suivante—following; according to

suivant que—following, next

supericie—suface area (of land)

supplice—corporal punishment

supplice-du-feu—punishment by fire

supplique—petition

support-chausettes—garters

sur—towards, about, over, in

surtout—a long cape with sleeves and a hood, a hooded wrap

syndic—elected official of the merchants who would speak on their behalf (He had to be elected before the intendant and approved); Originally were municipal officers appointed by the population of the cities to preserve public rights

T

tabac—tobacco

tabellion—men who were public scribes who would prepare legal agreements; they were to register their acts with a notary later.

tabellionage—the collected acts of a tabellion

tableaux communs et de prix—posting of prices of goods

tablier/tabliers (s/p)—apron/aprons

tablier de coton—cotton apron

tablier détamine—muslin apron

tafia—a kind of drink made from cane-sugar molasses imported from the French West Indies. It sold under the name of rhum.

taillandier—tool maker

tailleur—tailor

tailleur d'habits—tailor of clothes

tailleur de pierre—stone cutters

tambour—a closed vestibule

tambourineur—drummer

tambour-major—drum major

tanneur—tanner

tante—aunt (sl)

tapis—carpet; tablecloth

tapisseries—carpets; tapestries

tapissier—tapestry worker; carpet maker; upholsterer

tas—a heap or pile (a means of measuring weight)

tasse—cup; the Sunday collection (a cup was used)

tauraux—breeding bull

taureau, taureaux—buffalo hides, cut up and made into sacks to be filled with pemmican

taux—price, rate

tavernier—inn keeper

teinturier—dyer

témoignage—testimony, usually in writing to prove someone's status

témoignage de liberté au mariage—proof of freedom (to marry)

témoin/temoins (s/p)—witness/witnesses

temps—time

tenanciers—landholders; property managers

tenir feu et lieu—habitant had to occupy and cultivate the land

terrain—piece of land

terrains defriches—cleared land

terrasseur—person who does earth work, terraces, embankments; excavator

terre—land

Terre-Neuve, Terreneuve—Newfoundland

terrier—hole

terriere—earthen pot

testament—a will

testament olographe—written will

testament orale—oral will

tête—head

tête-a-tetê—a private conversation

têtu—stubborn

thé—tea

le tien—yours

tierce—third; third person

tierce—large wooden cask holding about 531 pounds used for shipping rice or peas during the British regime

tierson de lar—container of lard

timbre—bell

timonier—helmsman

tire—wax

tisanes—herb teas

tisserand—weaver

tisserand en toile—weaver of canvas

tisseur—weaver

tissier en toile—one who makes things of canvas

titre—title, heading; claim; voucher; title deed

tixier—spinner of wool

toile—canvas, cloth, linen

toile à coton—calico

toile à matelas—ticking

toile à voile—sailcloth

la toile—linen cloth

toile cirée—oil cloth

toise—unit of measurement equal to 6 feet 4 3/4 inches (about two yards); 6 pieds equals 1 toise

toit—rooftop, roof; house, home

tomba d'un échafaud—a fall from the scaffold

tomberee—load; a cart load (e.g., cart load of sand)

tonneau/tonneaux (s/p)—liquid measure equal to a barrique (barrel); drunkard (colloquial)

tonnelier—cooper; barrelmaker

tonnelier a la brasserie—person who fills beer barrels

tonnes—tons

toraux—breeding bulls

totaux—total

touliches—fillies

touque—see tuque

tour de lit—bed frame curtain

tourneur—turner or latheman

tourte d'entreé—meat pies

tourtière, tourtiere—in the seventeenth and eighteenth centuries, a pie dish used for cooking pigeon and eventually other meats. In time it came to mean the pie itself.

toutefois—yet, however, nonetheless

toux—cough

traine or traineau—a sledge or sleigh about seven feet long with the front end turned up so it could go over bushes and low obstructions; sled

traité—treaty

traiteur—caterer; restauranteur

transaction—arrangement; transaction

transport—transfer

travail—work

travail à gages—hired labor

travaillant—workman, laborer

travailleur—laborer

travail defini—limited forced labor punishment (would also be branded with a "T")

travail perpetual—life of hard labor (would also be branded with a "TP")

les travaux forces—punishment by hard labor

traver monté—crosscut saw

trèfle—clover

treize—thirteen

treizième—thirteenth

trente—thirty

trente-six mois—name given to tradesmen who signed three year contracts

trentième—thirtieth

trésorier—treasurer, paymaster

trésorier des deniers du Roi—Royal Treasurer

triples/triplees (m/f)—triplets

trois—three

troisième—third

trois jumeaux, trois jumelles—(three twins) triplets

troupe—troop

troupes de la marine—marines of the naval department

troupes de terre—regular army

tu—you

tué—killed, killed by

tués—killed

tués par—killed by

tués par la fondre—death by lightening

tuilier—tile maker

tumpline—see portage collier

tuque, touque—stocking cap with a tassle, worn by lower class men and boys of French Canada

tutelaire—guardian

tutelle—guardianship

tutelles et curatelles—guardianship deeds

tuteur/tutrice (m/f)—guardian; trustee

typhoide—typhoid

U

ulcères—ulcers

un, une—one

une belle terre—a fine piece of land

une masse de—a quantity; a lot of

un homme de peine—unskilled laborer

unième—first

union—agreement; marriage

unique—only; single

V

vache—a cow

vache, vachère—cowherd

vaches laitieres—milk cows

vaine pâture—right to pasture animals on the fallow (was regulated by the courts)

vaisseau—vessel, ship

vaisselier—hutch

valet—one who is employed to be at the personal service of a person, valet; man servant

valet de chambre—employed to be at the personal service of a hotel

valet de ferme—farm worker

valeur—worth, value

valeur au compant de la terre en dollars—cash value of farm in dollars

valeur au compant des instruments, aratoires ou machines en dollars—value of farming implements or machinery in dollars

valeur de travail sur les terres—value and labor of farms

valeur d'Iceux—value of same

valeur du travail à gages—value of hired labor

vannier—basket maker

varicelle—chicken pox

variole—smallpox

veau/veaux (s/p)—male calf

le veille—the day before, eve

velte—measurement of about seven quarts of liquid

vendredi—Friday

venndu frais—selling price

vente/ventes— sale of something

vente de droits et pretentions—sale of rights and claims

vente de meubles—sale of personal property

vente d'un emplacement—sale of a place or piece of land

verger—bell ringer; man who cares for orchards

vergers—orchards

verges—measuring standard used for measuring cloth, ribbon or similar items, almost one yard

vérole—pox

verrier—glass maker, glass blower

verrues—warts

vers—about, to, towards

vers—worms

vert—green

veste—vest

veston—top coat

veuf (vf)—widower

veuvage—widowed

veuve (vve)—widow

veux—eyes

viandes—meats

viandes et produits de tous animaux abattus sur la ferme—meats and products of all animals slaughtered on the farm

vicaire apostolique—intermediary between the French king and New France

vielle, vieil—old

le vielle—"Old woman of the wind"; oil cloth used for covering cargo and improvising a sail

vieille fille—old maid, spinster

vieillesse—old age

vieux/vieille, vieil (m/f)—aged, old

vieux garcon—old bachelor

vignobles—vineyards

vigneron/vignerons (s/p)—wine grower

vignes—grape vines

ville—town, city

vin—wine

vin du marché—See pot-de-vin

vinaigrier—vinegar maker

vingt—twenty

vingtième—twentieth

vingt un—twenty one

vingt-et-un—twenty one

vingt et unième—twenty first

vingtaine—about twenty

virez les crepes—tossing of pancakes

vison—mink

vitrier—glassmaker; varnisher; glazier

vivant—living, alive

voici—see here; these are, this is

voilier—sail maker; sailing ship

voiture/voitures (s/p)—vehicle, coach, conveyance, cart

voiture d'été—carriage (for summer)

voiture d'hiver—sleigh

voitures d'agrement—pleasure vehicles

voiturier—carrier, carter, transporter

volailles—fowls, poultry

voleur/voleurs (s/p)—thief/thieves

volontaire—volunteer; those who came to New France to work temporarily

volonté—a will

vos—your

votre—your

le votre—yours

vouloir—want, wants (because he deserves it)

vous—you, to yourself

vous-même (s)—yourself/yourselves

voyageur—manual laborer who carried goods and furs by canoe and on their backs; fur trader, trapper, canoeman

voyer—road surveyor

vrille— a piercer (a kitchen utensil)

vu/vus (m/f)—regarded, seen, observed

W

wattape—spruce roots used to sew pieces of bark together (An Indian word used by the French)

Y

yvrognerie, ivrognerie—drunkenness

Z

Zouave/Zouaves (s/p)—soldiers from French Canada who fought to protect the papacy in 1868-1870

Appendix C

Dates in French

By Patricia Keeney Geyh

French dates appearing in records are usually spelled out completely. Few Arabic numbers appear, although it is not uncommon to see the year written with Arabic numerals just before the first entry in a new year. Reading these dates creates a problem for the non-French-reading researcher. The chart on the opposite page is designed to assist genealogists decipher these dates.

Across the top of the chart can be seen numbers 1,2,3 and 4. Looking beneath #1, one sees the words "one thousand" in English. Beneath "one thousand" are the French words for one thousand: mil or mille. Unless researching records in the 21st century, all the French dates will begin with mil or mille.

Beneath #2 is an empty set of parentheses. Beneath the parentheses are the numbers, in French, for six, seven, eight and nine. One of these numbers will appear in lieu of the parentheses in every record written in the 1600's, 1700's, 1800's or 1900's.

Under #3 is the English word "hundred". Beneath that English word are the words cen, or cent which are the French words for hundred.

If a date of mil sept cen appears in a record, one can look under column #1 and see that mil means one thousand; under column #2 it can be seen that sept means seven, under column #3 cen means hundred. Therefore mil sept cen means one thousand seven hundred or 1700.

To the far right in this chart is #4. Beneath #4 is an empty set of parentheses. Beneath the parentheses are the numbers, in French, from one through ninety-nine. One of these numbers will appear, in lieu of the parentheses,

Notice the examples given in the box to the left. If mil sept cent dix-neuf is the date given in the record, the researcher knows that mil means one thousand; looking under #2 one learns that sept means seven; # 3 shows that cent means hundred; #4 shows that dix-neuf means nineteen. Therefore mil sept cent dix-neuf means one thousand seven hundred nineteen or 1719.

Look at the date given in the second example, mil huit cent trois Under #1 it can be seen that mil means one thousand; under #2 one can see that huit means eight,; #3 shows that cen is hundred and #4 shows us that the French for three is trois. Therefore mil huit cent trois is translated into one thousand eight hundred three or 1803.

In the box beneath the examples are the French words for the months of the year and the days of the week.

(1)	(2)	(3)	(4)
One thousand	**( )**	**hundred**	**( )**
mil or mille	6-six 7-sept 8-huit 9-neuf	cent or cen	

1-un	**40- quarante**
2-deux	41-quarante et un
3-trois	42-quarante-deux
4-quatre	43-quarante-trois
5-cinq	etc.
6-six	**50-cinquante**
7-sept	51-cinquante et un
8-huit	52-cinquante-deux
9-neuf	53-cinquante-trois
10-dix	etc.
11-onze	**60-soixante**
12-douze	61-soixante et un
13-treize	62-soixante-deux
14-quatorze	63-soixante-trois
15-quinze	etc
16-seize	**70-soixante-dix**
17-dix-sept	71-soixante-et onze
18-dix-huit	72-soixante-douze
19-dix neuf	73-soixante-treize
20-vingt	etc.
21-vingt et un	**80-quatre-vingt**
22-vingt-deux	81-quatre-vingt-un
23-vingt-trois	82-quatre-vingt-deux
etc	83-quatre-vingt-trois
30-trente	etc.
31-trente et un	**90-quatre-vingt-dix**
32-trente-deux	91-quatre-vingt-onze
33-trente-trois	92-quatre-vingt-douze
etc.	93-quatre-vingt-treize
	etc.

Examples:
1719=mil **sept** cent **dix-neuf**
1803=mil **huit** cent **trois**
1773=mil sept cent soixante-trieize
1957=mil **neuf** cent **cinquante-sept**

Months of the Year
January—janvier
February—février
March—mars
April—avril
May—mai
June—juin
July—juillet
August—août
September—septembre
October—octobre
November—novembre
December—décembre

Days of the Week
Sunday—dimanche
Monday—lundi
Tuesday—mardi
Wednesday—mercredi
Thursday—jeudi
Friday—vendredi
Saturday—samedi

Variations sometimes found when reading dates in French

• The superscript ^{e} acts as the th in English. Example: French: le 4e jour de avril; English: the 4th day of April

• The superscript ^{me} also acts as the th in English.

• Sometimes the words *premier* (first) or *dernier*(last) are used in the place of numbers. Example: French: *le premier septembre* ; English: the first of September

• Ordinal numbers are created by adding *ième* to a cardinal number. Sometimes the last letter of the cardinal number is eliminated. For example: *quatre* (four) becomes *quatrième* (fourth). At times a letter is added: For example *cinq* (five) becomes *cinquième* (fifth). Further examples:

first	unième
second	deuxième
third	troisième
fourth	quatrième
fifth	cinquième
twenty-fifth	vingt-cinquième
thirty-third	trente-troisième
seventy-second	soixante-douzième
ninety-first	quatre vingt-onzième

• Numbers over 20 are usually written in one of three ways.

As two words, with no connection i.e. *trente deux* (32)
Separated by the word "*et*" i.e. *trente et deux*
Separated by a hyphen i.e. *trente-deux*

• Abbreviations are sometimes used for the names of the months:

September	7bre
October	8bre
November	9bre
December	10bre
December	x^{bre}

• Other vocabulary relating to time appears in French Canadian records.

morning (the)	le matin
noon	midi
afternoon	après midi
evening(the)	le soir
night(the)	la nuit
midnight	minuit
hour (the)	l'heure
day(the)	le jour
today	aujourd'hui or aujourd 'huy
yesterday	hier
day before yesterday	avant hier
the previous day	le veille
two days before	après veille
the previous evening	la veille au soir
month	mois
year (the)	l'an, l'annèe

These are the standard French numbers. When reading ancient French Canadian records, one may find variations in the spelling that have not been noted here.

Appendix D

Charts of Canadian Census Records and Census Substitutes

By Patricia Keeney Geyh and Joyce Soltis Banachowski

The following chart shows many of the census records available for the provinces of New Brunswick, Newfoundland, Nova Scotia, Ontario, Prince Edward Island, and Quebec. In early history, parts of Nova Scotia and New Brunswick, including Cape Breton, were known as Acadia, and censuses listed for Acadia are noted separately. Census records for Upper Canada and Canada West are listed under Ontario. Records for Lower Canada and Canada East are listed under Quebec.

Some of the Ontario census records are listed on this chart as, "Ontario, Incomplete." This generally means that the census records for only a few towns or townships were located.

"Head of H." means head of household. In this kind of a census only the head of household is named, but other facts about those living in the household may be given. "Nominal" means that this census names every member of the household and possibly other facts.

At times a census is taken in only one village in a province. In this case, the specific community is listed. An example is the 1671 censuses noted on this chart. It indicates that one nominal census was taken in all of Acadia. It also indicates that a nominal census was taken in Newfoundland, but only in the village of Plaisance.

St. Pierre and Miquelon are island possessions of France. Because of their proximity to Canada, they are listed under "Prince Edward Island."

Cape Breton and Ile Royale are the same place and are used interchangeably depending on what they are named on the census/census substitute itself.

For further details about the contents of any census listed below, refer to Appendix D, *Census/Census Substitutes Descriptions*, which follows the chart. These descriptions are in chronological order.

258

Year	Acadia	New Brunswick	Newfound-land	Nova Scotia	Ontario	Prince Edward Island	Quebec
1659							Head of H., Fief LeChesnay
1666							Nominal
1667							Nominal
1671	Nominal		Nominal, Plaisance				
1673			Nominal, Plaisance				Head of H., Montreal
1675			Head of H.				
1677			Head of H.				Head of H., Seigneuries of Portneuf & Becancour
1678							Head of H., Seigneury of Silary
1678/9	Head of H. & Spouse, Port Royal						
1681							Nominal
1686	Nominal						
1691			Nominal, French Settlement				
1693	Nominal, French Settlement		1) Nominal, St. Pierre, Plaisance & Cotullonne 2) Nominal, all of Newfoundland				

Year	Acadia	New Brunswick	Newfound-land	Nova Scotia	Ontario	Prince Edward Island	Quebec
1694			Nominal				
1695	Head of H., Riviere St. Jean						
1698	Nominal		Head of H. & Spouse, Plaisance				
1699/00							Nominal, Mt. Louis, Gaspe
1700	Nominal						
1701	Nominal		Head of H., Seamen Only, Plaisance				
1703	Head of H.						
1704			1) Head of H. French Settle-Ment only. 2) Head of H. of those who wintered over in 1704				
1706			1) Head of H., Plaisance 2) Head of H. Petite Plaisance, Pointe Verte				
1707	Head of H.						
1708	Nominal						
1710			Head of H. Plaisance				

Year	Acadia	New Brunswick	Newfound-land	Nova Scotia	Ontario	Prince Edward Island	Quebec
1711			1) Head of H., Plaisance 2) Head of H., Plaisance, Pte. Verte, Petit Plaisance			Head of H.	
1713-1726	Head of H. Cape Breton					Head of H.	
1714	1) Head of H., Isle Royale & Antigonish 2) Head of H.						
1715	1) Head of H., Louisbourg 2) List Les Mines						
1716	Head of H., Louisbourg						Nominal, Quebec City
1717	1) Head of H., Louisbourg and Ile de Scataris 2) List Port Toulouse and Port Dauphine 3) Head of H. Ile Royale						
1718	1) List Port Toulouse & Port Dauphine 2) Head of H.. Indians of Isle Royal & Antigonish						
1719	Head of H., Port Dauphine					Head of H., Indians, La Havre	
1720	Head of H., Isle Royale					Head of H., Indians at La Havre	
1722	Head of H., Port Toulouse						
1723							Head of H., Fief Varennes & du Tremblay

Year	Acadia	New Brunswick	Newfound-land	Nova Scotia	Ontario	Prince Edward Island	Quebec
1724	Head of H., Isle Royale						Head of H., Fief Vincelotte
1725							Head of H., L'Isle, Compte St. Laurent, L'Ille de Orleans
1726	Head of H., Isle Royale						
1728						1) Head of H.; 2) Head of H. for different ports 3) Head of H. for Indians at LaHavre	
1730	Head of H.; Cape Breton					Head of H.	
1731							1) Head of H., Montreal 2) Head of H., Seigneury de St. Sulpice
1732	Head of H.						
1734	Head of H. Ile Royale					1) Head of H. 2) Head of H.	
1735	Head of H., Isle Royal					Head of H.	
1739	1) Head of H. 2) Head of H. Riveire St Jean (incomplete)	Head of H.					
1741	List of Landholders around Louisbourg					Head of H.	Head of H., Montreal
1744							Nominal, Quebec City
1745-1748	Head of H.						
1749	Nominal Ile Royale					Nominal	

Year	Acadia	New Brunswick	Newfound-land	Nova Scotia	Ontario	Prince Edward Island	Quebec
1749-50	1) Head of H.Cape Breton 2) Nominal Cape Breton						
1750	Nominal Ile Royal					Nominal	
1752	1) Nominal, Cape Breton 2) Head of H.	List of Principal Settlers				Nominal	
1753	Head of H. Isle Royale					Head of H.	
1760-2							Head of H., Trois Rivières
1761	List of Inhabitants	List of Inhabitants					
1762	Head of H., Isle Royale						Head of H.
1764							1) List of Protestant Housekeepers in Montreal 2) List of Protestant house-keepers in Quebec City
1765							1) Head of H., Baye des Chaleurs, Bonaventure, Gaspe 2) Head of H. Montreal & Trois Rivières 3) Head of H. Protestants in Montreal
1767						Nominal, Iles St. Pierre & Miquelon	
1769-1772							Head of H., Quebec City
1770		Head of H.					
1770-1771				Head of H. (incomplete)			

Year	Acadia	New Brunswick	Newfound-land	Nova Scotia	Ontario	Prince Edward Island	Quebec
1773				Head of H., Township of Yarmouth			
1774							Head of H. and spouse, Bonaventure
1775				Head of H., Conway			
1776						Nominal, St. Pierre & Miquelon	
1777							1) Head of H. and spouse, Bonaventure & Pespebiac, Gaspe 2) Head of H. and spouse, Perce, Bonaventure Island 3) Head of H. and spouse, Carleton, Gaspe 4) Head of H. Mal Bay & Bonventure Isle, 5) Head of H. and spouse, Gaspe & du Cap
1781							Head of H. Seigneury of St. Sulpice
1784						Nominal Miquelon Isle	
1787				Head of H. Queens Co.			Head of H., Seigneury of La Prairie de la Madeleine
1788					List. Charlottenberg Upper Canada		
1791-1795		Poll Tax		1) Poll Tax 2) Head of H			
1792							Head of H.
1795							Head of H.

Year	Acadia	New Brunswick	Newfound-land	Nova Scotia	Ontario	Prince Edward Island	Quebec
1796			Head of H. St. John's City		Head of H.. Augusta Twp., Granville		
1797					Head of H., Incomplete		
1798						Head of H.	Head of H.
1799					Head of H., Incomplete		
1800					Head of H. Incomplete		
1800-1801			Head of H. Trinity Bay				
1801					Head of H. Incomplete		
1802					Head of H. Incomplete		
1804					Head of H. Incomplete		
1805					Head of H., York Incomplete		Head of H.
1806					Head of H., Incomplete		
1807					Head of H., York Incomplete		
1808					Head of H. Incomplete		
1810					Head of H. Incomplete		

Year	Acadia	New Brunswick	Newfound-land	Nova Scotia	Ontario	Prince Edward Island	Quebec
1811				1) Head of H Incomplete; 2) Head of H., Cape Breton			List of Jurors in Montreal
1812					Head of H. Incomplete		
1813					Head of H. Incomplete		List of Jurors in Montreal
1814					Head of H., Incomplete		
1816					Head of H., Incomplete		List of Jurors in Montreal
1817				1) Head of H., Incomplete; 2) Head of H., Cape Breton	Head of H. Incomplete		
1818				Head of H., Cape Breton	Head of H., Incomplete		nominal, Quebec City
1819					Head of H., Incomplete		
1822					Head of H., Incomplete		
1823					Head of H. Incomplete		
1824/25					Head of H. Incomplete		
1825							Head of H.
1827				Head of H., Upper dist. Of Sydney Twp. Arisaig, Dorchester, St. Andrews & Traccadie			
1828					Head of H., Niagara Dist.		

Year	Acadia	New Brunswick	Newfound-land	Nova Scotia	Ontario	Prince Edward Island	Quebec
1831							Head of H.
1831-1835, 1833-1834, 1832-1835, 1833-1835							Lists of Jurors Montreal
1838				Head of H., Incomplete			
1841						Head of H.	
1842					Head of H.		Head of H.
1848					Head of H. Incomplete	Head of H.	
1850					Head of H.		
1851				Head of H., Incomplete			
1851/52		Nominal			Nominal		Nominal
1861		Nominal		Head of H.	Nominal	Head of H.	Nominal
1870				List, Ste Bridget of Transfiguration, Parrsboro			
1871		Nominal		Nominal	Nominal		Nominal
1881		Nominal		Nominal	Nominal	Nominal	Nominal

French-Canadian Sources: A Guide for Genealogists

Year	Acadia	New Brunswick	Newfound-land	Nova Scotia	Ontario	Prince Edward Island	Quebec
1885-1886							Nominal
1890							Nominal
1891		Nominal		Nominal	Nominal	Nominal	Nominal
1901		Nominal		Nominal	Nominal	Nominal	Nominal

Descriptions of Census and Census Substitutes

By Joyce Soltis Banachowski

The census records itemized in the preceding chart are discussed in more detail below. Note that they are listed in chronological order as is the chart. At the end of each description is a number in brackets. This refers to Appendix F, a list of primary and secondary sources where the census may be found.

1659 Census for *arriere-fief* Le Chesnay, Québec. Fief Census. *HEAD OF HOUSEHOLD*. Name of head of household; description of buildings; terms of rent. [7]

1666 Census for New France (Quebec). *NOMINAL*. Names head of household; names everyone in the household, their ages and occupations; maiden names of all women. Individual families found listed under the name of the community in which they live. (This is the first official census taken. Talon was responsible for it, and he also did a great deal of the data collecting himself.) [5,7,23,26,32,33,35]

1667 Census for New France (Quebec). *NOMINAL*. Names everyone in the household; their ages and occupations; Maiden names of all women; the number of horned animals, sheep, hogs; number of *arpents* of land held and the number of guns in the household. [5,26,33]

1671 Census for Acadia. *NOMINAL*. Name of head of household and all its members; their ages; number of *arpents* of land; number of cattle, sheep, goats and hogs. (This first French census of Acadia was done by Laurent Molin, a Grey Friar. In the enumeration, the first twenty-two families include the names of girls and boys. In the remainder, the names of boys are given but not the names of girls.) [2,3,4,14,18,27,33,34]

1671 Census for Plaisance (Newfoundland). *NOMINAL.* Names of *habitants*; some occupations; women married (named) and to whom they are married (named); names of daughters ready for marriage; names of children aged four to eight; names of boys and girls from birth to three years. [2,19]

1673 Census for Plaisance (Newfoundland). *NOMINAL.* Names of habitants; their ages; girls unmarried; women married and to whom; boys of the age of ten and lower; boys in the service of inhabitants, their ages, place of origin and for whom they work. [2,19]

1673 Roll of *habitants* de I'le of Montreal, Quebec. *HEAD OF HOUSEHOLD.* Only Names of head of household and assessment for each. [7]

1675 Census for Newfoundland. *HEAD OF HOUSEHOLD.* [3]

1677 Census for Newfoundland. *HEAD OF HOUSEHOLD.* [3]

1677 Census for the Fief and Seigneury of Portneuf and Seigneury of Becancour, Québec. Seigneurial Census. *HEAD OF HOUSEHOLD.* Name of head of household; description of land; amount of *rentes and cens* and other conditions; buildings [2,23]

1678 Census for Seigneury of Sillery, Quebec. Seigneurial Census. *HEAD OF HOUSEHOLD.* Name of head of household; description of land; amount of *rentes and cens* and other conditions; buildings. [23]

1678-1679 Census for Port Royal, Acadia. *HEAD OF HOUSEHOLD AND SPOUSE.* Name of head of household and his spouse; number of boys and their ages; number of girls and their ages; number of acres of land; number of cattle; number of firearms. [11,19]

1681 Census for New France (Quebec). *NOMINAL.* Names of all members of household; (maiden names of all women) ages and occupations of all members; number of horned animals, sheep, hogs; number of *arpents* of land held; number of guns in the household. [5,24,26,33]

1686 Census for Acadia. *NOMINAL*. Names of all members of household; ages of all members of household; number of *arpents* of land; number of guns; number of cattle, sheep, and hogs. [2,3,4,7,10,18,33,34]

1691 Census for Terre Neuve (Newfoundland) French settlement only. *NOMINAL*. Name of head of household; name of spouse; names of male children; names of daughters; number of guns; and residences of all persons. [2,3,19]

1693 Census for Acadia French settlement only. *NOMINAL*. Names and ages of all members of the household; number of *arpents* of land; number of guns; number of cattle, sheep, and hogs. [2,3,4,34]

1693 Census for Terreneuve (Newfoundland). *NOMINAL*. Names, ages, and residences of all persons. [2,3]

1693 Census for Terreneuve (Newfoundland) and St, Pierre, le Grand Plaisance and la premiere Colullonne. *NOMINAL*. Names of all in the household and number of domestics and places of residence. [2,19]

1694 Census for Terre Neuve (Newfoundland). *NOMINAL*. Names of men, women, children and domestics, and places of residence. [2,19]

1695 Census of Riviere St. Jean, Acadia. *HEAD OF HOUSEHOLD*. Name of head of household; whether there is a wife; number of children; number and kind of buildings; number of *arpents* in use, cultivated or prairie; number of cattle, hogs, and chickens; in 1694 harvest, number of *minots* of wheat, peas, corn, and oats; number of guns. [2,3,34]

1698 Census for Acadia. *NOMINAL*. Names and ages of all members of household; number of cattle, sheep, and hogs; number of *arpents* of land; number of fruit trees; number of guns. [2,3,4,34]

1698 Census for Plaisance (Newfoundland). *HEAD OF HOUSEHOLD AND SPOUSE*. Name of head of family; place of origin; age; name of spouse; number of years married; number of sons and daughters; number and description of boats; if they have a house and/ or garden; organized by district of town. [2,19]

1699-1700 Census of Mont Louis, Gaspe, Québec. *NOMINAL*. Name of head of household and his occupation, names of his wife and children. [2,26]

1700 Census for Acadia. *NOMINAL*. Names and ages of head of household and all its members; number of cattle, sheep, and hogs; number of *arpents* of land; number of firearms. [2,3,34]

1701 Census for Acadia. *NOMINAL*. Names and ages of all members of household; number of cattle, sheep, and hogs; number of *arpents* of land; number of firearms. [2,3,34]

1701 Census for Plaisance (Newfoundland). (Census of seamen, fishermen, the inhabitants hired for the year 1701). *HEAD OF HOUSEHOLD*. Name of habitant; name of fishermen who habitants kept for the winter; name of fishermen who returned to France; number of boats. [19]

1703 Census for Acadia. *HEAD OF HOUSEHOLD*. Name of head of household; whether there is a wife; number of boys; number of girls; number of household members capable of bearing arms. [2,3,34]

1704 Census for Terre Neuve (Newfoundland)French settlements only. *HEAD OF HOUSE-HOLD*. Name; whether he has a wife; number of daughters; number of sons; number of fishermen; number of men who came from France. [2,3]

1704 Census for Terre Neuve (Newfoundland). *HEAD OF HOUSEHOLD* (census of habitants and fishermen who wintered in Terre Neuve in 1704). Name of habitants; number of women; number of daughters; number of sons; number of fishermen; number of ship's boys; number of men who came from France; number of ships, and place of residence. [19]

1706 Census for Plaisance, Petite Plaisance, and Pointe Verte (Newfoundland). *HEAD OF HOUSEHOLD*. Name of habitant; whether he has a wife; number of boys over 12; number of boys under 12; number of daughters over 12; number of daughters under 12; number of fishermen; number of boy fishermen. [2,19]

1706 Census for Plaisance (Newfoundland). *HEAD OF HOUSEHOLD*. (Census of fishermen in the service of officers) Name; if he has a wife; number of sons; number of daughters; number of fishermen; number of ship's boys; number of men returned to France; number of small boats. [2]

1707 Census for Acadia. *HEAD OF HOUSEHOLD*. Name of head of household; name of his wife; number of boys younger than 14; number of boys 14 or older; number of girls younger than 12; number of girls 12 and older; number of *arpents* of land; number of cattle, sheep and hogs. At Port Royal, the number of firearms is also given. [2,3,34]

1708 Census for Acadia. *NOMINAL*. Names, sex, and usually ages of family members; residence. [4 (Ayer Library, Chicago)]

1710 Census for Plaisance (Newfoundland). *HEAD OF HOUSEHOLD*. Name of habitants; number of wives; number of children; number of fishermen; number of domestics; number of winterers. [2]

1711 Census for Plaisance (Newfoundland). *HEAD OF HOUSEHOLD*. Names of habitants and number of fishermen or hunters they kept for the winter. [2,19]

1711 Census for Plaisance, Pointe Verte, Petit Plaisance, and Isles St. Pierre (Newfoundland). *HEAD OF HOUSEHOLD*. Names of habitants; whether he has a wife; number of boys; number of daughters. [19]

1713-1726 Censuses for Ile St. Jean (Prince Edward Island) and Ile Royale (Cape Breton Island). *ANNUAL HEAD OF HOUSEHOLD*. Names and residences of head of household. [2]

1714 Census for Acadia. *HEAD OF HOUSEHOLD*. Name of head of household. Whether there is a wife; number of males and number of females. [2,3,4,18,34]

1714 Census for Isle Royale and Artigouech (Antigonish). *HEAD OF HOUSEHOLD*. Name of head of household; number or arms; number of wife and children. [2]

1715 Census of Louisbourg. *HEAD OF HOUSEHOLD*. Names; occupations; if there is a wife; number of boys; number of girls; others in the household. (Not organized in columns, but written in prose form.) [2]

1715 List of habitants of Les Mines. *HEAD OF HOUSEHOLD*. Name of head; if there is a wife; number of males and females. [2]

1716 Census for Quebec City, Quebec. *NOMINAL*. Names, ages and occupations of each member of household; street where they live. Includes a name index. [1,3,6,9,26, also in Ecclesiastical Archives, Quebec City]

1716 Census for Louisbourg. *HEAD OF HOUSEHOLD*. Name of head; location; if there is a wife; number of boys; number of girls; number of *compagnons* (number of fishermen and *garcons* who wintered). [2]

Liste de Ceux qui sont hors d'état de
payer pour les ramonages et de ceux qui sont
parti sans payer depuis le mois de p[...]68
Jusqu'à la fin d'octobre 1769

Rue Champlain

Veuve Castagnil Pauvre		6
Simon hot Charpentier d°		6
Claude hot d°		6..6
f. Amiot Journalier d°		6
Jn Cardy d° d°		6
François Dallee d° d°		6
f. Griffart Journalier d°		6
Lavictoire d°		3
Jn Duca Journalier d° Blanchisseuse		6
Ve Jacques d'alleran		6
~~[struck out]~~ d°		6
~~[struck out]~~ d°		1..6
Pierre Dupuis Journalier d°		3
x François Bertrand parti d°		6
x Js Millot Ve		6
x Js Maranda Lave d°		6
x M Duchesne Lave d°		6
Etienne Marchand Lave		6
René Babineau Cordonier t		6
Ve Tourangeau		6
Lave Doucet		6
Ch. Cameron Anglais Pauvre Journalier		4..6
Ch. Tyinga Galfa		6
Js Le Boeuf Journalier		6
Ve Lanoix		6
Jve Miguel fils		6

Part of a census substitute: A list of poor whose chimneys have been swept from 8 November 1768 to 31 October 1769 as recorded by Franks, overseer of the chimneys. National Archives of Canada, Ottawa. Microfilm No. H-1758.

1717 Census for Louisbourg and L'Isle De Scataris. *HEAD OF HOUSEHOLD.* Name of habitant; if there is a wife; number of boys; number of girls; number of domestics or *equipage* (personnel or crew) who wintered. [2]

1717 List for Port Toulouse and Port Dauphine, Cape Breton. Principal Settlers and Heads of Family. *HEAD OF HOUSEHOLD.* Names of head; occupation; if there is a wife; number of boys; number of girls. (Port Dauphine Census also includes number of domestics). [2,4]

1717 Census for Isle Royale. *HEAD OF HOUSEHOLD.* Name of habitant; number of women; number of boys; number of girls. [2]

1718 List for Port Toulouse and Port Dauphine, Cape Breton. Principal Settlers and Heads of Family. [4]

1718 List of Indians of Isle Royale and Artigouche (Antigonish). *HEAD OF HOUSEHOLD.* Name, number of men with guns; total number; number of women and children. [2]

1719 List for Port Dauphin, Cape Breton only. Principal Settlers and Heads of Family. *HEAD OF HOUSEHOLD.* Name of head; occupation; total number in household. [2,4]

1719 Census of Indians at La Havre. *HEAD OF HOUSEHOLD.* Name; year of establishment; number of houses; number of women; number of older boys; number of younger boys; number of younger girls; number of older girls; number of valets; number in the family; number of *bateaux* or *goélettes*; number of *chaloupes.* [2]

1720 Census of Indians at la Havre. *HEAD OF HOUSEHOLD.* Name; year of establishment; number of houses; number of women; number of older boys; number of younger boys; number of younger girls; number of older girls; number of *valets*; number in the family; number of *bateaux* or *goélettes*; number of *chaloupes.* [2]

1720 Census for Isle Royale. *HEAD OF HOUSEHOLD.* Surnames of inhabitants; number of *chaloupes*; number of women; number of children; number of domestics. [2]

1722 Census for Port Toulouse, Cape Breton only. *HEAD OF HOUSEHOLD.* Name of head; number of persons in household. [2,4]

1723 Census for Fief Varennes and du Tremblay, Québec. Seigneurial Census. *HEAD OF HOUSEHOLD.* Name of head of household; amount of *rente and cens* and other conditions; buildings. [23]

1724 Census for Fief Vincelotte, Québec. Seigneurial Census. *HEAD OF HOUSEHOLD*. Name of head of household; amount of *rente and cens* and other conditions; buildings. [2,23]

1724 Census for Isle Royale. *HEAD OF HOUSEHOLD*. Location; name of habitant; place of birth; quality (habitant, fisherman, etc); number of women; number of boys under and over 15; number of daughters; number of servants; number of *engages*; number of fishermen; total number of persons; number of *chaloupes*; number of *bateaux* or *goélettes*. [2]

1725 Census for L'isle and Comte St. Laurent a L'Ile de Orleans, Québec. Seigneurial Census. *HEAD OF HOUSEHOLD*. Names of head of family; description of land; amount of *rente and cens* and other conditions; buildings. [23]

1726 Census for Isle Royale. *HEAD OF HOUSEHOLD*. Location; name of habitant; place of birth; quality; wife and if in France so noted; number of boys under and over 15; number of daughters; number of domestics and servants; number of seamen and fishermen; total number; number of *chaloupes, bateaus* and *goélettes* for fish; number of *bateaus* and *goélettes* for commerce. [2]

1728 Census of Indians at La Havre. *HEAD OF HOUSEHOLD*. Name; year of establishment; number of houses; number of women; number of older boys; number of younger boys; number of younger girls; number of older girls; number of *valets*; number in the family; number of *bateaux* or *goélettes*; number of *chaloupes*. [2]

1728 Census of those established at different ports and La Havre of Isle St. Jean. *HEAD OF HOUSEHOLD*. Name; year of establishment; number of houses; number of women; number of younger boys; number of older boys; number of younger girls; number of older girls; number of *valets*; number in the family; number of *bateaux* or *goélettes*; number of *chaloupes*. [2]

1728 Census for Isle St. Jean. *HEAD OF HOUSEHOLD*. Location; name of habitants; place of birth; conditions; number of men; number of women; number of boys and girls; number of *domiciles* or *engages*; number of seamen or fishermen; total number of persons; number of *chaloups, goélettes,* and *bateaux*. [2]

1730 Census for Ile St Jean (Prince Edward Island) and Ile Royale (Cape Breton). *HEAD OF HOUSEHOLD*. Names and residences of head of household; number of men, women, children and domestics; number of *bateaux, goélettes* and *chaloupes*. [2,3]

1731 Census for Ile de Montréal, Québec. Seigneurial Census. *HEAD OF HOUSEHOLD.* Name of head of household; description of land; amount of *rentes and cens*; buildings. [3,23]

1731 Census for Fief and Seigneury of St. Sulpice, Québec. Seigneurial Census. *HEAD OF HOUSEHOLD.* Name of head of household; description of land; amount of *rentes and cens*; buildings. [3,23]

1732 Census for Acadia. *HEAD OF HOUSEHOLD.* Name of head of household; whether he has a wife; number of children. [2,34]

1734 Census for Isle Royale (Cape Breton). *HEAD OF HOUSEHOLD.* Location; Name of habitant; place of birth; occupation; wife (if in France, so noted); number of sons under 15; number of sons over 15; number of daughters; number of servants and domestics; number of seamen and fishermen in the service of habitant; number of persons; number of *chaloupes* of habitant in fishing; number of *bateau* and *goélettes* of habitant in fishing; number of ships and vessels to destination for commerce and coasting trade. [2,3]

1734 Census for Isle St. Jean (Prince Edward Island). *HEAD OF HOUSEHOLD.* Name of head of household; age; if there is a wife; her age; number of boys; their ages; number of girls; their ages; number of personnel or crew; number of *chaloupes*; number of beef; number of cows; number of heifers; number of *thoreaux*; number of sheep; number of *igneaux*. [2,3]

1734 Census of Isle St. Jean (month of 7bre 'September'). *HEAD OF HOUSEHOLD.* Location; name of habitant; place of birth; occupation; if there is a wife; number of sons over 15; number of sons under 15; number of daughters; number of servants and domestics; number of seamen and fishermen; number of persons; number of beef and cows; number of sheep, number of fishing boats; number of *bateaux* and *goélettes*; number of vessels for commercial use and coasting trade. [2]

1735 Census for Ile Royale (Cape Breton) and Ile St. Jean (Prince Edward Island). *HEAD OF HOUSEHOLD.* [2,3]

1735 Census for Isle St. Jean (Prince Edward Island). *HEAD OF HOUSEHOLD.* Place; name of habitant; place of birth; occupation; if he has a wife; number of sons under 15; number of sons over 15; number of daughters; number of servants and other domestics; number of seamen and fishermen; total number; number of *grand betail* (oxen etc.); number of *petite betail* (sheep, goats etc.); number of fishing boats, *bateaux* and *goélettes* for fishing; number of vessels for commerce; number of bushels of grain in 1735. [2]

1739 Census for Acadia. *HEAD OF HOUSEHOLD.* [2,3]

1739 Census for Riviere St. Jean, Acadia, (not complete). *HEAD OF HOUSEHOLD.* Names head of household; if he is married; and number of children. [2]

1739 Census for New Brunswick. *HEAD OF HOUSEHOLD.* [3]

1741 Census for Ile St. Jean (Prince Edward Island) and Ile Royale (Cape Breton). *HEAD OF HOUSEHOLD.* [2]

1741 Census for Montreal, Quebec. *HEAD OF HOUSEHOLD.* This census was taken by order of the governor general, Charles de Beauharnois, and the intendant, Giles Hocquart. It was taken by La Compagnie des Indes. It was to be taken at Quebec, Trois Rivières, and Montreal. It names the proprietor of the house; the name of the occupant, the person there when they were visited; and the mark or signature of those who could sign. (It appears Montreal's is the only one in existence.) [21, Archives of the Palais de Justice of Montreal]

1741 List of Landholders around Louisbourg, Cape Breton. [2,3]

1744 Census for Quebec City, Quebec. *NOMINAL.* Names, ages, and occupations of all members of household; street where they live. [1,23,26]

1745-1748 List of families who were at Isle Royale (Cape Breton) from 1745- September 1748. *HEAD OF HOUSEHOLD.* Occupations; name of head of household; total number of wife and children; location. [2]

1749 Census for Ile St-Jean (Prince Edward Island) and Ile Royale (Cape Breton Island). *NOMINAL.* Names and ages of family members; relationships; birth place of adults. [2,4]

1749-1750 Census for Cape Breton. *HEAD OF HOUSEHOLD.* [4]

1749-1750 Census for Isle Royale (Cape Breton) (Officers and *Habitants*). *NOMINAL.* Dates when there; names of all household members; occupations; relationships. [2]

1750 Census for Ile St. Jean (Prince Edward Island) and Ile Royale (Cape Breton Island). *NOMINAL.* Names and ages of family members; relationships; birth place of adults. [2,4]

1752 Census for Acadia. *HEAD OF HOUSEHOLD.* Name of head of household; whether there is a wife; number of boys; number of girls. [34]

1752 Census of Isle Royale (Cape Breton Island). *NOMINAL.* Names and ages of all members of household; occupations; place of origin; number of boats, *bateaux*, schooners or skiffs; number of livestock (cows, oxen, heifers, horses, chickens, ducks, fowl, pigs, horses); some description of homesteads; whether settler, bachelor, hired fisherman, or thirty-six month man. [5,27,29]

1752 Census for Prince Edward Island. *NOMINAL.* [3]

1752 List of principal settlers of New Brunswick. [3]

1753 Census for Ile St. Jean (Prince Edward Island) and Ile Royale (Cape Breton). *HEAD OF HOUSEHOLD.* [2]

1753 Census for Isle Royale (Cape Breton). *HEAD OF HOUSEHOLD.* Location; name of head of household; number of men; number of women; number of boys; number of girls; number of fishermen; number of *chaloupes*; number of platforms for drying fish; number of cleared land; number of *toises* in gardens. [2]

1760-1762 Census for the government region of Trois Rivières, Quebec. *HEAD OF HOUSEHOLD.* Name of head of household; number of male and female children; number of women; number of male and female domestic servants; number of buildings. [1,23,26]

1761 List of inhabitants of Acadia (the area from Gaspe to Baie Verte only). Names and residence of Acadians who did not surrender at Fort Cumberland 8 Nov. 1761. [2]

1761 List of inhabitants of New Brunswick. [3]

1762 Census for the government region of Quebec, Quebec. *HEAD OF HOUSEHOLD.* Name of head of household; number of women; number of male children over and under age fifteen; number of female children; number of male domestic servants over and under age fifteen; number of foreigners; number of *arpents* of land; number of steers, cows, sheep, horses and pigs. [1,23,26]

1762 Roll of habitants of Isle Royale (Cape Breton) and of Quebec. *HEAD OF HOUSE-HOLD.* Names and surnames of officials and principal habitants. [7]

1764 List of Protestant Housekeepers (one who occupied a house) in Montreal. [2,7]

1764 List of Protestant Housekeepers (one who occupied a house) in the District of Quebec (city) [2,7]

1765 Census for the government regions of Montreal and Trois Rivières, Québec. *HEAD OF HOUSEHOLD.* Name of head of household; number of houses; number of men; number of women; number of male children over and under age fifteen; number of female children; number of male servants over and under age fifteen; number of female servants; number of foreigners; number of *arpents* of land; number of steers, cows, sheep, horses and pigs. [23,26]

1765 Census for la Baye des Chaleurs, Bonaventure, and Gaspez (Gaspe), Québec. *HEAD OF HOUSEHOLD.* Name of head of household; number of houses; number of men; number of women; number of male children above fifteen; number of male children under fifteen; number of female children; number of male domestics above fifteen; number of male domestics below fifteen; number of female domestics; number of foreigners; number of *arpents* of land; number of steers; cows, *taurailles*, sheep and horses. [19]

1765 Census of Protestant Inhabitants of the District of Montreal. *HEAD OF HOUSEHOLD.* Name; where born; former calling (occupation); present calling (occupation); residence; freeholds. (This census is followed by lists of marriages, births and deaths which include names and dates and locations for deaths. [2]

1767 Census for Iles St. Pierre and Miquelon. *NOMINAL.* Names of head of family; names of his wife and children; ages of all members of household. [2,27]

1769-1772 Name Returns of householders in the city of Quebec. *HEAD OF HOUSEHOLD.* Names of head of household and amount they paid for chimney sweeping. There is a separate listing for those who were too poor to pay for the cleaning. (These returns were taken for the years 1769-1772 by the chimney inspector.) [2]

1770 Census for New Brunswick. *HEAD OF HOUSEHOLD.* [2,3]

1770-1771 Census for Nova Scotia (Not complete: Cornwallis, Liverpool, Newport, and Yarmouth Townships are missing.) *HEAD OF HOUSEHOLD.* Names of head of family; number of men; number of boys; number of women; number of girls; total, Protestant, Catholic; English, Scots, Irish, American, German and Others, Acadians. [1,2,3,12,28]

1773 Census for Nova Scotia (Township of Yarmouth). *HEAD OF HOUSEHOLD.* Names of head of family; number of men, number of boys; number of women; number of girls; total, American, German, English. [some in 1,2,3,12,28]

1774 Census for Bonaventure, Québec. *HEAD OF HOUSEHOLD AND SPOUSE.* Names of head of household and name of wife; number of sons; number of daughters; number of foreigners; number of cattle; number of sheep. In some cases the place of origin. [19]

1775 Census for Nova Scotia (Township of Conway). *HEAD OF HOUSEHOLD.* Name of head of family; number of men; number of boys; number of women; number of girls; total persons; Protestant or Roman Catholic; English, Scots, Irish, American, German and other foreigners, and Acadians. [3,12]

1776 Census for Isles Miquelon and St. Pierre. *NOMINAL.* Names of all in household; ages; number of members in household; possessions. [2]

1777 Census for Bonaventure and Paspebiac, Gaspe, Québec. *HEAD OF HOUSEHOLD AND SPOUSE.* Name of head of household; name of his wife; number of boys and number of girls less than 16; number of boys and number of girls more than 16. [2,19]

1777 Census for Perce (on Bonaventure Island), Québec. *HEAD OF HOUSEHOLD AND SPOUSE.* Name of head of household; name of his wife; number of children; number of cows; number of boats; number of servants. [19]

1777 Census for Carleton, Gaspe, Québec. *HEAD OF HOUSEHOLD AND SPOUSE.* Name and age of head of household; name and age of his spouse; number of boys; number of daughters. [19]

1777 Census for Mal Bay and I'le de Bonaventure, Québec. *HEAD OF HOUSEHOLD.* Name of head of household; whether he has a wife; number of children; number of cows; number of boats; and number of servants. [19]

1777 Census for Gaspe and du Cap, Québec. *HEAD OF HOUSEHOLD AND SPOUSE.* Name of head of household; where he is from; name of his wife; number of sons over and under sixteen; number of daughters over and under sixteen. [19]

1781 Census for Fief and Seigneury of St. Sulpice, Québec. Seigneurial Census. *HEAD OF HOUSEHOLD.* Name of head of household; description of land, buildings and *bâtiments*; revenues of *cens and rentes*. [23]

1784 Census of Miquelon. *NOMINAL.* (Alphabetical by name of head of household). Names; ages; number of men, women, daughters; boys, and domestics; number of houses; number of fishing shacks; number of *goélettes, chaloupes,* canoes and *voisies;* number of warehouses. [2]

1787 Census for Nova Scotia (County of Queens). *HEAD OF HOUSEHOLD.* Name of head of family; number of men; number of women; number of children; totals. [some in 1,2,3,12,28]

1787 Census for the Seigneury de la Prairie de la Madeleine, Québec. Seigneurial Census. *HEAD OF HOUSEHOLD.* Name of head of household; number of *arpents* in cultivated land, in prairie, and wooded land; buildings identified. [3,25]

1788 List of Protestant inhabitants of Charlottenberg, Upper Canada (Ontario). [2]

1791-1795 Rolls for New Brunswick and Nova Scotia. Poll tax rolls. [2,3]

1791-1795 Census for Nova Scotia. *HEAD OF HOUSEHOLD.* [2]

1792 Census for Quebec. Taken by the *curé* of Notre Dame de Québec. *HEAD OF HOUSEHOLD.* Name of head of household; occupation; if Protestant, so stated, number of parishioners, number of communicants; number and street where they live. Indexed in *RAPQ,* (see bibliography). [1,23]

1795 Census for Quebec. Taken by the *curé* of Notre Dame de Québec. *HEAD OF HOUSE-HOLD.* Name and occupation of head of household; if Protestant, so stated; Number of parishioners; number of communicants; number of Protestants; number and street where they live. Indexed in *RAPQ* (See bibliography). [1,23]

1796 Census for St. John's City, Newfoundland only. *HEAD OF HOUSEHOLD.* [3]

1796 Census for Augusta Township, Granville (Grenville),* Ontario. *HEAD OF HOUSE-HOLD.* [1,2]

1797 Census for Upper Canada,* (Ontario). (Incomplete) *HEAD OF HOUSEHOLD.* Name of head of household; number of males; number of females. [3, 22 (York)]

1798 Census for Quebec. Taken by L'Abbe Joseph-Octave Plessis,the *curé* of Notre Dame de Québec. *HEAD OF HOUSEHOLD.* Name and occupation of head of household; if

Protestant, so stated; number of parishioners; number of communicants; number of Protestants; number and street where they live. Indexed in *RAPQ* (See bibliography). [1,23]

1798 Census for Prince Edward Island. *HEAD OF HOUSEHOLD.* [1,8]

1799 Census for Upper Canada (Ontario)*. (Incomplete) *HEAD OF HOUSEHOLD.* Name of head of household; number of males; number of females; place of abode. [4,22 (York)]

1800 Census for Upper Canada (Ontario)*. (Incomplete) *HEAD OF HOUSEHOLD.* Name of head of household; number of males; number of females; place of residence. [4,22 (York)]

1800-1801 Census for Trinity Bay, Newfoundland. *HEAD OF HOUSEHOLD.* [3]

1801 Census for Upper Canada (Ontario)*. (Incomplete) *HEAD OF HOUSEHOLD.* Name of head of household; number of males; number of females; place of residence. [2,3,4,22 (York)]

1802 Census for Upper Canada (Ontario)*. (Incomplete) *HEAD OF HOUSEHOLD.* Name of head of household; males 16 and older; women; number of male and female children; total number. [3,4,22 (York)]

1804 Census for Upper Canada (Ontario)*. (Incomplete) *HEAD OF HOUSEHOLD.* Name of head of household; males 16 and older; women; number of male and female children; total number. [2,3,4,22 (York)]

1805 Census for Quebec. Taken by the *curé* of Notre Dame de Québec. *HEAD OF HOUSE-HOLD.* Name and occupation of head of household; if Protestant, so stated; number of parishioners; number of communicants; number of Protestants; number and street where they live. Indexed in *RAPQ* (See bibliography). [1,3,23]

1805 Census for Upper Canada (Ontario)*. (Incomplete) *HEAD OF HOUSEHOLD.* Names heads of family, number of men; number of women; number of male children over and under sixteen; number of female children over and under sixteen; number of servants; total number. [2,3,22 (York)]

1806 Census for Upper Canada (Ontario).* (Incomplete) *HEAD OF HOUSEHOLD.* Names of heads of family; number of men; number of women; number of male children over

No 8

1978

[1] RETOUR de l'Enumération des HABITANTS de *Parish of Chateauguay* ainsi

MAISONS avec leurs positions locales dans aucun Rang, Concession, Rue, &c.	MAISONS habitées.	MAISONS inhabitées.	MAISONS en construction.	NOM du Chef de chaque Famille.	PROPRIÉTAIRE de Biens-Fonds.	NON PROPRIÉTAIRE de Biens-Fonds.	LOCATAIRE ayant droit de Voter à aucune Élection de Cté, Ville, &c.	MÉTIER ou PROFESSION.	NOMBRE TOTAL de Personnes dans chaque Famille, Mâles et Femelles, y résidant ordinairement.	NOMBRE de Personnes appartenant à la Famille, Mâles ou Femelles, et temporairement absentes.
1				Etienne Farrar	1	—		Farmer	4	
2				Ignace Coté	1			Do	15	
3				Edward Perrian	1			Black Smith	6	
4				Michel Lafabure		1		Farmer	8	1
5				Ignace Desay	1			Farmer	16	
6				Robt Findley	1			Do	8	
7				Jacquin Doucans	1			Do	10	
8				Bapt Livernois dit	1			Do	6	
9				Phillipe Curot	1			Do	8	
10				Etienne Bourget	1				10	
11		1		Louis Curot	1			Lumberer		1
12				Toussaint St Marie	1			Labourer	6	
13				Jeremy Green				Do	5	
14		1		Etienne Bourget				Farmer		
15				Ignace Reid	1			Do	5	2
16				Louis Perrot	1			Do	9	
17				Francois Bourier	1			Labourer	3	
18		1		Dominique Dupont	1			Farmer		
19				Jr Bapt View			1		9	
20				Jr Bapt Durandsault			1		8	1
21		1		Pierre Latour			1	Mason		
22				Md Durandsault				Widow	7	
23				Etienne Durandsault	1			Labourer	9	
24				Jr Bapt Bourier	1			Mason	10	
25				Charles Amiot	1			Cabler	2	
26				Antoine Lafabure			1	Carpenter	9	

Census Return for the Head of Family 1842 Census, Chateauguay, Huntingdon Co. Wisconsin State Historical Society, microfilm # P73-3110.

and under sixteen; number of female children over and under sixteen; number of servants; total number. [1 (for Augusta Twp),2,3,22 (Granville in York Dist.)]

1807 Census for Upper Canada (Ontario)*. (Incomplete) *HEAD OF HOUSEHOLD.* Name of head of family; number of men; number of women; number of male children over and under sixteen; number of female children over and under sixteen; number of servants; total number. [2,3,4,22]

1808 Census for Upper Canada (Ontario)*. (Incomplete) *HEAD OF HOUSEHOLD.* Name of head of family; number of men; number of women; number of male children over and under sixteen; number of female children over and under sixteen; number of servants; total number. [2,3,4,22]

1810 Census for Upper Canada (Ontario)*, (Incomplete). *HEAD OF HOUSEHOLD.* Name of head of family; number of men; number of women; number of male children over and under sixteen; number of female children over and under sixteen; number of servants; total number. [3,22]

1811 Census of Cape Breton. *HEAD OF HOUSEHOLD.* Names of head of household, occupations; males between fourteen and sixty; females between fourteen and sixty; males and females unmarried; males and females over sixty; males under fourteen; females under fourteen; male and female servants; number of cattle, sheep, horses; vessels; station. (This census is not complete especially on the east coast. It is bound in vol. 333, Public Archives of Nova Scotia.) [3,16]

1811 Census Nova Scotia (not complete). *HEAD OF HOUSEHOLD.* [2]

1811 List of persons qualified to serve as jurors in Montreal and its surrounding area. [2]

1812 Census of Upper Canada (Ontario)*. (Incomplete) *HEAD OF HOUSEHOLD.* Name of head of household; number of males over sixteen; number of males under sixteen; number of females over sixteen; number of females under sixteen; total number. [1 (Woodhouse Twp.),2,4,22 (York only)]

1813 Census for Upper Canada (Ontario)*. (Incomplete) *HEAD OF HOUSEHOLD.* Names of heads of family; number of males over sixteen; number of males under sixteen; number of females over sixteen; number of females under sixteen; total number. [1 (Augusta Twp., Granville),2,3,4,22 (York only)]

1813 List of persons qualified to serve as jurors in Montreal and its surrounding area. [2]

1814 Census for Upper Canada (Ontario)*. (Incomplete) *HEAD OF HOUSEHOLD.* Names of head of family; number of males over sixteen; number of males under sixteen; number of females over sixteen; number of females under sixteen; total number. [2,3,4,22 (York)]

1816 Census for Upper Canada (Ontario)*.(Incomplete) *HEAD OF HOUSEHOLD.* Names of heads of family; number of males over sixteen; number of males under sixteen; number of females over sixteen; number of females under sixteen; total number. [2,3,22 (York)]

1816 List of persons qualified to serve as jurors in Montreal and its surrounding area. [2]

1817 Census for Upper Canada (Ontario)*. (Incomplete) *HEAD OF HOUSEHOLD.* Name of head of family; number of males over sixteen; number of males under sixteen; number of females over sixteen; number of females under sixteen; total number. [2,3,22 (York)]

1817 Census for Nova Scotia (not complete). *HEAD OF HOUSEHOLD.* [2,3]

1817 Census for Cape Breton. *HEAD OF HOUSEHOLD.* [36]

1818 Census for Cape Breton Island. *HEAD OF HOUSEHOLD.* Name of head of household; age; time on the island; country (of origin); country of parents; situation; trade, marital status and number of children. [3,16]

1818 Census Church of Notre Dame of Quebec Census for the city of Quebec, Quebec. *NOMINAL.* Names, ages, occupations of all members of household; number of parishioners, number of Communicants, number of Protestants. Indexed in *Recensements de la Ville de Québec* by Joseph Signay (see bibliography). [30]

1818 Census for Upper Canada (Ontario)*. (Incomplete) *HEAD OF HOUSEHOLD.* Name of head of family; number of males over sixteen; number of males under sixteen; number of females over sixteen; number of females under sixteen; total number. [2,4,22 (York)]

1819 Census for Upper Canada (Ontario)*. (Incomplete) *HEAD OF HOUSEHOLD.* Name of head of family; number of males over sixteen; number of males under sixteen; number of females over sixteen; number of females under sixteen; total number. [2,3,22 (York)]

1822 Census for Upper Canada (Ontario)*. (Incomplete) *HEAD OF HOUSEHOLD.* Name of head of family; number of males over sixteen; number of males under sixteen; number of females over sixteen; number of females under sixteen; total number. [2,3,4,22 (York)]

1823 Census for Upper Canada (Ontario)*. (Incomplete) *HEAD OF HOUSEHOLD.* [1 (Augusta Twp.),2,3]

1824 or 1825 Census for Upper Canada (Ontario)*. (Incomplete) *HEAD OF HOUSEHOLD.* Name of head of family; males under sixteen; females under sixteen; males above sixteen; females above sixteen; total number. [1 (Augusta Twp.),2,3, 22 (Town of York only)]

1825 Census for Lower Canada (Quebec). *HEAD OF HOUSEHOLD.* Name of head of household; name of parish of residence; number of members of household sorted by age, sex and married or single; number absent from the province. [1,2]

1827 census for Nova Scotia (not complete; available for Upper District of Sydney County— the townships of Arisaig, Dorchester, St. Andrews, and Traccadie). *HEAD OF HOUSE-HOLD.* Name of head of the family; number of males; number of females; number of male servants; number of female servants; total in the family; occupation, religion; number of births, marriages and deaths; number of acres cultivated; number of bushels of wheat; number of bushels of other grains; number of tons of hay; number of horses, horned cattle, sheep, and swine; number of bushels of potatoes. [2,3,12]

1828 Census for Upper Canada (Ontario)*. (Incomplete) [2,3,20 (Niagara Dist.)]

1831 Census for Lower Canada (Quebec). *HEAD OF HOUSEHOLD.* Sorted by parish, seigneury or township. Name of owner or non-owner of home; occupation of head of household; total number in family; number of family members temporarily out of the province; total number of persons under age five; total number between age five and fourteen; children grouped by age, sex, and marital status; number in subsistence agricultural occupation; number of male farm servants employed; number in family engaged in commerce and trade; number of persons subsisting on alms; number of acres or *arpents* occupied by each family; number of acres or *arpents* cultivated; number of *minots* of wheat, peas, oats, barley, rye, corn, potatoes and buckwheat; tenure of land— rate of seigneurial rent, price of rent in cash, proportion of goods allowed to proprietor for land to farm or cultivate; number of horned animals, horses, sheep, pigs; number of academic colleges, convents of parishes, seigneury, township, quarters or division of city; number of elementary schools; number of males and females attending college, convent, or elementary schools; number of public houses or public service buildings; number of storehouses or shops of strong liquor; number of flour, saw, and carding mills; number of manufacturers of iron goods, foundrys, distilleries, and manufacturers of potash; number of manufacturers of other kinds; average value of wheat last harvest; average value of monthly wages of those employed in agriculture; average value of day wages of journalier; number of persons actually established who arrived in province by sea since 1 May 1825; number of persons established in province who came other than by sea since 1 May 1825; number of persons established in province who came since 1 May 1825 and are foreigners, names of persons. [1,2,3]

1832-1835 List of persons qualified to serve as grand jurors in Montreal. [2]

1831-1835, 1833-1834, 1832-1835, 1833-1835 Lists of persons qualified to serve on various juries in Montreal (*petit Jure*, special juries; grand and *petite* juries). Some of these lists include not only their name but their occupation, parish they are in, if they are proprietors or tenants, and if they qualified or not. [2]

1838 Census for Nova Scotia (not complete). *HEAD OF HOUSEHOLD.* Name of head of household; occupation; number of male and female children under six; number of males and females under fourteen number of males (not head of family) and females over fourteen; total number in family; number of male heads of family; location. [2,17]

1841 Census for Prince Edward Island. *HEAD OF HOUSEHOLD.* [1,2]

1842 Census for Lower Canada (Quebec) and Upper Canada (Ontario). *HEAD OF HOUSE-HOLD.* Name of head of household; name of person from whom land is leased; whether tenant is allowed to vote; occupation; total number in the family; non-resident when not native thereof; number of family members absent; number in family who are: natives of England, Ireland, Scotland, Canadians of French origin, or Canadians of British origin, Europe, U.S.A.; number of years each person has been in the province; number of aliens not naturalized; number of persons five years of age and under by gender; number of persons above five and under fourteen by gender; marital status of males fourteen to eighteen years; marital status of males eighteen and not twenty-one; marital status of males twenty-one and not thirty; males thirty and not sixty; males sixty and upwards; marital status of females fourteen and not forty; marital status of females forty-five and upwards; number of deaf and dumb by gender and occupation; number of blind by gender; number of idiots by gender; number of lunatics by gender; number of those in various denominations (Church of England, Church of Scotland, Church of Rome, Methodist, Presbyterian, Congregationalist, Baptists and Anabaptists, Lutherans, Quakers,

Moravians and Tunkers, Church of Holland (Dutch Reformed), Jewish and other denominations); number of colored persons by gender; number of male farm servants employed; number of other servants employed; number of male servants in private families; number of female servants in private families; number engaged in trade or commerce; number of family members existing on alms or paupers; number of acres or *arpents* of land occupied; number of acres or *arpents* of improved land occupied; commercial and agricultural statistics (number of *minots* of various crops, animals, textiles, land tenure, educational institutions, mills, manufacturing businesses and values of such). Houses with their local situations in any range, concession, street etc., divided by houses inhabited, houses vacant and houses under construction. [1,2,3]

1848 Census for Upper Canada or Canada West (Ontario).(not complete; Johnstown, New Castle and Huron counties have survived as well as various locations in a number of counties of Ontario.) *HEAD OF HOUSEHOLD.* Lot number; concession number; occupied or vacant houses; public buildings; name of head of household; owned or not owned property; occupation; total number of persons in the family; number of absent family members; Native of Ireland, Scotland, Canada (French), Canada (British), U.S.A., Germany and Holland, and unspecified countries; male and female under 5 years of age; number of male and female 5-14 years; males, married and single 14-18 years; 18-21 years, 21-30 years, 30-40 years, 40-60 years, 60 years or older; females, married and single 14-45 years, 45 years or older; number of births the preceding year; number of marriages the preceding year; number of deaths the preceding year; deaf and dumb, male and female; blind male and female; lunatics and idiots male and female; colored male and female; male farm servants; domestic servants male and female; religion (Church of England, Church of Scotland, Church of Rome, Episcopal Methodist, Wesleyan Methodist; Other Methodist, Baptist/Anabaptist, Congregationalist/ Independent, Lutheran, Quaker, Jew, Free Presbyterian, Other Presbyterian, Universalist/Unitarian, Mennonites, Others, no creed or denomination; acres held or occupied; acres in crops; acres in pasture; acres in wood/wild; acres unfit for cultivation; average value of cleared land per acre; average value of wild land per acre; rent if held by a tenant; acres in wheat, barley, rye, oats, corn, buckwheat, potatoes; number of lbs. of flax/hemp, tobacco, maple sugar and wool; number of yards of fulled cloth manufactured by the family; number of yards of linen/cotton/other manufactured by family; number of yards of flannel/woolen manufactured by family; number of lbs. of cheese and butter for market; number of barrels of beef/pork for market; number of neat cattle (oxen), horses, sheep and hogs; number of grist, oatmeal, barley, saw, fulling and carding mills; number of distilleries, breweries, tanneries, pot and pearl ash manufactures, and woolen factories; number employed; number of children 5-15. [1,2,3,4, Parts of this census can be found at these locations and at the D.B. Weldon Library,

University of Western Ontario, London, Ontario and Hiram Walker Historical Museum, Windsor Ontario. Parts may be at one location and not at the others. It would prove useful to look at Jonasson, Eric, "Pre 1851 Census Records of Ontario," in *Genealogical Journal*, vol. 13 no. 2, summer 1984, pp. 43-55.]

1848 Census for Prince Edward Island. (In one volume in Public Archives of Prince Edward Island.) [1,3]

1850 Census for Canada West (Ontario) *HEAD OF HOUSEHOLD.* Lot number; concession number; occupied or vacant houses; public buildings; name of head of family; owner or non-owner of land; trade or occupation (profession, trade and commerce, agriculture, laborer, handicraft, employed in factories, employed in lumber trade, navigation or fisheries); number of family members; number of non family members; number of absent family members; number of natives of Ireland, Scotland, Canada (French), Canada (British), U.S.A., Germany and Holland, countries not specified; number of persons male and female under 1 year, 1-2 years, 2-5 years, 5-10 years, 10-14 years; number of males married/single 14-18 years, 18-21 years, 21-30 years, 30-40 years, 40-60 years, 60-100 years, 100 or over; number of females married/single 14-30 years, 30-40 years, 40-60 years, 60-100 years, 100 or older; number of single and twin births male and female; number of marriages in preceding year; number of deaths, male and female under 5 years, 5-10 years, 10-21 years, 21 or older; number of male and female deaf and dumb; number male and female blind; number male and female lunatics and idiots; number of male farm servants; number of domestic servants, number of male/female attending school/college; religion; number of acres or *arpents* held or occupied; number of acres in crops, pasture, wood/wild land, unfit for cultivation; average value of cleared and wild land per acre; rent paid if held by tenant; acreage in wheat, barley, rye, oats, peas, corn, buckwheat, potatoes and other produce; number of lbs. of flax/hemp, tobacco, maple sugar and wool; number of bushels of beans, mangel wurtzel and turnips; number of tons of hay; number of barrels of apples; number of yards of fulled cloth, linen/cotton/other, flannel/woolen produced by the family; number of pounds of cheese and butter for market; number of barrels of beef/pork for market; number of neat cattle (oxen), horses sheep and hogs; number of grist, oatmeal, barley, saw, fulling and carding mills; number of distilleries, breweries, tanneries, pot and pearl ash manufacturers, and woolen factories; number of children 5-15. [1,2,3, Hiram Walker Historical Museum, Windsor Ontario; D.B. Weldon Library, University of Western Ontario, London, Ontario. See reference above in 1848 for Upper Canada.]

1851 Census for Nova Scotia (not complete). *HEAD OF HOUSEHOLD.* Name of head; number of inhabited homes; number of homes now under construction; number of uninhabited homes; number of other buildings (stables, barns, outhouses); number of males and females under 10, 10-20, 20-30, 30-40, 40-50, over 50; information on mills and factories (number of different types of mills, their value and number employed; number of hand looms; their value); information on articles manufactured (number of yards of cloth not fulled, number of yards of flannel; value of boots and shoes, leather goods, candles, soap, agricultural implements, chairs and cabinets, carriages, woolen, iron castings; quantity of coal mined; amount of iron smelted and their value); number of schools; number of children attending; religious denomination; number of tons of hay; number of bushels of wheat, barley, rye, oats, buckwheat, corn, timothy, potatoes, turnips and other root crops; number of neat cattle, milk cows, horses, sheep, and swine; number of vessels in fishing; number of men aboard; amount of tonnage in fisheries; number of boats engaged in fisheries; number of men aboard; number of nets and seins; quantity of dry fish cured; amount of salmon, shad, smoked herring, mackerel, herring and ale wives caught and cured; their value; amount of fish oil; its value; number of married, number of widowed; number of paupers; number of male and female deaf and dumb, blind, lunatics/idiots; Indians, colored; amount of assessment; value of property; number of births, deaths and marriages the preceding year; the number engaged in specified occupations; number of churches; acres of dike land and its value; number of acres of other improved land. [2]

1851/52 Census for New Brunswick, Quebec, and Ontario. *NOMINAL.* Names of all people living in household; occupations; place of birth (*note—those born of Canadian parents were to be marked with an F); religion; absent family members; age next birthday; sex; marital status; whether individual is colored or Indian; male and female resident members; male and female non-resident members; male and female members absent; number of deaf, dumb, blind, or lunatic by gender; number attending school by gender; births during year 1851 by gender; deaths in 1851 by gender, age and cause of death; type of residence (brick, stone, frame, log, shanty or other kind); number of stories of residence; number of families occupying residence; number of vacant residences; number building homes; number of different kinds of businesses (shops, stores, inns, taverns); public buildings; places of worship; information concerning mills, factories etc. concerning their cost, power source, production, number of persons employed etc.; general remarks of enumerator. Agriculture and industrial schedules are attached. Lot and concession numbers are given on the agricultural census. (This is the first census where the ages and place of origin of all members of the household are indicated.) (The 1851/52 census was taken more carefully in Lower Canada than in Upper Canada. Throughout the colony, there was a general feeling that the census would affect taxation. The agriculture census consisted of 55 columns. In the agriculture census, enumerations were taken in a more careless and imperfect manner than the personal census portion.) (*Archivo Histoirie* has individually indexed some of the parishes of Quebec for the 1851 census). The census day was 12 January 1852. [5]

1861 Census for Canada East (Quebec), Canada West (Ontario)and New Brunswick. *NOMINAL.* Names of all living in the household; occupation; place of birth; married during the year; religion (religious denominations were entered in a number of ways); residence if out of the district; age at the next birthday (not the age at the time of enumeration); sex, marital status; colored, Mulatto or Indian; residents of household by gender; non-member residents by gender; number absent; deaf and dumb; blind; lunatic or idiot; number attending school within the year by gender; number over 20 who cannot read or write by gender; number of births in 1860 by gender; number of deaths in 1860, by gender; age and cause of those deaths; type of residence (brick, stone, frame, log etc.), number of stories; number of families living in the home; whether dwelling is vacant or being built; ^number of horses, cows, sheep and pigs; value of livestock; number of carriages for personal use or for hire and their value;^ name of business or manufacture; capital invested in business; quantity, kind and value of raw materials used in business; power used for machinery; number of people employed, by gender and average cost per month; quantity, cost and value of products produced; general remarks of enumerator. An Agricultural Census is also available. (Items between ^'s: these columns were intended to be asked of those who were *not* farmers and who lived in a village, town or city. This and other information for farmers was included on the agriculture schedule.) The census day was 13 January 1861. [5]

1861 Census for Nova Scotia. *HEAD OF HOUSEHOLD.* [2]

1861 Census for Prince Edward Island. *HEAD OF HOUSEHOLD.* [1,2]

1870 List of parishioners of Ste. Bridget of the Transfiguration, Parrsboro, Nova Scotia. (Includes names from Amherst, Gulf Short, Point Brule, Acadian Mines and Talonagouche Mountains). [1]

1871 Census for Quebec, Ontario, Nova Scotia and New Brunswick. *NOMINAL.* This is the first national census. From the 1871 census on, it was determined that "population de jure" would be used. (A person would be counted where he usually resides, not where he was located on the census day. eg. a person absent because he was at fisheries, at sea, in the forest, wilderness etc., would be registered in the place in which his home, family or abode was located.) There are nine schedules of the 1871 Census: (1) Return of the Living (2) Return of Deaths within 12 months (3) Public institutions, real estate, vehicles and implements (4) Public cultivated land of field products and of plants and fruit (5) Livestock, animal production, home-made fabrics and furs (6) Return of industrial establishments (7) Return of forest products (8) Shipping and fisheries (9) Mineral products. The Return of the Living Schedule includes: vessels (those inhabited as dwellings, abode or domicile of a family not having a domicile on shore); shanties (hut or cheap dwelling put up in a settlement for a temporary abiding place—e.g., lumbering or public work shanties, fishermen's huts, Indian wigwams, etc.); dwelling houses in construction; dwellings uninhabited; dwellings inhabited (There may be several families in the same house. A separate house is counted whenever there is a separate entrance from outside.); families; names; sex; age (age for infants under one year is given in fractions of 1/12 to 11/12); born in last 12 months (month was to be given); country or province of birth; religion; racial origin (The enumerator was to indicate the paternal place of origin. Therefore, a mother's place of origin would be indicated as that of her husband although in reality she may be of a different place of origin. In previous censuses, origin was place of birth.); occupation (Only young men at college were to be enumerated as students, but not school children); marital status; married within last 12 months; number going to school; number over 20 who cannot read or write; number of deaf and dumb, blind or unsound mind (those deprived of reason); and enumerator's remarks. The enumerator was to use a " —- " (dash) to indicate if an answer to a question was no, not concerned or unknown, and a " / " (slash) to indicate if the answer to a question was yes. (") was to be used for idem or ditto. In schedules 2-9, any quantities given were to include the total whether the producer sold, exported, consumed or still had the item on hand. (The Ontario Genealogical Society has indexed the census of 1871 for Ontario by county or groups of counties. The National Archives of Canada has the province of Ontario index on its web site <http://www.archives.ca>. The census day for the 1871 census was 2 April 1871. [5]

1881 Census for Canada except Newfoundland. *NOMINAL.* There were eight schedules taken. However, only the Schedule of the living has survived. Vessels (those inhabited by families); shanties (dwellings, hurriedly put up or are moveable lodges of nomadic people); houses under construction; houses uninhabited; houses inhabited; families; names of all in the household; sex; age; born within last 12 months; country or province of birth; religion (Mennonites are included among the Baptists. In the 1891 census, they are separate.); origin; occupation; marital status; number attending school; number of deaf and dumb; number blind; number of unsound mind; remarks of enumerator. (There are some county indexes for Quebec and Ontario) The census day was 4 April 1881. [5]

1885-1886 Census for the parishes of Quebec. *NOMINAL.* Names and ages of members of the household; relationship to the head of the family; domestics; occupations. These parish censuses were taken by the local priest. There may be differences in the information which was noted. Some of these parish censuses have been published. [Church or Ecclesiastical Archives, 13]

1890 Census for the parishes of Quebec. *NOMINAL.* Names and ages of members of the household; relationship to the head of the family; domestics; occupations. These censuses were taken by the local priest. Therefore, there may be differences in the information which was noted. Brigitte Hamel has published some of these. [Church or Ecclesiastical Archives, 13,(The Archives of Canada has those published by Hamel.)]

1891 Census for Canada except Newfoundland. *NOMINAL.* Nine schedules were taken, but only the schedule of the living has survived. Vessels and shanties (those inhabited by families); houses in construction; houses uninhabited; houses inhabited; families; name; sex; age; relation to head of family; country or province of birth; French Canadians (to include French Canadians and Acadians); place of birth of father; place of birth of mother; religion (Episcopal Church is included with the general column, "Church of England." They had been separate in the 1881 census.); occupation; employer; wage earner; unemployed during week preceding census; employer to state number employed during the year; number who can read; number who can write; number of deaf and dumb; number of blind; number of unsound mind. The census day was 5 April 1891. [5]

1901 Census for Canada except Newfoundland. *Nominal.* There were eleven schedules of the 1901 census: (1) Return of the Living (2) Return of building and lands, churches and schools (3) Return of deaths (4) Return of farm land, fruits and plantations (5) Return of field products (6) Return of livestock and animal products (7) Return of agricultural value (8) Return of manufactures (9) Return of forest products and furs (10) Return of fisheries (11) Return of mines. Schedules one and two are available with random examples of the other schedules found throughout. They are, however, not of consistent quality. The Return of the Living Schedule includes: House number; name of each person in household; sex, color; relationship to head of household; marital status; month and day of birth; year of birth; age; place of birth (by country except for Canada, where it is listed by province. To know whether a person was rural (r) or urban (u) born, an "r" or "u" is added to the place of birth. (eg. if born on a farm in Quebec, it is noted as "Q.r."); year of immigration to Canada; year of naturalization ("pa" indicates, he has applied for his papers.); racial or tribal origin (origin is traced through the father by name of country and if Indian, by name of tribe. For mixed white and red, the addition of "b" is added. For example, f.b (French breed), e.b. (English breed), s.b. (Scotch breed); i.b. (Irish breed) and o.b. (other breeds); nationality; religion; occupation; living on own means; employer; employee; working on own account; working at trade in factory or home (f-factory, h-home); month employed in trade at factory; months employed in trade at home; months employed other than factory or home; earnings from occupation or trade; extra earnings other than occupation or trade ("r" indicates retired from that trade); number of months at school in a year (applied to those of age 5-21); can read; can write; can speak English; can speak French; mother tongue (is the language of his race, but not necessarily the one in which he thinks or speaks most fluently or uses chiefly in conversation); deaf and dumb; blind; unsound mind. Note-a " / " (slash) is a yes answer and a " —- " (dash) is a negative answer. (Note-Schedule 2: "Buildings and Lands, Churches and Schools" has the lot and concession numbers for land owners enumerated in Schedule 1 (Return of the Living). (The page number and line number of the person enumerated in Schedule 1 is necessary to locate the lot and concession number in Schedule 2. The lot and concession numbers are essential when you are searching land records.) The census day for the 1901 census was 31 March 1901. [5]

* Upper Canada had a census taken each year. Many of the Ontario censuses are lost. The few which have survived are scattered. Many are not complete. Some appear at the National Archives of Canada in Ottawa. They often appear in provincial, regional, or local archives or libraries. Some have appeared in local clerk offices. No one location has all copies of any one district. You will have to search in various locations. A number of censuses for a single district or town (eg. Augusta Township, Grenville) have been indicated on the previous list. This does not mean to imply that only the Grenville District had an enumeration. It indicates a census was taken and as a genealogist, you may have to do some extensive research to see if there is a return available for your particular area. A good place to start might be a branch of the Ontario Genealogical Society that is located in your area of research.

**There is no evidence of names of French families in Acadia prior to 1636. Many of the church records of Acadia have been lost. Censuses are, therefore, a major source for reconstructing Acadian families.

Sources for Locating Census Records in Appendix E

By Joyce Soltis Banachowski

The numbers in brackets in Appendix E, correspond to the following locations, both primary and secondary, where those particular censuses can be found.

[1]   FHL (Family History Library)

[2]   National Archives of Canada, Ottawa

[3]   Appropriate Provincial Archives

[4]   Other Major Libraries in the U.S. and Canada

[5]   All of the above

[6]   Beaudet, Abbe L. *1716 Recensement de la Ville de Québec.* Québec: Imprimerie Generale a Cote et Cie, 1887. A name index is included at the back.

[7]   *Bulletin des Recherches Historiques,* 70 volumes, 1895-1968. Roy, Pierre-Georges, director for vols. 1-54; Roy, Antoine, director for volumes 55-70, Quebec. (vol. 28, 1659 census; vol. 37, 1666 census; vol. 38,1686 census; vol. 36, rolls of 1673 and 1762; vol. 39, rolls of 1762, L'Isle Royale and Quebec; vol. 38 and 39, Protestant Housekeepers)

[8] Campbell, Duncan. *History of Prince Edwards Island.* Charlottetown, Nova Scotia, 1875.

[9] *Canadiana Monographs Collection* (CIHM). Ottawa: Canadian Institute of Historical Reproductions. This is a collection on microfiche of over 70,000 books and periodicals documenting the development of Canada from mid 16th century to 1900.

[10] DeVille, Winston. *The Acadian Families in 1686.* Ville Platte, Louisiana, 1986. This is an English translation of the 1686 census made by Intendant Meulles of areas he personally visited in 1686. There is a name index.

[11] *French Canadian and Acadian Genealogical Review,* vol. 7, no. 1 (Spring 1979): 47-66. (The 1678 census is translated into English).

[12] Harvey, Dr. D. C. *Report of the Board of Trustees of the Public Archives of Nova Scotia for 1934,* Provincial Secretary, Halifax, Appendix B (1770 census: townships of Amhurst, Annapolis, Barrington, Cumberland, Falmouth, Granville, Hillsborough, Horton, Londonderry, New Dublin, Onslow, Donegall or Pictou, Sackville and Truro; 1773 census: township of Yarmouth; 1775 census: township of Conway; and 1787 census: county of Queens). *Report of the Board of Trustees of the Public Archives of Nova Scotia for 1938,* Appendix B (1827 census).

[13] Hamel, Brigitte has published the following parish censuses for 1885: St. Severe, Comte Maurice. For 1886: St. Francois-Xavier-de-Batiscan, Ste. Flore, St. Barnabe-Nord, St. Leon-le-Grand, St. Etienne-des-Gras, St. Luc-de-Vincennes, St. Mathieu du Lac-Bellemare, St. Maurice, Ste. Ursule, and the combined parishes of St. Francois-de-la-Croche, *dit* St. Hippolyte, St. Jean-Baptiste-de-la-Riviere-Rats, St. Theodore-de-la-Grand Anse, St. Nicolas-de-la-Mattawin, Mekanic, and St. Zephrin-de-la-Tuque. There is an alphabetical name index at the back of each.

[14] Hannay, James. "Our First Families," in *The New Brunswick Magazine,* vol. 1, no. 3, (Sept 1898): 121-131. (It includes the 1671 Acadian census.)

[15] Hebert, Donald J. *Acadians in Exile.* Cecilia, Louisiana: Hebert Publications, 1980. A photocopy of the original census as well as an alphabetical name index for the 1671, 1686, and 1714 censuses are included.

[16] *Holland's Description of Cape Breton Island and Other Documents,* (introduction by Harvey, D.C.). Publication no. 2. Halifax: Board of Authority of Board of Trustees of Public Archives of Nova Scotia, 1935.

[17]   Howard, Mildred, compiler. *Census of Cape Breton Island: Province of Nova Scotia 1838-1841*. Sydney: Cape Breton Genealogical Society, 1991.

[18]   Le Blanc, Dudley J. *The Acadian Miracle*. Lafayette, Louisiana: Evangeline Publishing Company, 1966 (1671 census, pp. 21-26; 1686 census, pp. 377-383; 1714 census, pp. 383-402).

[19]   *Memoires de la Société Généalogique Canadienne-Francaise*, (vol. 9; vol. 10, no. 3 & 4, July & Oct 1959 and vol. 11 no. 1 & 2 Jan-Apr 1960: 1671, 1673, 1698, 1701, 1706, 1710, 1711 censuses of Plaisance; vol.12 no. 4, Oct-Dec 1971: 1678 census; vol. 13, no. 10 & 12, Oct & Dec 1962: 1691 Census for I'le Terre Neuve, 1693 census,1694 census and 1704 census; vol. 13 no. 11, Nov 1962: 1765 census; vol. 14, no. 6, June 1963: 1774 and all 1777 censuses).

[20]   *Niagara District Census for 1828*. Niagara Genealogical Society.

[21]   Massicote, E.Z. "Un Recensement inedit de Montréal, en 1741," in *Memoires de la société royale du Canada*, Series 3, vol. 15, May 1921, Section I, pp. 1-61. This covers the census of 1741 in Montreal only. The author has added information which he extracted from Tanguay to help identify those enumerated.

[22]   Mosser, Christine, ed. *York, Upper Canada Minutes of Town Meetings and Lists of Inhabitants 1797-1823*, Metropolitan Toronto Library Board, Toronto, 1984. A cumulative name index is at the back of the book. (In addition to census rolls and list of habitants, there is a section entitled, "A record of marks of horn cattle, sheep and swine. For the inhabitants of the Townships of York, Scarborough, and Etobeconk.")

[23]   *Rapport de l'Archivist de la Province de Québec (RAPQ)*, 1920-1921 to 1982, Quebec (1925-1926: 1677, 1723, 1724 seignorial and 1762 censuses; 1935-1936: 1936-1937: 1765 census; 1666 census; 1939-1940: 1744 census; 1941-1942: 1731 census with name index; 1943-1944: 1678 census; 1945-1946: 1725 census; 1946-1947: 1760 census; 1948-1949: 1792, 1795, 1798, 1805 Quebec church censuses plus a name index of the combined four censuses; 1949-1951: 1734 and 1781 censuses; 1933: list of officers and principal families of Isle Royale and Quebec).

[24]   *Recensement Nominal de Québec Envoye en 1681* (Reprinted from Sulte, Benjamin, *Histoire des Canadiens-Francais, 1608-1880*), Danbury House, Oakland, Maine, 1989.

[25] *Recensements 1787: Seigneurie de La Prairie de La Magdeleine.* Societe Historique de la Prairie de la Magdeleine.

[26] *Repertoire des Actes de Bapteme, Mariage, Sepulture et des Recensements du Québec Ancien* (*Programme de recherche en demographie historique*) (PRDH) University of Montreal, Montreal (vol. 6: 1666, 1667, 1681, 1699 census; vol. 8: 1716 census; vol. 11: 1700 census; vol. 18: 1744 census; vol. 47: 1760, 1762 and 1765 censuses).

[27] *Report of Canadian Archives for 1905*, 3 vols., S.E. Dawson, Ottawa, and 1906, (vol. 2, Appendix A, Part I: 1752 Census, a name index follows the census; vol. 2, Appendix A, Part III: 1671 Census; vol. 2, Appendix A Part III, Appendix G: 1767 Census) There is a reprint of volume 2, part I and II of this report entitled, *Report Concerning the Canadian Archives 1905.* Bowie, Maryland: Heritage Books, 1994.

[28] Richard, Bernice C., *Nova Scotia 1770 Census (Some 1773 and 1787),* (Taken from Nova Scotia Public Archives Bulletin), Chicago Genealogical Society, Chicago, 1975. There is a cumulative name index at the back of the book. (1773 Census includes Yarmouth; 1787 Census includes Queen's County, Liverpool Township, Port Mutton, Port Hebear, Jones Habour in Hebron, Savel River, and Ragged Islands in Hebron.)

[29] *The 1752 Census of Isle Royale.* Pawtucket, Rhode Island: Quintin Publications, 1997. This is a reprint of the Sieur de La Roque's census which appeared in the *Report of Canadian Archives, 1905.*

[30] Signay, Joseph, *Recensement de la Ville de Québec en 1818* (Cahiers d'Histoire, no. 29). Québec: La Societe Historique de Québec, 1976. This is a photocopy of the 1818 census. A supplement provides a typed list of the names of the Catholic clergy of the city, the seminary of Quebec, the Ursulines of Quebec, the Hôtel Dieu of Quebec, the Hopital-General, the Chateau Louis, and the garrison of Quebec. There is a name index at the back.

[31] Simard, Georges, Pierre Rioux, and Christian Fournier. *St-Thomas Paroisse, Comte de L'islet Recensement 1851*, Société généalogique de l'est du Québec, Rimouski. This gives the names of the persons in the household, occupations, name of spouse, place of birth of each, religion, age, sex and the page on which this person can be located.

[32] *1666 Census for Nouvelle France.* Pawtucket, Rhode Island: Quintin Publications, 1997.

[33] Sulte, Benjamin. *Histoire des Canadiens-Francais 1608-1880*, 8 vols., Wilson and cie, editors, Montreal, 1882 (vol. 4: 1666, 1667 and 1671 Census; vol. 5: 1681 Census; vol. 6: 1686 Census).

[34] Trahan, Charles C. *Acadian Census 1671-1752*. Rayne, Louisiana: Hebert Publications, 1994. There is a name index for each of the Acadian Censuses and a cumulative name index of all the Acadian Censuses combined.

[35] Trudel, Marcel. *La Population du Canada en 1666: Recensement Reconstitue*. Québec: Editions du Septentrion, 1995. Trudel has arranged the information of the 1666 census into a chart format. Names are listed alphabetically within the three regions of Quebec, Trois Rivières and Montreal. He has added information which is not included in the census (ie. whether one can sign his name; his place of origin). The charts for the three regions include the name, sex, marital status, age, whether he can sign his signature, his occupation or profession and his place of origin. In addition he has a similar chart of the troops which arrived in 1665. Another chart of the officers and soldiers in 1666 includes rank, company, age, whether they can sign their name, place of origin and whether they were called habitants in 1668.

[36] There are some lists and censuses we have found mentioned as existing, but we were unable to verify where they are located. We presume they might be found in [2,3, or 4].

French-Canadian Research Addresses

Compiled by Patricia Sarasin Ustine

T here are many hundreds of addresses that the French Canadian researcher may need. The goal of this section is to provide some of those of major importance. This information was taken from four sources:

1. Barclay-Lapoint, Elizabeth. *Sourcing Canada, Genealogy Addresses Edition*, 1997. 10 des Castors, Buckingham, Quebec, Canada: Buckingham Press, 1997.

2. St. Louis-Harrison, Lorraine and Mary Munk. *Tracing Your Ancestors in Canada*. 395 Wellington St., Ottawa, Ontario K1A 0N3, Canada: National Archives of Canada.

3. Bentley, Elizabeth Petty, *The Genealogist's Address Book, 3rd Edition*, 1001 N. Calvert St., Baltimore Md. 21202: Genealogical Publishing Co. 1995.

4. Various websites on the Internet.

Researchers are encouraged to check these sources for other addresses.

CANADA-NATIONAL ARCHIVES AND LIBRARIES

National Archives of Canada
395 Wellington St.
Ottawa, Ontario, K1A 0N3
Canada
Phone: 613-995-5138
Website : http://www.archives.ca
E-mail: through website extension
 http://www.archives.ca/09/09_e.html

National Library of Canada
395 Wellington St.
Ottawa, Ontario, K1A 0N4
Canada
Phone: 819-997-7227
Website: http://www.nlc-bnc.ca
E-Mail: through website extension
http://www.nlc-bnc.ca/10/2/a2-140-e.html

CANADA-PROVINCES

The Provincial Archives of Alberta
12845-102nd Ave, N.W.
Edmonton, Alberta T5J 3L2
Canada
Phone: 403-427 -1750
Website: http://www.cd.gov.ab.ca/preserving/provincial_archives/index.asp
E-mail: paa@ww.mcd.gov.ab.ca

The Provincial Archives of British Columbia
P.O. Box 9419 Stn. PROV GOVT
Victoria, British Columbia V8W 9V1
Canada
Phone: 250-387-1952
Website: http://www.bcarchives.gov.bc.ca/
E-Mail: access@bcarchives.gov.bc.ca

The Provincial Archives of Manitoba

200 Vaughan St.

Winnipeg, Manitoba, R3C 1T5

Canada

Phone: 204-945-3971

Website: http://www.gov.mb.ca/chc/archives/index.html

E-Mail: pam@chc.gov.mb.ca

The Provincial Archives of New Brunswick

Bonar Law-Bennett Building

23 Dinnen Drive

U.N.B. Campus, Fredericton, New Brunswick

mailing address:

P.O. Box 6000

Fredericton, New Brunswick

E3B 5H1

Canada

Phone: 506-453-2637

Website: http://archives.gnb.ca/Archives/Default.aspx

E-Mail: provincial.archives@gnb.ca

Centre d'etudes acadiennes

University of Moncton, Moncton, New Brunswick,

E1A 3E9 Canada

Phone: 506-858-4085

Website: http://www.umoncton.ca/etudeacadiennes/centre/cea.html

New Brunswick Genealogical Society

P.O. Box 3235, Station B

Fredericton, New Brunswick, E3A 5G9 Canada

Website: http://www.bitheads.com/nbgs/

(There are many branches of the New Brunswick Genealogy Society. Refer to *Sourcing Canada* for addresses.)

Provincial Archives of Newfoundland and Labrador

Colonial Building, Military Road,

St. John's, Newfoundland A1C 2C9

Phone: 709-729-3065

Website: http://www.gov.nf.ca/panl/

Centre for Newfoundland Studies, Queen Elizabeth Library, Memorial University

St. John's, Newfoundland A1B 3Y1
Canada
Phone:709-737-7475

Maritime History Archives, Memorial University of Newfoundland

St. John's, Newfoundland A1C 5S7
Canada
Phone: 709-737-8428/8429
Website: http://www.mun.ca/mha/about.html

Newfoundland and Labrador Genealogical Society.

354 Water Street, Suite 202,St. John's, Newfoundland
mailing address:
Colonial Building, Military Rd.,
St. John's Newfoundland, A1C 2C9
Canada
Phone: 709-754-9525
Website: http://www3.nf.sympatico.ca/nlgs/
E-Mail: NLGS@nf.simpatico.ca

The Public Archives of Nova Scotia

6016 University Ave.
Halifax, Nova Scotia B3H 1W4
Canada
Phone: 902-423-9115

Archives du Centre Acadien, Louis R. Comeau Library,

University of Ste. Anne
Church Point, Nova Scotia B0W 1M0
Canada
Phone: 902-749-2114

Genealogical Association of Nova Scotia

P.O. Box 641, Station "Central" Halifax, Nova Scotia. B3J 2T3 Canada
Website: http://www.chebucto.ns.ca/Recreation/GANS/
E-Mail: ip-gans@chebucto.ns.ca
Phone: 902-454-0322

The Provincial Archives of Ontario

77 Grenville St.

Toronto, Ontario M7A 2R9

Canada

Phone: 416-965-4030

Website: http://www.archives.gov.on.ca/english/index.html

Toronto Public Library

789 Yonge St.

Toronto, Ontario M4W 2G8

Canada

Phone: 416-393-7131

Website: http://www.tpl.toronto.on.ca

North York Public Library

5120 Yonge St.

North York, Ontario M2N 5N9

Canada

Phone: 416-395-5535

Website: http://www.nypl.north-york.on.ca

Ontario Genealogical Society

Suite 102, 40 Orchardview Blvd

Toronto, Ontario M4R 1B9

Canada

Phone: 416-4890-0734

Website: http://www.ogs.on.ca/

E-Mail: ogs@bellnet.ca

(There are many branches of the Ontario Genealogical Society. Check for their addresses in *Sourcing Canada*.)

Public Archives of Prince Edward Island

Honourable George Coles Building,

Richmond St., Charlottetown, Prince Edward Island, (mailing address: P.O. Box 1000, Charlottetown, Prince Edward Island, C1A 7M4 Canada)

Phone: 902-368-4290

Website: http://www.gov.pe.ca/infopei/onelisting.php3?number=54179

E-Mail: archives@gov.pe.ca

Prince Edward Island Genealogical Society

P.O. Box 2744, Charlottetown, Prince Edward Island, C1A 8C4 Canada

Phone: 902-368-6600

E-Mail: rghughes@isn.net

Prince Edward Island Museum & Heritage Center

2 Kent Street., Charlottetown, Prince Edward Island, C1A 1M6 Canada

Phone: 902-892-9127

The National Archives of Quebec

1210 avenue du Seminaire

Ste.- Foy, Québec, Canada

(mailing address: C.P.10450 Québec Succ.,Ste Foy, Québec. G1V 4N1 Canada)

Phone: 418-643-8904

Website: http://www.anq.gouv.qc.ca

E-Mail: anq@mccq.gouv.qc.ca

National Archives of Quebec Bas-Saint Laurent et Gaspesie-Iles-de-la-Madeleine

337 rue Moreault

Rimouski, Québec,G5L 1P4, Canada

National Archives of Quebec
Saguenay-Lac-Saint Jean

930 rue Jacques-Cartier Est

Bureau C-103, 1er etage

Chicoutimi, Québec G7H 2A9 Canada

Telephone: (418)698-3516

National Archives of Quebec/Maurice Centre du Québec

225 rue des Forges;

 Bureau 208

Trois Rivières, Québec G9A 2G7

Tel: (819) 371-6015

National Archives of Quebec Estrie

740 rue Galt Oest

Gureau R-11

Sherbrooke, Québec J1H 1Z3

Tel: (819) 820 3010

National Archives of Quebec-Montreal

535 Avenue Viger Est

Montréal, Québec H2L 2P3

Tel: (514) 873-6000

National Archives of Quebec Outaouais

170 Rue de l'Hôtel de Ville

Hull, Québec J8X 4C2 Canada

Tel: (819) 772-3010

Montreal Central Library, Salle Gagnon,

1210 rue Sherbrooke est.,

Montréal, Québec H2L 1L9

Canada

Phone: 514-872-1616

Website: http://www2.ville.montreal.qc.ca/biblio/info/biblio04.htm

Quebec Family History Society

P.O. Box 1026, Pointe Claire, Québec

H9S 4H9

Canada

Phone: 514-695-1502

Website: http://www.cam.org/~qfhs/index.html

(This is an English-speaking group)

Societe genealogie canadienne-francaise

C.P. 335, Station Place d'Armes

Montréal, Québec H2Y 3H1

Canada

Societe de genealogie de Québec

C.P. 9066, Ste-Foy, Québec, G1V 4A8

Canada

Phone: 418-651-9127

(There are many, many other genealogy societies in the province of Quebec.
Many of their addresses are found in *Sourcing Canada*)

The Saskatchewan Archives Board, Regina Office
University of Regina
Regina, Saskatchewan, S4S 0A2
Canada
Phone: 306-565-4068

The Saskatchewan Archives Board
Saskatoon Office
Murray Memorial Building, University of Saskatchewan,
Saskatoon, Saskatchewan, S7N 0W0
Canada
Phone: 306-644-5832
Website: http://www.saskarchives.com/

Yukon Archives
P.O. Box 2703
Whitehorse, Yukon Y1A 2C6
Phone: 403-667-5321
Website: http://www.urova.fi/home/arktinen/polarweb/polar/lbcdykar.htm

UNITED STATES—ARCHIVES AND LIBRARIES

Allen County Public Library
900 Webster St.
P.O. Box 2270
Fort Wayne, IN 46802
USA
Phone: 219-424-7241 ext 3315

Family History Library
35 North West Temple
Salt Lake City, UT 84150
USA
Phone: 801-240-2331

Library of Congress

Thomas Jefferson Building,

Room LJ 20

10 First St., S.E.

Washington, DC 20540-5554

USA

Phone: 202-707-5537

National Archives and Records Administration

700 Pennsylvania Avenue. N.W.,

Washington, DC 20408

USA

Phone: 1-866-272-6272

(This is Archives 1. There are also regional centers throughout the USA. Their addresses can be found in *The Genealogist's Address Book*.)

Wisconsin Historical Society

816 State Street

Madison, WI 53706

USA

Phone: 608-264-6460

UNITED STATES—GENEALOGICAL SOCIETIES

American-French Genealogical Society

P.O. Box 2113

Pawtucket, RI 02861-2113

USA

French-Canadian/Acadian Genealogists of Wisconsin

P.O. Box 414,

Hales Corners, WI 53130

USA

French-Canadian Heritage Society of Michigan

P.O. Box 10028

Lansing, MI 48901-0028

USA

Phone: 517-372-9707

Northern New York American-Canadian Genealogical Society

P.O. Box 1256

Plattsburg, N.Y. 12901-1256

USA

Phone: 518-846-7707

Northwest Territory Canadian and French Heritage Center-Minnesota Genealogical Society

P.O. Box 29397

Brooklyn Center, MN 55443

USA

Family History Library Microfilm Numbers for the Loiselle Marriage Index

Names	FHL US/CAN Film
Abbé, Sara - Allard, Hermine	543721
Allard, Hertel - Archambault, Frédéric	543722
Archabault, Gabrielle - Asselin, Alphonsine	543723
Asselin, Alphonsine - Audet, Charlotte	543724
Audet, Claire - Ayotte, Rosalia	543725
Ayot, Rosanna - Barbier, Louis	543726
Barbier, Marguerite - Baudin, Delphis	543727
Beaudin, Denise - Beaudet, Louise	543728
Beaudet, Lubain - Beaulac, Marguerite	543729
Beaulac, Maria - Beauregard, Marguerite	543730
Beauregard, Marg. - Bégin, Henri	543731
Bégin, Henriette - Bélanger, Gérardine	543732
Bélanger, Germain - Bellrose, Edmond	543733
Belrose, Edmond - Bergeron, Adelia	543734
Bergeron, Adélard - Bernard, Sara	543735
Bernard, Scolastique - Bertrand, Jos.	543736
Bertrand, Jos. - Begras, Frs.	543737
Bigras, Genev. - Bissonnet, Théophile	543738
Bissonnet, Théothiste - Blanchet, Ferdinand	543739
Blanchet, Firmin - Boissel, Rossana	543740
Boissel, Simonne - Bomard, Pierre	543741
Bolduc, Pierre - Bouchard, Edwige	543742
Bouchard, Edwilda - Boucher, M.	543743
Boucher, M. - Bourassa, Félix	543744
Bourassa, Ferdinand - Bourque, Joseph	543745
Bourque, Joséphine - Brébant, Jos.	543746

Brabant, Josephine - Brien-Desrochers, Marg. 543747
Brien, Marg. - Brodeur, Zephirine 543748
Brodeur, Zoé - Brunel, Anne Laura 543749
Beaufort, Anne Rosalie 543750
Charon, Euphrosine - Cantin, Edouard 543751
Cantin, Elénore - Caron, Auguste 543752
Caron, Auréa - Cartier, Paul-Hormisdas 543753
Cartier, Pauline - Chabot, Caroline 543754
Chabot, Caroline - Chanpoux, Albetine 543755
Champoux, Alcide - Charby, Thérèse 543756
Charby, Virginie - Ducharme, Joseph 543757
Charron, D. Joseph - Chenette, Malvina 543758
Chenette, Marceline - Chouinard, Marie 543685
Chouinard, Marilda - Cloutier, Wilfrid 543686
Cloutier, William - Comtois, F. Xavier 543687
Comtois, Gaspé - Cossette, Normand 543688
Cosset, Numidique - Coté, Madeleine 543689
Coté, Magloire - Courtemanche, Elénore 543690
Courtemanche, Eliz. - Coyle, Patrick 543691
Coyle, Rose - Cyr, Eloi 543692
Cyr, Elzéar - Damien, Anna 543693
Damien, Bernard - David, Francois 543694
Davis, Frederic - Delisle, Eliz. 543695
Delisle, Elise - Deneau, William 543696
Deneau, Aulma - Deschamps, Amable 543697
Deschamps, Amanda - Desjarlais, Armand 543698
Desjarlais, Augustin - Descrochers, Primat 543699
Desrochers, Rachel - Dicaire, Siméon 543700
Dicaire, Sophie - Dominique, Joseph 543701
Dominique, Lse. - Drainville, Louise 543702
Drainville, Madeleine - Dubeau, Zoé 543703
Dubeau, Abraham - Ducharme, Olympe 543704
Ducharme, Omer - Dugas, Lydia 543705
Dugas, Mad. - Duplin, Pomela 543706
Duplain, Rachel - Duquet, Honoré 543707
Duquet, Ignace - Eberts, Ignace 543708
Eccher, Denis - Faribault, Rachel 543709
Faries, Charles - Filion, Samuel 543710
Filion, Sara - Fontaine, Armaide 543711
Fontaine, Armand - Fortier, Annette 543712
Fortier, Anselme - Fournier, Florence 543713
Fournier, Florent - Fréchette, Ovila 543714
Fréchette, Paméla - Gagné, Jacques 543715
Gagné, Jacques - Gagnon, Athalia 543716
Gagnon, Athanase - Garand, Arthur 543717
Garand, Azilda - Gaudreau, Césaire 543718
Gaudreau, Chs. - Gauthier, Joseph 543719
Gauthier, Joséphine - Gendreau, Jeannette 543720

Gendreau, Josephie - Germain, Abel 543759
Germain, Adeé - Giguére, J. B. 543760
Giguére, Jean - Girard, Arthemise 543761
Girard, Arthur - Godbout, Alilda 543762
Godbout, Edmond - Gourgon, Azilda 543763
Gourgon, Cath. - Grégoire, Armeline 543764
Grégoire, Arséne - Groleau, Emma 543765
Groleau, Esther - Guertin, Josephie 543766
Guertin, Joseph - Gwndon, Pauline 543767
Guindon, Phloméne - Handfield, Clerinda .543768
Handfield, Cordélia - Hébert, Edgar 543769
Hébert, Edith - Houle, Césarine 543770
Houle, Charles - Hudon, Antoine 543771
Hudon, Antoinette - Louise (illegitime de M-Rene Philippe) 543772
Louise (1825-14/2) - Lachenaie, Jacques Jazia 543773
Jean, Maurice - Joncas, Abraham 543774
Joncas, Achille - Kirouac, Rosaire 543775
Kirouac, Samuel - Labouriére, Remi 543776
Labouriére, Rose - Lachance, Octavie 543777
Lachance, Odélie - Laeerriére, Marg. Ant. .543778
Laferriére, Marie - Lafrance, Camille 543779
Lafrance, Caroline - Lalime, Isaac 543780
Lalime, Israel - Lamontagne, Léonce 543781
Lamontagne, Léonidas - Lanory, Francoise 543782
Landry, Frédéric - Langlois, Frédérica 543783
Langlois, Gaétan - Laplante, Malvina 543784
Paradis, Siméon - Paris, Azilda 543803
Paris, Béatrice - Pelland, Lucienne 543804
Pelland, Malvina - Pelletier, Priscille 543805
Pelletier, Prosper - Perreau, L. S. 543806
Perreau, L. S. - Lapres, Céline 543807
Petit, Chs. - Pechette, Aziline 543808
Pichet, Béatrice, - Pineau, David 543809
Pineault, Edouard - Pleau, Joséphine 543810
Pleau, Julie - Poitras, Joséphine 543811
Poitras, Julie - Pouloit, Adelme 543812
Pouliot, Adjutor - Proulx, Eugénie 543813
Paquet, Delvina - Paradis, Sieroy 543802
Proulx, Eulalie - Quenneville, Jos. 543814
Quenneville, Joséphine - Rajotte, Clarisse .543815
Rajotte, Damase - Rémy, Lumina 543816
Remy, Valvina - Richard, Lionel 543817
Laplante, Marcel - Laroche, Lucie 543785
Laroche, Lucien - Latour, Lse. 543786
Latour, Luce - Lavallée, Marielle 543787
Lavallée, Marthe - Lemoine, Adolphe 543788
Lebeau, Joseph - Lebrun, Joachim 543839
Lebrun, Jos. - Lécuyer, Célina 543840

Lécuyer, Charles - Lefebvre, Judith 543841
Lefebvre, B. Julie - LeGault, Christine 543842
LeGault, D. Christophe - LeMay, Egide 543843
LeMay, Elénore - Lemoine, Adolphe 543844
Lemoine, Aglae - Lessard, Augusie 543845
Levart, Augustin - Lessard, Aurélie 543846
Linteau, Celina - Levart, Benjamin 543847
Linteau, Chs. - Loyer, Johnny 543848
Loyer, Josephie - McHugh, Patrick 543849
McHugh, Peter - Mailloux, Michel 543850
Mailloux, Michel - Marchand, Frédérik Lorenzo 543851
Marchand, Gabrielle - Marien, Azéline 543852
Marien, Célina - Martel, Dominique 543853
Martel, Comithilde - Martin, Elisa 543854
Martin, Emilie - Mathieu, Irene 543789
Mathieu, Isaac - Ménard, Eulalie 543790
Ménard, Euphémie - Messier, M. 543791
Messier, Maurice - Michelin, Benjamin 543792
Michelin, Claire - Moufet, Monique 543793
Moffet, Hap - Monplaisir, Jos. 543794
Monplaisir, Julie - Morin, Henriette 543795
Morin, Hercule - Morissette, Lindée 543796
Morissette, Lorraine - Madeau, Prosper 543797
Madeau, Rachel - Nolin, Guillaume 543798
Nolin, Hékè - Ouellet, Aldéric 543799
Ouellet, Alexis - Paiement, Berthe 543800
Paiement, Caroline - Paquet, Delphine 543801
Paquet, Delvina - Paradis, Sieroy 543802
Richard, Lise - Rival, Frs. 543818
Rival, Genev - Roberge, Prudent 543819
Roberge, Raphael - Robin, Auréle 543820
Robin, Brigitte - Rodrique, Lépold 543821
Rodrique, Lorenzo - Rousseau, Benjamin 543822
Rousseau, Benoit - Roy, Onésime 543823
Roy, Onésiphore - Roy, Sara 543824
Roy, Scolastique - St. Hilaire, Elisa 543825
St. Hilaire, Elmire - St. Roch, Alexandre 543826
St. Roch, Alice - Saulnier, Thomas 543827
Solquin, Anne - Sèguin, Luisella 543828
Sequin, Madeleine - Simard, Rose 543829
Simard, Sara - Stoecklin, Chs. 543830
Stoke, Cyrille - Tardif, Georgiana 543831
Tardif, Géard - Tetreau, Appoline 543832
Tetreau, Archange - Therien, Zotique 543833
Therrien, Abraham - Thiffault, Gerard 543834
Thiffault, Germaine - Touzin, Gustave 543835
Touzin, Hélène - Trottier, Julienne 543836
Trottier, Laura - Turcote, Malvina 543837

Turcotte, Marcel - Vaillancourt, Marthe 543838
Vaillancourt, Martial - Vaudry, Luce 543855
Vaudry, Mad. - Vezina, Justine 543856
Vezina, Laisa - Vincelet, Jacques 543857
Vincelet, J. Bte. - Zuberbuhler, Maximilien 543858

Supplément à
la Collection Loiselle

Note	FHL US/CAN Film Number
Abbott, Anne - Audet, Eusèbe	1571024
Audet, Eustache - Beaudoin, Flore	1571025
Beaudoin, Florentin - Bellan, Prudant	1571026
Bellard, Victor - Biage, Alfred	1571027
Biage, Blanche - Boivin, Régina	1571028
Boivin, Robert - Bourgeois, Adélaide	1571029
Bourgeois, Adéline - Brisson, Jeannette	1571030
Brisson, Jennie - Campeau, Frs-Xavier	1571031
Campeau, François - Chamberland, Rose	1571032
Chamberland, Rosanna - Chatelain, Jean	1571033
Chatelain, Joseph - Conlon, Thomas	1571034
Conlon, William - Crevier, Hormisdas	1571035
Crevier, Hortence - David, Eugène	1571036
David, Exilda - Deschamps, Onésime	1571037
Deschamps, Onésiphore - Dicaire, Jean-Bpt	1571038
Dicaire, Josephte - Dubrule, Salomée	1571039
Dubrule, Théophile - Duquet, Joséphine	1571040
Duquette, Jovite - Fleury, Ida-May	1571041
Fleury, Jean-Bte - Fytgat, Camille	1571042
Gabard, Jean-Marcel - Gauthier, Alexandrine	1571043
Gauthier, Alfred - Girard, Appoline	1571044
Girard, Arcade - Goyette, Albert	1571045
Goyette, Albina - Guillemet, Anita	1571046
Guillemet, Ann - Houle, Cyrille	1571047
Houle, Damase - Jutras, Zéphirin	1571048
Kaible, André - Lacroix, Adélard	1571049
Lacroix, Adjutor - Lalonde, Hermine	1571050
Lalonde, Hilaire - Lanthier, Aimé	1571051
Lanthier, Albertine - Laurin, Basile	1571052
Laurin, Benoit - Lecavalier, Amégée	1571053
Lecavalier, Angélique - Legault, Joséphine	1571054
Legault, Judith - Letang, Anselme	1571055
Letang, Charles - Lytte, Jane-Elisa	1571056

Index

W